Praise for *Cilium: Up and Running*

Comprehensive, without being intimidating, this book is a good starting point for beginners and also dives deep into nuances that even experienced readers will find insightful.

—*Nimisha Mehta, Senior Software Engineer, Confluent*

Cilium: Up and Running guides the reader through common use cases and provides a comprehensive overview of internal components and architecture. Together with code examples and the authors' comments, this is a good reference for running Cilium in production.

—*Tony Norlin, Proact IT Group*

Cilium: Up and Running is an essential guide for novices and veterans in the Kubernetes networking space, taking you on a comprehensive journey to building robust and performant Kubernetes networking in production using Cilium's powerful eBPF capabilities.

—*Glen Yu, Principal Consultant at Trident Consulting*

The authors' real feat is how they share their experience to explain what Cilium does and provide you with all the keys to run it in production promptly. Turns any Cilium Padawan into a fully-grown Jedi!

—*Quentin Monnet, Principal Dataplane Engineer at Hedgehog*

Cilium: Up and Running

Cloud Native Networking, Security, and Observability

Nico Vibert, Filip Nikolic, and James Laverack

O'REILLY®

Cilium: Up and Running

by Nico Vibert, Filip Nikolic, and James Laverack

Published by O'Reilly Media, Inc., 141 Stony Circle, Suite 195, Santa Rosa, CA 95401.

O'Reilly books may be purchased for educational, business, or sales promotional use. Online editions are also available for most titles (*https://oreilly.com*). For more information, contact our corporate/institutional sales department: 800-998-9938 or *corporate@oreilly.com*.

Acquisitions Editor: Megan Laddusaw
Development Editor: Gary O'Brien
Production Editor: Christopher Faucher
Copyeditor: Rachel Wheeler
Proofreader: Tim Stewart
Indexer: Judith McConville
Cover Designer: Susan Brown
Cover Illustrator: José Marzan Jr.
Interior Designer: David Futato
Interior Illustrator: Kate Dullea

February 2026: First Edition

Revision History for the First Edition

2026-02-18: First Release

See *https://oreilly.com/catalog/errata.csp?isbn=9798341622999* for release details.

979-8-341-62299-9

[LSI]

Table of Contents

Foreword

When we started working on Cilium, none of us imagined how far the journey would take us. What began as an ambitious idea—to rethink networking and security for cloud native systems using eBPF—turned into a mission shared by an incredible group of engineers, users, and open source contributors. The journey of Cilium has been nothing short of amazing: from working with the very first wave of users trying to get Kubernetes into production, to partnering with some of the largest enterprises running massive fleets of Kubernetes clusters powered by Cilium and eBPF.

Cilium was built in the open, shaped by a community that believed in a better way of doing cloud native networking and security. Every design decision, feature, and improvement was influenced by real-world feedback from operators running production systems, contributors pushing boundaries, and users who trusted us with their most critical workloads. The community didn't just adopt Cilium—it helped build it. For that, I am deeply grateful.

I vividly remember the early days when simply getting a basic ping working between two Kubernetes pods felt like a breakthrough. The days when we had to support Docker, Kubernetes, and Mesos at the same time, because the ecosystem had not yet settled on a single orchestration standard. The excitement when we got `traceroute` working properly by implementing full ICMP support. The moment we scaled our first Kubernetes cluster to 5,000 nodes and realized we were entering an entirely new class of infrastructure. I remember the first Hubble flow that worked end to end, unlocking a completely new way to observe and troubleshoot distributed systems. Donating Cilium to the CNCF and later celebrating its graduation marked a significant milestone that validated the technology and the strength and maturity of the community behind it.

And I remember the moment when we realized Cilium was no longer just an exciting open source project. Today, Cilium is critical infrastructure powering stock exchanges, massive AI training clusters, sports stadiums, high-scale gaming platforms, financial institutions, and some of the most demanding production environments in the world. We do not take that responsibility lightly.

What has always mattered most is the people. Cilium exists because of the contributors, users, operators, maintainers, and advocates who invested their time, energy, and trust into the project. It exists because platform teams around the world were willing to deploy something new and push it to its limits. It exists because engineers believed that open source could build infrastructure that is faster, more secure, and more observable than anything that came before it. It has been one of the greatest privileges of my career to be part of that journey.

And it has been especially meaningful to share this journey with Nico, Filip, and James. Working closely with all three of them at Isovalent has been a true pleasure. We've shared countless architecture discussions, roadmap debates, customer conversations, conference stages, and community milestones. We've debugged complex networking issues late into the night, pushed each other to raise the bar, and celebrated every hard-earned success.

James has a rare gift for making complex systems understandable without oversimplifying them. Filip brings deep operational experience and an instinctive understanding of what platform teams actually need to succeed. Nico combines architectural clarity with hands-on engineering excellence and a relentless drive to make things better. Together, they represent the very best of what the Cilium community stands for: technical excellence, pragmatism, and a genuine desire to help others.

This is why *Cilium Up and Running* feels so special to me. This book reflects years of real-world experience building, operating, and scaling cloud native infrastructure. It captures the philosophy behind Cilium: that networking and security should be simple to operate, powerful by design, and deeply observable. It explains not only how Cilium works, but why it was built the way it is—from eBPF and identity-based security to service load balancing, observability, and multicluster architectures.

What truly sets this book apart is the care that went into writing it. You can feel the authors' respect for the reader. Their love for the technology. And you can feel their commitment to helping others succeed. This is a book written by practitioners, for practitioners—by people who have been in the trenches, running production systems and solving real problems.

Cilium was built by a community. This book is written by people who helped build that community. I am incredibly proud of what we've built together. I am deeply grateful to the global Cilium community for how far it has brought us. And I am honored to call James, Filip, and Nico not just collaborators, but friends.

This book is a celebration of everything we have achieved together—and an exciting glimpse into what comes next.

— Thomas Graf
Cocreator of Cilium, Cofounder & CTO Isovalent

Preface

Over the past decade, Kubernetes has evolved from a cutting-edge project spawned at Google into the universal standard for how modern applications are built and operated. Brendan Burns et al.'s description of the platform in *Kubernetes: Up and Running* (O'Reilly) as "an open source orchestrator for deploying containerized applications" doesn't quite do it justice. Today, Kubernetes is the preferred platform not only for containers but also for virtual machines, databases, batch processing jobs, development environments, and AI and machine learning workloads. It has followed in the footsteps of infrastructure-as-a-service, virtualization, and bare-metal servers and now provides engineers with unique abilities to run applications that have superior agility, resilience, and orchestration.

Regardless of the compute stack flavor of the year—and Kubernetes will, eventually, be replaced by something else—the networking and security requirements remain the same. Connectivity to, from, and between apps is still needed. Regulatory goals still need to be met, with data confidentiality, integrity, and resiliency remaining critical requirements. Application performance still needs to be closely monitored.

Whether you're a seasoned platform engineer or a newcomer to the cloud native world, you may be perplexed by the vast choice of networking tools that appear to be needed to meet the aforementioned requirements. It's a common phenomenon, and as a consequence, many clusters today are cluttered with collections of purpose-built tools: Container Network Interface (CNI) implementations, proxies, service meshes, ingress controllers, load balancers, multicluster utilities, and more.

But things are changing. Users are yearning for simplification. Addressing the cognitive exhaustion that comes with maintaining dozens of tools is at the forefront of engineers' minds.

A new layer is developing in the infrastructure stack—we call it "cloud native networking, security, and observability." You might call it something else, but regardless of the name, a clear leader in this category is emerging.

Cilium.

Powered by a kernel technology called eBPF, Cilium has taken the Kubernetes space by storm. It has been adopted by thousands of users and selected as the standard for Kubernetes networking by the likes of Google, AWS, and Microsoft. At the time of writing, it remains the only graduated Cloud Native Computing Foundation (CNCF) project in the Cloud Native Networking category, highlighting its broad scale, adoption, and maturity.

This book aims to show you the fastest way to get up and running with Cilium—but not just that: we want you to run Cilium *well*.

Who This Book Is For

This book was written for anyone who wants to accelerate and develop their proficiency in Cilium.

We expect readers to have some familiarity with Kubernetes. While Cilium can be used outside this platform, for now its primary purpose remains to provide networking, security, and observability for workloads running inside a Kubernetes cluster.

We also expect readers to have a fundamental understanding of IP networking. While we don't necessarily expect you to have mastered every routing protocol, we will assume you are familiar with IP addressing, CIDR ranges, `iptables`, NAT, DNS, and the OSI layer model in addition to network security concepts such as firewalls and encryption.

Why We Wrote This Book

We knew up front that writing a book about a technology that evolves as quickly as Cilium would be a challenge—but given its ever-growing popularity and importance within the cloud native ecosystem, we thought it was important to provide a starting point for anyone considering using it. We hope that this book will expedite your learning and help even uninitiated users feel confident installing, managing, and configuring Cilium.

What This Book Covers

Thanks to its broad and healthy community of contributors, Cilium is constantly evolving to meet the demands of its users and adapt to changes in the Kubernetes platform. For this reason, we will focus on the core and stable features and principles of Cilium, rather than exploring every possible use case. We will focus on the version of Cilium that was available at the time of writing (v1.18) and will not cover deprecated features.

Chapter 1 begins by answering the question "Why Cilium?" and provides a broad overview of its role within Kubernetes and the core use cases. We present the major components in Chapter 2 before moving on to more concrete examples in Chapter 3, which provides code samples to follow to install and monitor Cilium.

We then dive into the networking aspects of Cilium. Chapter 4 describes IP address management, and Chapter 5 introduces the datapath and explains how connectivity is delivered. Chapters 6 and 7 cover Kubernetes service networking and Ingress and Gateway API, respectively. Chapter 8 concentrates on performance-focused features, and Chapter 9 explains how Cilium enables multicluster communication.

Next, we turn to cluster access. Chapter 10 shows how external clients reach applications, and Chapter 11 outlines the options available for outbound traffic.

From there, we move into security. Chapter 12 introduces the core ideas behind network policy, and Chapter 13 expands on this with more advanced policy capabilities. Chapter 14 covers encryption before we shift to observability in Chapter 15 with Hubble. Finally, Chapter 16 focuses on operating Cilium.

Example Code and Exercises

You will find code examples and manifests throughout this book, and we encourage you to try them yourself to build a solid understanding of Cilium. Example files are available for download at *https://github.com/isovalent/cilium-up-and-running*. Most Cilium features work well on Kubernetes in Docker (using kind), meaning you can test almost everything at no cost by running kind on your own machine. When we cover features that cannot run in nested network namespace environments such as kind, we will point out suitable alternatives.

You can also follow along with this book using the free online companion lab (*https://isovalent.com/labs/cilium-up-and-running*) on Isovalent.com.

Command outputs shown in the book may be trimmed so they remain readable and to keep the examples focused on what matters.

If you have a technical question or a problem using the code examples, please send email to *support@oreilly.com*.

This book is here to help you get your job done. In general, if example code is offered with this book, you may use it in your programs and documentation. You do not need to contact us for permission unless you're reproducing a significant portion of the code. For example, writing a program that uses several chunks of code from this book does not require permission. Selling or distributing examples from O'Reilly books does require permission. Answering a question by citing this book and quoting example code does not require permission. Incorporating a significant amount of example code from this book into your product's documentation does require permission.

We appreciate, but do not require, attribution. An attribution usually includes the title, author, publisher, and ISBN. For example: "*Cilium: Up and Running* by Nico Vibert, Filip Nikolic, and James Laverack (O'Reilly). Copyright 2026 O'Reilly Media, Inc., 979-8-341-62299-9."

If you feel your use of code examples falls outside fair use or the permission given above, feel free to contact us at *permissions@oreilly.com*.

Conventions Used in This Book

The following typographical conventions are used in this book:

Italic
: Indicates new terms, URLs, email addresses, filenames, and file extensions.

`Constant width`
: Used for program listings, as well as within paragraphs to refer to program elements such as variable or function names, databases, data types, environment variables, statements, and keywords.

`Constant width italic`
: Shows text that should be replaced with user-supplied values or by values determined by context.

This element signifies a tip or suggestion.

This element signifies a general note.

This element indicates a warning or caution.

O'Reilly Online Learning

For more than 40 years, *O'Reilly Media* has provided technology and business training, knowledge, and insight to help companies succeed.

Our unique network of experts and innovators share their knowledge and expertise through books, articles, conferences, and our online learning platform. O'Reilly's online learning platform gives you on-demand access to live training courses, in-depth learning paths, interactive coding environments, and a vast collection of text and video from O'Reilly and 200+ other publishers. For more information, visit *https://oreilly.com*.

How to Contact Us

Please address comments and questions concerning this book to the publisher:

O'Reilly Media, Inc.
141 Stony Circle, Suite 195
Santa Rosa, CA 95401
800-889-8969 (in the United States or Canada)
707-827-7019 (international or local)
707-829-0104 (fax)
support@oreilly.com
https://oreilly.com/about/contact.html

We have a web page for this book, where we list errata, examples, and any additional information. You can access this page at *https://oreil.ly/cilium-up-and-running*.

For news and information about our books and courses, visit *https://oreilly.com*.

Find us on LinkedIn: *https://linkedin.com/company/oreilly-media*.

Watch us on YouTube: *https://youtube.com/oreillymedia*.

Acknowledgments

We are deeply grateful to our technical reviewers for their meticulous work, painstakingly going through the manuscript and strengthening it at every step. Their input made this book far better than it would otherwise have been. Our thanks go to Tony Norlin, Joseph Ligier, Glen Yu, Grace Nguyen, Hemanth Malla, Quentin Monnet, James Strong, Nimisha Mehta, Pedro Ignácio, and Marco Iorio.

We would also like to thank the O'Reilly team, including John Devins, Megan Laddusaw, Christopher Faucher, Rachel Wheeler, Kate Dullea and especially Gary O'Brien. His dedication, support, and kindness were exceptional. Gary worked through the

Thanksgiving holidays to help ensure the book was completed on time, something for which we are all extremely grateful.

Our thanks extend to Isovalent for sponsoring this book, and to all our colleagues who helped throughout the writing process. In particular, we want to recognize Roland Wolters, Cornelia Hertzman, Carla Gaggini, Raphaël Pinson, Toufic Arabi, Liz Rice, Thomas Graf, and the broader Isovalent team for their steady encouragement and assistance.

James would like to express his thanks to all of his nerd friends for keeping him (mostly) sane during this last year, with special thanks for their endless support to his wife Britnee, his aunt and uncle David and Kathy, and finally his mother Kay.

Filip wishes to express his gratitude to his loved ones, who not only supported him throughout the writing of this book but, more importantly, helped shape him into the person he is today. Filip would also like to share this thought; "At times, we may wonder whether we have truly made a difference in the world, but please know that you have made a lasting impact on me. From the bottom of my heart, thank you."

Nico would like to thank his family (Claire, Noah, Inès, and Mathieu) for their unwavering support throughout the creation of this book. He would also like to thank them in advance for their patience as he begins working on the next one.

Finally, we would like to thank the entire community for making Cilium the platform it is today. This includes not only the more than 1,000 contributors to the codebase, but also everyone who has supported Cilium's growth by writing about it, presenting it, answering questions on Slack, or simply sharing their appreciation for the project. This book would not exist without this collective effort.

CHAPTER 1
Why Cilium?

Kubernetes is now the accepted standard platform for running cloud native applications. Originating at Google and inspired by the company's experience with its internal cluster manager Borg, the platform was open sourced in 2014.

Kubernetes transformed containerization, which was already gaining popularity, into a scalable framework for managing distributed systems. It quickly evolved from a container orchestrator into what Brendan Burns, Joe Beda, Kelsey Hightower, and Lachlan Evenson describe as "the standard API for building cloud native applications" and "a proven infrastructure for distributed systems that is suitable for cloud native developers of all scales" in their book *Kubernetes: Up and Running* (O'Reilly).

The open source nature of Kubernetes has been fundamental to its success. Like Linux before it, Kubernetes thrives thanks to its community of contributors, from individual developers to the largest cloud providers. Google's decision to donate it to the Cloud Native Computing Foundation (CNCF) gave Kubernetes a neutral home, which in turn enabled it to become the foundation for an entire ecosystem of open source projects.

As use of Kubernetes and containerization spread, one reality became obvious: regardless of the underlying computing platform, workloads have the same basic network and security requirements. Whether you run them on bare metal, virtual machines (VMs), or containers, you expect your applications to:

- Have accessible IP addresses
- Be able to communicate with other applications
- Be able to reach the outside world when they need outbound access
- Be reachable from the outside world when inbound access is required
- Be secured, with data protected in transit and at rest

- Remain resilient and highly available on a global scale
- Meet regulatory goals and compliance requirements
- Provide the visibility you need to operate and troubleshoot when things go wrong

For decades, these goals were met with traditional networking stacks—but those approaches were not designed for the speed and scale of Kubernetes. Microservices, by their very nature, create a storm of ephemeral connections as workloads spin up and down across clusters.

From Early CNIs to Modern Datapaths

As Kubernetes gained traction, the community introduced the Container Network Interface (CNI) specification to standardize how Kubernetes interfaces with a network implementation. Early implementations like Flannel and Weave Net focused on basic connectivity, with only limited support for network policy. Calico added policy enforcement and route distribution using the Border Gateway Protocol (BGP), but like the others, it depended on `iptables` for packet filtering, network address translation (NAT), and load balancing. These rules had to be continually updated as pods and services appeared and disappeared, making them inefficient at scale.

This is where timing mattered. Coincidentally, 2014 was also the year in which another technology appeared: eBPF. Once known as *extended Berkeley Packet Filter* but now considered a standalone term (*https://oreil.ly/W0SDp*), eBPF began as a low-level kernel feature but has since become one of the most influential technologies in modern infrastructure. It provides a safe way to run custom programs inside the kernel, allowing developers to observe, modify, and extend kernel behavior without writing kernel modules or recompiling the kernel. Brendan Gregg once described it as giving Linux "superpowers" (*https://oreil.ly/GACbb*), and the label has stuck.

Like Kubernetes, eBPF succeeded because it was open source. It is merged into the upstream Linux kernel, ensuring neutrality and enabling rapid innovation. Its in-kernel verifier guarantees safety, preventing programs from crashing the system.

eBPF is often described as playing the same role for the kernel that JavaScript does for the browser. Just as JavaScript made the web programmable and extensible in a safe way, eBPF brings that same level of flexibility to the operating system kernel. This balance of power and safety paved the way for a wave of new projects.

To better understand the origins of eBPF, we highly recommend watching the fascinating documentary *eBPF: Unlocking the Kernel* (*https://oreil.ly/Hm0px*). Released in 2024 to celebrate eBPF's 10th anniversary, it is an insightful look at how a small group of kernel engineers created a technology that is now at the heart of modern networking, security, and observability.

For readers who want to dive deeper into the details of how eBPF works and how to write eBPF programs, Liz Rice's *Learning eBPF* (O'Reilly) is an excellent companion.

eBPF's primary use cases span a wide range: observability (early use cases included flame graphs for performance profiling), runtime security (Tetragon (*https://tetragon.io*), a companion project to Cilium, provides low-overhead and high-context security observability and enforcement), load balancing (at Meta, engineers used eBPF to build Katran, a high-performance load balancer capable of handling millions of packets per second (*https://oreil.ly/ETcsf*)).

But eBPF has had its most significant impact on container networking. The parallel rise of Kubernetes and eBPF was more than a coincidence. Kubernetes needed a networking and security foundation that could keep up with its scale and dynamism. eBPF provided the programmable power in the kernel to make it possible.

Time for *Cilium* to enter the scene.

Cilium: Origins and Evolution

The story of Cilium begins in December 2015, with a very modest first commit (*https://oreil.ly/rmwOm*). The initial vision was bold: to build a new networking layer for Linux containers based on the emerging power of eBPF.

The first releases of Cilium were focused on providing a scalable networking and security datapath across multiple container schedulers (Kubernetes had not yet established itself as the dominant container management platform). From there, new capabilities followed at a rapid pace:

- Multicluster connectivity with Cluster Mesh
- Transparent Encryption
- Observability through Hubble
- Service mesh functionality without the need for sidecars

As Kubernetes emerged as the winner among container orchestration systems, Cilium's development solidified around its Kubernetes integration. Powered by eBPF, Cilium excelled in performance benchmarks and, supported by its expanding set of features, quickly gained traction across the community.

Industry Adoption

Cilium's adoption by Google (for GKE Dataplane V2), Amazon (for EKS Anywhere), and Microsoft (for Azure CNI powered by Cilium) marked critical milestones. These announcements demonstrated that the creators of Kubernetes and the world's largest cloud providers all trusted Cilium to be the default networking layer for their platforms. Other cloud vendors and distributions, from DigitalOcean to Alibaba Cloud, soon followed.

Consequently, for many users, Cilium became the networking layer they ran without ever making an explicit choice. For those not using Kubernetes on these public managed services, the fact that the largest cloud providers independently chose Cilium was a powerful signal that it met the demanding requirements of multitenant, hyperscale environments.

That industry adoption served as more than just a seal of approval. It demonstrated that Cilium could run reliably at any scale—from small development clusters to global, multitenant cloud platforms—while managing the operational pressures and performance expectations of each. For organizations running Kubernetes on premises or in self-managed clusters, this validation meant that adopting Cilium was a safe, future-proof choice aligned with the direction of the wider ecosystem.

Becoming a CNCF Graduated Project

With broad technical maturity and adoption in place, Cilium reached another landmark in 2023: graduation from incubating status at the CNCF after just two years. To graduate, a project must demonstrate not only technical stability but also governance, security processes, active contributions from multiple organizations, and a sustainable community.

Achieving this status is no small feat. It is a recognition that a project has moved beyond being a promising technology and become trusted, open infrastructure. In fact, Cilium remains the only project in the Cloud Native Networking category to have reached graduated status. This milestone underscores its unique position as the standard networking and security layer for Kubernetes.

An Open Source Success Story

Cilium's success is not only technical but also communal. From its early days, the project has drawn contributors from across the open source ecosystem—individual developers, start-ups, and some of the largest technology companies in the world. This diversity of perspectives has been central to Cilium's rapid innovation and resilience.

Today, Cilium is among the most active projects in the CNCF ecosystem, consistently ranking in the top three by contributor activity. Design discussions happen in the open through Cilium Feature Proposals (CFPs) (*https://oreil.ly/STddL*), and regular community meetings welcome new participants. The project also offers a list of "good first issues" that make it easy for new contributors to get started.

Cilium's Use Cases

Cilium is fluid. It adapts as the cloud native ecosystem evolves, continuously improving and adjusting to new demands. It is also modular. In this book, you will learn about a wide range of Cilium features. Cilium's versatility can sometimes feel overwhelming: it can do a *lot*. But you don't need to enable every feature. You can begin with Cilium as a simple CNI and, over time, enable capabilities such as encryption, observability, service mesh, or multicluster connectivity as your requirements grow.

The technical components that make up this versatile platform—such as the agent, operator, CLI, and Hubble—are described in detail in Chapter 2. In this section, we will focus on the major use cases where Cilium is applied. Each of these will be explored in greater depth in later chapters.

Networking with Cilium as a CNI

At its core, Cilium acts as a network fabric for Kubernetes (Figure 1-1).

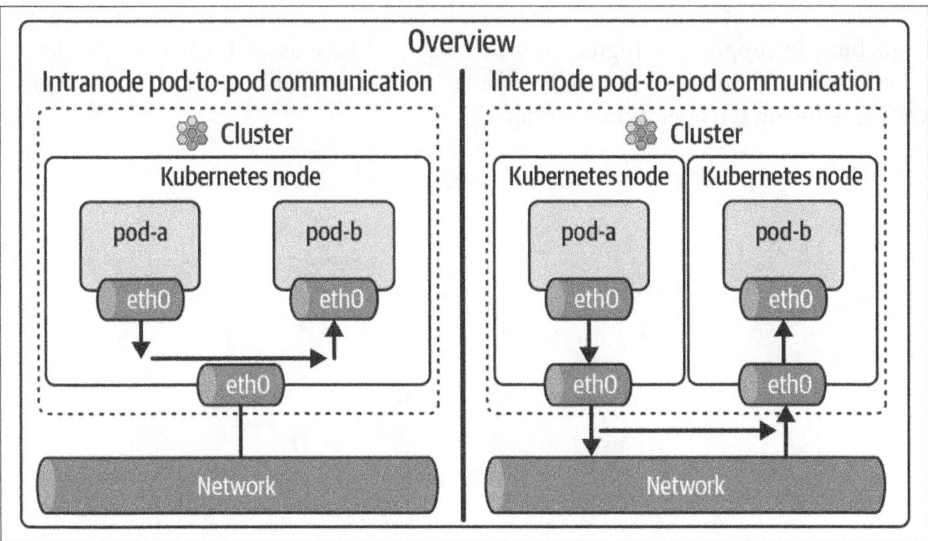

Figure 1-1. Cilium as a network fabric

Its job is to:

- Provide connectivity between pods located on the same node, or on different nodes within the same cluster, or even in different clusters.
- Build a network overlay between nodes, or leverage the underlying physical network directly.
- Provide IP address management (IPAM), similar to the role the Dynamic Host Configuration Protocol (DHCP) plays in traditional networks.

This fabric is what allows applications running across a cluster to communicate reliably and securely. Earlier CNIs used `iptables` to implement it, but `iptables` was never designed for the scale and churn of Kubernetes workloads. Cilium instead relies on eBPF-based datapath logic, resulting in a more scalable, more observable, and higher-performance foundation. We'll talk more about this in Chapters 4 and 5.

Ingress and Gateway API

Most applications need to be accessed by external clients and therefore require a reliable way for traffic to enter the cluster. Kubernetes introduced Ingress for this purpose, but its design was limited, and it has gradually been superseded by the newer Gateway API project (Figure 1-2). Cilium implements both.

Using Cilium, you can expose services through ingress rules or, increasingly, through Gateway API objects that provide more expressive and standardized control. Thanks to its built-in support for Ingress and Gateway API (discussed further in Chapter 7), Cilium users do not need to install and manage a third-party tool for cluster ingress traffic, reducing the operational burden.

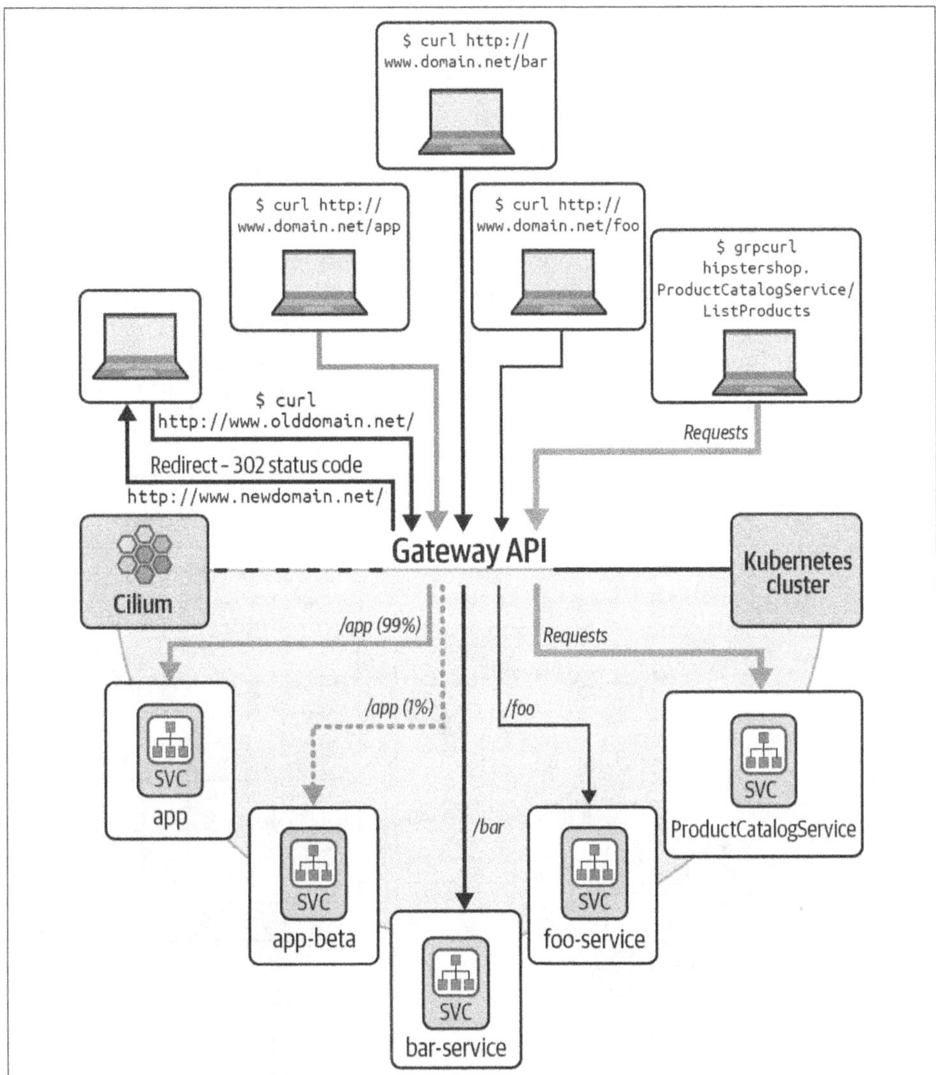

Figure 1-2. Cilium Gateway API support

Service Mesh Without the Sidecars

Service meshes emerged to provide features such as service-to-service encryption, load balancing, A/B testing, and observability. Most early meshes relied on a sidecar model, injecting an additional proxy into every pod. This approach worked but introduced resource overhead, operational complexity, and debugging challenges.

Cilium takes a different approach. By using eBPF (and a host-level Envoy for when layer 7 functionality is needed), it provides service mesh functionality directly in the datapath without requiring sidecars (Figure 1-3). This means you can enable features such as encryption and observability cluster-wide without adding another layer of infrastructure. Importantly, Cilium Service Mesh is not a distinct product but a set of features that extend the existing platform. This makes it a natural evolution of the network fabric rather than a separate system to deploy and operate.

Although Cilium pioneered the sidecarless model, other projects have since adopted similar designs, recognizing the efficiency and simplicity of this approach.

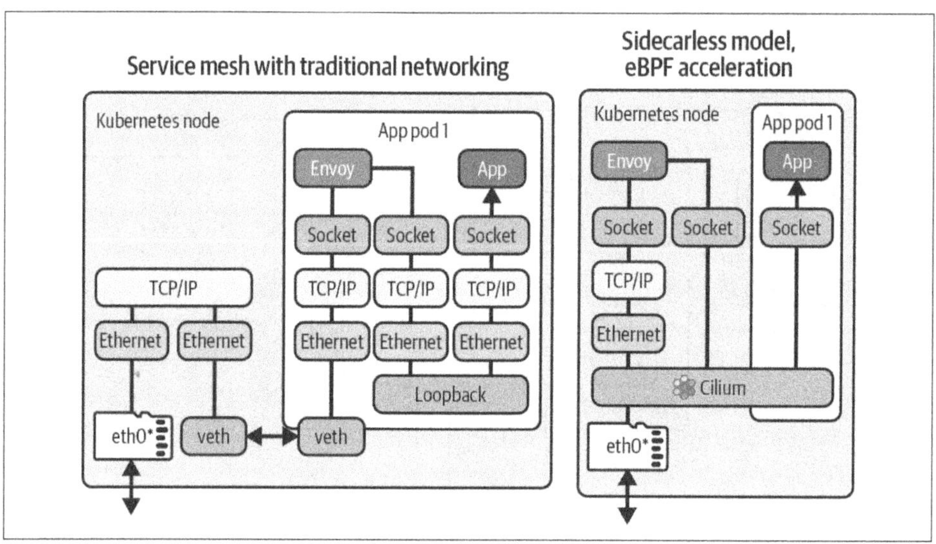

Figure 1-3. The sidecarless service mesh model

Service mesh features are not covered in a dedicated chapter in this book but will be discussed in context with ingress (Chapter 7), encryption (Chapter 14), and observability (Chapter 15).

Multicluster Networking and Load Balancing

For organizations that require multicluster topologies for high availability, disaster recovery, or geographic distribution, Cilium Cluster Mesh provides service discovery and east–west load balancing between clusters with affinity support, ensuring that traffic can be steered intelligently while keeping it as close as possible to the workloads it needs to reach (Figure 1-4).

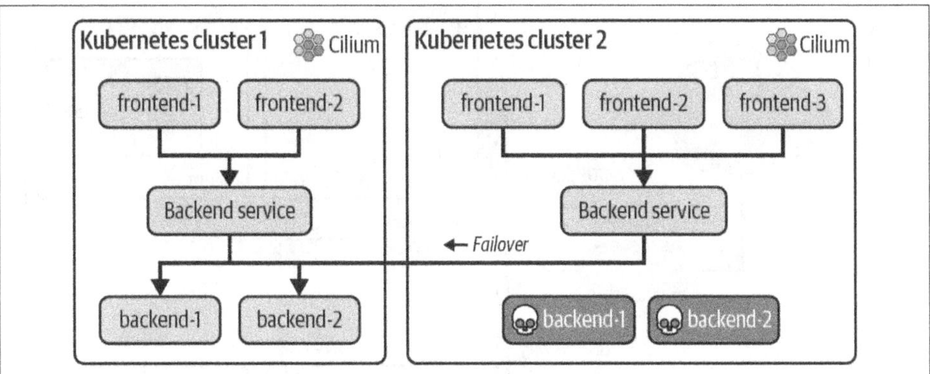

Figure 1-4. Multicluster networking with Cilium Cluster Mesh

More broadly, load balancing is an area where Cilium shines. Traditional `kube-proxy` implementations are replaced with eBPF-based logic, supporting advanced algorithms such as Maglev.[1] This ensures that traffic is distributed efficiently both within a cluster and across multiple clusters, helping applications remain available and performant. We'll talk more about these features in Chapters 8 and 9.

Interconnectivity with the Wider Network

Kubernetes clusters do not exist in isolation. Applications often need to be reachable by clients residing outside the cluster, in a different part of the network. Cilium supports this by:

- Connecting back to the core network, such as top-of-rack (ToR) devices, to advertise Kubernetes service IP addresses
- Enabling Kubernetes applications to be accessible to workloads and users outside the cluster

1 Maglev is a consistent hashing algorithm originally developed at Google to achieve stable and efficient load balancing at scale; it is covered in detail in Chapter 8.

By providing built-in support for BGP (Figure 1-5), Cilium becomes more than a cluster network; it extends the cluster into the enterprise fabric. This is especially valuable in hybrid deployments, where Kubernetes needs to coexist with VMs, bare-metal, and/or legacy infrastructure.

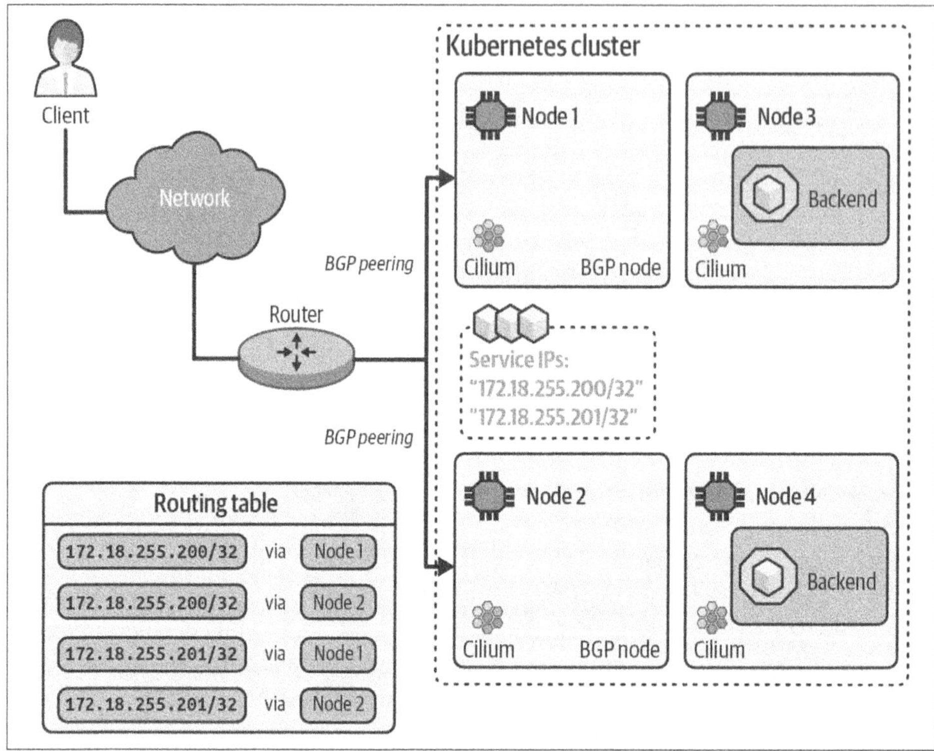

Figure 1-5. Cilium's built-in BGP support

We discuss BGP and layer 2 connectivity in detail in Chapter 10.

Firewalling and Network Policy

Kubernetes introduced the concept of NetworkPolicy to restrict access to and from pods. While this was a major step forward, the built-in NetworkPolicy model is limited to layer 3 and 4 controls: you can allow or deny traffic based on IPs, ports, and protocols, but not on higher-level application concepts.

Cilium extends this model. It enforces Kubernetes NetworkPolicies using eBPF and also provides its own CiliumNetworkPolicy resource, which supports application-level rules such as filtering based on Domain Name System (DNS) names or Hypertext Transfer Protocol (HTTP) methods. Importantly, Cilium policies operate on Kubernetes labels and identities. Policies can thus reflect intents such as "allow traffic from the frontend namespace to the payments service" rather than "allow traffic from `10.42.0.23` to `10.42.0.42`." This identity-based approach is better aligned with dynamic Kubernetes environments and helps meet regulatory requirements.

See Chapters 12 and 13 for more details on network policy.

Encryption and Secure Connectivity

As workloads communicate across nodes, and increasingly across clusters or even across clouds, encryption becomes essential. Cilium supports Transparent Encryption of traffic between nodes using either IPsec or WireGuard (Figure 1-6). This provides confidentiality and integrity without requiring changes to applications.

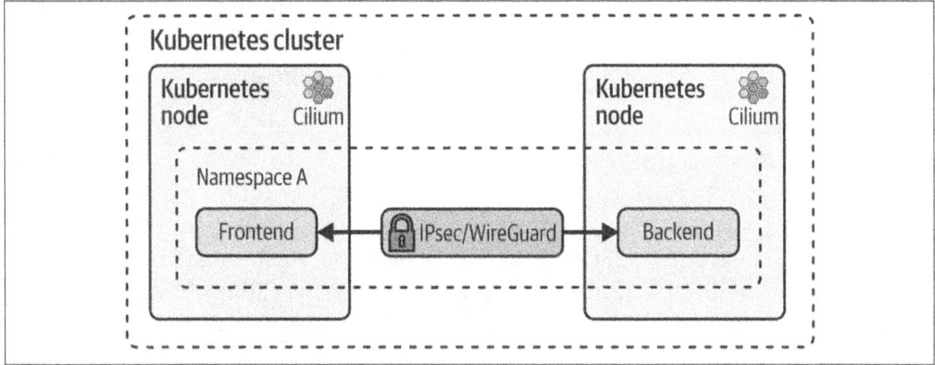

Figure 1-6. Cilium Transparent Encryption

In practice, enabling encryption with Cilium is extremely simple. It is described as transparent because applications do not need to be modified to benefit from it. Encryption can be enabled with a simple configuration flag, and when WireGuard is used, even key management is handled automatically. This allows operators to secure internode and intercluster communication at scale without adding operational burden.

See Chapter 14 for more on Transparent Encryption.

Observability with Hubble

Operating a network is not only about making packets flow or enforcing security rules. Day-to-day operations require visibility: you need to understand why a connection failed, which services depend on each other, and whether policies are being enforced as intended. Cilium integrates Hubble, a fully distributed observability system built on eBPF. Hubble captures detailed information about network flows, service dependencies, and policy decisions directly in the kernel.

Because only relevant events are exported to the user space, Hubble provides rich insights with minimal overhead. Operators can see not just IPs and ports, but also Kubernetes identities and namespaces. This makes troubleshooting and auditing far more intuitive than with traditional tools. Data can be visualized in the terminal or in a user interface. Cilium and Hubble can also be configured to serve Prometheus metrics, which can then be visualized in Grafana dashboards.

See Chapter 15 for more on Hubble and observability.

Looking Ahead

Cilium's story is still being written. What began as a container networking and security platform has expanded to include a broad set of capabilities for connectivity, security, and observability in Kubernetes environments. As the needs of cloud native infrastructure continue to evolve, Cilium is evolving with them.

One important trend is the expansion beyond microservices. Databases are already widely deployed on Kubernetes, despite early reservations about running stateful workloads. More recently, many organizations have begun running artificial intelligence and machine learning workloads on Kubernetes, often spanning clusters of graphics processing units (GPUs). These workloads place extreme demands on networking, requiring both high throughput and low latency. Cilium is well positioned to meet these needs with its programmable datapath.

Another significant development has been the rise of virtual machines managed by Kubernetes. More and more users want to bring their VM estates under the same operational model as their container workloads, rather than relying on traditional VM management platforms. Projects such as KubeVirt make this possible, and Cilium extends its networking, security, and observability features seamlessly to VMs.

Performance improvements also continue to shape the trajectory of Cilium. The introduction of *netkit*, a successor to the long-standing virtual Ethernet (veth) device, has shown that container networking can match the performance of host networking. Early adopters are already benefiting from deploying netkit—Bytedance, for example, has reportedly increased throughput by 10% across its entire fleet (*https://oreil.ly/MWRl2*)—and its use is likely to spread rapidly. By embedding eBPF programs even closer to the workload, Cilium can continue to reduce overhead and bring new capabilities to the datapath.

Beyond Linux, eBPF itself is becoming a standard across operating systems. Work on eBPF for Windows is progressing quickly, making it possible for technologies like Cilium and Tetragon to extend their capabilities to Windows environments in the future. This marks an important turning point: eBPF is no longer just a Linux innovation but an industry-wide platform for building networking and security.

Because it is open source, Cilium is shaped not only by its original creators but also by a wide and active community. Contributions from hyperscalers, enterprises, and independent developers ensure that it adapts to the ecosystem around it. This momentum, which as we saw earlier made it the first (and so far, only) CNCF project in the Cloud Native Networking category to graduate from the CNCF, has not slowed. New contributors are always welcome; don't hesitate to join the project!

The future of Cilium is tied to the future of cloud native development itself. As Kubernetes expands to new workloads and new forms of infrastructure, Cilium will continue to evolve in parallel.

In the chapters that follow, we will look more closely at how Cilium achieves these goals. Chapter 2 opens the box to examine the internal components of Cilium, showing how the agent, operator, and other components work together to provide the foundation on which all these capabilities are built. Understanding these building blocks will make it easier to understand how the Cilium features and use cases described earlier function.

CHAPTER 2

Inside Cilium

In Chapter 1 we explored the main use cases for Cilium—networking, security, and observability—and how eBPF enables them. In this chapter, we will take a closer look at the components that make up Cilium. Understanding how these pieces fit together will make it easier to follow how each feature works in later chapters.

Cilium's architecture is modular, with each component focusing on a specific responsibility. Some are present on every node, while others are optional and become relevant only when certain features are enabled.

Cilium at a Glance

Cilium's versatility comes from a modular design built around several key components:

Cilium agent
: Runs on every node and forms the core of Cilium. It loads and manages the eBPF programs and maps in the kernel, and it watches Kubernetes objects and Cilium custom resources to keep the datapath state up-to-date.

Cilium CNI plugin
: Connects Cilium to Kubernetes through the Container Network Interface framework. It is responsible for wiring new pods into the network when they are created, using the configuration files and binaries installed by the agent.

Cilium operator
: Provides cluster-level coordination. It manages Cilium's custom resources and allocates IP addresses, as well as other cluster-wide operations.

eBPF programs and maps
: Provide the foundation of the datapath. Programs handle connection tracking, NAT, load balancing, and policy enforcement, while maps store shared state between programs and the agent.

Cilium CLI
: Offers administrators a simple command-line interface for installation, configuration, and troubleshooting.

Proxies
: Handle traffic that requires inspection beyond simple packet filtering. Envoy processes HTTP and Transport Layer Security (TLS) traffic, providing layer 7 visibility and enforcement, while the built-in DNS proxy enables policies based on fully qualified domain names (FQDNs) by intercepting DNS requests and responses.

Hubble
: Optional component that provides observability through the per-node Hubble server, Hubble Relay for cluster-wide aggregation, and visualization tools such as the Hubble CLI and UI.

Cluster Mesh API Server
: Enables multicluster networking by sharing service and endpoint metadata across clusters. It allows each cluster to discover and route to remote services as if they were local, providing a consistent networking model when Cluster Mesh is enabled. You'll learn more about this component in Chapter 9, which covers Cluster Mesh in detail.

Let's dive into how they interact with each other to get a better understanding of the big picture, illustrated in Figure 2-1.

The Cilium operator is responsible for creating and managing various Cilium-specific custom resources, such as CiliumNetworkPolicy, CiliumNode, and CiliumEndpoint resources. These, along with standard Kubernetes objects, are continuously monitored by the Cilium agent. Based on this state, the agent loads and configures eBPF maps and programs that implement policy enforcement, load balancing, and visibility features. The agent also installs the CNI plugin and handles networking setup when new pods are created.

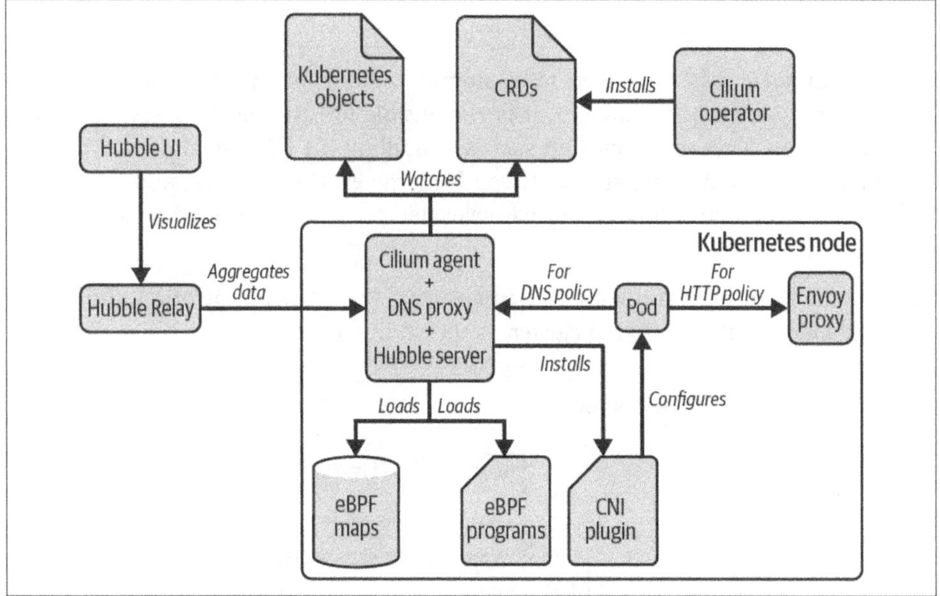

Figure 2-1. How all the Cilium components work together

When a pod sends traffic, it reaches a kernel hook point where an eBPF program is triggered. This program inspects the packet and determines whether to forward or drop it. If a layer 7 policy or FQDN-based rule is in effect, the eBPF program may redirect the packet to the appropriate user space proxy: the DNS proxy for domain name resolution, or the Envoy proxy for HTTP and TLS traffic.

The Envoy proxy processes layer 7 traffic and makes policy decisions based on application-level metadata, such as HTTP paths or TLS Server Name Indication (SNI). The DNS proxy captures DNS responses, maps the returned IP addresses to domain names, and updates the relevant eBPF maps so that future traffic to those IPs can be allowed or denied based on FQDN policies.

Meanwhile, the Hubble server observes network flows directly on each node. It collects metadata from eBPF events and, when available, enhances it with information from the DNS proxy. This enriched data can be viewed locally using the Hubble CLI or aggregated across the cluster by Hubble Relay. Finally, the Hubble UI visualizes this cluster-wide traffic information, making it easier to explore and troubleshoot networking behavior.

The Cilium Agent

The Cilium agent, often referred to as simply "Cilium" or the "Cilium daemon," is the core component of the system. It is responsible for orchestrating several critical tasks across the Kubernetes cluster, such as installing the CNI plugin, loading eBPF programs, and maintaining state between Kubernetes, the datapath, and the Cilium operator. To accomplish this, it runs with elevated privileges as a DaemonSet on every node.

The Cilium agent plays a pivotal role in ensuring the efficient operation of both the network and security within the cluster, as shown in Figure 2-2.

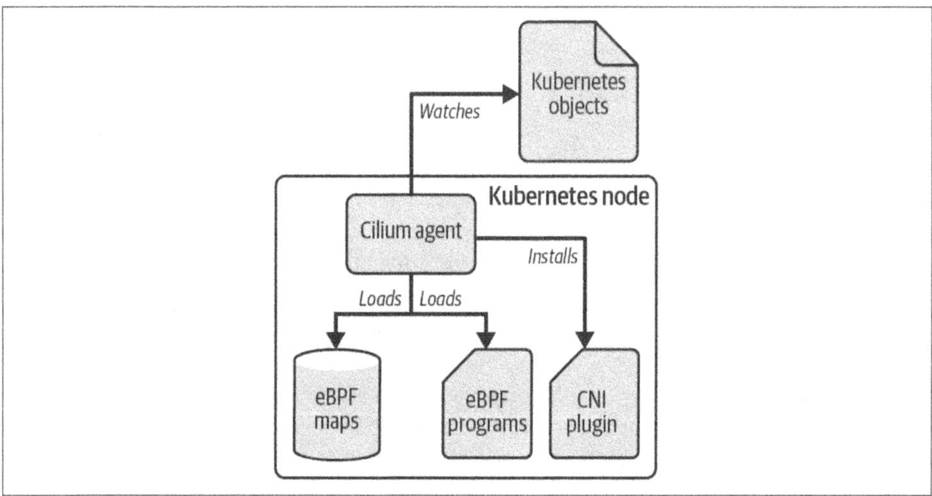

Figure 2-2. Cilium agent lifecycle responsibilities

Its responsibilities include:

Installing the CNI plugin
: The agent ensures that the Cilium CNI plugin is available on each node so that pod networking can be configured correctly when workloads are created. The plugin itself and its operation are described later in this chapter.

Loading eBPF programs and maps
: The agent loads and manages eBPF programs and maps on each node. The programs enforce network policy, perform NAT and load balancing, and apply encryption when Transparent Encryption is enabled. The agent not only loads these programs but also reads from and writes to several maps, for example to update service backends, track identities, or collect metrics that Hubble later consumes for observability.

Reconciling Kubernetes state
: The agent continuously monitors the desired Kubernetes state by communicating with the `kube-apiserver` and by watching Cilium's own custom resources maintained by the Cilium operator. It reacts to changes in these objects and updates eBPF maps and datapath configuration accordingly to maintain consistency between Kubernetes and the kernel.

Applying configuration
: Configuration for Cilium can come from both the `cilium-config` ConfigMap and Cilium's custom resource definitions (CRDs). The ConfigMap often carries cluster-level defaults, while CRDs hold more specific or feature-focused settings. The agent reads these values at start-up and uses them to control its runtime behavior.

Exposing debugging and troubleshooting interfaces
: For debugging and troubleshooting, the Cilium agent provides a suite of tools that can be invoked via the Cilium agent pod. The most notable is `cilium-dbg`, which gathers detailed diagnostic information from the node. It should not be confused with the Cilium CLI, a cluster-level tool for installing, managing, and operating Cilium described in the following section.

Prior to Cilium 1.15, `cilium-dbg` was named `cilium`, which caused confusion since it was unclear whether references to `cilium` described the CLI or the agent's debugging tool. Keep this in mind when reviewing older issues or documentation.

The Cilium CNI Plugin

Cilium is often described as a CNI, but this refers only to one part of the system: the plugin that connects Cilium to Kubernetes through the Container Network Interface framework. While this plugin is essential, Cilium itself provides a much broader set of capabilities for networking, security, and observability. The CNI plugin is simply how Cilium integrates with Kubernetes to handle pod networking.

The CNI specification defines a standard interface that allows container runtimes such as containerd or CRI-O to attach containers to a network. A CNI plugin must support four basic operations: adding (`ADD`) and deleting (`DEL`) containers, verifying (`CHECK`) that the container's network is functioning correctly, and reporting the plugin's version (`VERSION`).

When a user creates a pod, typically by applying a manifest with `kubectl`, the request is sent to the Kubernetes API server. After the scheduler assigns the pod to a node, the API server notifies the kubelet. The kubelet delegates container creation to the container runtime, which prepares the pod environment, including a new network namespace.[1]

The runtime then executes the CNI plugin defined in the host's configuration directory, which by default is */etc/cni/net.d/*. The corresponding plugin binary is typically located in */opt/cni/bin/*. These paths are standard for all CNIs in Kubernetes. When Cilium is installed, the Cilium agent populates these locations with its own configuration file (*05-cilium.conflist*) and plugin binary (*cilium-cni*).[2]

A typical configuration file looks like this:

```
{
  "cniVersion": "0.3.1",
  "name": "cilium",
  "plugins": [
    {
       "type": "cilium-cni",
       "enable-debug": false,
       "log-file": "/var/run/cilium/cilium-cni.log"
    }
  ]
}
```

When following the practical examples later in this book using the kind-based environment, you can view this configuration file on any worker node once the cluster is up and running with this command:

```
$ docker exec -it kind-worker \
    cat /etc/cni/net.d/05-cilium.conflist
```

1 If you're not familiar with network namespaces, see the sidebar "Linux Networking Essentials for Cilium" on page 74 for a brief explainer.

2 Some clusters use CNI chaining, where the configuration file lists several plugins in order, allowing Cilium to run alongside another CNI that handles tasks such as IP assignment or specific network setup. We don't particularly recommend this model and will not cover it in this book.

This process is illustrated in Figure 2-3.[3]

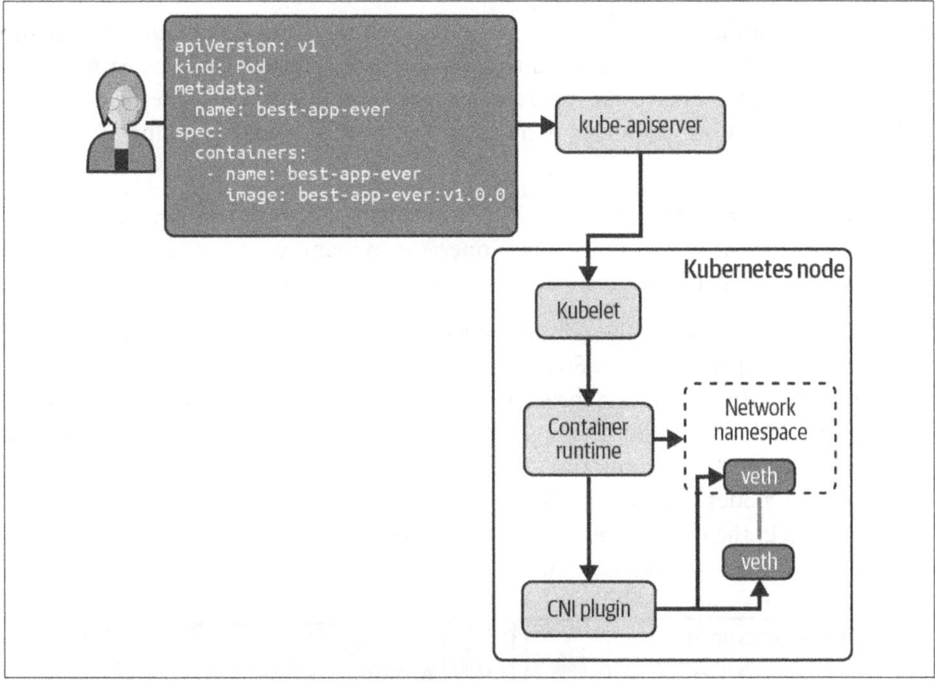
apiVersion: v1
kind: Pod
metadata:
  name: best-app-ever
spec:
  containers:
    - name: best-app-ever
      image: best-app-ever:v1.0.0
kube-apiserver
Kubernetes node
Kubelet
Container runtime
Network namespace
veth
veth
CNI plugin

Figure 2-3. Pod creation workflow and CNI integration

The Cilium CNI plugin acts as the link between the container runtime and the Cilium agent. When the runtime creates or removes a pod, it executes the CNI plugin binary with the details of the request. The plugin passes this information along to the Cilium agent, which then sets up or tears down the network interface and updates the relevant eBPF maps so the new endpoint is fully registered in the datapath.

CNIs typically do not handle traffic forwarding or load balancing. By default, `kube-proxy` serves as the default network proxy in Kubernetes, using technologies such as `iptables`, IPVS, or, more recently, `nftables` to direct incoming network traffic to the relevant pods within the cluster. Cilium can replace `kube-proxy` entirely, achieving the same tasks with significantly better performance, especially at scale. For more information on this topic, see Chapter 6.

3 For more details on the process of a CNI, consult *Networking and Kubernetes* by James Strong and Vallery Lancey (O'Reilly) or visit repos such as *https://github.com/f1ko/demystifying-cni* and *https://github.com/containernetworking/cni*.

The Cilium Operator

While the Cilium agent operates at the node level, the Cilium operator runs at the cluster level as a deployment within the Kubernetes cluster. Certain features and environments may modify the operator's responsibilities, but two key tasks stand out: managing custom resources defined by Cilium CRDs and handling IP address management.

Unlike many other projects, when Cilium is installed, it does not automatically install CRDs. This approach allows the Cilium operator to manage custom resources across versions, ensuring backward compatibility where needed.

Beyond CRD registration, the Cilium operator is also responsible for managing IP address allocation, as shown in Figure 2-4. The operator creates a CiliumNode object for each node (after registering the CRDs) and populates it with relevant information, such as the PodCIDRs (the IP ranges from which pods on this node are assigned addresses). Since the operator runs at the cluster level, it is aware of the IP ranges used by other nodes and can ensure there are no overlaps.[4] The Cilium agent then reads the data in the CiliumNode object to configure the local datapath. You will learn more about IP address management in Chapter 4.

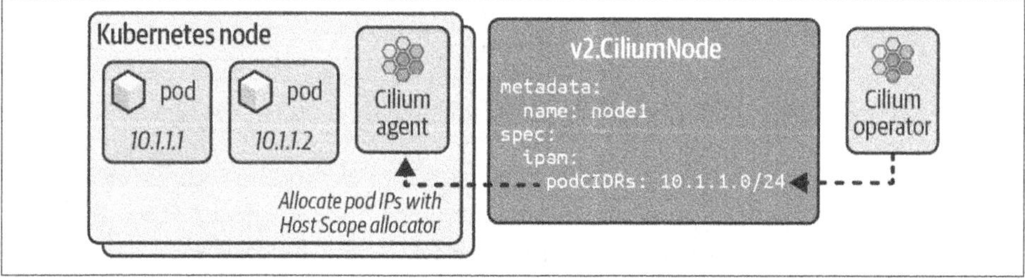

Figure 2-4. The Cilium operator manages IP address allocation

eBPF Programs and eBPF Maps

As discussed in Chapter 1, eBPF is a revolutionary technology that allows developers to extend the behavior of the Linux kernel without modifying or recompiling it. Instead of submitting kernel patches and waiting for them to be merged and released, they can write custom code that is safely injected into the running kernel, enabling immediate changes in behavior without a reboot.

4 Although the operator can run with multiple replicas, leader election ensures that only one instance is active at a time, preventing race conditions.

One of the reasons eBPF has gained such widespread adoption is its combination of safety and performance. Programs are verified before they are allowed to run in the kernel to ensure that they cannot compromise system stability[5] and then just-in-time (JIT) compiled into native machine code for near-native execution speed.[6] Together, these features allow for highly efficient and secure extensions to kernel functionality.

Two key concepts are fundamental to understanding how eBPF powers Cilium:

eBPF programs
: User-defined, stateless, event-driven pieces of code that are triggered by specific events within the kernel. These programs are attached to hook points, such as when a packet enters or leaves a network interface. When that event occurs, the corresponding eBPF program is executed. When applied to packet processing hook points, programs can inspect, modify, or drop packets based on policy or connection state.

eBPF maps
: Serve as in-kernel data storage. These maps allow eBPF programs and user space processes to store and retrieve data, enabling dynamic decision making. Just as a stateless microservice might query a database to make a decision, eBPF programs can perform lookups in eBPF maps to determine how to handle packets. Maps can also be updated to record connection state, update load-balancing entries, or increment metrics that Hubble later consumes for observability.

eBPF programs and maps enable Cilium to implement critical datapath functions entirely within the kernel, including:

- Connection tracking and stateful inspection
- NAT and service load balancing
- Network policy enforcement
- Flow and event observability through Hubble

When the Cilium agent starts, it loads the required eBPF programs for datapath operations and then continuously updates the relevant maps as Kubernetes objects change.

5 The eBPF verifier ensures that all programs are safe to execute within the kernel, preventing invalid memory access and infinite loops.

6 JIT compilation refers to the process of converting verified eBPF bytecode into native CPU instructions immediately before execution, avoiding interpretation overhead and significantly improving runtime performance.

The Cilium CLI

To manage and configure Cilium, you can install a separate command-line binary called the *Cilium CLI* on your machine. It provides a simple interface for managing and troubleshooting Cilium.

With the Cilium CLI, you can:

- Monitor the status and health of Cilium
- Run a battery of connectivity and performance tests
- Execute operational commands, such as rotating encryption keys and collecting sysdumps
- Install or uninstall Cilium
- Upgrade or downgrade to a different Cilium version
- Enable and disable Cilium features

The most commonly used command is `cilium status`. You can use it to easily check the health of the Cilium components described in this section:

```
$ cilium status
    /¯¯\
 /¯¯\__/¯¯\    Cilium:             OK
 \__/¯¯\__/    Operator:           OK
 /¯¯\__/¯¯\    Envoy DaemonSet:    OK
 \__/¯¯\__/    Hubble Relay:       disabled
    \__/       ClusterMesh:        disabled

DaemonSet              cilium            Desired: 4, Ready: 4/4, Available: 4/4
DaemonSet              cilium-envoy      Desired: 4, Ready: 4/4, Available: 4/4
Deployment             cilium-operator   Desired: 1, Ready: 1/1, Available: 1/1
Containers:            cilium            Running: 4
                       cilium-envoy      Running: 4
                       cilium-operator   Running: 1
Cluster Pods:          3/3 managed by Cilium
Helm chart version:    1.18.4
Image versions         cilium            quay.io/cilium/cilium:v1.18.4
                       cilium-envoy      quay.io/cilium/cilium-envoy:v1.34.10
                       cilium-operator   quay.io/cilium/operator-generic:v1.18.4
```

The Cilium CLI reads from your *kubeconfig* file to interact with the cluster via the Kubernetes API. We recommend downloading and installing it on your local machine if you intend to follow along with the examples in this book—you'll be using it extensively. The Cilium CLI is available for Linux, macOS, and Windows.

If you recall from "The Cilium Agent" on page 18, a separate utility called `cilium-dbg` is available inside each Cilium pod. Unless stated otherwise, references in this book to the Cilium CLI refer to the external cluster-level tool.

Hubble

Hubble is Cilium's observability component. It provides real-time visibility into network traffic and security events by collecting flow data directly from eBPF programs running in the kernel.

Hubble consists of several subsystems that work together, as illustrated in Figure 2-5:

Hubble server
: Runs on every node as part of the Cilium agent and observes network events locally. It enriches flow data with metadata such as pod names, namespaces, and policy verdicts.

Hubble Relay
: An optional component that adds multinode visibility. It discovers Hubble instances across the cluster, queries their gRPC APIs, and maintains connections to each peer to present a unified view of flow events.

Hubble CLI
: A command-line tool that connects to the Relay or directly to an agent, allowing users to query and filter observed network flows.

Hubble UI
: A web interface that visualizes communication patterns between services, namespaces, and endpoints.

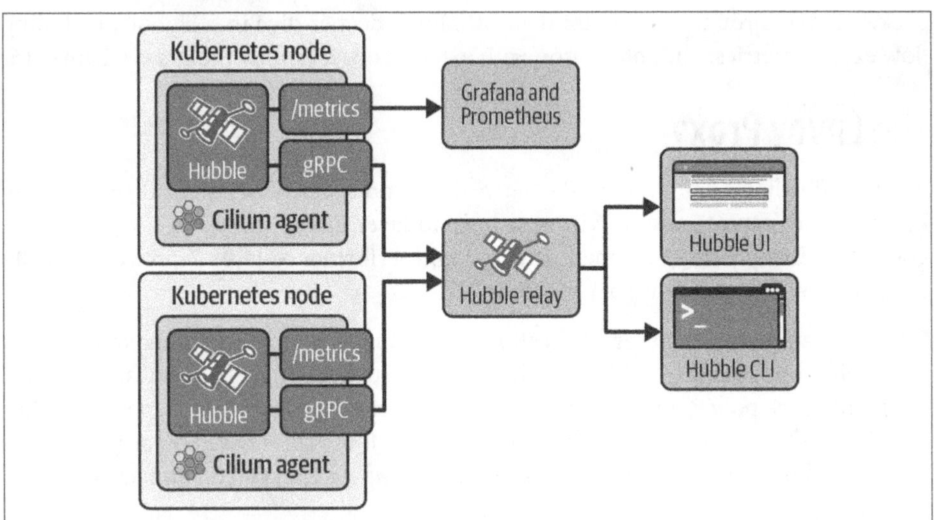

Figure 2-5. Hubble, the observability component of Cilium

Hubble Relay and the Hubble UI are not enabled by default and must be deployed separately.

Once Hubble Relay is enabled, you can observe network activity using the Hubble CLI.

Here is an example of a flow log for an ICMPv6 (Internet Control Message Protocol for IPv6) packet sent from a pod named `pod-worker` on a node named `kind-worker` to a pod named `pod-worker2` located on the node `kind-worker2`:

```
$ hubble observe --ipv6 --from-pod pod-worker
Sep  7 15:11:18.288: default/pod-worker (ID:3211) ->
  default/pod-worker2 (ID:50760)
  to-overlay FORWARDED (ICMPv6 EchoRequest)

Sep  7 15:11:18.289: default/pod-worker (ID:3211) ->
  default/pod-worker2 (ID:50760)
  to-endpoint FORWARDED (ICMPv6 EchoRequest)
```

The `--from-pod` flag filters flows originating from the specified pod, while `--ipv6` limits the output to IPv6 traffic. Each log entry contains metadata about the packet, including its timestamp, source and destination pods, forwarding decision, and protocol type. In this example, the two log lines represent the same ICMPv6 echo request as it traverses the overlay network and then reaches the destination endpoint.

The Hubble UI provides a visual representation of the same data, displaying a live service map of network interactions within the cluster. It can be accessed through a browser once the relay and UI components are deployed.

You will use Hubble throughout this book to verify network activity and observe how packets move through the Cilium datapath. For a deeper dive into Hubble, including flow export, metrics, and integration with external observability tools, see Chapter 15.

The Envoy Proxy

While eBPF allows Cilium to make networking and security decisions directly in the kernel, some features require visibility beyond layer 4. For these cases, Cilium integrates the Envoy proxy, an open source, high-performance layer 7 proxy originally developed by Lyft and now part of the CNCF.

Cilium uses Envoy whenever application-layer context is required to make decisions or provide observability. This includes features such as Ingress and Gateway API, layer 7 network policy, and application protocol visibility. Envoy can inspect and filter HTTP, gRPC, or TLS traffic, enabling Cilium to enforce rules based on attributes like HTTP methods, paths, or hostnames and to terminate encrypted connections when necessary.

Envoy is deployed as a DaemonSet, giving each node its own dedicated Envoy instance that the Cilium agent communicates with locally. Only traffic that requires application-layer inspection or policy enforcement is redirected to Envoy, while all other traffic remains within the eBPF datapath.

To confirm that Envoy is running in your cluster, you can list the DaemonSet:

```
$ kubectl get daemonset -n kube-system cilium-envoy
NAME           DESIRED   CURRENT   READY   UP-TO-DATE   AVAILABLE
cilium-envoy   3         3         3       3            3
```

The DNS Proxy

In addition to Envoy, Cilium includes a lightweight DNS proxy that enables FQDN-based policies at layer 4. The proxy intercepts DNS queries and responses, ties resolved IPs to domain names in eBPF maps, and lets Cilium enforce policies based on names rather than static IPs.

Although the DNS proxy is considered a separate component in Cilium, it operates on every node within the cluster as part of the Cilium agent pod. This approach minimizes performance overhead by ensuring that DNS traffic is intercepted and processed locally, avoiding unnecessary internode communication.

FQDN-based policies are especially useful in dynamic environments, where services are accessed via domain names rather than hardcoded IP addresses. This is common when workloads communicate with third-party APIs or cloud services. Instead of tracking and maintaining lists of changing IPs, Cilium allows operators to define policies based on domain names. We will revisit DNS and FQDN-based network policies in Chapter 13, which covers advanced policy concepts and configuration.

Summary

In this chapter, we have explored the individual components of Cilium. At the heart of Cilium's architecture is the Cilium agent. It installs the Cilium CNI plugin; loads the eBPF programs and maps used to forward, filter, and observe traffic; and monitors the custom resource definitions managed by the Cilium operator. When a pod sends traffic, an eBPF program decides whether to forward or drop the traffic and may send it to a proxy for further processing (Envoy for HTTP-related traffic, or DNS for DNS-related requests). The Cilium CLI is a binary that primarily helps install and manage Cilium. Meanwhile, the Hubble server observes and enriches traffic data, and Hubble Relay aggregates it across all cluster nodes. The Hubble UI and CLI provide options to visualize network activity in a web browser and a terminal, respectively.

With that, we've established a solid understanding of the various components that make up Cilium, allowing us to explore each one in greater depth in the following chapters.

CHAPTER 3

Getting Started with Cilium

Now that you're familiar with the core components of Cilium, let's go ahead and put it to use. The best way to become familiar with Cilium is to deploy it and try out some of the core capabilities. In this chapter, you will learn how to:

- Install Cilium in a Kubernetes cluster
- Deploy an application
- Access, secure, and monitor the application

In later chapters, we will dive further into various areas of Cilium, but the practical, hands-on experience you gain here will give you a strong foundation to build on. To get started, you will need access to a Kubernetes cluster. We'll create one locally.

If you don't have local compute resources available to run a Kubernetes cluster, feel free to use the free online hands-on labs provided by Isovalent. Head over to *https://isovalent.com/labs* to begin your evaluation of Cilium.

Setting Up Your Environment

Throughout this book, you will find code snippets and scripts to install, test, and configure Cilium. This implies that you have access to a Kubernetes cluster. Do not try any of the scripts in a production cluster: they may cause some disruption or, even worse, a complete cluster outage.

Cilium works with any distribution conformant with "vanilla" Kubernetes and is often even packaged and included by default with many Kubernetes distributions and services.

Not everyone has the financial or computing resources to run a Kubernetes cluster. Therefore, the environment we will recommend for the vast majority of the exercises in the book is based on Kubernetes in Docker (kind) (*https://kind.sigs.k8s.io*), a popular tool used to run Kubernetes clusters locally in Docker containers. We recommend kind over alternatives because it is a lightweight, CNCF-certified conformant Kubernetes installer that works across multiple platforms (Linux, macOS, and Windows).

If you prefer another lightweight Kubernetes solution, check the documentation to make sure it's compatible with Cilium (*https://oreil.ly/760L8*).

Kubernetes in Docker (kind)

This chapter assumes you have Docker or another container runtime installed, as kind requires it to launch Kubernetes clusters. If you need help installing Docker, refer to the official documentation (*https://oreil.ly/WE0Wp*) for your operating system.

If you don't have kind installed yet, let's do that now. For those of you on macOS, you can use Homebrew (*https://brew.sh*) to install it:

```
$ brew install kind
```

The instructions for other platforms can be found on the kind website (*https://oreil.ly/sCjfW*).

Installing the Cilium CLI

To manage and inspect Cilium deployments, we will use the Cilium CLI. It should be available in your operating system's package manager. For example, you can run the following Homebrew command to install it on macOS:

```
$ brew install cilium-cli
```

You can also download and install Cilium CLI from its GitHub repository (*https://github.com/cilium/cilium-cli*). You'll find detailed instructions in the Cilium docs (*https://oreil.ly/GSZuP*). Once that's done, verify that it has been installed correctly:

```
$ cilium version --client
cilium-cli: v0.18.7 compiled with go1.25.0 on darwin/arm64
cilium image (default): v1.18.1
cilium image (stable): v1.18.4
```

Installing the Hubble CLI

To observe network traffic in the cluster, we will use Hubble and its binary client, the Hubble CLI. You can also install Hubble with a package manager like Homebrew:

```
$ brew install hubble
```

Alternatively, download and install the tarball from the Hubble GitHub repository (*https://github.com/cilium/hubble*). Again, detailed installation instructions are available in the Cilium docs (*https://oreil.ly/OjN8S*).

You can verify that the Hubble CLI has been installed correctly by running the following command:

```
$ hubble version
hubble v1.16.4@HEAD-4b765dc compiled with go1.23.3 on darwin/arm64
```

Installing Helm

We will use the Kubernetes package manager Helm throughout the book. If you don't have it installed on your machine yet, install it via your package manager (e.g., with `brew install helm`) or refer to the official Helm installation docs (*https://helm.sh/docs/intro/install/*). We've used Helm v3 in this book.

Deploying a kind Cluster

The following YAML manifest, available in the book's GitHub repository, includes the specification of the cluster:

```
kind: Cluster                          # Declares a kind cluster
apiVersion: kind.x-k8s.io/v1alpha4   # Kind API version
nodes:
- role: control-plane                  # One control-plane node
- role: worker                         # Two worker nodes
- role: worker                         # Two worker nodes
networking:
  disableDefaultCNI: true              # Disables kindnetd prior to Cilium install
```

The most notable aspect of the configuration is the `networking.disableDefaultCNI: true` setting. It specifies that the cluster must be deployed without kind's built-in CNI (`kindnetd`).

As you'll recall from Chapter 1, a CNI plugin is required in order for the cluster to host and connect applications. We intentionally disable kind's default built-in CNI so that we can install Cilium instead in the next section.

You can find all the YAML manifests you will use in this chapter to deploy and test Cilium in the *chapter03* directory of the book's GitHub repository (*https://github.com/isovalent/cilium-up-and-running*). Navigate to this folder before proceeding.

Let's now deploy the kind cluster. To do that, you'll use the following command:

```
$ kind create cluster --config kind.yaml
Creating cluster "kind" ...
 ✓ Ensuring node image (kindest/node:v1.33.4) 🖼
 ✓ Preparing nodes 📦 📦 📦
 ✓ Writing configuration 📜
 ✓ Starting control-plane 🕹️
 ✓ Installing StorageClass 💾
 ✓ Joining worker nodes 🚜
 Set kubectl context to "kind-kind"
You can now use your cluster with:

kubectl cluster-info --context kind-kind

Thanks for using kind! 😊
```

With the cluster deployed, let's use `kubectl` to verify its status:

```
$ kubectl get nodes
NAME                 STATUS     ROLES           AGE   VERSION
kind-control-plane   NotReady   control-plane   6m    v1.33.4
kind-worker          NotReady   <none>          6m    v1.33.4
kind-worker2         NotReady   <none>          6m    v1.33.4
```

The preceding terminal output shows that three nodes (one control plane and two workers) have been deployed, but they are in the `NotReady` state. This indicates the nodes are unhealthy and will not accept workloads. You may have already guessed the reason, but let's confirm it by inspecting the status of one of our worker nodes:

```
$ kubectl get nodes kind-worker -o yaml
[...]
message: >
  container runtime network not ready: NetworkReady=false
  reason: NetworkPluginNotReady
  message: Network plugin returns error: cni plugin not initialized
```

As you can see, since no network plugin has been deployed, the kubelet reports it is not ready to run pods. We'll resolve that by installing the Cilium CNI plugin in the next section.

Installing Cilium

Cilium supports multiple installation methods, but the two most common are using the Cilium CLI (`cilium install`) for quick setup and environment autodetection or Helm, which provides explicit control and aligns better with GitOps and long-term operations.

Installing Cilium Using the Cilium CLI

The Cilium CLI simplifies the initial experience by inspecting your current Kubernetes context and generating a set of recommended Helm values based on your environment. To preview the configuration without performing the installation, run:

```
$ cilium install --dry-run-helm-values
```

For your kind cluster, this should return:

```
cluster:
  name: kind-kind
ipam:
  mode: kubernetes
operator:
  replicas: 1
routingMode: tunnel
tunnelProtocol: vxlan
```

In this configuration:

- The Cilium operator will be deployed with a single replica.
- The IPAM mode is set to Kubernetes Host Scope mode.
- The routing mode is set to encapsulation, with VXLAN tunnels used to encapsulate traffic between nodes.

We'll explore IPAM and routing modes in more detail in Chapters 4 and 5. For now, note that Cilium will form VXLAN tunnels between all nodes to enable cross-node pod communication, and it will allocate pod IPs from the subnets assigned to each node by Kubernetes.

To verify the PodCIDRs Kubernetes has assigned, run:

```
$ kubectl get nodes kind-worker -o yaml | yq .spec.podCIDR
10.244.1.0/24

$ kubectl get nodes kind-worker2 -o yaml | yq .spec.podCIDR
10.244.2.0/24
```

When you deploy the sample app shortly, you will observe that Cilium assigns IPs from these ranges.

Running `cilium install` now will install Cilium using the autogenerated settings:

```
$ cilium install
🔮 Auto-detected Kubernetes kind: kind
ℹ️ Using Cilium version 1.18.4
🔮 Autodetected cluster name: kind-kind
🔮 Autodetected kube-proxy has been installed
```

Installing Cilium Using Helm (Recommended)

Helm is already widely used to manage other Kubernetes applications, such as Prometheus, Grafana, cert-manager, and so on. Using it for Cilium as well ensures a consistent deployment workflow and makes it easier to integrate with continuous integration/continuous deployment (CI/CD) and GitOps practices.

First, set up the Helm repository:

```
$ helm repo add cilium https://helm.cilium.io/
```

Then install Cilium with Helm:

```
$ helm install cilium cilium/cilium -n kube-system \
    --version 1.18.4 \
    --values helm-values.yaml
```

You should see something like this:

```
NAME: cilium
LAST DEPLOYED: Fri Dec 19 09:03:46 2025
NAMESPACE: kube-system
STATUS: deployed
REVISION: 1
TEST SUITE: None
NOTES:
You have successfully installed Cilium with Hubble.
```

You'll find Helm values files to use throughout the rest of the book in the folders corresponding to each chapter in the book's GitHub repository. Use them with the Helm install command shown earlier to deploy Cilium with the appropriate settings.

Instead of using a values file, you can pass values inline:

```
$ helm upgrade --install cilium cilium/cilium -n kube-system \
    --version 1.18.4 \
    --set cluster.name=kind-kind \
    --set ipam.mode=kubernetes \
    --set operator.replicas=1 \
    --set routingMode=tunnel \
    --set tunnelProtocol=vxlan
```

The `cilium install` command also accepts these Helm-style `--set` flags for customization.

By default, both `cilium install` and Helm will install the latest stable version of Cilium.[1] However, you can explicitly specify a version to ensure consistency across environments or to avoid unexpected changes. This is especially useful in production, where you may want to pin versions and manage upgrades intentionally.

1 To be precise, the Cilium CLI will install the version of Cilium that was most recent when the CLI was built.

To install a specific version, use the `--version` flag:

```
$ helm upgrade --install cilium cilium/cilium \
    -n kube-system --version 1.18.4 --values helm-values.yaml
```

You can watch the progress of the installation by typing `cilium status --wait`. After a couple of minutes, Cilium should be successfully installed. Verify the installation with the `cilium status` command:

```
$ cilium status
```

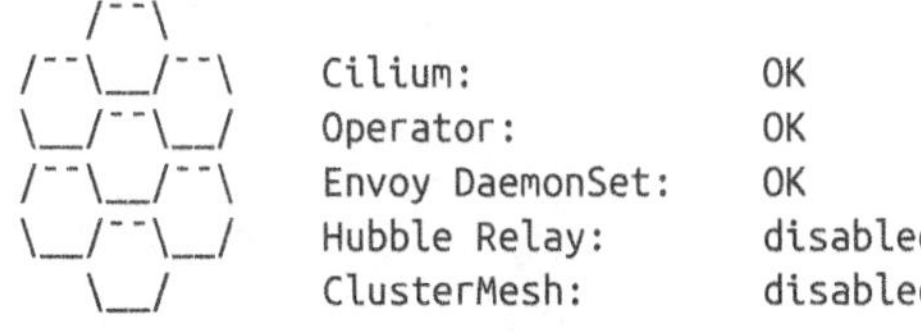

```
Cilium:             OK
Operator:           OK
Envoy DaemonSet:    OK
Hubble Relay:       disabled
ClusterMesh:        disabled

DaemonSet          cilium                  Desired: 3, Ready: 3/3
DaemonSet          cilium-envoy            Desired: 3, Ready: 3/3
Deployment         cilium-operator         Desired: 1, Ready: 1/1
Containers:        cilium                  Running: 3
                   cilium-envoy            Running: 3
                   cilium-operator         Running: 1
                   clustermesh-apiserver
                   hubble-relay
Cluster Pods:      3/3 managed by Cilium
[...]
```

In the output, you can see how the components we described in Chapter 2 are deployed. Since the Cilium agent and Envoy components are both deployed through a DaemonSet, there is an instance of each deployed on every cluster node. As you might have seen in the earlier `cilium install --dry-run-helm-values` output, a single Cilium operator was deployed as part of the deployment. You can verify this with the following `kubectl` commands:

```
$ kubectl get -n kube-system daemonset cilium cilium-envoy
NAME           DESIRED   READY   NODE SELECTOR
cilium         3         3       kubernetes.io/os=linux
cilium-envoy   3         3       kubernetes.io/os=linux

$ kubectl get -n kube-system deployment cilium-operator
NAME              READY   AVAILABLE
cilium-operator   1/1     1
```

Deploying a Sample Application

Let's now deploy a sample application. The following example is a common first application deployed in Kubernetes: the lightweight NGINX web server app. We'll use the *nginx-deployment.yaml* manifest file from the book's GitHub repository:

```
apiVersion: apps/v1
kind: Deployment
metadata:
  name: nginx-deployment
spec:
  replicas: 1
  selector:
    matchLabels:
      app.kubernetes.io/name: nginx
  template:
    metadata:
      labels:
        app.kubernetes.io/name: nginx
    spec:
      nodeSelector:
        kubernetes.io/hostname: kind-worker2
      containers:
        - name: nginx
          image: nginx
```

"Pinning" the `nginx-server` pod to a specific worker node (`kind-worker2`) isn't a best practice in production, but it's useful here to illustrate internode traffic, which Cilium handles through VXLAN tunneling in the selected configuration mode. Let's deploy the manifest:

```
$ kubectl apply -f nginx-deployment.yaml
deployment.apps/nginx-deployment created
```

We can verify that the pod was scheduled on the expected node and that it was assigned an IP address by running the following command:

```
$ kubectl get pods -o wide
NAME                               READY   IP             NODE
nginx-deployment-979f5455f-tjd2w   1/1     10.244.2.127   kind-worker2
```

Next, we'll deploy a pod on a different worker node (`kind-worker`), using the following manifest (*netshoot-client-pod.yaml*). We're using a networking utility called netshoot (*https://github.com/nicolaka/netshoot*), which we'll use throughout the book because it includes many helpful networking tools. Given that it's a debugging utility, it typically runs once and exits.

To keep it running, we instruct it to run `sleep infinity`:

```
apiVersion: v1
kind: Pod
metadata:
  name: netshoot-client
  labels:
    app.kubernetes.io/name: netshoot-client
spec:
  nodeSelector:
    kubernetes.io/hostname: kind-worker
  containers:
    - name: netshoot
      image: nicolaka/netshoot
      command: ["sleep", "infinity"]
```

Let's deploy the pod and verify that it was scheduled on the `kind-worker` node:

```
$ kubectl apply -f netshoot-client-pod.yaml
pod/netshoot-client created

$ kubectl get pods -o wide
NAME                              READY   IP            NODE
netshoot-client                   1/1     10.244.1.67   kind-worker
```

We should also check that we can connect from `netshoot-client` (located on `kind-worker`) to the `nginx-server` (located on `kind-worker2`):[2]

```
$ kubectl exec pod/netshoot-client -- curl -s http://10.244.2.127
<!DOCTYPE html>
<html>
<head>
<title>Welcome to nginx!</title>
[OUTPUT TRUNCATED]
```

To verify HTTP connectivity, we really only need the HTTP status code. In our case, we expect a `200` to show a successful access. The following `curl` command will output just the status code:

```
$ kubectl exec pod/netshoot-client -- \
    curl -s -o /dev/null \
    -w "%{http_code}\n" \
    http://10.244.2.127
200
```

We've successfully deployed two pods across different nodes in the cluster, confirmed IP address assignments, and verified successful internode connectivity using Cilium's VXLAN-based tunneling. We'll dive deeper into VXLAN and the datapath in Chapter 5.

2 Use the pod IP you got from the previous step, which probably won't match ours.

While a successful connection from a client to the IP of a destination pod is a good first step, you might already know it's not the preferred approach in Kubernetes. Kubernetes provides the *service* abstraction as a deterministic method for accessing applications.

Upon creation, Kubernetes will assign a service a virtual IP address. When a client connects to the service's virtual IP, traffic will be forwarded to one of the service's endpoints.

Kubernetes uses Endpoints and EndpointSlices to track the backends of a service. These objects are used for load-balancing decisions for each service. EndpointSlices, in particular, offer a more scalable way to track backends across large clusters. By contrast, Cilium uses CiliumEndpoints (CEPs) and CiliumEndpointSlices (CESs) to support network routing and policy enforcement (you will see how CEPs are used later in this book).

To better understand how Kubernetes services work, let's create one using the following manifest (*nginx-service.yaml*). This service listens on TCP port 80 and load-balances traffic randomly toward pods labeled `app.kubernetes.io/name: nginx`:

```
apiVersion: v1
kind: Service
metadata:
  name: nginx-service
spec:
  selector:
    app.kubernetes.io/name: nginx
  ports:
    - protocol: TCP
      port: 80
      targetPort: 80
  type: ClusterIP
```

Once you've deployed the service, inspect it:

```
$ kubectl get svc nginx-service -o yaml
apiVersion: v1
kind: Service
metadata:
[...]
  name: nginx-service
  namespace: default
spec:
  clusterIP: 10.96.242.74 ❷
  clusterIPs:
  - 10.96.242.74
  internalTrafficPolicy: Cluster
  ipFamilies:
```

```
  - IPv4
  ipFamilyPolicy: SingleStack
  ports:
  - port: 80
    protocol: TCP
    targetPort: 80
  selector:
    app.kubernetes.io/name: nginx
  sessionAffinity: None
  type: ClusterIP ❶
```

❶ The service type is ClusterIP, which means it's only accessible from within the cluster.

❷ It was assigned a cluster-internal IP (`10.96.242.74`) in the `10.96.0.0/16` CIDR range (the default IPv4 service subnet in kind).

You can confirm that the service is working by sending an HTTP request to its ClusterIP:

```
$ kubectl exec netshoot-client -- curl http://10.96.242.74
<h1>Welcome to nginx!</h1>
```

ClusterIP is one of several Kubernetes service types, alongside NodePort and LoadBalancer. Chapter 6 will provide a refresher on service types. While ClusterIP is used for internal communication, most of your applications will need to be accessible from outside the cluster. Chapter 7 will introduce Ingress and Gateway API for handling external traffic, and Chapter 10 will explain the networking options available to expose your applications.

Although the client connects to the service IP, the request is forwarded to one of the backend pods selected by the service. The backend pod generates the response, but Cilium's eBPF-based service handling rewrites it so that the client still sees the service IP as the source. Kubernetes tracks which pods belong to the service through EndpointSlices, which list the IPs of all pods matching the service's label selector:

```
$ kubectl get endpointslices.discovery.k8s.io nginx-service-66q4l
NAME                  ADDRESSTYPE   PORTS   ENDPOINTS      AGE
nginx-service-66q4l   IPv4          80      10.244.2.127   2m13s
```

If you scale the deployment, Kubernetes automatically updates the endpoints:

```
$ kubectl scale deployment nginx-deployment --replicas=2
deployment.apps/nginx-deployment scaled
```

After scaling, both pods will be running and the EndpointSlices object will reflect both IPs:

```
$ kubectl get pods -l app.kubernetes.io/name=nginx
NAME                               READY   STATUS    RESTARTS   AGE
nginx-deployment-979f5455f-9pm7d   1/1     Running   0          4m29s
nginx-deployment-979f5455f-xw8nz   1/1     Running   0          13s

$ kubectl get endpointslices.discovery.k8s.io nginx-service-66q4l
NAME                  ADDRESSTYPE   PORTS   ENDPOINTS                     AGE
nginx-service-66q4l   IPv4          80      10.244.2.127,10.244.2.189     14m
```

Behind the scenes, these endpoint IPs are what Kubernetes uses to route traffic to pods. In many clusters, `kube-proxy` runs on every node and programs `iptables`, IPVS, or `nftables` rules to implement service forwarding. In our setup, `kube-proxy` is installed, but Cilium still intercepts ClusterIP traffic and resolves services through its eBPF datapath. `kube-proxy` remains present on the node, although it is not used for service lookup in this case.

You can confirm that `kube-proxy` is running with:

```
$ kubectl get -n kube-system daemonset kube-proxy
NAME         DESIRED   READY   NODE SELECTOR
kube-proxy   3         3       kubernetes.io/os=linux
```

In Chapter 6, you'll learn how Cilium replaces `kube-proxy` entirely using eBPF, eliminating the need for `iptables`, IPVS, or `nftables`.

Another benefit of leveraging a service is the automatic service DNS name generation. You can verify successful DNS resolution by accessing the `nginx-service` name from the client:

```
$ kubectl exec netshoot-client -- curl nginx-service.default.svc.cluster.local
<h1>Welcome to nginx!</h1>
```

Given that the client and the NGINX servers reside in the same namespace, you only need the service name, and `curl http://nginx-service` would also be successful.

Cilium is not responsible for DNS activities; however, as we saw briefly in Chapter 2, it sometimes leverages a component called the DNS Proxy when users define domain-based network policies. You will learn more about that in Chapter 13.

Securing the Application with Cilium Network Policies

With the application deployed and reachable, let's apply a network policy to restrict access, allowing only trusted systems to access it. We will create a network policy that allows access only from the `netshoot-client` to the `nginx-server` pod, blocking the traffic from unauthorized systems.

First, to help us demonstrate network policies, we'll create another client pod with the following manifest (*unauthorized-client.yaml*):

```
apiVersion: v1
kind: Pod
metadata:
  name: unauthorized-client
spec:
  containers:
    - name: netshoot
      image: nicolaka/netshoot
      command: ["sleep", "infinity"]
```

Deploy it and verify it has access to the `nginx-server` prior to deploying network policies.

You might already be familiar with Kubernetes network policies. Cilium network policies (CNPs) build on them and provide more granular controls. Chapter 12 will cover the concepts of identity, endpoints, labels, and how to construct CNPs. For now, just know that they're defined through the use of Kubernetes labels.

Next, take a look at the following network policy (*policy.yaml*):

```
apiVersion: cilium.io/v2
kind: CiliumNetworkPolicy
metadata:
  name: ch03-policy
  namespace: default
spec:
  endpointSelector: ❶
    matchLabels:
      app.kubernetes.io/name: nginx
  ingress: ❷
    - fromEndpoints: ❸
        - matchLabels:
            app.kubernetes.io/name: netshoot-client
      toPorts: ❹
        - ports:
            - port: "80"
              protocol: TCP
```

❶ `endpointSelector` selects the pods the policy applies to: here we're selecting pods with the label `app.kubernetes.io/name: nginx`.

❷ `ingress` defines the traffic direction the policy applies to. In this instance we are defining a rule that will authorize traffic *to* the pods with the `app.kubernetes.io/name: nginx` label (`egress` would instead apply to traffic *from* the pods).

❸ `fromEndpoints` determines which sources pods are allowed to connect to (here, those with the `app.kubernetes.io/name: netshoot-client` label).

❹ `toPorts` specifies which TCP/UDP ports are permitted.

By default, all egress and ingress traffic is allowed for all endpoints. When an endpoint is selected by a network policy, it transitions to a default deny state, where only explicitly allowed traffic is permitted.

Given that our rule has an ingress section, the endpoint goes into default deny mode for ingress. In other words, when traffic enters endpoints with the `app.kubernetes.io/name: nginx` label, only traffic from clients with the `app.kubernetes.io/name: netshoot-client` label going to port 80 will be allowed. Any other traffic to these endpoints will be denied.

Isovalent offers a free online Network Policy Editor tool (*https://editor.cilium.io*) to help create and manage network policies.

Let's check that our `netshoot-client` has the right label and that `unauthorized-client` does not:

```
$ kubectl get pods --show-labels
NAME                   READY   LABELS
netshoot-client        1/1     app.kubernetes.io/name=netshoot-client
nginx-server           1/1     app.kubernetes.io/name=nginx
unauthorized-client    1/1     <none>
```

Once you've deployed the policy (*policy.yaml*) with `kubectl`, verify that the `unauthorized-client` pod can no longer access the NGINX server, while the `netshoot-client` still can:

```
$ kubectl exec unauthorized-client -- curl --max-time 3 -s \
    http://nginx-service
command terminated with exit code 28

$ kubectl exec netshoot-client -- curl --max-time 3 -s http://nginx-service
<h1>Welcome to nginx!</h1>
```

Unlike standard Kubernetes network policies, Cilium network policies can apply at up to layer 7. This is particularly useful for securing API calls, such as those made over REST or gRPC. With layer 7 network policies, you can restrict access based on HTTP methods, headers, and paths.

Traffic matching layer 7 rules is directed to Envoy, which performs HTTP inspection before forwarding or denying the request. We introduced Envoy in Chapter 2, and you will see more use cases for it in Chapter 7.

By default, the NGINX server we deployed includes an error page named *50x.html*. The current CiliumNetworkPolicy lets you access it with no restrictions:

```
$ kubectl exec -t netshoot-client -- curl http://nginx-service/50x.html
<html><title>Error</title><body>
<h1>An error occurred.</h1>
<p>Sorry, the page you are looking for is currently unavailable.</p>
<em>Faithfully yours, nginx.</em>
</body>
```

You can refine the previous policy to allow access only to the *index.html* page via the HTTP `GET` method by adding a layer 7 rule such as the following:

```
      toPorts:
        - ports:
            - port: "80"
              protocol: TCP
          rules:
            http:
              - method: "GET"
                path: "/index.html"
```

Deploy the updated network policy (*policy-with-l7.yaml*), overwriting the previously configured policy, and then verify access to */50x.html* and */index.html*. You should see that the former is now blocked, while the latter is still allowed:

```
$ kubectl exec netshoot-client -- curl -s http://nginx-service/50x.html
Access denied

$ kubectl exec netshoot-client -- curl http://nginx-service/index.html
<h1>Welcome to nginx!</h1>
```

Notice that this time you receive an "access denied" error, rather than a timeout as you saw earlier when you used a layer 3 policy. While enforced layer 3 rules lead to dropped packets, enforced layer 7 rules applied by Envoy return deny codes for the application protocol. In this case, we're parsing HTTP traffic, so it returns `403` for a denied request.

Now that we have set up a security policy to control who can access our application, let's observe its effect on actual flows.

Monitoring the Application with Hubble

Hubble is the observability subsystem of Cilium. You cannot use Hubble without Cilium because it leverages the data collected through eBPF to provide deep visibility into network traffic and policy enforcement. Chapter 15 will cover Hubble in depth.

By default, Hubble runs on the individual node on which the Cilium agent runs. This confines the network insights to the traffic observed by the local Cilium agent. As mentioned in Chapter 2, the Hubble Relay component provides a cluster-wide view of network flows. To enable Hubble Relay, use the following command:

```
$ helm upgrade cilium cilium/cilium --version 1.18.4 \
    --namespace kube-system \
    --reuse-values \
    --set hubble.relay.enabled=true
```

Alternatively, you can use the Cilium CLI command `cilium hubble enable` to enable Hubble. Once it is enabled, verify that the status of Hubble Relay is `OK` using `cilium status`.

To access the observability data collected by Hubble, you can use the `port-forward` feature of Kubernetes. The following command connects the Hubble client to the local port 4245, enabling you to access the Hubble Relay service in your Kubernetes cluster. The `&` lets you run Hubble in the background rather than having to keep the terminal open:

```
$ cilium hubble port-forward &
[1] 71325
ℹ️ Hubble Relay is available at 127.0.0.1:4245
$
```

You can now connect to the Hubble server using the Hubble UI or CLI. Let's start by using the CLI. First, verify the status of Hubble using `hubble status`. This command provides a real-time snapshot of Hubble's health, including metrics such as the rate of flows observed per second and the volume of flows currently stored locally:

```
$ hubble status
Healthcheck (via localhost:4245): Ok
Current/Max Flows: 16,380/16,380 (100.00%)
Flows/s: 9.43
Connected Nodes: 3/3
```

You can list all the nodes that Hubble Relay is connected to with the following command:

```
$ hubble list nodes
NAME                          STATUS      FLOWS/S   CURRENT/MAX-FLOWS
kind-kind/kind-control-plane  Connected   1.05      4095/4095 (100.00%)
kind-kind/kind-worker         Connected   1.06      4095/4095 (100.00%)
kind-kind/kind-worker2        Connected   4.32      4095/4095 (100.00%)
```

Next, use hubble observe to list all the flows collected by Hubble:

```
$ hubble observe
Mar 14 11:22:41.654: default/netshoot-client:50976 (ID:18901) ->
  kube-system/coredns-668d6bf9bc-qdkn6:53 (ID:23236)
  to-overlay FORWARDED (UDP)

Mar 14 11:22:41.655: default/netshoot-client:50976 (ID:18901) <-
  kube-system/coredns-668d6bf9bc-qdkn6:53 (ID:23236)
  to-endpoint FORWARDED (UDP)

Mar 14 11:22:41.656: default/netshoot-client:36998 (ID:18901) ->
  default/nginx-deployment-979f5455f-xw8nz:80 (ID:4437)
  policy-verdict:L3-L4 INGRESS ALLOWED (TCP Flags: SYN)

Mar 14 11:22:41.657: default/netshoot-client:36998 (ID:18901) ->
  default/nginx-deployment-979f5455f-xw8nz:80 (ID:4437)
  http-request FORWARDED
  (HTTP/1.1 GET http://nginx-service/index.html)

Mar 14 11:22:41.658: default/netshoot-client:36998 (ID:18901) <-
  default/nginx-deployment-979f5455f-xw8nz:80 (ID:4437)
  http-response FORWARDED
  (HTTP/1.1 200 1ms (GET http://nginx-service/index.html))
```

The (verbose) output shows traffic from the netshoot-client pod, including a DNS query to CoreDNS (UDP/53) in a different namespace, followed by a successful HTTP request to the NGINX service. The arrow direction (<- or ->) indicates the flow of traffic, and you can see which namespace (default or kube-system) it originated from and where it was sent. The logs also show the identity of each pod and whether traffic was forwarded, dropped, or denied by a network policy. Notice the to-overlay flag in the first flow log, indicating the path the packet has followed: since the DNS server was located on a different node from the client, the traffic was sent via the VXLAN tunnel.

Sending DNS traffic outside of the node is inefficient, as it adds latency and creates unnecessary internode traffic. In Chapter 8 you will learn how Cilium can optimize DNS by intercepting these requests locally, using a feature called Local Redirect Policy.

You can use filters to narrow down the Hubble output. For example, to list only the flows originating from netshoot-client, use:

```
$ hubble observe --from-pod netshoot-client
Jul  2 10:39:11.325: default/netshoot-client:42214 (ID:7613) ->
  default/nginx-deployment-979f5455f-qcbjh:80 (ID:42054)
  to-overlay FORWARDED (TCP Flags: SYN)
```

```
Jul  2 10:39:11.325: default/netshoot-client:42214 (ID:7613) ->
  default/nginx-deployment-979f5455f-qcbjh:80 (ID:42054)
  policy-verdict:L3-L4 INGRESS ALLOWED (TCP Flags: SYN)

Jul  2 10:39:11.325: default/netshoot-client:42214 (ID:7613) ->
  default/nginx-deployment-979f5455f-qcbjh:80 (ID:42054)
  to-proxy FORWARDED (TCP Flags: SYN)
```

The output was recorded shortly after executing the `kubectl exec netshoot-client -- curl nginx-service/index.html` command. The `to-proxy` confirms that traffic was redirected to the Envoy proxy because of the layer 7 policy we put in place.

You can combine multiple filters. For example, here we show only traffic from `netshoot-client` to the HTTP path `"/index.html"`:

```
$ hubble observe --from-pod netshoot-client --http-path "/index.html"
Jul  2 10:41:55.108: default/netshoot-client:59110 (ID:7613) ->
  default/nginx-deployment-979f5455f-qcbjh:80 (ID:42054)
  http-request FORWARDED
  (HTTP/1.1 GET http://nginx-service/index.html)
```

Another useful Hubble CLI filter, `--label`, lets you select flows based on labels:

```
$ hubble observe --label app.kubernetes.io/name=nginx
Mar 14 11:28:32.002: 10.244.1.218:51932 (ID:18901) ->
  default/nginx-deployment-979f5455f-9pm7d:80 (ID:4437)
  to-endpoint FORWARDED (TCP Flags: ACK, FIN)

Mar 14 11:28:32.002: 10.244.1.218:51932 (host) <-
  default/nginx-deployment-979f5455f-9pm7d:80 (ID:4437)
  to-stack FORWARDED (TCP Flags: ACK, FIN)
```

You can also filter based on the network policy verdict and check only the flows where a network policy decision was made. You can find the full list of available filters with `hubble observe --help`:

```
$ hubble observe -t policy-verdict
Mar 21 11:18:51.917: default/netshoot-client:34898 (ID:11661) ->
  default/nginx-deployment-979f5455f-bnxh7:80 (ID:5834)
  policy-verdict:L3-L4 INGRESS ALLOWED (TCP Flags: SYN)

Mar 21 12:12:27.525: default/netshoot-client-worker2:48768 (ID:11661) ->
  default/nginx-deployment-979f5455f-bnxh7:80 (ID:5834)
  policy-verdict:L3-L4 INGRESS ALLOWED (TCP Flags: SYN)

Mar 21 12:15:40.016: default/unauthorized-client:41212 (ID:8087) <>
  default/nginx-deployment-979f5455f-bnxh7:80 (ID:5834)
  policy-verdict:none INGRESS DENIED (TCP Flags: SYN)
```

The Hubble CLI provides useful insights into what's happening in your cluster, but as we mentioned in Chapter 2, the Hubble UI can also consume the flows aggregated from Hubble Relay. This is a good solution for those of you who prefer a more visual representation of the network traffic.

You can use the following Helm command to enable the Hubble UI:

```
$ helm upgrade cilium cilium/cilium --version 1.18.4 \
    --namespace kube-system \
    --reuse-values \
    --set hubble.relay.enabled=true \
    --set hubble.ui.enabled=true
```

You can also enable the UI via the Cilium CLI (with `cilium hubble enable --ui`), but you'll first need to temporarily disable Hubble using `cilium hubble disable`. This is necessary because the Hubble UI cannot be enabled when Hubble is already running.

Once you enable the Hubble UI, you will see a Hubble UI deployment being created and a Hubble UI pod consisting of a backend container and a frontend UI:

```
$ kubectl -n kube-system get deployment/hubble-ui
NAME        READY   UP-TO-DATE   AVAILABLE   AGE
hubble-ui   1/1     1            1           2m22s

$ kubectl get pod hubble-ui-76d4965bb6-m8s78 -n kube-system -o yaml
 containerStatuses:
  - containerID:
[...]
    name: backend
  - containerID:
[...]
    name: frontend
```

To access the Hubble UI, we will once again use the Kubernetes `port-forward` functionality (note that the Hubble UI can also be accessed over Ingress):

```
$ cilium hubble ui &
ℹ️ Opening "http://localhost:12000" in your browser...
```

A browser should automatically open. If it doesn't, navigate to *http://localhost:12000* in your preferred browser. You will see the Hubble UI landing page.

Just like the Hubble CLI, the Hubble UI can display flows filtered by namespace. Select the `default` namespace, and you'll see the same flows you observed earlier, now shown as a visual service map that illustrates communication between services. Click on any of the pods to see the equivalent representation to `hubble observe --pod`. For example, you can see the flows to and from `netshoot-client` in Figure 3-1.

You might also notice an "L7 info" column in the user interface, populated with details such as HTTP path, method, and latency. This is a side effect—and added benefit—of the layer 7–based Cilium network policy we enforced earlier. Layer 7 rules not only provide more granular control, they also enhance observability. As Envoy intercepts traffic, it enriches the network flow information with application-layer context.

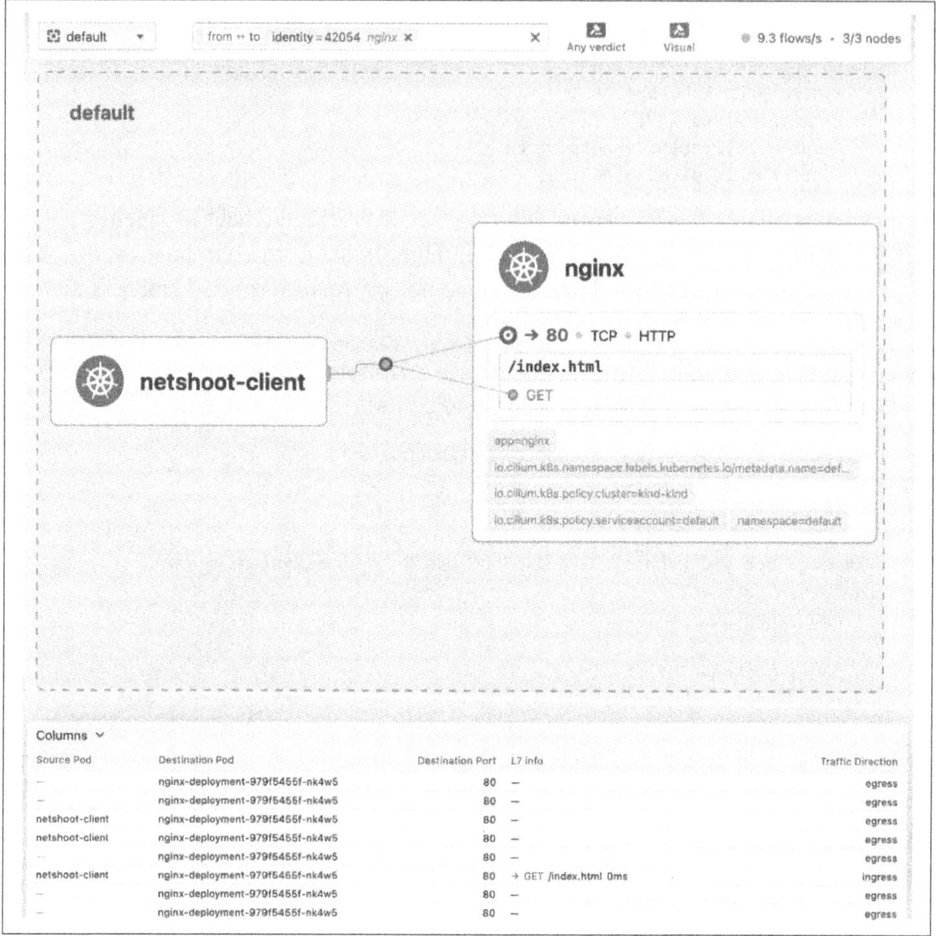

Figure 3-1. Hubble UI service map

Summary

We hope this chapter has demonstrated that getting started with Cilium is straightforward. You've deployed Cilium in a Kubernetes cluster and taken your first steps toward using it to secure, observe, and manage application traffic. In the next chapter, we'll take a closer look at how Cilium handles IP address management and establishes network connectivity for pods. You'll learn how to choose the right IPAM mode for your environment and discover the implications of using IPv4, IPv6, or both.

CHAPTER 4

IP Address Management

Before deploying Cilium in a Kubernetes cluster, platform engineers need to make two fundamental networking decisions: how pod IP addresses are allocated, and whether to use IPv4, IPv6, or both. Selecting the right IP address management mode is essential, as changing it later may disrupt connectivity for running workloads or may not be supported at all.

Broader organizational requirements typically drive the choice between IPv4, IPv6, or dual stack, but the options also demand careful consideration by platform teams during initial cluster design. This chapter will help you make an informed decision. We will start by examining the different IPAM modes supported by Cilium and highlighting the pros and cons of each. We will then explore the dual stack and IPv6 deployment models. Sample manifests are included for you to try in your own test environments; you can find all the YAML manifests in the *chapter04* directory of the book's GitHub repository (*https://github.com/isovalent/cilium-up-and-running*).

IPv4 and IPv6 Support in Cilium

We'll start with a brief overview of IPv4 and IPv6 support before we explain how IP addresses are assigned and how pods communicate with each other. Kubernetes supports single-stack IPv4, single-stack IPv6, and dual-stack networking, depending on the CNI you choose to implement the required functionality.

With single-stack IPv4/IPv6 networking, each pod and service can be assigned a single IPv4 or IPv6 address. With dual-stack networking, each pod and service can be assigned both an IPv4 and an IPv6 address. This enables off-cluster egress routing (e.g., to the internet) via both IPv4 and IPv6 interfaces.

When Cilium was first introduced, it supported only IPv6. This was a deliberate and forward-looking decision by the development team, who saw IPv6 as a natural fit for Kubernetes. Its expansive address space aligned well with the scale and dynamic nature of container workloads, where traditional IPv4 ranges can become limiting.

However, it soon became clear that most users—and the broader cloud native ecosystem—were not yet prepared for IPv6-only clusters. Many tools, services, and operational practices were still built around IPv4. In response, the Cilium team added IPv4 support early in the project's lifecycle, making it possible to run clusters in dual stack or IPv4-only mode.

IPv6 has remained a core part of Cilium's design. In some cases, new features have even been implemented with IPv6 support before IPv4. While most of the examples in this book use IPv4 (reflecting its continued prevalence in Kubernetes environments), we include IPv6 examples where relevant and note any important caveats or considerations along the way.

IP Address Management

Assigning IP addresses to entities is one of Cilium's core responsibilities. In non-containerized environments, you would have relied on DHCP or SLAAC (Stateless Address Autoconfiguration for IPv6) to dynamically assign IP addresses to machines. In Kubernetes, assigning IP addresses to pods is called *IP address management* (IPAM).

The CNI plugin is often responsible for assigning an IP address to your pod. Cilium offers several options for this, which we will discuss in this section.

Pod IP Address Allocation

Figure 4-1 illustrates the process for allocating pod IP addresses. When a new pod is added in Kubernetes, the Kubernetes scheduler assigns it to a node. The kubelet running on that node is notified and begins creating the pod's containers.

First, the kubelet checks the CNI configuration on the node, located in */etc/cni/net.d/*. When Cilium is installed on the cluster, it creates a configuration file in this folder (*05-cilium.conf*) that instructs the kubelet on how to configure pod networking.

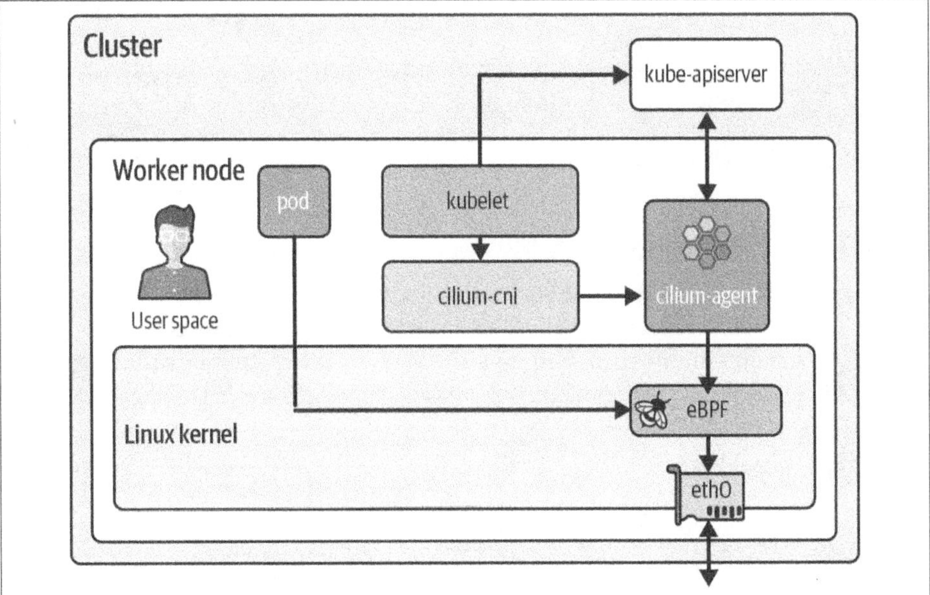

Figure 4-1. Pod IP address allocation

Each pod receives an IP address from a subnet referred to as a *PodCIDR*. CIDR (short for Classless Inter-Domain Routing) defines IP address blocks using subnet prefixes. In Kubernetes, each node is assigned one or more PodCIDRs, and pods on that node receive their IPs from those ranges via the IPAM process.

Cilium supports multiple IPAM modes. Some are specific to a cloud provider (such as AWS or Google Cloud), while others can be used across any Kubernetes environment. We won't cover all of them in this book, but we will cover the ones we see used most commonly:

Kubernetes Host Scope
: Uses PodCIDRs assigned to each node by Kubernetes. Simple but inflexible.

Cluster Scope
: Cilium manages PodCIDR allocation via the operator. The default mode.

Multi-Pool
: Allows pods to be assigned IPs from multiple IP pools based on namespaces or annotations. Ideal for multitenant setups.

ENI IPAM
: Exclusive to Amazon Elastic Kubernetes Service (EKS) environments. Allocates pod IPs from AWS elastic network interfaces.

This chapter focuses on the management of pod IP addresses. Other components of Kubernetes also require IP addresses. Nodes typically receive theirs via DHCP or SLAAC. Kubernetes services receive theirs either from the Kubernetes API server or, in the case of LoadBalancer services, via a cloud provider or a dedicated system. We'll explore service networking in more detail in Chapter 6.

Kubernetes Host Scope IPAM Mode

We'll begin with Kubernetes Host Scope, the simplest IPAM mode to understand and deploy. In this mode, Kubernetes allocates a cluster-wide prefix and assigns each node a subnet from it. Cilium then assigns pod IPs from these subnets, relying on the PodCIDRs set by the Kubernetes controller manager, as illustrated in Figure 4-2.

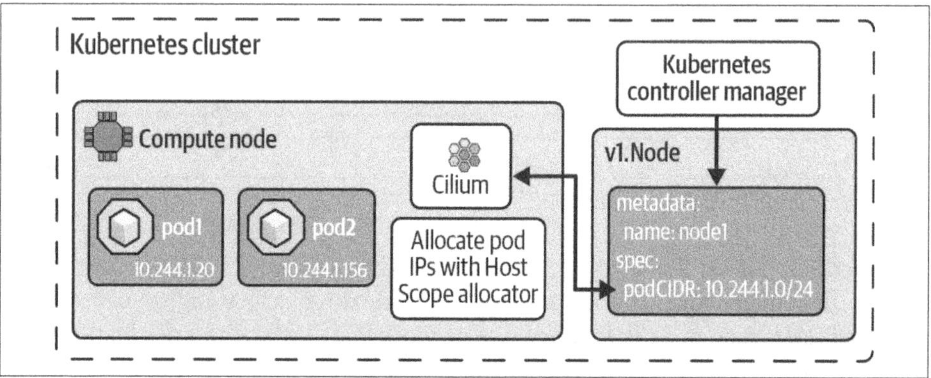

Figure 4-2. Kubernetes Host Scope mode

This is the IPAM mode we used in the Chapter 3 walk-through (`ipam.mode=kubernetes` was set in the Helm values file). You can follow the same steps here, running `kind create cluster -config kind.yaml` to create the cluster and `cilium install` (or the equivalent Helm config) to install Cilium.

After installation (whose progress you can observe with `cilium status --wait`), let's inspect the IP addressing situation.

By default, kind uses `10.244.0.0/16` as the cluster-wide prefix. Kubernetes assigns /24 subnets to the various nodes in the cluster. You can verify this in your own cluster—you should see something like the following, although the assigned prefixes may differ in your environment since subnet allocation is random:

```
$ kubectl get node kind-worker -o jsonpath='{.spec.podCIDRs}'
["10.244.1.0/24"]
```

You can now deploy a pod and verify that it receives an IP address from the node's subnet:

```
$ kubectl apply -f netshoot-client-pod.yaml
pod/netshoot-client created

$ kubectl get pods -o wide
NAME              READY   STATUS    IP            NODE
netshoot-client   1/1     Running   10.244.1.20   kind-worker
```

While Host Scope mode is straightforward, it comes with a few limitations:

- You cannot configure the size of the PodCIDRs allocated to each node, only globally for the cluster.
- You cannot add CIDRs to or remove them from the cluster or individual nodes.

This makes it difficult to grow the pool of IP addresses available to your cluster as it grows. Next, we'll take a look at a more flexible IPAM mode.

Cluster Scope IPAM Mode

In Cluster Scope mode, Cilium (not Kubernetes) allocates PodCIDRs to nodes. As this mode doesn't require a specific configuration of the Kubernetes cluster, it is the default IPAM option in Cilium.

In Chapter 2 we explained that one of the Cilium operator's responsibilities is IPAM. In Cluster Scope mode, the operator assigns subnets to each node by updating the CiliumNode custom resources (as illustrated in Figure 4-3).

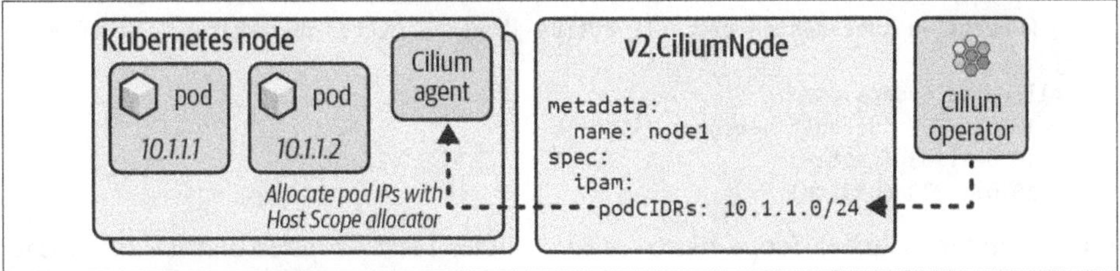

Figure 4-3. Cluster Scope IPAM mode

To deploy Cilium in this mode, we'll create a new cluster. If you previously deployed a cluster, delete it first:

```
$ kind delete cluster --name kind
$ kind create cluster --config kind.yaml
```

We recommend deleting the cluster because changing the IPAM mode in a live environment can cause persistent connectivity issues for existing workloads.

Next, install Cilium (*cilium-ipam-cluster-scope.yaml*). This mode is sometimes also referred to as "Cluster Pool mode," as you can see from the Helm value:

```
ipam:
  mode: cluster-pool
```

By default, Cilium uses the cluster-wide `10.0.0.0/8` prefix and assigns `/24` subnets to CiliumNode resources. You can verify this in your cluster by checking the Cilium configuration with the Cilium CLI command `cilium config view`:

```
$ cilium config view | grep cluster-pool
cluster-pool-ipv4-cidr                          10.0.0.0/8
cluster-pool-ipv4-mask-size                     24
ipam                                            cluster-pool
```

You can also list the CIDRs associated with each node:

```
$ kubectl get ciliumnode -o json | jq -r '.items[] |
    "NODE: \(.metadata.name) CIDR: \(.spec.ipam.podCIDRs[0])"'
NODE: kind-control-plane CIDR: 10.0.0.0/24
NODE: kind-worker CIDR: 10.0.1.0/24
NODE: kind-worker2 CIDR: 10.0.2.0/24
```

Deploy a sample pod (*netshoot-client-pod.yaml*) and check the verbose output of `cilium-dbg status` on the Cilium agent on the node hosting the pod:

```
$ kubectl -n kube-system exec -ti cilium-jhhpp -- cilium-dbg status --verbose
[...]
Allocated addresses:
  10.0.1.235 (default/netshoot-client)
  10.0.1.133 (router)
  10.0.1.238 (health)
```

One advantage Cluster Scope has over Kubernetes Host Scope is that it can allocate multiple CIDRs to the cluster instead of just one. This mode can thus provide more flexibility, although it doesn't necessarily overcome the problem of IP address exhaustion if the overall address pool was too small to begin with. Let's simulate such a scenario.

Once again, starting with a new cluster is preferable, so rerun the commands you used earlier to delete the previously created one and create a new one. Use the following values for Cilium's starting configuration (*cilium-ipam-cluster-scope-small.yaml*). In this example, Cilium will assign two small CIDRs (`/28`) to the cluster, and each node will receive a `/29` subnet from one of the CIDRs. As two IPs are reserved for the `cilium-host` and `cilium-health` interfaces, each node will get six usable addresses:

```
ipam:
  mode: cluster-pool
  operator:
    clusterPoolIPv4MaskSize: 29
    clusterPoolIPv4PodCIDRList:
      - 10.0.42.0/28
      - 10.0.84.0/28
```

Let's install Cilium in this mode and check the subnets assigned to the nodes:

```
$ kubectl get ciliumnode -o json | jq -r '.items[] |
    "NODE: \(.metadata.name) CIDR: \(.spec.ipam.podCIDRs[0])"'
NODE: kind-control-plane CIDR: 10.0.42.8/29
NODE: kind-worker              10.0.42.0/29
NODE: kind-worker2             10.0.84.8/29
```

As a /28 prefix only allows two /29 allocations, the third node receives its subnet from the second block.

Next, create a deployment with 10 pods (*nginx-deployment-10-replicas.yaml*) and pin them to `kind-worker2`. When you run `kubectl get pods -o wide`, you'll notice that several pods remain stuck in the `ContainerCreating` stage—meaning they are not running properly. If you run `cilium-dbg status` on the Cilium agent running on `kind-worker2`, you'll see that all available IP addresses have been allocated:

```
$ kubectl exec -it cilium-qrw2f -n kube-system -- cilium-dbg status
IPAM:                     IPv4: 6/6 allocated from 10.0.84.8/29,
```

While this mode provides greater flexibility than the Kubernetes Host Scope mode, it still has important limitations. The address space assigned to the cluster is static: you cannot add or expand PodCIDRs once the cluster is running, which means IP exhaustion cannot be remedied without redeploying. In addition, Cluster Scope mode offers limited control over how pods receive IP addresses, as all pods draw from the same shared pools regardless of workload or namespace.

To see how to get around these restrictions, let's take a look at Multi-Pool IPAM mode.

Multi-Pool IPAM Mode

Multi-Pool is the most flexible IPAM mode in Cilium. It enables you to allocate PodCIDRs from multiple distinct pools, depending on user-defined workload properties such as annotations or namespaces. Pods on the same node can receive IP addresses from different ranges, and new CIDRs can be dynamically added to a node as needed.

This flexibility makes Multi-Pool the recommended mode, especially for multitenant clusters or when granular IP addressing control is preferred. The IP allocation process used in Multi-Pool IPAM mode is described in Figure 4-4.

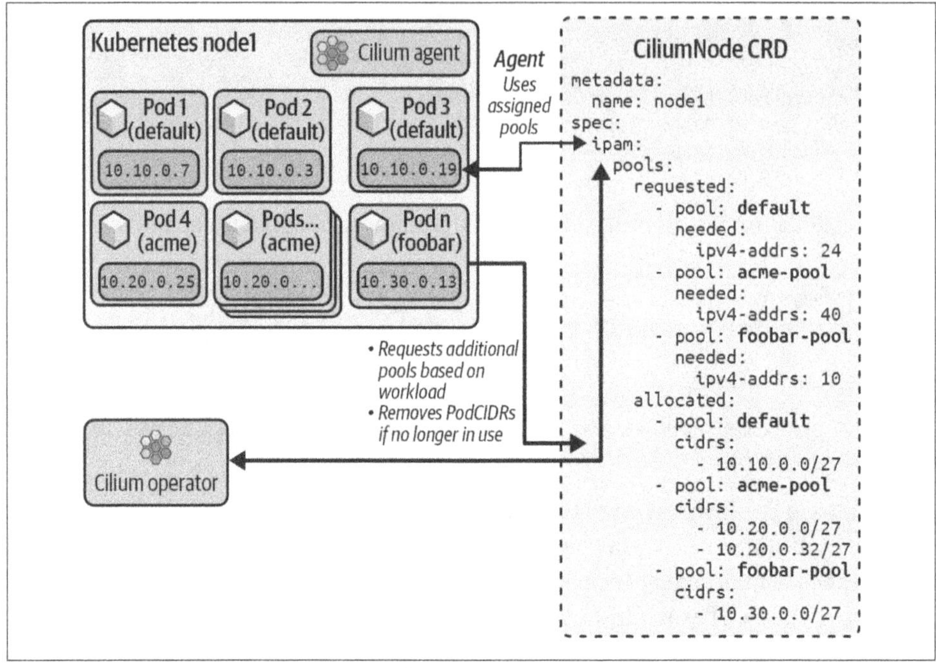

Figure 4-4. Multi-Pool IPAM mode

Let's deploy Cilium in Multi-Pool mode. First, delete the existing cluster and create a new one. Use the following values for Cilium's starting configuration (*cilium-ipam-multi-pool.yaml*):

```
ipam:
  mode: multi-pool
  operator:
    autoCreateCiliumPodIPPools:
      default:
        ipv4:
          cidrs: ["10.10.0.0/16"]
          maskSize: 27

routingMode: native
endpointRoutes:
  enabled: true

autoDirectNodeRoutes: true
ipv4NativeRoutingCIDR: 10.0.0.0/8
```

In Chapter 3 we introduced the encapsulation routing mode (using VXLAN). This time we will use native routing, which sends packets directly between nodes without encapsulating them in tunnels. We will explain this in more detail in Chapter 5.

The `autoCreateCiliumPodIPPools` option configures Cilium to create a default pool of IP addresses at start-up and to assign prefixes to nodes based on the `ipam.operator.autoCreateCiliumPodIPPools.ipv4.maskSize` value (in our case, 27).

Once Cilium is installed, verify that a default pool has been created:

```
$ kubectl get ciliumpodippools.cilium.io default -o yaml
apiVersion: cilium.io/v2alpha1
kind: CiliumPodIPPool
spec:
  ipv4:
    cidrs:
    - 10.10.0.0/16
    maskSize: 27
```

Let's also verify that the `kind-worker` node received a `/27` subnet from this pool:

```
$ kubectl get ciliumnode kind-worker -o yaml | yq '.spec.ipam'
pools:
  allocated:
    - cidrs:
        - 10.10.0.64/27
      pool: default
  requested:
    - needed:
        ipv4-addrs: 16
      pool: default
```

Deploy a pod on this specific node using the *netshoot-client-pod.yaml* manifest we used previously. When you verify its IP address, you should again see that the pod received an IP address from the allocated subnet (e.g., `10.10.0.93`):

```
$ kubectl get pods -o wide
NAME              READY   STATUS    RESTARTS   AGE   IP            NODE
netshoot-client   1/1     Running   0          24s   10.10.0.93    kind-worker
```

So far, Multi-Pool mode functions similarly to Cluster Scope IPAM mode. One advantage it has over other IPAM modes, however, is that it gives you more control over how IP addresses are assigned to pods. You can force a pod—or all pods in a particular namespace—to receive IPs from a particular range.

This is handy for multitenant environments. For example, suppose you have two tenants, *ACME Corp.* and *Foobar Inc.* Namespaces are often used in Kubernetes to differentiate tenants. While the IPAM modes we looked at previously are not namespace-aware, with Multi-Pool IPAM each namespace can draw pod IPs from its own defined address pool. This capability is particularly useful when traffic exits the cluster, as it helps engineers understand which tenant the traffic originated from.[1]

In Chapter 11, you will learn more about what to consider when traffic leaves the cluster, including another method to map outbound traffic to a particular IP or interface: Egress Gateway.

Let's create namespaces for our two tenants:

```
$ kubectl apply -f namespaces.yaml
namespace/acme-corp created
namespace/foobar-inc created
```

We'll then deploy two separate pools (*acme-pool.yaml* and *foobar-pool.yaml*):

```
apiVersion: cilium.io/v2alpha1
kind: CiliumPodIPPool
metadata:
  name: foobar-pool
spec:
  ipv4:
    cidrs:
    - 10.30.0.0/16
    maskSize: 27
---
apiVersion: cilium.io/v2alpha1
kind: CiliumPodIPPool
metadata:
  name: acme-pool
spec:
  ipv4:
    cidrs:
    - 10.20.0.0/16
    maskSize: 27
```

To ensure that all workloads in a particular namespace receive an IP address from a particular IP pool, you can annotate the namespace with `ipam.cilium.io/ip-pool=`*`pool_name`*:

```
$ kubectl annotate ns acme-corp ipam.cilium.io/ip-pool=acme-pool
namespace/acme-corp annotated

$ kubectl annotate ns foobar-inc ipam.cilium.io/ip-pool=foobar-pool
namespace/foobar-inc annotated
```

1 Although Multi-Pool IPAM can assign ranges at the namespace level, pods may also request a pool directly through an annotation. This means pool selection should be treated as an operational aid rather than an isolation mechanism.

When deploying workloads, they will be allocated an IP address from the appropriate pool:

```
$ kubectl apply -f nginx-deployment-10-replicas.yaml -n acme-corp
deployment.apps/nginx-deployment created

$ kubectl apply -f nginx-deployment-10-replicas.yaml -n foobar-inc
deployment.apps/nginx-deployment created
```

Here is a trimmed version of the output:

```
$ kubectl get pods -o wide -n acme-corp
NAME                                READY   STATUS    IP           NODE
nginx-deployment-979f5455f-5tkws    1/1     Running   10.20.0.25   kind-worker2
nginx-deployment-979f5455f-6dw7n    1/1     Running   10.20.0.6    kind-worker2
[...]

$ kubectl get pods -o wide -n foobar-inc
NAME                                READY   STATUS    IP           NODE
nginx-deployment-979f5455f-2p7mc    1/1     Running   10.30.0.28   kind-worker2
nginx-deployment-979f5455f-82g98    1/1     Running   10.30.0.13   kind-worker2
[...]
```

Check the CiliumNode to see which PodCIDRs are assigned to each node:

```
$ kubectl get ciliumnode kind-worker2 -o yaml | yq .spec.ipam
pools:
  allocated:
    - cidrs:
        - 10.20.0.0/27
      pool: acme-pool
    - cidrs:
        - 10.10.0.0/27
      pool: default
    - cidrs:
        - 10.30.0.0/27
      pool: foobar-pool
  requested:
    - needed:
        ipv4-addrs: 10
      pool: acme-pool
    - needed:
        ipv4-addrs: 16
      pool: default
    - needed:
        ipv4-addrs: 10
      pool: foobar-pool
```

If you need more IPs, Cilium dynamically assigns additional subnets to the node. For example, let's scale up the ACME deployment from 10 replicas to 40:

```
$ kubectl scale -n acme-corp deployment nginx-deployment --replicas=40
deployment.apps/nginx-deployment scaled
```

Note the needed field in the following output. Since the number of required IPs significantly increased, another /27 subnet from the cluster-wide 10.20.0.0/16 was allocated to the node:

```
$ kubectl get ciliumnode kind-worker2 -o yaml | yq '.spec.ipam'
pools:
  allocated:
    - cidrs:
        - 10.20.0.0/27
        - 10.20.0.32/27
      pool: acme-pool
    - cidrs:
        - 10.10.0.0/27
      pool: default
    - cidrs:
        - 10.30.0.0/27
      pool: foobar-pool
  requested:
    - needed:
        ipv4-addrs: 40
      pool: acme-pool
    - needed:
        ipv4-addrs: 16
      pool: default
    - needed:
        ipv4-addrs: 10
      pool: foobar-pool
```

In some environments (e.g., in the telecom or finance industries), pods may have multiple interfaces (for example, for out-of-band management and for signaling or data). The Isovalent Enterprise Platform extends Multi-Pool mode with a feature called Multi Network that lets you connect a pod to multiple networks.

CRD-Backed IPAM Mode

Cilium also supports a lesser-known IPAM mode called CRD-backed IPAM, which delegates IP address management to an external operator. This mode gives you significant flexibility, but using it can be complex. When using CRD-backed mode, Cilium is not automatically programmed to route traffic to the assigned CIDRs, so administrators must assign IP ranges to nodes and ensure proper routing between them.

CRD-backed IPAM is often used in managed Kubernetes environments, where the cloud provider handles IP address management and routing outside of Cilium.

ENI IPAM Mode

The final IPAM mode we will review is specific to Amazon Elastic Kubernetes Service, but as it's widely adopted by AWS users, it deserves a detailed look.

In ENI IPAM mode, Cilium tightly integrates with AWS networking by assigning pod IP addresses from secondary IP addresses on elastic network interfaces (ENIs) (*https://oreil.ly/zBkqF*). At start-up, Cilium contacts the EC2 metadata ENI to retrieve the instance ID, instance type, and virtual private cloud (VPC) information and populates each CiliumNode custom resource with this information (as illustrated in Figure 4-5). Cilium then allocates pod IPs directly from the pool of secondary addresses associated with those ENIs. This provides a clear benefit: pods receive IPs that are directly routable within the AWS VPC. No NAT is required, simplifying networking and improving observability for operators.[2]

Note that Cilium does not currently support IPv6 ENIs. This is being tracked in GitHub issue #18405 (*https://oreil.ly/OrbDU*).

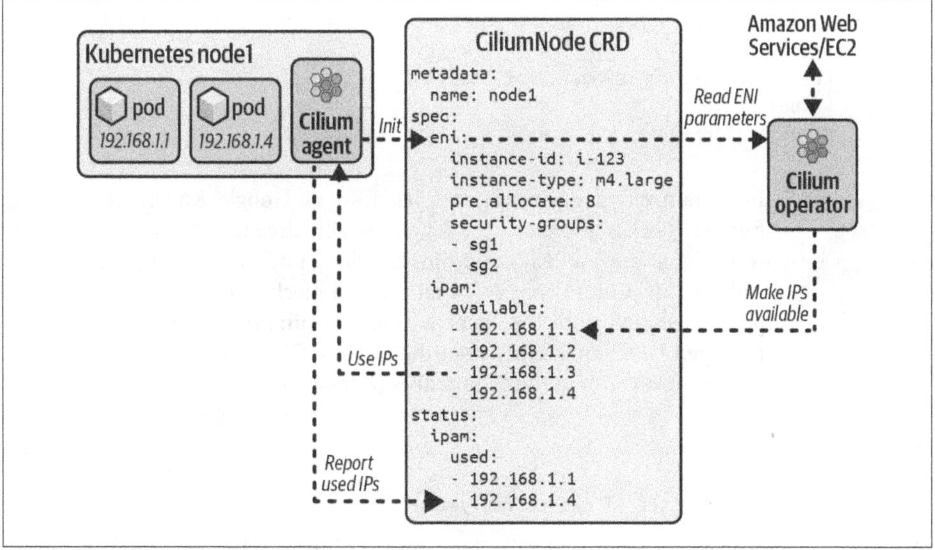

Figure 4-5. ENI mode

2 ENI mode also affects how packets reach pods. Each pod IP is tied to the ENI it was allocated from, so traffic arrives through that ENI rather than the node's usual network path, and Cilium applies its policies when packets enter the pod. Because the ENI is the attachment point, AWS security groups apply cleanly at the pod level.

ENI mode is only relevant when running Cilium on Amazon EKS, where ENIs and their IPs are managed by AWS. Let's explain it by walking through an example.

Unlike the previous examples where we were using kind, deploying a cluster on EKS comes with a cost. Proceed carefully before deploying a managed cloud-hosted cluster.

To deploy an EKS cluster, we recommend the eksctl tool (*https://oreil.ly/1EoiB*). Follow the instructions in the documentation to install and configure it.

The `eksctl` configuration shown here will create a cluster with two nodes in the `eu-west-1` region (you can change this to the region of your choice):

```
apiVersion: eksctl.io/v1alpha5
kind: ClusterConfig
metadata:
  name: cuar
  region: eu-west-1
managedNodeGroups:
- name: ng-1
  desiredCapacity: 2
  privateNetworking: true
  taints:
   - key: "node.cilium.io/agent-not-ready"
     value: "true"
     effect: "NoExecute"
```

In certain cloud environments, like EKS or Google Kubernetes Engine (GKE), another CNI plugin might already be installed, which can prevent Cilium from handling pod networking. To address this, Cilium supports a taint-based mechanism that delays pod scheduling until the agent is ready, helping ensure pods are managed by Cilium rather than the existing CNI plugin. You can read more about it in the Cilium docs (*https://oreil.ly/n9Oxf*).

To deploy the cluster, run:

```
$ eksctl create cluster -f eks-config.yaml
```

When it's ready (after about 15–20 minutes), install Cilium (*cilium-eni-values.yaml*). ENI mode requires the `ipam.mode=eni` and `eni.enabled=true` values.

Let's deploy five pods with a sample deployment. All pods should receive an IP address, as you would expect:

```
$ kubectl apply -f echo-deployment.yaml
deployment.apps/echoserver created
```

```
$ kubectl get pods -o wide
NAME                          READY   STATUS    IP
echoserver-79974b75cd-fwd9r   1/1     Running   192.168.168.230
echoserver-79974b75cd-kn9fz   1/1     Running   192.168.156.61
echoserver-79974b75cd-p5q9b   1/1     Running   192.168.131.53
echoserver-79974b75cd-wgdzf   1/1     Running   192.168.170.2
echoserver-79974b75cd-whjvc   1/1     Running   192.168.142.65
```

The pod IPs are actually taken from the EC2 instance's network interface and listed as secondary private IPs, as you can see in the AWS Console under EC2→Instances→<*instance_name*>→Networking (Figure 4-6).

Figure 4-6. The AWS Console

You can also see the IPs being populated on the CiliumNode resource:

```
$ kubectl get cn ip-192-168-132-54.eu-west-1.compute.internal -o yaml
[...]
enis:
  eni-02f39382678db84b5:
    addresses:
      - 192.168.159.141
      - 192.168.156.61
      - 192.168.149.241
      - 192.168.142.65
      - 192.168.139.147
```

```
- 192.168.158.35
- 192.168.135.116
- 192.168.131.53
- 192.168.157.103
```

When using ENI mode, you should be aware of certain scaling limitations. In this mode, the number of IPs that can be allocated per node is limited by the instance type's ENI and secondary IP capacity (e.g., an m5.large instance supports only 3 ENIs with 10 IPs each). This restricts the number of pods a node can run (with an m5.large instance able to support just 30 pods—far below the 110 pods per node limit Kubernetes imposes by default).

Cilium supports AWS prefix delegation (*https://oreil.ly/weI5C*), a feature that assigns entire CIDR blocks (e.g., a `/28`) to each ENI. This significantly increases per-node pod density, without requiring you to scale the cluster horizontally or vertically.

If you created a cluster to test this feature, remember to delete it to avoid further costs.

IPv6 Clusters

Apart from which IPAM mode to use, the other essential decision you will need to make regarding IP addressing is which version of IP to use: IPv4, IPv6, or both. While this choice will often be dictated by broader organizational directives, it has direct implications for your Kubernetes networking architecture that it is important to be aware of.

Cilium provides strong IPv6 support across the board, with the notable exception of the ENI IPAM mode described in the previous section. The vast majority of Cilium features are IPv6-ready and can operate seamlessly in single-stack or dual-stack clusters.

In this section, we will explore two common deployment models:

- *Dual stack* (IPv4 and IPv6), where pods and services receive both an IPv4 and an IPv6 address
- *Single stack* (IPv6 only), where pods and services receive only an IPv6 address

The decision of whether to use single-stack IPv4 or IPv6 or dual-stack networking should be based on a combination of technical readiness and organizational strategy. You should consider the following aspects:

Organizational IPv6 strategy
: Is your company actively working toward IPv6 adoption or still primarily reliant on IPv4? Some enterprises mandate IPv6 for all new workloads; in some regions, governments and public sector institutions go even further, requiring IPv6 compliance for all digital infrastructure and services.

Operational readiness
: Do your teams have the tooling and expertise to monitor and troubleshoot IPv6 traffic? Logging, observability, and security tooling must be IPv6-aware.

Ecosystem limitations
: While Kubernetes and Cilium support IPv6 well, other tools and common services (including some popular container registries) may not. This means IPv6-only environments may need to rely on mechanisms like NAT64/DNS64[3] to reach IPv4-only endpoints, adding complexity.

As a general guide:

- IPv4 only is the default and safest option for most organizations. It ensures broad compatibility, but it does not help you future-proof your stack.
- Dual stack is often a transitional strategy. It allows IPv6 experimentation while maintaining full IPv4 compatibility. However, it introduces operational complexity, especially in IP management and observability.

IPv6 only is viable in greenfield deployments where external dependencies are well understood and NAT64/DNS64 can be reliably deployed. It demands a mature operational model and close awareness of third-party IPv6 support.

With those considerations in mind, let's look at how to configure and operate Cilium in dual-stack and IPv6-only modes.

Dual Stack (IPv4/IPv6)

In dual-stack mode, each pod is allocated both an IPv4 and an IPv6 address. This enables communications with IPv6 systems as well as legacy apps that only use IPv4.

3 NAT64 and DNS64 are mechanisms that allow IPv6-only clients to communicate with IPv4-only servers. DNS64 synthesizes AAAA records from A records, enabling IPv6 clients to resolve IPv4-only domain names. NAT64 then translates the IPv6 traffic to IPv4 at the network edge. Together, they provide access to legacy IPv4 services from IPv6-only environments.

To test it, we will use the following kind configuration for Linux (*kind-dual-stack.yaml*). Notice that the `ipFamily` is set to `dual` to enable dual-stack functionality, supporting both IPv4 and IPv6 protocols:

```
kind: Cluster
apiVersion: kind.x-k8s.io/v1alpha4
nodes:
  - role: control-plane
  - role: worker
  - role: worker
networking:
  disableDefaultCNI: true
  ipFamily: dual
```

This configuration works on Linux machines with IPv6 support enabled. On macOS, set `apiServerAddress` to `127.0.0.1` under `networking` to work around Docker's lack of IPv6 forwarding. For additional platform-specific guidance, see the kind docs (*https://oreil.ly/2XDhi*).

Deploy the cluster and verify with the following command that the nodes receive both an IPv4 and an IPv6 address:[4]

```
$ kubectl get node kind-worker -o jsonpath='{.status.addresses}' | jq
[
  { "address": "172.18.0.4", "type": "InternalIP" },
  { "address": "fc00:f853:ccd:e793::4", "type": "InternalIP" },
  ...
]
```

With Cilium, IPv6 is disabled by default and has to be explicitly enabled in the Helm values (with `ipv6.enabled=true`).

Install Cilium (*cilium-dual-stack-values.yaml*) and run the following command to see the PodCIDRs from which IPv4 and IPv6 addresses will be allocated to your pods:

```
$ kubectl describe nodes | grep PodCIDRs
PodCIDRs:                     10.244.0.0/24,fd00:10:244::/64
PodCIDRs:                     10.244.1.0/24,fd00:10:244:1::/64
PodCIDRs:                     10.244.3.0/24,fd00:10:244:3::/64
PodCIDRs:                     10.244.2.0/24,fd00:10:244:2::/64
```

Let's again deploy a couple of sample pods (*pod1.yaml* and *pod2.yaml*) that will be pinned to specific nodes to validate internode connectivity. In this instance we're

4 Alongside its IPv4 address, `172.18.0.4`, the node is also given an IPv6 address such as `fc00:f853:ccd:e793::4`. This belongs to an IPv6 unique local address range, which is reserved for private internal networking and is not routable on the public internet. `fc00:f853:ccd:e793::/64` is the default IPv6 range in Docker.

using the Kubernetes Host Scope IPAM mode, so IP addresses are assigned from the PodCIDR assigned to each node:

```
$ kubectl describe pod pod-worker | grep -A 2 IPs
IPs:
  IP:  10.244.1.117
  IP:  fd00:10:244:1::8204

$ kubectl describe pod pod-worker2 | grep -A 2 IPs
IPs:
  IP:  10.244.3.29
  IP:  fd00:10:244:3::833f
```

Let's verify that pods can communicate. We'll test a ping from `pod-worker` to `pod-worker`'s IPv6 address. Because the pods were pinned to different nodes, it should show successful IPv6 connectivity between pods on different nodes:[5]

```
$ IPv6="$(kubectl get pod pod-worker2 -o jsonpath='{.status.podIPs[1].ip}')"

$ echo "$IPv6"
fd00:10:244:3::833f

$ kubectl exec -it pod-worker -- ping6 -c 2 "$IPv6"
PING fd00:10:244:3::833f (fd00:10:244:3::833f) 56 data bytes
64 bytes from fd00:10:244:3::833f: icmp_seq=1 ttl=63 time=0.330 ms
64 bytes from fd00:10:244:3::833f: icmp_seq=2 ttl=63 time=0.156 ms

--- fd00:10:244:3::833f ping statistics ---
2 packets transmitted, 2 received, 0% packet loss, time 4087ms
rtt min/avg/max/mdev = 0.133/0.181/0.330/0.074 ms
```

Next, we'll create a deployment with five pods (*echo-deployment.yaml*) and deploy a service fronting them (*echo-service-dualstack.yaml*). Note that we specify `PreferDualStack` in the service configuration:

```
spec:
  ipFamilyPolicy: PreferDualStack
  ipFamilies:
    - IPv6
    - IPv4
```

We can verify that both IPv4 and IPv6 addresses are assigned with:

```
$ kubectl describe svc echoserver
[...]
IP Family Policy:          PreferDualStack
```

5 Note that we deployed Cilium in VXLAN mode in this particular instance. At the time of writing, when using dual-stack mode, IPv6 packets are encapsulated in an IPv4 tunnel. You can check this yourself by opening the *dual_stack.pcap* packet capture (available in the */pcaps* directory of the book's GitHub repository) in Wireshark or `tcpdump`. In Cilium 1.19 onward, IPv6 is supported as an underlay for dual-stack clusters.

```
IP Families:                IPv6,IPv4
IP:                         fd00:10:96::d4d5
IPs:                        fd00:10:96::d4d5,10.96.181.159
Port:                       <unset>  80/TCP
TargetPort:                 80/TCP
Endpoints:                  10.244.1.206:80,10.244.3.235:80,...
[...]
```

Let's also verify access to the service name from the `pod-worker` client. We'll use `curl -4` and `curl -6` to show connectivity works over both IPv4 and IPv6:

```
$ kubectl exec -it pod-worker -- bash

pod-worker:~# nslookup -q=AAAA echoserver
Server:         10.96.0.10
Address:        10.96.0.10#53

Name:   echoserver.default.svc.cluster.local
Address: fd00:10:96::d4d5

pod-worker:~# curl -sw '%{http_code}\n' -o /dev/null -4 http://echoserver
200

pod-worker:~# curl -sw '%{http_code}\n' -o /dev/null -6 http://echoserver
200
```

Single Stack (IPv6 Only)

Let's now explore an IPv6-only cluster with Cilium. In the dual-stack example, we used the default IPv6 prefixes that kind assigns (`fd00:10:244::/56` for pods and `fd00:10:96::/112` for services). For our single-stack IPv6 cluster, however, we will use documentation-specific prefixes defined in RFC 9637 (*https://oreil.ly/k4EMW*). These fall within the `2001:db8::/32` range and are reserved exclusively for examples and instructional material.

While this section uses documentation-specific prefixes from RFC 9637 for clarity, these should not be used in production. For real clusters, we recommend drawing pod IPv6 ranges from your organization's public IPv6 allocation, even when pods are not intended to be reachable from outside the network. With native routing, pods can use their assigned IPv6 addresses directly without NAT, and the available IPv6 space easily accommodates large node counts. For example, a `/116` per node supports more than 4,000 pods per node, and a `/96` for the cluster can support over a million nodes.

For cluster services, use IPv6 unique local addresses, as these services are designed to be internal only.

The following configuration creates an IPv6-only kind cluster with Cilium, disabling the default CNI and explicitly defining pod and service subnets using the documentation-specific prefixes:

```
kind: Cluster
apiVersion: kind.x-k8s.io/v1alpha4
nodes:
  - role: control-plane
  - role: worker
  - role: worker
networking:
  ipFamily: ipv6
  disableDefaultCNI: true
  podSubnet: "2001:db8:10:244::/48"
  serviceSubnet: "2001:db8:10:96::/112"
```

Deploy the cluster with `kind create cluster --config kind-ipv6-only.yaml` and check that the nodes only receive an IPv6 address:

```
$ kubectl get nodes -o wide
NAME                 STATUS     ROLES           INTERNAL-IP
kind-control-plane   NotReady   control-plane   fc00:f853:ccd:e793::3
kind-worker          NotReady   <none>          fc00:f853:ccd:e793::2
kind-worker2         NotReady   <none>          fc00:f853:ccd:e793::4
```

You should see that only IPv6 PodCIDRs are assigned to the node:

```
$ kubectl describe node kind-worker
[...]
PodCIDR:                      2001:db8:10:1::/64
PodCIDRs:                     2001:db8:10:1::/64
[...]
```

As IPv4 is enabled by default in Cilium, make sure to disable it during the Cilium installation. Use the following Helm values (*cilium-ipv6-only-values.yaml*):

```
ipv6:
  enabled: true
ipv4:
  enabled: false
ipam:
  mode: kubernetes
routingMode: native
autoDirectNodeRoutes: true
ipv6NativeRoutingCIDR: 2001:db8:10:244::/48
```

Let's deploy our two sample pods again (*pod1.yaml* and *pod2.yaml*) and check that they have only been assigned IPv6 addresses:

```
$ kubectl get pods -o wide
NAME          READY   AGE   IP
pod-worker    1/1     43s   2001:db8:10:1::4d69
pod-worker2   1/1     43s   2001:db8:10:2::c7cf
```

Next, we'll try out our five-pod deployment (*echo-deployment.yaml*) and sample service (*echo-service-ipv6.yaml*). Notice that a slight change in the `ipFamilyPolicy` and `ipFamilies` settings is required to deploy IPv6-only services:

```
apiVersion: v1
kind: Service
metadata:
  name: echoserver
spec:
  ipFamilyPolicy: SingleStack
  ipFamilies:
  - IPv6
[...]
```

After deploying these, we can check that pod-to-pod connectivity tests are successful:

```
$ IPv6="$(kubectl get pod pod-worker2 -o jsonpath='{.status.podIPs[0].ip}')"

$ echo "$IPv6"
2001:db8:10:2::c7cf

$ kubectl exec -it pod-worker -- ping6 -c 3 "$IPv6"
PING 2001:db8:10:2::c7cf (2001:db8:10:2::c7cf) 56 data bytes
64 bytes from 2001:db8:10:2::c7cf: icmp_seq=1 ttl=60 time=0.370 ms
64 bytes from 2001:db8:10:2::c7cf: icmp_seq=2 ttl=60 time=0.239 ms
64 bytes from 2001:db8:10:2::c7cf: icmp_seq=3 ttl=60 time=0.513 ms

--- 2001:db8:10:2::c7cf ping statistics ---
3 packets transmitted, 3 received, 0% packet loss, time 2029ms
rtt min/avg/max/mdev = 0.239/0.374/0.513/0.111 ms
```

We can also verify pod-to-service connectivity and DNS resolution:

```
$ ServiceIPv6="$(kubectl get svc echoserver -o jsonpath='{.spec.clusterIP}')"

$ echo "$ServiceIPv6"
2001:db8:10:96::6f43

$ kubectl exec -it pod-worker -- bash

pod-worker:~# nslookup -q=AAAA echoserver
Server:         2001:db8:10:96::a
Address:        2001:db8:10:96::a#53

Name:   echoserver.default.svc.cluster.local
Address: 2001:db8:10:96::6f43

pod-worker:~# curl -sw '%{http_code}\n' -o /dev/null  -6 http://echoserver
200
```

Summary

This chapter introduced the basics of Cilium networking by covering IP address management and IPv6/dual-stack support. We explored the various IPAM modes Cilium offers—from simple Kubernetes Host Scope setups to more flexible options like Cluster Scope and Multi-Pool—and discussed how to deploy clusters using IPv4, IPv6, or both.

These decisions are critical; changing them later can be disruptive, unsupported, or simply impractical. Our goal is to help you make informed, durable choices that align with your environment's long-term needs.

Now that you understand how Cilium assigns IP addresses to pods, the next step is to understand how traffic actually flows between them. In the next chapter, we'll dive into how packets are forwarded within and across nodes, examine the role of encapsulation, and compare native routing with overlay tunnels. We'll even dissect packet headers to see how Cilium, and the underlying network, moves traffic across your cluster.

CHAPTER 5

The Cilium Datapath

In the previous chapter, we explored how Cilium allocates IP addresses to pods. With each pod now assigned an IP, the next logical step is to understand how traffic flows between them. This is the role of the Cilium datapath: the set of technologies Cilium uses to process, route, and forward packets within a Kubernetes cluster.

In this chapter, we'll examine how packets are delivered both within and across nodes, how different routing models work, and how encapsulation protocols like VXLAN and Geneve come into play when native routing isn't possible. You can find all the YAML manifests you will use in this chapter in the *chapter05* directory of the book's GitHub repository (*https://github.com/isovalent/cilium-up-and-running*).

We'll begin with the simplest case (intranode, for communication between pods on the same node), then move on to internode traffic (connectivity between pods located on different nodes) and the differences between native and overlay modes (Figure 5-1).

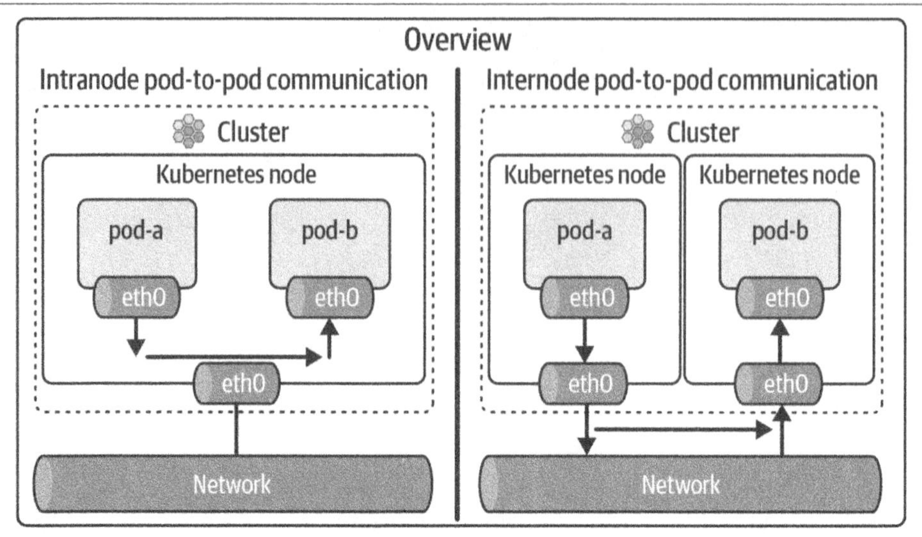

Figure 5-1. Intranode versus internode communication

Linux Networking Essentials for Cilium

This chapter does not attempt to cover Linux and container networking comprehensively. For a broader introduction, see *Networking and Kubernetes* by James Strong and Vallery Lancey (O'Reilly), especially Chapters 2 and 3. Here, we will briefly cover the essentials you need in order to understand how Cilium integrates with the kernel datapath.

The core kernel primitives underlying most container networking implementations are:

Network namespaces
: In Linux, a network namespace provides an isolated copy of the network stack (interfaces, routing tables, firewall rules). Each Kubernetes pod runs in its own network namespace, giving it the illusion of having a dedicated network stack. The host itself also has a network namespace that is shared by system processes (including the Cilium agent).

Veth pairs
: Virtual Ethernet devices come in pairs. Packets sent into one end of the pair appear on the other end. Most CNIs use veth pairs to connect pod namespaces to the host's network namespace. Inside the pod, you see an interface such as `eth0`; on the host, you see its peer, usually named `lxc*`.

Figure 5-2 shows an example of what this looks like.

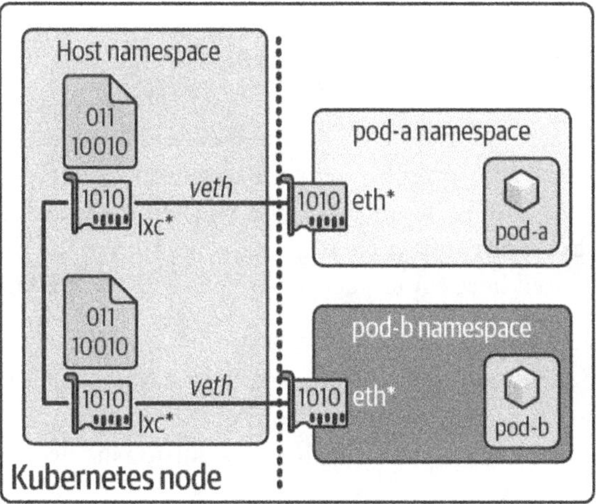

Figure 5-2. High-level view of container networking

Intranode Connectivity

Let's start by looking at how two pods (`pod-a` and `pod-b`) on the same node communicate. To do that, we will trace a successful ping from one pod to another running on the same node.

As explained in "Linux Networking Essentials for Cilium", each pod connects to the host through a veth pair. Cilium attaches eBPF programs to the interfaces on the host side so that packets are inspected and forwarded as soon as they leave or enter the pod. This early interception allows Cilium to consult its eBPF maps for identity, policy, or connection tracking information and apply decisions immediately.

This is different from the behavior of many traditional CNIs, where packets are typically bridged or passed through `iptables` chains for filtering and routing. With Cilium, the decision is made directly in the datapath at the earliest possible moment, avoiding the extra layers of processing.

Let's test it. In a generic kind cluster (`kind create cluster --config kind.yaml`), with a default Cilium installation (`cilium install`), deploy two pods (`pod-a` and `pod-b`) on the same node (`kind-worker`) with the manifest *intra-node-example.yaml*.

Check their IP addresses and verify the successful intranode ping:

```
$ kubectl get pods -o wide
NAME     READY   STATUS    RESTARTS   AGE   IP             NODE
pod-a    1/1     Running   0          58m   10.244.1.203   kind-worker
pod-b    1/1     Running   0          58m   10.244.1.69    kind-worker
```

```
$ kubectl exec -it pod-a -- ping 10.244.1.69
PING 10.244.1.69 (10.244.1.69) 56(84) bytes of data.
64 bytes from 10.244.1.69: icmp_seq=1 ttl=63 time=0.223 ms
64 bytes from 10.244.1.69: icmp_seq=2 ttl=63 time=0.073 ms
```

Both pods are connected to the host's network namespace via their veth pairs. The host namespace acts as the common network domain where these veth pairs terminate and provides the link between otherwise isolated pod stacks. For two pods on the same node to exchange traffic, their packets must leave the pod namespace and pass through this shared host namespace, where Cilium's datapath logic is applied.

Enter the pod-a shell with `kubectl exec -it pod-a -- bash` and check its eth0 interface details and routing table. From inside pod-a, the output shows that its eth0 interface, with the index 23, is connected to a peer with index 24 (eth0@if24). This indicates that the other end of the veth pair exists outside the pod's namespace:

```
pod-a:~# ip address show eth0
23: eth0@if24: <BROADCAST,MULTICAST,UP,LOWER_UP> mtu 65520 qdisc noqueue
    state UP group default qlen 1000
    link/ether 76:43:9c:d5:bd:2a brd ff:ff:ff:ff:ff:ff link-netnsid 0
    inet 10.244.1.203/32 scope global eth0
       valid_lft forever preferred_lft forever
    inet6 fe80::7443:9cff:fed5:bd2a/64 scope link proto kernel_ll
       valid_lft forever preferred_lft forever

pod-a:~# ip route
default via 10.244.1.198 dev eth0 mtu 65470
10.244.1.198 dev eth0 scope link
```

The @if24 suffix shows the peer index. To confirm what this peer is, we look at the host's network namespace. On the host, the other end of the veth pair appears as an lxc* interface with the corresponding peer index (if23 in this case):

```
$ docker exec -it kind-worker bash

root@kind-worker:/# ip address | grep -A 3 if23
24: lxcbee302eb186c@if23: <BROADCAST,MULTICAST,UP,LOWER_UP> mtu 65520
    qdisc noqueue state UP group default qlen 1000
    link/ether a2:cf:c3:e6:e4:c7 brd ff:ff:ff:ff:ff:ff
      link-netns cni-d35c64e3-0ea6-5967-0698-427e7255cdc8
    inet6 fe80::a0cf:c3ff:fee6:e4c7/64 scope link
       valid_lft forever preferred_lft forever
```

This pairing (eth0@if24 inside the pod, lxc*@if23 on the host) is how traffic leaves the pod's isolated namespace and enters the host's network namespace, where Cilium's eBPF programs can process it.

You will see a similar pairing for pod-b:

```
pod-b:~# ip address show eth0
25: eth0@if26: <BROADCAST,MULTICAST,UP,LOWER_UP> mtu 65520 qdisc noqueue
    state UP group default qlen 1000
    link/ether 46:9c:c0:5f:ec:1c brd ff:ff:ff:ff:ff:ff link-netnsid 0
    inet 10.244.1.69/32 scope global eth0
       valid_lft forever preferred_lft forever
    inet6 fe80::449c:c0ff:fe5f:ec1c/64 scope link proto kernel_ll
       valid_lft forever preferred_lft forever
```

On the host:

```
root@kind-worker:/# ip address | grep -A 3 if25
26: lxcc5b0a1b7ddfb@if25: <BROADCAST,MULTICAST,UP,LOWER_UP> mtu 65520
    qdisc noqueue state UP group default qlen 1000
    link/ether fa:a2:c6:90:65:f7 brd ff:ff:ff:ff:ff:ff
      link-netns cni-f4803bdf-3eb6-a209-831e-b93beac138a3
    inet6 fe80::f8a2:c6ff:fe90:65f7/64 scope link
       valid_lft forever preferred_lft forever
```

This confirms that both pods exchange traffic through the host namespace, with their veth pairs terminating there. This intranode pod-to-pod connectivity is depicted in Figure 5-3.

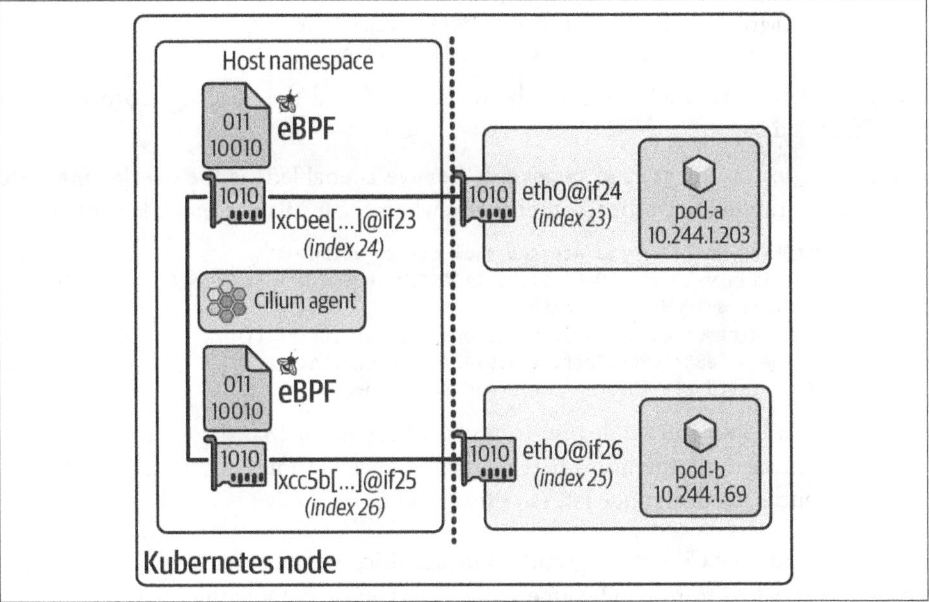

Figure 5-3. Intranode pod-to-pod connectivity

Cilium also installs a set of interfaces during initialization, which can be confusing the first time you see them in the `ip address` output. Let's break them down:

- For traffic leaving the pod, `pod-a` uses its default gateway (`10.244.1.198` in this example). This gateway address maps to the `cilium_host` device in the host's network namespace:

  ```
  root@kind-worker:/# ip address show cilium_host
  13: cilium_host@cilium_net: <BROADCAST,MULTICAST,NOARP,UP,LOWER_UP>
      mtu 65520 qdisc noqueue state UP group default qlen 1000
      link/ether 2e:62:71:74:47:90 brd ff:ff:ff:ff:ff:ff
      inet 10.244.1.198/32 scope global cilium_host
         valid_lft forever preferred_lft forever
      inet6 fe80::2c62:71ff:fe74:4790/64 scope link
         valid_lft forever preferred_lft forever
  ```

- `cilium_net` is a companion device paired with `cilium_host`. Together, they form the two ends of a veth pair, which is why the output shows `cilium_host@cilium_net` and `cilium_net@cilium_host`:

  ```
  root@kind-worker:/# ip address show cilium_net
  12: cilium_net@cilium_host: <BROADCAST,MULTICAST,NOARP,UP,LOWER_UP>
      mtu 65520 qdisc noqueue state UP group default qlen 1000
      link/ether ba:6c:63:bb:3a:f8 brd ff:ff:ff:ff:ff:ff
      inet6 fe80::b86c:63ff:febb:3af8/64 scope link
         valid_lft forever preferred_lft forever
  ```

  This construction allows traffic between a pod and the host to be processed by Cilium's datapath.

- `cilium_vxlan` (or `cilium_geneve`, if Geneve is enabled) is the overlay interface used for tunneling traffic to other nodes when encapsulation mode is configured:

  ```
  root@kind-worker:/# ip address show cilium_vxlan
  14: cilium_vxlan: <BROADCAST,MULTICAST,UP,LOWER_UP> mtu 65520 qdisc noqueue
      state UNKNOWN group default
      link/ether c2:6e:2a:c2:91:42 brd ff:ff:ff:ff:ff:ff
      inet6 fe80::c06e:2aff:fec2:9142/64 scope link
         valid_lft forever preferred_lft forever
  ```

  It is not used for intranode pod-to-pod traffic; packets that stay on the same node are forwarded via the host's network namespace without encapsulation. We will cover encapsulation mode later in this chapter.

To understand how Cilium programs control traffic, we can inspect which eBPF programs are attached to the node's interfaces. This can be done with either `cilium-dbg` (introduced in Chapter 2 and first used in Chapter 4) or the kernel's `bpftool` (*https://bpftool.dev*), a command-line tool for inspecting and managing BPF objects. Here we will use `bpftool` so you can see exactly which programs are attached to which devices:

```
$ kubectl -n kube-system exec -it cilium-gq458 -c cilium-agent -- bash

root@kind-worker:/home/cilium# bpftool net show
xdp:

tc:
eth0(11)            tcx/ingress cil_from_netdev       prog_id 617 link_id 16
cilium_net(12)      tcx/ingress cil_to_host           prog_id 609 link_id 15
cilium_host(13)     tcx/ingress cil_to_host           prog_id 607 link_id 13
cilium_host(13)     tcx/egress  cil_from_host         prog_id 601 link_id 14
cilium_vxlan(14)    tcx/ingress cil_from_overlay      prog_id 598 link_id 11
cilium_vxlan(14)    tcx/egress  cil_to_overlay        prog_id 599 link_id 12
lxc_health(16)      tcx/ingress cil_from_container    prog_id 633 link_id 17
lxc0090ec0fed69(18) tcx/ingress cil_from_container prog_id 643 link_id 18
lxcefc945dce028(20) tcx/ingress cil_from_container prog_id 666 link_id 20
lxce97d7b72b3aa(22) tcx/ingress cil_from_container prog_id 657 link_id 19
lxcbee302eb186c(24) tcx/ingress cil_from_container prog_id 1668 link_id 37
lxcc5b0a1b7ddfb(26) tcx/ingress cil_from_container prog_id 1695 link_id 38
[...]
```

The listing shows several important things:

- Host devices (`cilium_host`, `cilium_net`, `cilium_vxlan`) all have programs attached, handling traffic into and out of the node.
- Pod veth devices (`lxc*`) each have ingress programs attached. These entries are shown as `cil_from_container-*`. The attachment point is ingress on the veth, which corresponds to packets leaving the container. In other words, whenever a packet exits a pod, it first passes through this eBPF program before entering the host's network namespace.

Putting this together, packets from `pod-a` traverse its veth into the host-side `lxc*` device, where Cilium's ingress program (`cil_from_container-*`) runs. The packet is then delivered to `pod-b` if the traffic stays on the same node.

You can confirm the packet path with a simple packet capture on the host-side veth for `pod-b (lxcc5b0a1b7ddfb)` by using `tcpdump` on the worker node. The ICMP echo request and reply shown here are the ping traffic we initiated earlier from `pod-a` (`10.244.1.203`) to `pod-b` (`10.244.1.69`):

```
root@kind-worker:/# tcpdump -i lxcc5b0a1b7ddfb
14:12:34.847472 IP 10.244.1.203 > 10.244.1.69:
  ICMP echo request, id 51, seq 1, length 64

14:12:34.847589 IP 10.244.1.69 > 10.244.1.203:
  ICMP echo reply, id 51, seq 1, length 64
```

This confirms the intranode path: packets leave `pod-a`, enter the host's network namespace, are processed by Cilium's eBPF datapath, and are delivered to `pod-b` without encapsulation.[1]

From Cilium 1.16 on, an alternative to veth called the netkit device is supported. Introduced in Linux 6.7, netkit allows eBPF programs to run directly inside pod namespaces for improved performance. This is covered in more detail in Chapter 8.

Internode Connectivity

While intranode pod-to-pod communication is handled entirely on the local host, internode traffic must be forwarded across the physical network connecting cluster nodes. This introduces additional complexity, since each node must know which pod IP ranges are assigned to other nodes and how to reach them.

A fundamental rule of Kubernetes networking (*https://oreil.ly/0zLYq*) is that *every pod must be able to communicate with every other pod using its IP address, without any form of network address translation*. In other words:

- The source IP of a packet sent by a pod must be visible, unmodified, at the destination pod.
- The destination pod must be reachable directly by its pod IP, not by a translated node IP or service address.

To meet this requirement, Cilium supports two primary routing models for internode connectivity:

- Native routing, where the nodes and the underlying network are aware of all pod networks and can forward the traffic accordingly.
- Encapsulation (overlay) routing, where Cilium builds a mesh of tunnels between nodes and hides pod network details from the underlay.

Let's explore both models, how Cilium implements them, and the trade-offs of each.

Native Routing Mode

In native routing, packets sent by pods to other pods are routed through the host networking stack, just like packets from any other local process. Once a packet exits

1 If you'd like to truly understand how packets make their way across the Linux networking stack, you can try out `pwru` (*https://github.com/cilium/pwru*) ("Packet, where are you?"), an eBPF-based Linux kernel networking debugger that is part of the broader Cilium project.

a pod and enters the host's networking namespace, it is routed based on the host's routing table.

This mode requires either that each Kubernetes node knows the PodCIDRs assigned to all other nodes, or that the underlying network can route pod IPs directly (for example, through a pod IP–aware fabric such as BGP). In the first case, nodes maintain explicit routes between one another. For instance, if the subnet `10.10.0.32/27` is allocated to `kind-worker2`, then `kind-worker1` must have a route sending traffic for that range to `kind-worker2`'s node IP.

Table 5-1 shows a simple example with three nodes, their PodCIDRs, and the corresponding next hops.

Table 5-1. Native routing example

Destination prefix	Destination node	Next hop
`10.10.0.0/27`	`kind-worker`	`172.18.0.3`
`10.10.0.32/27`	`kind-worker2`	`172.18.0.4`
`10.10.0.64/27`	`kind-control-plane`	`172.18.0.5`

The same example is illustrated in Figure 5-4.

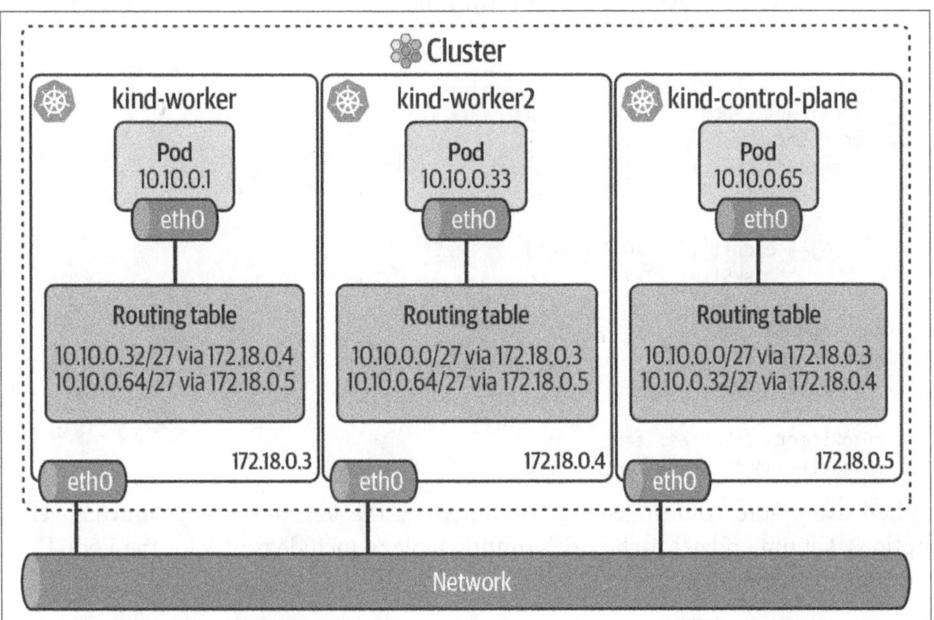

Figure 5-4. Native routing mode

Since encapsulation is Cilium's default routing mode, native routing must be enabled explicitly with the `routingMode: native` Helm value.

The other required value when using native routing is the CIDR range that is already routable by the underlying network, which can be defined with the `ipv4NativeRoutingCIDR` (or `ipv6NativeRoutingCIDR`) option. This tells Cilium to hand packets in that range directly to the Linux kernel's routing subsystem, without applying NAT to the node's IP on egress.

For the nodes to learn about each PodCIDR, you have three main options: auto route injection, static routing, and dynamic routing with BGP. Let's review each of these.

Auto route injection

Auto route injection (also known as *auto-direct node routes*) is the simplest way to propagate the pod network information, but it requires each node to be on the same layer 2 network.

Let's try it. First, create a generic kind cluster:

```
kind create cluster --config kind.yaml
```

Then install Cilium with the following Helm values (*cilium-native-auto-node-routes.yaml*). We're reusing the values from the Multi-Pool example from Chapter 4 here:

```
ipam:
  mode: multi-pool
  operator:
    autoCreateCiliumPodIPPools:
      default:
        ipv4:
          cidrs: ["10.10.0.0/16"]
          maskSize: 27

routingMode: native
endpointRoutes:
  enabled: true

autoDirectNodeRoutes: true
ipv4NativeRoutingCIDR: 10.0.0.0/8
```

When using auto route injection (indicated by the `autoDirectNodeRoutes: true` option), Cilium updates each node's routing table to include routes for the PodCIDRs owned by other nodes.

Let's check the PodCIDRs first. You may recall from our discussion of Multi-Pool mode and the previous Helm configuration that Cilium will automatically create PodCIDRs on each node. We can verify this with the following commands:

```
$ kubectl get ciliumnodes kind-worker -o yaml | yq .spec.ipam.pools
- cidrs:
    - 10.10.0.64/27
  pool: default

$ kubectl get ciliumnodes kind-worker2 -o yaml | yq .spec.ipam.pools
- cidrs:
    - 10.10.0.32/27
  pool: default

$ kubectl get ciliumnodes kind-control-plane -o yaml | yq .spec.ipam.pools
- cidrs:
    - 10.10.0.0/27
  pool: default
```

Now, let's inspect the routing tables on the nodes in our kind cluster. With `autoDirectNodeRoutes` enabled, Cilium has automatically populated each table with routes to the PodCIDRs, using the corresponding node IPs as next hops:

```
$ docker exec kind-worker ip route
[...]
10.10.0.0/27 via 172.18.0.4 dev eth0 proto kernel
10.10.0.32/27 via 172.18.0.2 dev eth0 proto kernel

$ docker exec kind-worker2 ip route
[...]
10.10.0.0/27 via 172.18.0.4 dev eth0 proto kernel
10.10.0.64/27 via 172.18.0.3 dev eth0 proto kernel

$ docker exec kind-control-plane ip route
[...]
10.10.0.32/27 via 172.18.0.2 dev eth0 proto kernel
10.10.0.64/27 via 172.18.0.3 dev eth0 proto kernel
```

Static routing

In a very small cluster with a fixed set of nodes, such as a two-node lab environment or a development setup where nodes rarely change, you can configure PodCIDRs manually using `ip route` or a configuration management tool.

For instance, if the PodCIDR `10.10.0.32/27` is allocated to `kind-worker2` (node IP `172.18.0.4`), then every other node in the cluster must be told how to reach that range. On `kind-worker`, you would configure:

```
ip route add 10.10.0.32/27 via 172.18.0.4 dev eth0
```

This ensures that any packets destined for `10.10.0.32/27` are forwarded to `kind-worker2`. The same principle applies in reverse: each node must have static routes installed for the PodCIDRs owned by all of the other nodes.

While simple and explicit, this approach does not scale. Whenever nodes are added, removed, or rescheduled, static routes need to be updated manually across the cluster. This quickly becomes error-prone and operationally unmanageable outside of very small test setups.

Dynamic routing with BGP

In production environments with many nodes or frequent churn, such as deployments spanning multiple racks, the most scalable option is to distribute PodCIDRs dynamically using BGP. With BGP enabled, each node advertises its PodCIDRs to the network fabric. This ensures routes are kept up-to-date automatically. With Cilium's BGP support (covered in Chapter 10), pod prefixes can be advertised directly.

With a Cilium BGP configuration like the one that follows, nodes can dynamically advertise their PodCIDRs to the underlying network (typically, by peering with top-of-rack devices):

```
apiVersion: cilium.io/v2
kind: CiliumBGPPeerConfig
metadata:
  name: peer-config-generic
spec:
  families:
    - afi: ipv4
      safi: unicast
      advertisements:
        matchLabels:
          advertise: "pod-cidr"
---
apiVersion: cilium.io/v2
kind: CiliumBGPAdvertisement
metadata:
  name: pod-cidr
  labels:
    advertise: pod-cidr
spec:
  advertisements:
    - advertisementType: "PodCIDR"
```

This approach allows the cluster to scale without manual configuration. When nodes join or leave the cluster, the routing fabric is updated automatically.

Encapsulation Mode

Native routing works well when the underlying network can carry PodCIDRs directly or when you can extend the routing fabric with static routes or BGP. But in many environments, especially in cloud or multitenant infrastructures, you do not have the ability to influence the underlay. In those cases, Cilium cannot rely on the network to forward pod IPs.

To solve this problem, Cilium provides *encapsulation mode*, where pod traffic is tunneled between nodes. From the underlay's perspective this is just ordinary node-to-node traffic, but the original pod packets are preserved inside the tunnel. In encapsulation mode—also known as tunnel or overlay mode—all nodes form a full set of overlay tunnels using a User Datagram Protocol (UDP)-based encapsulation protocol such as VXLAN or Geneve. This is Cilium's default routing mode.

Encapsulation is most useful in environments where you cannot control the underlay routing. Instead of requiring the physical network to carry pod prefixes, Cilium hides pod addressing behind node IPs. From the underlay's perspective, all pod-to-pod traffic looks like node-to-node traffic between Kubernetes nodes.

Encapsulation mode with VXLAN

Virtual eXtensible LAN (VXLAN) is a tunneling protocol that encapsulates layer 2 Ethernet frames inside UDP packets, allowing networks to extend layer 2 segments across layer 3 boundaries. It was designed to overcome the scalability limits of VLANs by supporting up to 16 million unique VXLAN network identifiers (VNIs), compared to the 4,096 VLAN IDs (VIDs) supported by VLAN.

In practical terms, VXLAN provides a way to build overlay networks on top of an existing IP underlay. The underlay only needs to deliver UDP traffic between nodes, while the overlay preserves the original Ethernet and IP headers of pod-to-pod traffic.

When Cilium is installed in VXLAN mode, a `cilium_vxlan` device appears on each node:

```
root@kind-worker:/# ip address show cilium_vxlan
14: cilium_vxlan: <BROADCAST,MULTICAST,UP,LOWER_UP> mtu 65520
    qdisc noqueue state UNKNOWN group default
    link/ether c2:6e:2a:c2:91:42 brd ff:ff:ff:ff:ff:ff
    inet6 fe80::c06e:2aff:fec2:9142/64 scope link
       valid_lft forever preferred_lft forever
```

Routes to remote PodCIDRs point to this device. Packets destined for another node's PodCIDR are encapsulated and sent via the VXLAN interface, as illustrated in Figure 5-5.

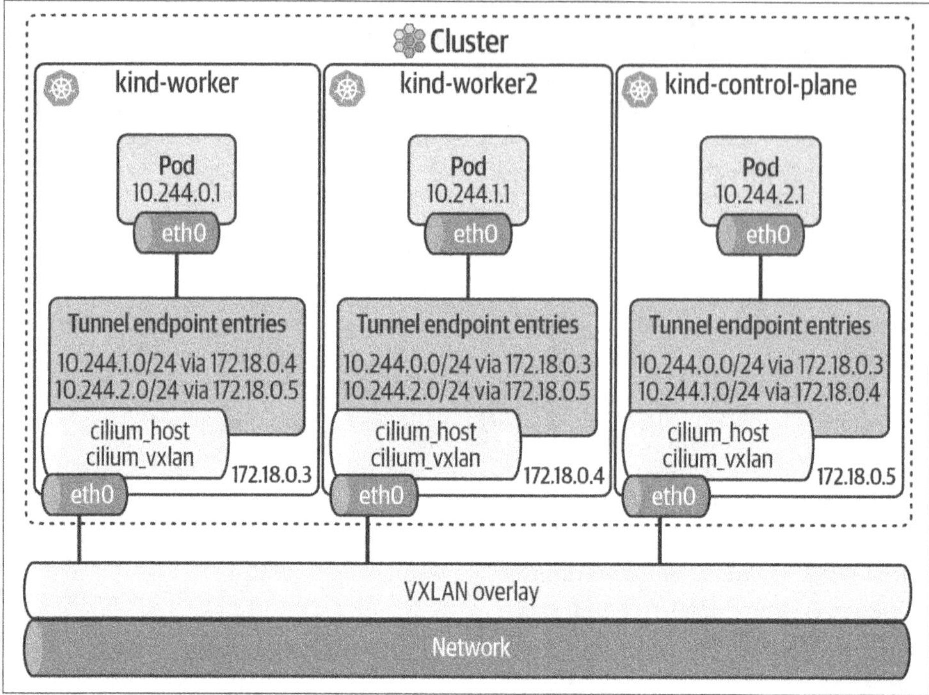

Figure 5-5. Encapsulation routing mode

You can verify this using a generic kind cluster (`kind create cluster --config kind.yaml`) with a default Cilium installation.

The routing table is updated to direct PodCIDRs via the `cilium_host` device. For example:

```
$ docker exec kind-worker ip route
[...]
10.244.0.0/24 via 10.244.2.63 dev cilium_host [...]
10.244.1.0/24 via 10.244.2.63 dev cilium_host [...] mtu 65470
10.244.2.0/24 via 10.244.2.63 dev cilium_host [...] mtu 65470
[...]
```

Similar routes are installed on the other nodes, always pointing PodCIDRs to the local `cilium_host`.

If this looks familiar, it should. We saw a similar pattern in native routing mode with auto route injection: Cilium updated the host routing table with PodCIDRs and directed them to the appropriate node IPs. The difference here is that in VXLAN mode the routes point to the local `cilium_host` device. From there, Cilium intercepts the traffic, encapsulates it, and sends it through the `cilium_vxlan` interface to the destination node.

Figure 5-6 illustrates the packet format:

- The outer IP header holds the node IPs (for example, `172.18.0.5 > 172.18.0.3`).
- The outer UDP header identifies the tunnel. Cilium uses UDP port 8472 by default, although the IANA-assigned VXLAN port is 4789.
- The VXLAN header contains the VNI. In traditional VXLAN, the VNI is used to distinguish overlay networks. In Cilium, it is repurposed to carry the identity of the source pod. This provides a minor performance boost, as it allows the destination node to enforce policy without performing a separate identity lookup.[2]
- The inner packet is the original pod-to-pod traffic, preserved unmodified.

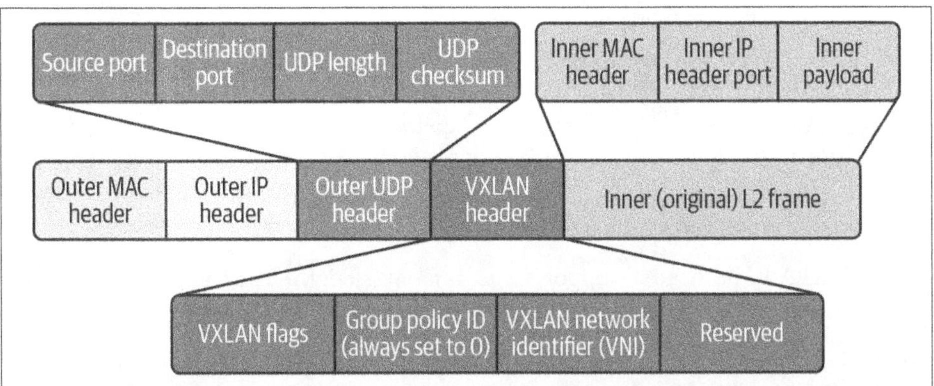

Figure 5-6. VXLAN encapsulation

You can inspect this traffic using the sample capture file *vxlan_traffic.pcap*, available in the */pcaps* directory of the book's GitHub repository. To view the packet flow directly on the command line, use this command:

```
$ tcpdump -r vxlan_traffic.pcap
IP 172.18.0.3.51713 > 172.18.0.4.8472: OTV, flags [I]
IP 10.244.0.185.52442 > 10.244.1.212.4240: Flags [.], ack 1439317725, length 0
```

This shows that the packet was encapsulated with VXLAN on UDP port 8472.
The outer IP header (`172.18.0.3 > 172.18.0.4`) corresponds to the node-to-node communication between `kind-worker` and `kind-worker2`. Inside the VXLAN header, the original pod-level packet (`10.244.0.185 > 10.244.1.212`) is preserved, which is the actual application traffic.

2 Don't worry if you find the concepts of identity and policy confusing—they will be explained in detail in Chapter 12.

From the network's point of view, this is just internode traffic. The nodes do not need to be on the same subnet, and they do not need to understand or route pod IPs.

Once the packet reaches the destination node, Cilium removes the VXLAN header and delivers the original packet to the receiving pod. The key benefit of encapsulation mode is that it abstracts the pod network from the underlying infrastructure. As long as nodes can reach each other over IP, pod-to-pod communication will work. The downside is the encapsulation overhead. Each packet includes an additional VXLAN header and outer IP/UDP headers. This adds approximately 50 bytes per packet (depending on configuration), which reduces the effective MTU (*maximum transmission unit*, the largest amount of data that can be transmitted over a network in a single packet) and can impact performance. For most clusters, this overhead is acceptable. However, in performance-sensitive environments, native routing is typically preferred when possible.

Encapsulation mode with Geneve

Like VXLAN, Geneve (Generic Network Virtualization Encapsulation) lets Cilium tunnel pod traffic between nodes when the underlay cannot route PodCIDRs. The effect is the same: the underlay only sees node-to-node IP traffic, while the original pod packet is preserved inside the tunnel.

Unlike VXLAN, its header supports custom type–length–value (TLV) fields. TLVs allow Geneve to carry extra metadata in the tunnel.

To test Geneve, we will use another managed Kubernetes service: Azure Kubernetes Service (AKS). This gives you the opportunity to try Cilium in a different cloud environment. The choice of AKS is deliberate because it offers a convenient and flexible networking mode: *bring your own Container Network Interface* (BYOCNI). In this mode, the cluster is deployed without a CNI, leaving you free to install the CNI of your choice—in this case, Cilium.

As mentioned in Chapter 4, keep in mind that creating clusters and infrastructure in cloud environments may incur costs. Be sure to clean up any resources when you're done.

To deploy an AKS cluster, we'll use the Azure CLI (`az`). Follow the documentation (*https://learn.microsoft.com/en-us/cli/azure/?view=azure-cli-latest*) to install it, sign in with `az login`, and then use the following commands to create a managed cluster in AKS (*aks-byocni.md*). In this example we use names prefixed with `geneve-` to make their purpose clearer:

```
az group create -l canadacentral -n geneve-rg ❶

az network vnet create \ ❷
  -g geneve-rg \
  --location canadacentral \
```

```
    --name geneve-vnet \
    --address-prefixes 192.168.8.0/22 \
    -o none

  az network vnet subnet create \ ❸
    -g geneve-rg \
    --vnet-name geneve-vnet \
    --name geneve-subnet \
    --address-prefixes 192.168.10.0/24 \
    -o none

  SUBNET_ID=$(az network vnet subnet show \ ❹
    --resource-group geneve-rg \
    --vnet-name geneve-vnet \
    --name geneve-subnet \
    --query id -o tsv)

  az aks create \ ❺
    -l canadacentral \
    -g geneve-rg \
    -n geneve-cluster \
    --network-plugin none \
    --vnet-subnet-id "$SUBNET_ID"

  az aks get-credentials --resource-group geneve-rg --name geneve-cluster ❻
```

❶ Create a new Azure resource group in the `canadacentral` region (customize this to the region of your choice).

❷ Set up a virtual network (`geneve-vnet`) with a `/22` address space.

❸ Create a subnet (`geneve-subnet`) within the VNet using a `/24` prefix.

❹ Dynamically retrieve the subnet ID.

❺ Provision an AKS cluster (`geneve-cluster`) in BYOCNI mode (indicated by the `--network-plugin none` flag).

❻ Fetch the kubeconfig for the created cluster.

Once the cluster is ready, you can install Cilium in Geneve mode with the following Helm values (*cilium-geneve-values.yaml*):

```
aksbyocni:
  enabled: true
ipam:
  mode: cluster-pool

tunnelProtocol: geneve
```

When the installation is complete, check the cluster nodes' IP addresses:

```
$ kubectl get nodes -o wide
NAME                              INTERNAL-IP
aks-nodepool1-30411986-vmss000000  192.168.10.4
aks-nodepool1-30411986-vmss000001  192.168.10.5
aks-nodepool1-30411986-vmss000002  192.168.10.6
```

Next, confirm which PodCIDRs have been allocated to each node. This is available from the CiliumNode objects:

```
$ kubectl get ciliumnodes -o yaml | grep -C 1 CIDR
ipam: { podCIDRs: [10.0.2.0/24] }
ipam: { podCIDRs: [10.0.0.0/24] }
ipam: { podCIDRs: [10.0.1.0/24] }
```

Deploy a set of pods (*netshoot-deployment.yaml*) and verify that they each get an IP address from the expected pools:

```
$ kubectl get pods -o wide
NAME                            READY   STATUS    IP            NODE
pod-worker-54f8b77c97-fm22b 1/1     Running   10.0.0.125    vmss000001
pod-worker-54f8b77c97-kxcr9 1/1     Running   10.0.1.219    vmss000002
pod-worker-54f8b77c97-pbgv6 1/1     Running   10.0.2.75     vmss000000
```

Now let's verify internode connectivity between pods to confirm that Geneve encapsulation is working:

```
$ kubectl exec -it pod-worker-54f8b77c97-fm22b -- ping 10.0.2.75
PING 10.0.2.75 (10.0.2.75) 56(84) bytes of data.
64 bytes from 10.0.2.75: icmp_seq=1 ttl=63 time=0.129 ms
64 bytes from 10.0.2.75: icmp_seq=2 ttl=63 time=0.064 ms
^C
--- 10.0.0.249 ping statistics ---
2 packets transmitted, 2 received, 0% packet loss, time 3077ms
rtt min/avg/max/mdev = 0.064/0.080/0.129/0.027 ms
```

We explained earlier how, when using native routing with auto route injection or VXLAN, PodCIDR routes are installed in the node's routing table and point to the destination node's IP address. The same applies in Geneve mode, but in this case the mapping can be confirmed by checking the Cilium agent. For example, on the agent located on `aks-***-vmss000001`, the route to `10.0.2.0/24` (the PodCIDR on `aks-***-vmss000000`) maps to the tunnel bound to the node's IP address (`192.168.10.4`):

```
$ kubectl -n kube-system exec -it cilium-8z49v -- cilium-dbg bpf ipcache list

IP PREFIX        ADDRESS IDENTITY
10.0.2.0/24      encryptkey=0 tunnelendpoint=192.168.10.4 flags=hastunnel
10.0.1.0/24      encryptkey=0 tunnelendpoint=192.168.10.6 flags=hastunnel
```

Similar to VXLAN encapsulation, the original pod packet is wrapped inside a UDP packet for transmission between nodes, as illustrated in Figure 5-7.

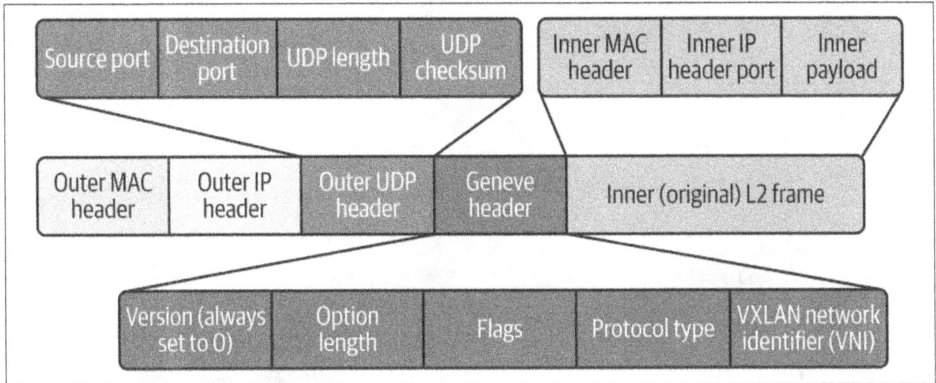

Figure 5-7. Geneve encapsulation

The main differences between VXLAN and Geneve are the ability to use TLVs and the UDP port: Cilium uses UDP port 6081 for Geneve and 8472 for VXLAN.

Most of the Geneve header fields remain fixed in Cilium's implementation:

- The version is always `0`.
- The flags are set to `0x00`.
- The protocol type is usually `0x6558`, meaning Ethernet.

The other two fields are more interesting to examine. The option length field indicates whether any TLVs are present. In our example it is `0`, meaning no TLVs are used. The TLV fields are populated when using Direct Server Return (covered in Chapter 8) with Geneve. As with VXLAN, the VNI field in Geneve is used by Cilium to carry the identity of the source pod. This allows the destination node to enforce network policy without having to perform a separate identity lookup.

You can inspect the Geneve-encapsulated traffic using the sample capture file *geneve.pcap* in the */pcaps* directory of the book's GitHub repository. To view the packet flow directly on the command line, use this command:

```
$ tcpdump -r geneve.pcap
IP 192.168.10.5.49135 > 192.168.10.4.6081: Geneve, vni 0x382e:
  IP 10.0.0.125 > 10.0.2.75: ICMP echo request, length 64
```

The outer header (`192.168.10.5 > 192.168.10.4`) represents node-to-node traffic sent over UDP port 6081. Inside the tunnel, the original pod-to-pod packet (`10.0.0.125 > 10.0.2.75`) is preserved unchanged.

The VNI field in the Geneve header is set to `0x382e`, which converts to the decimal value 14382. This value corresponds to the CiliumIdentity associated with the source pod. You can verify that this is the identity of the source pod with `kubectl get ciliumid`:

```
$ kubectl get ciliumid 14382 -o yaml
apiVersion: cilium.io/v2
kind: CiliumIdentity
metadata:
[...]
  name: "14382"
security-labels:
  k8s:app: pod-worker
[...]
```

If you created a cloud-hosted cluster to test this feature, remember to delete it to avoid further costs.

Summary

Understanding how packets move between pods (both within the same node and across nodes) is fundamental to mastering Kubernetes networking with Cilium. In this chapter, we traced a packet from one pod to another, examined how Cilium leverages Linux primitives like veth pairs, and explored the role of Cilium in forwarding decisions. We also looked at the two main models of internode connectivity—native routing mode, where the underlying network must be able to route PodCIDRs, and encapsulation mode, where Cilium builds a tunnel mesh using VXLAN or Geneve to abstract the pod network from the infrastructure—and explained how each approach has trade-offs in terms of performance, simplicity, and control.

In the next chapter, we'll turn our attention to Kubernetes service networking: we'll explore how it works and see how Cilium handles service discovery, load balancing, and proxying.

CHAPTER 6

Service Networking

In Kubernetes, pod-to-pod communication enables direct connectivity between workloads—but this model alone does not scale well for dynamic, distributed applications. Instead, most real-world applications interact through *services*, which provide stable virtual IPs and load balancing across dynamic backend pods. This abstraction is critical for scalability, reliability, and operational simplicity in distributed systems.

Service networking is at the core of how applications discover and reach each other in a cluster. It enables decoupling of workloads, supports horizontal scaling, and provides mechanisms for high availability.

In this chapter, we will examine how Kubernetes manages service communication, the traditional role of `kube-proxy`, and how Cilium enhances and ultimately replaces it with an eBPF-based datapath. Along the way, we will explore concepts such as headless services, session affinity, and external access through LoadBalancer services. You can find all the YAML manifests you will use in this chapter in the *chapter06* directory of the book's GitHub repository (*https://github.com/isovalent/cilium-up-and-running*).

Kubernetes Service Refresher

To better understand some of the principles referred to in later sections of this book, a brief overview of Kubernetes services may be useful. This is not meant to be a comprehensive explanation, given that there are various books dedicated to this topic already (including O'Reilly's *Networking and Kubernetes* and *Container Networking*). Instead, it serves as a concise refresher on the concepts most relevant to service communication.

Kubernetes is built for ephemeral workloads. New pods are constantly being created, while old ones are removed. The IP addresses assigned to pods are not reserved: once a pod terminates, the cluster returns its IP to the pool and may reassign it to another pod. Because of this, relying solely on IPs for connectivity in Kubernetes is impractical. Instead, we typically use services and DNS to provide stable names and a single virtual IP for a set of ready pods.

A service defines a consistent way for clients to reach a group of pods. It acts as a tiny virtual load balancer that targets pods with specific labels. Each service is assigned a unique virtual IP address (VIP) that exists only inside the cluster. Traffic sent to that VIP is load-balanced across pods that are marked as `Ready` based on a readiness probe.

Kubernetes supports several types of services for different use cases:

ClusterIP (default)
: Provides an in-cluster VIP so that other pods can reach the service.

NodePort
: Exposes the service on the same static port across all nodes, which allows basic external access. Chapter 10 will explain some of the limitations of NodePort and how to address them.

LoadBalancer
: Provisions an external IP by integrating with a cloud provider's load balancer or with Cilium's LoadBalancer IPAM (LB IPAM). We will cover external reachability and announcements in Chapters 7 and 10.

Headless
: Skips allocating a VIP. DNS lookups return the individual pod IPs directly, which works well with StatefulSets, where each pod keeps a stable identity.

Inside the cluster, Kubernetes services rely on `kube-proxy`. Let's take a look at this component and consider its role and limitations before walking through how Cilium addresses them.

kube-proxy Refresher

This component is deployed as a DaemonSet, so it runs on every node. Its job is to program the networking rules required to forward traffic from a service VIP to one of its backend pods. To do this, `kube-proxy` watches for changes to services and their backends, recorded as Endpoints or EndpointSlices, and updates the node's networking tables accordingly. When a packet is addressed to a service IP, the kernel applies one of these rules and performs destination network address translation (DNAT) to rewrite the destination address to a selected backend pod, as illustrated in Figure 6-1.

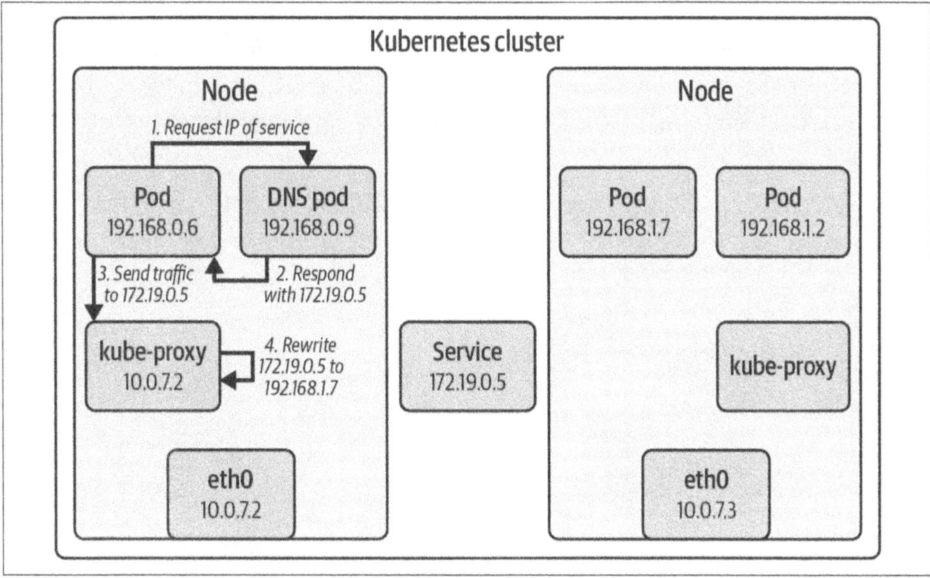

Figure 6-1. Kubernetes service networking

`kube-proxy` supports multiple modes for programming these rules, and each mode influences how load-balancing decisions are made. In `iptables` mode (*https://oreil.ly/LWilK*), packets are matched against large chains of NAT rules, with a random selection from the available endpoints. IPVS (*https://oreil.ly/9rGkm*) introduces a richer set of algorithms, such as round-robin and least connections. `nftables` (*https://oreil.ly/-mWyy*) provides a more modern alternative to `iptables` while offering similar functionality. Regardless of the backend, the outcome is the same: traffic sent to a single service IP is distributed across the set of healthy pods.

For a long time, most clusters relied on the `iptables` backend. However, `iptables` was originally designed more than two decades ago for static firewalling, not for the highly dynamic nature of Kubernetes. Each time a pod is added or removed, the `iptables` rules must be rewritten, which can become extremely expensive at scale—a well-known KubeCon talk in 2017 (*https://oreil.ly/tXZuF*) described how updating `iptables` rules for 20,000 services could take as long as five hours. Even without large updates, every packet must traverse the `iptables` chains one rule at a time, which is an operation that grows linearly with the number of rules.[1]

1 In mathematics, this would be referred to as an algorithm of $O(n)$ complexity.

To understand why iptables does not scale well as a backend for kube-proxy, we can create a large number of services and observe how many rules get inserted into the kernel. Recall that kube-proxy installs NAT rules for every service and every backend endpoint. As the number of services grows, so does the size of the iptables chains. Let's try it.

First, we'll deploy a kind cluster. We won't use Cilium yet, but rather the built-in CNI for kind clusters, kindnet. We'll also use the iptables-based kube-proxy (*kind-cluster-config-no-cilium.yaml*):

```
kind: Cluster
apiVersion: kind.x-k8s.io/v1alpha4
nodes:
- role: control-plane
- role: worker
- role: worker
networking:
  kubeProxyMode: iptables
```

Let's start with a simple deployment (*httpd-deployment.yaml*) and service (*httpd-service.yaml*) for httpd. Once this service is deployed, you can check out the worker nodes and the raw iptables rules yourself:

```
$ docker exec -it kind-worker iptables -t nat -L -n --line-numbers
Chain KUBE-SERVICES (2 references)
num target         prot source    destination comment
1   KUBE-SVC-*     tcp  0.0.0.0/0 10.96.0.10  /* kube-dns:dns-tcp */ dpt:53
3   KUBE-SVC-*.    tcp  0.0.0.0/0 10.96.1.252 /* httpd */ dpt:80
6   KUBE-NODEPORTS all  0.0.0.0/0 0.0.0.0/0   /* service nodeports */ dst-type LOCAL
```

You will observe that, even with a single service, multiple rules have been added to the NAT tables.

Now let's generate 100 services pointing to the httpd deployment, with this short for loop:

```
$ for i in {1..100}; do
  kubectl expose deployment httpd --port=80 --name="httpd-$i"
done

service/httpd-1 exposed
service/httpd-2 exposed
[...]
service/httpd-99 exposed
service/httpd-100 exposed
```

We can count the total number of rules created using grep:

```
$ docker exec kind-worker iptables-save | grep KUBE-SEP | wc -l
787
```

This illustrates the problem with iptables: every new service requires more rules, each rule must be evaluated linearly, and updating rulesets becomes increasingly expensive. This is one of the main reasons to consider replacing kube-proxy. Cilium's implementation, which we will examine next, uses eBPF maps in the kernel—a far more efficient way to store and update service state.

kube-proxy Replacement

Cilium approaches service connectivity differently. In this section we'll explore its eBPF-based kube-proxy replacement, commonly referred to as *KPR*.

KPR is a highly customizable feature. It exposes a wide range of options that control how services are implemented in the datapath, including translation modes, load-balancing algorithms, traffic policies, and acceleration features. (The user experience is due to be simplified in future releases so that common configurations require fewer manual settings.) Covering every option in detail is beyond the scope of this book. In this chapter, we will focus on the most important features relevant to day-to-day use, while pointing you to later chapters for further information on advanced topics such as Direct Server Return, XDP acceleration, and Maglev load balancing. For full details, see the Cilium documentation (*https://oreil.ly/pLmu_*).

When KPR is enabled, Cilium loads eBPF programs into the Linux kernel on every node. These programs attach to key networking interfaces, as described in Chapter 2, and intercept packets destined for a service. Instead of relying on long iptables chains, the program performs a lookup in an eBPF map that stores the current set of backends for that service. It then selects one of the available pods according to the load-balancing policy, rewrites the destination address (using DNAT), and forwards the packet, as illustrated in Figure 6-2. Because hash table lookups and insertions are done by key instead of by matching against chains of rules, the lookup time[2] stays the same regardless of how many services you have.

2 In computer science, this would be known as $O(1)$, or constant time complexity.

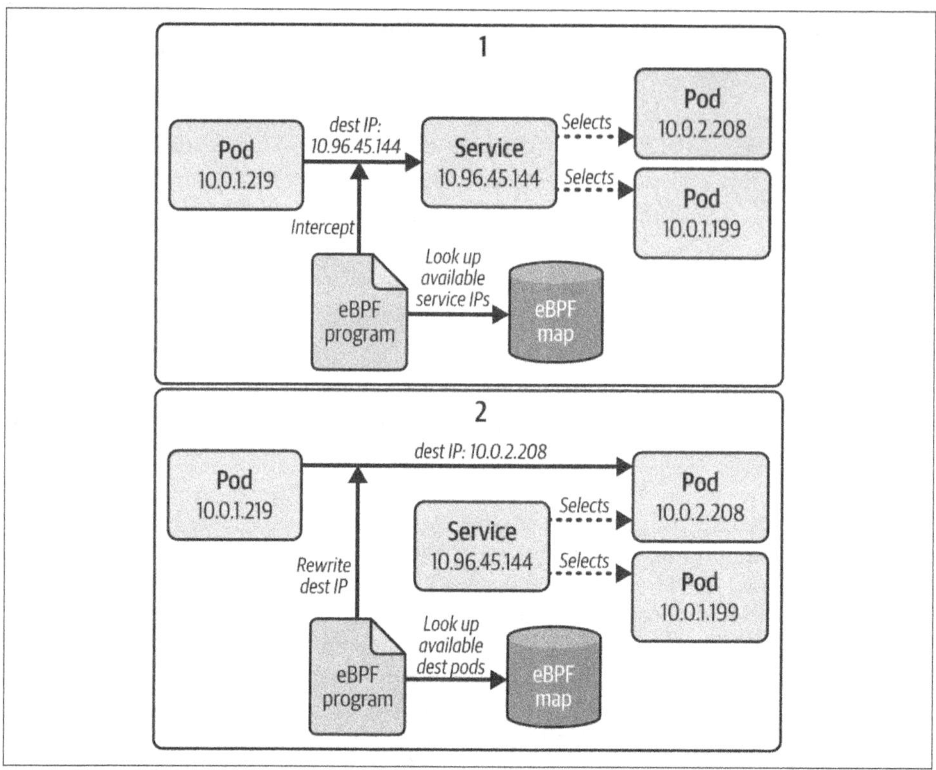

Figure 6-2. Cilium's eBPF-based `kube-proxy` replacement

When Cilium is installed, even without the `kube-proxy` replacement enabled, ClusterIP services are still implemented using eBPF.

Let's demonstrate this in practice. Deploy a kind cluster, using the kind configuration (*kind.yaml*) without the built-in `kube-proxy`:

```
networking:
  kubeProxyMode: "none"
```

Then, install Cilium in KPR mode. When using Helm, you'll need to specify the Kubernetes API server IP and port (*cilium-kpr-values.yaml*):

```
kubeProxyReplacement: true
k8sServiceHost: kind-control-plane
k8sServicePort: 6443
```

Why? When `kube-proxy` is in place, it handles service traffic toward Kubernetes services, including the Kubernetes API server itself. Pods can connect to kubernetes.default.svc, and kube-proxy will DNAT the service IP (usually 10.96.0.1 in kind) to the actual API server endpoint.

But given that we deployed our cluster without kube-proxy, there's no component to program the rules that let the Cilium agent and operator talk to the API server through the service IP. To avoid a chicken-and-egg problem, Cilium needs to know how to contact the API server directly, bypassing the service abstractions. That's why you need to set k8sServiceHost and k8sServicePort in the Helm values when enabling KPR. When using kind, we can just use kind-control-plane, as that hostname is resolvable from the worker containers.

One advantage of using the Cilium CLI in this instance is that it can detect the Kubernetes API server's IP address and port automatically from the kubeconfig:

```
$ cilium install --set kubeProxyReplacement=true
🔮 Auto-detected Kubernetes kind: kind
ℹ️ Using Cilium version 1.18.2
🔮 Auto-detected cluster name: kind-kind
ℹ️ Detecting real Kubernetes API server addr and port on Kind
🔮 Auto-detected kube-proxy has not been installed
ℹ️ Cilium will fully replace all functionalities of kube-proxy
```

Let's first verify that KPR was enabled by checking the detailed configuration status with the Cilium agent's cilium-dbg binary (introduced in Chapter 2):

```
$ kubectl -n kube-system exec ds/cilium -- cilium-dbg status --verbose
[...]
KubeProxyReplacement Details:
  Status:                 True ❶
  Socket LB:              Enabled
  Socket LB Tracing:      Enabled
  Socket LB Coverage:     Full
  Devices:                eth0    172.18.0.3 [...] (Direct Routing) ❷
  Mode:                   SNAT ❸
  Backend Selection:      Random ❹
  Session Affinity:       Enabled ❺
  Graceful Termination:   Enabled
  NAT46/64 Support:       Disabled
  XDP Acceleration:       Disabled
  Services: ❻
  - ClusterIP:      Enabled
  - NodePort:       Enabled (Range: 30000-32767)
  - LoadBalancer:   Enabled
  - externalIPs:    Enabled
  - HostPort:       Enabled
  Annotations:
  - service.cilium.io/node
  - service.cilium.io/src-ranges-policy
  - service.cilium.io/type
[...]
```

❶ This confirms that KPR is active.

❷ This shows the network devices where Cilium has attached its eBPF programs, with (direct) native routing enabled on `eth0`. Note that KPR works for both native and encapsulation routing modes.

❸ The translation mode is SNAT, which means incoming packets are source-NATed with the IPs of the nodes. We will see an alternative translation mode (DSR) in Chapter 8.

❹ Backend selection uses random choice by default. For more consistent load balancing across nodes, Cilium also supports Maglev hashing, which we cover in Chapter 8.

❺ Session affinity is enabled. This ensures that packets from the same client IP can be steered to the same backend pod. We discuss session affinity later in this chapter.

❻ Here we can see the service types that are implemented by KPR: ClusterIP, NodePort, LoadBalancer, externalIPs, and HostPort.

Throughout this book, you'll notice that some `cilium-dbg` commands are run against the entire Cilium DaemonSet (e.g., `ds/cilium`), while others target a specific Cilium agent pod. This is intentional. We use the DaemonSet form when querying cluster-wide or uniform information (configuration, enabled features, or service maps), because it doesn't matter which instance we land on. In contrast, when inspecting node-local state (like tunnel maps or health checks), we explicitly target a specific Cilium pod associated with the node of interest. Running a command against the DaemonSet causes Kubernetes to pick one of the available Cilium pods at random.

Next, we'll create the same httpd deployment (*httpd-deployment.yaml*) and service (*httpd-service.yaml*) we used in the previous section. Take note of the pod IPs, as well as the service IP:

```
$ kubectl get pods -o wide
NAME                      READY   STATUS    IP           NODE
httpd-77b5fcff59-k6svw    1/1     Running   10.0.1.199   kind-worker2
httpd-77b5fcff59-vfnxt    1/1     Running   10.0.2.208   kind-worker

$ kubectl get service
NAME    TYPE        CLUSTER-IP     EXTERNAL-IP   PORT(S)   AGE
httpd   ClusterIP   10.96.45.144   <none>        80/TCP    17s
```

We can check that there are no `iptables` rules created to handle traffic for this service by running the same command we used earlier:

```
$ docker exec kind-worker iptables-save | grep KUBE-SEP | wc -l
0
```

Instead, eBPF entries are populated with the healthy (active) backends. We can use `cilium-dbg` to inspect the current services and their backends:

```
$ kubectl exec -n kube-system -it ds/cilium -- cilium-dbg service list
ID   Frontend               Service Type   Backend
6    10.96.45.144:80/TCP    ClusterIP      1 => 10.0.1.199:80/TCP (active)
                                           2 => 10.0.2.208:80/TCP (active
```

Now, let's launch a client pod (*netshoot-client.yaml*) and, from its shell, send traffic to the service IP (`10.96.45.144`) and immediately inspect */proc/<pid>/net/tcp*:

```
$ kubectl exec -it netshoot-client -- bash

netshoot-client:~# curl 10.96.45.144 && cat "/proc/$$/net/tcp"
<html><body><h1>It works!</h1></body></html>
  sl  local_address     rem_address    st
   0: DB01000A:D316     D002000A:0050  06
```

When we run `curl 10.96.45.144`, the request goes to the service we just created. The HTML response confirms that the request successfully reached one of the httpd pods. Traffic was forwarded appropriately to the right backend, even though there are no matching `iptables` rules.

On Linux, every process has a directory under */proc/<pid>/* (where *<pid>* is the process ID) that contains details about that process. The command `cat "/proc/$$/net/tcp"` lists the TCP connections for the current process (`$$` expands to the current process ID). In that file, the `rem_address` field shows the remote IP address. Instead of being displayed in a human-readable format, the address appears in hexadecimal.

For example, the value `0xD002000A` corresponds to the IPv4 address `D0.02.00.0A`. Splitting it into byte pairs gives us the four octets of the address, and converting them to decimal produces `208.2.0.10`. Because the kernel stores addresses in little-endian order (least significant byte first), we reverse the sequence to obtain the real address: `10.0.2.208`. This IP belongs to one of the httpd pods.

This confirms what is happening under the hood. Although we connected to the service IP `10.96.45.144`, the eBPF program in the kernel rewrote the destination early in the networking stack, allowing us to observe the pod's actual IP as the backend.

If we repeat the request, we may see another value, such as 0xC701000A, which translates to 10.0.1.199—the address of the second httpd pod:

```
netshoot-client:~# curl 10.96.45.144 && cat "/proc/$$/net/tcp"
<html><body><h1>It works!</h1></body></html>
  sl  local_address     rem_address    st
   0: DB01000A:ED76     D002000A:0050  06
   1: DB01000A:85B0     C701000A:0050  06
```

The value 0x0050 is the port number in hexadecimal. Converting 0x0050 to decimal gives us 80, which is the default port for HTTP.

Finally, let's repeat the service scaling test and verify there are still no iptables rules being created:

```
$ for i in {1..100}; do
  kubectl expose deployment httpd --port=80 --name="httpd-$i"
done

service/httpd-1 exposed
service/httpd-2 exposed
[...]
service/httpd-99 exposed
service/httpd-100 exposed

$ docker exec kind-worker iptables-save | grep KUBE-SEP | wc -l
0
```

Agent Availability and Datapath Resiliency

Cilium separates control-plane work from datapath forwarding. As you saw in Chapter 2, the Cilium agent watches the Kubernetes API server and pushes updates about changes to pods and their readiness. It computes the state and writes service and backend information into eBPF maps. eBPF programs in the Linux kernel read those maps to steer packets to pod backends. The programs themselves are stateless; they do not have any built-in knowledge of pods but rely entirely on the data maintained by the agent.

This architecture provides a significant advantage: the datapath itself continues to operate as long as the kernel state is intact. This design means that service connectivity does not immediately break if the agent is restarted or temporarily unavailable.

This resiliency is important because rolling upgrades, node restarts, and other operational events should not disrupt applications. Since the eBPF programs and maps live in the kernel, packets continue to be forwarded while the agent restarts. In fact, service connectivity is preserved even if the Cilium agent crashes or is temporarily removed. To demonstrate this, we will simulate the removal of the agent by modifying its DaemonSet:

```
$ kubectl -n kube-system patch ds cilium --type=merge \
    -p '{"spec":{"template":{"spec":{"nodeSelector":{"foo":"bar"}}}}}'
daemonset.apps/cilium patched
```

Setting the DaemonSet's `nodeSelector` to an unused label removes all Cilium agent pods from the cluster:

```
$ kubectl get daemonset -n kube-system cilium
NAME     DESIRED   READY   NODE SELECTOR
cilium   0         0       foo=bar,kubernetes.io/os=linux
```

Despite the Cilium agent being absent, however, traffic is still able to reach the service:

```
$ kubectl exec -it netshoot-client -- curl httpd
<html><body><h1>It works!</h1></body></html>
```

As you can see, the datapath continues forwarding packets even though the control-plane component has disappeared.

However, the design does have a limitation—while the agent is unavailable, eBPF maps are not updated to reflect changes in the cluster. If a pod on a remote node restarts during this time, the map still contains its IP address, and the datapath continues to forward traffic to it:

```
$ kubectl delete pod httpd-77b5fcff59-vfnxt
pod "httpd-77b5fcff59-vfnxt" deleted

$ curl -m 2 10.96.45.144
curl: (28) Connection timed out after 2004 milliseconds
```

The timeout occurs because the datapath is trying to send traffic to the failed backend. Only when the agent is brought back online (by applying the correct label to the DaemonSet's node selector) are the maps reconciled and stale entries removed:

```
$ kubectl -n kube-system patch ds cilium --type=json \
    -p='[{"op":"remove","path":"/spec/template/spec/nodeSelector/foo"}]'
daemonset.apps/cilium patched

$ kubectl get ds -n kube-system cilium
NAME     DESIRED   READY   NODE SELECTOR
cilium   3         3       kubernetes.io/os=linux
```

Now everything is working as expected again, and all the healthy backends are listed for our service:

```
$ kubectl get pods -o wide
NAME                     READY   IP
httpd-7ffb6c7dd7-8lxjg   1/1     10.244.1.233
```

```
httpd-7ffb6c7dd7-m65rg   1/1     10.244.1.183
httpd-7ffb6c7dd7-vj6r8   1/1     10.244.2.112

$ kubectl exec -n kube-system ds/cilium -- cilium-dbg service list
ID   Frontend               Service Type   Backend
6    10.96.130.157:80/TCP   ClusterIP      1 => 10.244.1.233:80/TCP
                                           2 => 10.244.1.183:80/TCP
                                           3 => 10.244.2.112:80/TCP
```

This behavior highlights one of Cilium KPR's design principles: the data plane is independent of the control plane. In summary, the datapath continues to forward traffic without the Cilium agent, giving operators resiliency during upgrades or restarts. But until the agent resumes, eBPF maps remain stale, which can lead to timeouts if backends fail. Minimizing agent downtime is therefore essential to maintain both connectivity and accuracy.

KPR Service Behavior Support

So far we have seen how Cilium replaces `kube-proxy`, how it handles service load balancing at scale without the `iptables` burden, and how it continues to operate even if the agent is temporarily unavailable.

The next question is what this means for the behaviors that users expect from services. Kubernetes supports a variety of options that influence how traffic is routed, including session affinity, external and internal traffic policies, and NodePort and LoadBalancer services. As you'll see here, Cilium's `kube-proxy` replacement implements all of these features, so users can rely on the same semantics that `kube-proxy` has while also gaining the efficiency of eBPF in the datapath.

Session Affinity

Services managed by Cilium's KPR support *session affinity*, or *sticky sessions*. By default, when a client sends multiple requests to a service, the requests may be distributed across different pods. With session affinity enabled, the same client consistently reaches the same pod for the duration of the session. This behavior can be useful for applications that require consistent routing to a single pod, such as when storing in-memory state or maintaining a shopping cart. However, sticky sessions should be used sparingly. In most cases it is better to design applications so that they do not depend on affinity, since it can skew load distribution and reduce resiliency.

Sticky sessions can provide short-term relief for applications that expect stateful behavior, but they are best considered a workaround for workloads that are not cloud native. Wherever possible, refactor applications to avoid this dependency and allow requests to be load-balanced freely.

To demonstrate how sticky sessions work, let's create a simple deployment and service (*affinity-deployment.yaml*) in our KPR-enabled cluster. The backend pods will reply to the client with its own hostname, so we'll know which pod serves each request and if the same one replies as we make multiple connections.

We'll use the client pod we deployed in the previous section and, from its shell, make a couple of requests to the `podinfo` service:

```
$ kubectl exec -it netshoot-client -- bash

netshoot-client:~# curl podinfo:9898
{ "hostname": "podinfo-849bfb5c8d-mp8l7" }

netshoot-client:~# curl podinfo:9898
{ "hostname": "podinfo-849bfb5c8d-bk452" }
```

As shown here, the hostname in the response changes depending on which `podinfo` instance serves the request. By enabling sticky sessions, we can ensure the client reaches the same pod for subsequent requests. To do this, we'll use the `sessionAffinity` field in the service specification. There are only two possible values:

`None` *(the default)*
: Requests from the same client can be distributed across different pods.

`ClientIP`
: Requests from the same client IP are consistently directed to the same pod.

Let's update the service specification so it looks like this:

```
apiVersion: v1
kind: Service
metadata:
  name: podinfo
spec:
  sessionAffinity: ClientIP
  selector:
    app.kubernetes.io/name: podinfo
  ports:
  - port: 9898
```

Now, let's check again what happens when we make multiple requests from our client pod:

```
netshoot-client:~# curl podinfo:9898
{ "hostname": "podinfo-849bfb5c8d-4v8sc", ... }

netshoot-client:~# curl podinfo:9898
{ "hostname": "podinfo-849bfb5c8d-4v8sc", ... }
```

This time the hostname remains consistent across requests, indicating that we are always reaching the same pod.

As this simple example shows, sticky sessions provide a way to keep traffic from a client directed to the same pod, which can help applications that rely on in-memory state. Be sure to use them only when necessary, though, since they reduce load-balancing flexibility and resiliency.

Traffic Policies

As mentioned previously, KPR supports both of the standard Kubernetes traffic management policies: `externalTrafficPolicy` and `internalTrafficPolicy`. Let's briefly explore each of them.

internalTrafficPolicy

By default, services use a cluster-wide internal traffic policy that distributes traffic randomly to all ready endpoints across the cluster (Figure 6-3).

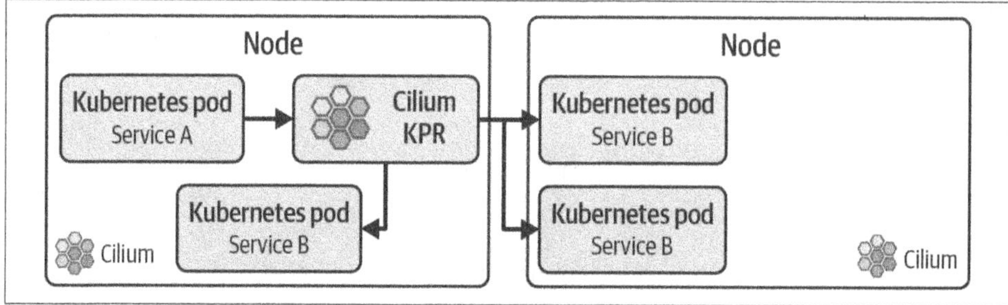

Figure 6-3. Cluster-wide internal traffic policy

When you set `internalTrafficPolicy` to `Local`, however, Cilium only forwards internal traffic to endpoints that are on the same node (Figure 6-4).

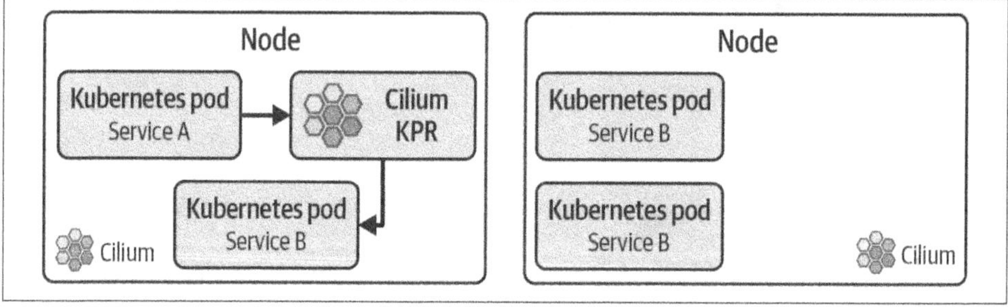

Figure 6-4. Local internal traffic policy

This option is useful for cases where locality matters, such as when you want to direct traffic to a node-local logging daemon or metrics agent, and for avoiding the latency or cross-node transfer costs of sending traffic elsewhere. Cilium itself leverages this feature for Hubble's `hubble-peer` service, which uses node-local routing for observability traffic.

If a node has no local endpoints for a service configured with `internalTrafficPolicy: Local`, pods on that node will see the service as having no backends, even if endpoints exist on other nodes.

We'll cover more traffic engineering features in Chapter 8.

externalTrafficPolicy

The external traffic policy controls how traffic that originates from outside the cluster is forwarded. It's used for external-facing services like NodePort and LoadBalancer services (discussed in the following section).

By default, `externalTrafficPolicy` (like `internalTrafficPolicy`) is set to `Cluster`. In this mode, any node that receives a connection can forward it to any ready backend in the cluster. This maximizes availability but comes with two caveats: it replaces the client source IP with the inbound node's Cilium internal IP (in other words, the client IP is not preserved), and it might add an additional hop as traffic won't necessarily enter the node closest to the backend.

Figure 6-5 illustrates this: even if `service-A` only has one backend (on `Node-1`), both nodes will forward any traffic they receive for this service to that backend. For traffic entering via `Node-2`, the source IP will be changed to `Node-2`'s.

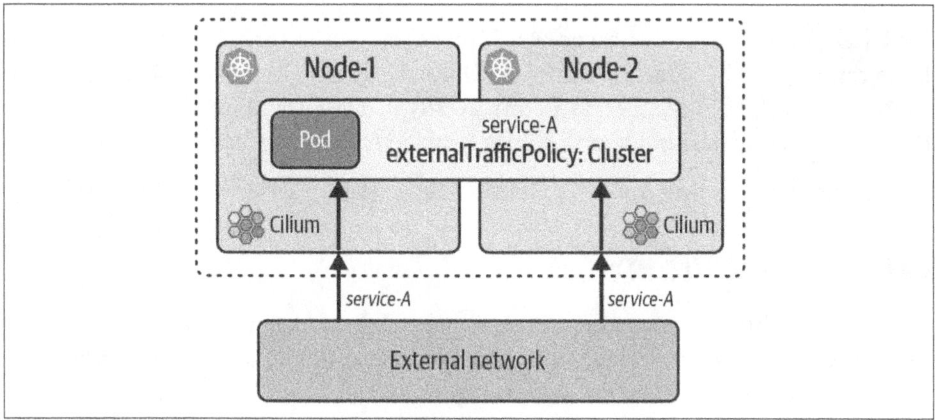

Figure 6-5. Cluster-wide external traffic policy

When `externalTrafficPolicy` is set to `Local`, on the other hand, nodes will only forward the incoming traffic to local backends (Figure 6-6).

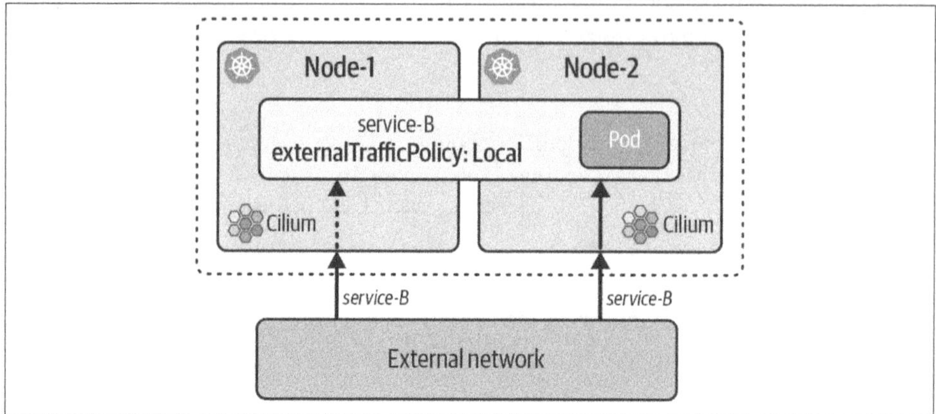

Figure 6-6. `Local` external traffic policy

This preserves the original client IP. Just be aware that, if the node has no local backends, it will drop external traffic for that service, even if other nodes have healthy backends.

The external traffic policy on LoadBalancer services also impacts how BGP announcement functions, if used with Cilium's LoadBalancer IP address management (LB IPAM) and BGP features. IP addresses for such services will be announced from all nodes if the policy is set to `Cluster`, but only from nodes with backends if it's set to `Local`. See Chapter 10 for more details on BGP announcement of services in Cilium.

KPR fully supports both `internalTrafficPolicy` and `externalTrafficPolicy`, so users can rely on the same semantics as with `kube-proxy`. In Chapter 8, we'll look at alternatives such as Direct Server Return (DSR) that are useful for cases where client IP preservation matters but you also want to avoid source translation side effects.

This brings us to another common requirement: exposing services outside the cluster.

External-Facing Services

Services have different types for different purposes. By default, a service is of type ClusterIP. This means it provides an in-cluster virtual IP and acts as an internal load balancer. However, a ClusterIP service is not accessible from outside the cluster.

When workloads outside the cluster must access an application running inside Kubernetes, two other types of services can be used. The first is a service of type NodePort. A NodePort service exposes a port on every node in the cluster. Traffic sent to that port is forwarded to the application, but while the port number is the same across nodes, each node has a different IP address. Clients must therefore be aware of all node IPs and handle load balancing themselves, or an external load balancer application must be in front of the nodes.

A service of type LoadBalancer addresses this limitation by providing a single external IP. In cloud environments such as GKE, EKS, or AKS, this process is handled automatically by the cloud controller manager. When a LoadBalancer service is created, the controller provisions a cloud-specific load balancer instance, points it at the cluster nodes, and assigns the external IP to the Kubernetes service object.

The situation is different in environments without a cloud controller manager. A LoadBalancer service can still be created, but no external IP will be assigned to it. This is where Cilium's LoadBalancer IP address management comes in. Enabling LB IPAM allows Cilium to assign IP addresses directly to LoadBalancer services, making them externally reachable even in on-premises or bare-metal environments. These IPs can then be announced using Cilium's BGP or layer 2 announcement features, which we will cover in Chapter 10.

This section focuses on assigning external IP addresses to LoadBalancer services. IP address management for pods was covered in Chapter 4. ClusterIP services are given IP addresses by Kubernetes and are not affected by Cilium's LB IPAM.

This feature is always enabled in Cilium but is dormant until the first IP pool is configured. Let's test it (you can find the files used here in the */chapter06/lb-ipam* directory of the book's GitHub repository). If you created a cluster with Cilium earlier, you can reuse it for this example. Otherwise, create a kind cluster using the generic configuration (*kind.yaml*) and install Cilium as covered previously. Kind does not come with a cloud controller manager; instead, Cilium will be the system assigning the IP to our external LoadBalancer service.

Create a simple service of type LoadBalancer (*httpd-lb-service.yaml*). Once the service is created, it will show a pending external IP:

```
$ kubectl get svc httpd
NAME    TYPE           CLUSTER-IP     EXTERNAL-IP   PORT(S)        AGE
httpd   LoadBalancer   10.96.72.137   <pending>     80:31478/TCP   20s
```

No matter how long we wait, no external IP will be assigned. To get an IP assigned, we must create a CiliumLoadBalancerIPPool object (*lb-pool.yaml*):

```
apiVersion: "cilium.io/v2"
kind: CiliumLoadBalancerIPPool
metadata:
  name: "lb-pool"
spec:
  blocks:
  - cidr: "172.16.0.0/24"
```

Once this object is created, the Cilium operator takes responsibility for assigning IPs from the defined pool to LoadBalancer services. If we check the service again, we will see that an external IP from the pool has been assigned:

```
$ kubectl get svc
NAME    TYPE           CLUSTER-IP     EXTERNAL-IP   PORT(S)        AGE
httpd   LoadBalancer   10.96.72.137   172.16.0.0    80:31478/TCP   48s
```

By default, the Cilium operator may assign any IP within that block. In conventional networking, however, the first and last IP addresses are usually reserved. The first is the network address and the last is the broadcast address; in many cases, we want to avoid assigning these addresses to services.

There are two ways to prevent the use of the first and last addresses:

1. Define a custom start and stop range that explicitly excludes these addresses.
2. Set `allowFirstLastIPs: "No"`. This is the most scalable option and requires the least manual configuration.

We'll start with the first option. Update the pool object as follows (*lb-pool-start-stop.yaml*):

```
apiVersion: "cilium.io/v2"
kind: CiliumLoadBalancerIPPool
metadata:
  name: "lb-pool"
spec:
  blocks:
  - start: 172.16.0.1
    stop: 172.16.0.254
```

Now the Cilium operator will only assign IPs from `172.16.0.1` to `172.16.0.254`. Since we updated the existing pool, it will automatically reassign the external IP of the service:

```
$ kubectl get svc
NAME    TYPE           CLUSTER-IP     EXTERNAL-IP   PORT(S)        AGE
httpd   LoadBalancer   10.96.72.137   172.16.0.1    80:31478/TCP   1m14s
```

When managing multiple blocks, it can be tedious to define start and stop values for each one manually. Instead, we can use `allowFirstLastIPs: "No"` to automatically exclude those IPs. Let's update the pool object again (*lb-pool-no-allow-first-last.yaml*):

```
apiVersion: "cilium.io/v2"
kind: CiliumLoadBalancerIPPool
metadata:
  name: "lb-pool"
spec:
  allowFirstLastIPs: "No"
  blocks:
  - cidr: "192.168.9.0/24"
  - cidr: "10.234.9.0/24"
```

By specifying `allowFirstLastIPs: "No"`, we ensure that the Cilium operator does not assign `192.168.9.0`, `192.168.9.255`, `10.234.9.0`, and `10.234.9.255`.[3] We can verify the IP assignment by checking the service again:

```
$ kubectl get svc
NAME    TYPE           CLUSTER-IP     EXTERNAL-IP   PORT(S)        AGE
httpd   LoadBalancer   10.96.72.137   192.168.9.1   80:31478/TCP   2m11s
```

You might want to create multiple CiliumLoadBalancerIPPools for different use cases. For example, you might want to reserve a specific block of addresses for services that are part of a production workload. This example restricts the use of the `100.16.38.0/24` block to services that carry the label `environment: production`:

```
apiVersion: "cilium.io/v2"
kind: CiliumLoadBalancerIPPool
metadata:
  name: "production-pool"
spec:
  allowFirstLastIPs: "No"
  blocks:
  - cidr: "100.16.38.0/24"
  serviceSelector:
    matchLabels:
      environment: production
```

Note that CiliumLoadBalancerIPPool is a cluster-wide resource, so any service in any namespace with the matching label can receive an IP from this pool.

If you want to further restrict the pool to a specific namespace, you can use the special selector `io.kubernetes.service.namespace`:

```
serviceSelector:
  matchLabels:
    io.kubernetes.service.namespace: payments
    environment: production
```

3 You must enclose the `"No"` in quotes in your YAML, as Cilium expects this to be a string. Writing it without the quotes will cause it to be interpreted in YAML as a Boolean, and the change will fail to apply with a type error.

In this case, only services in the `payments` namespace with the label `environment: production` will be allocated IPs from the pool.

When using `serviceSelector`, avoid overlapping selectors. If multiple CiliumLoadBalancerIPPools match the same service, the outcome is undefined. This can lead to services receiving an IP from the wrong pool, which may cause incorrect or even unsafe configurations. As a best practice, either do not use selectors at all and let pools serve all services, or ensure that each selector is unique and unambiguous.

Cilium LB IPAM only assigns external IPs to services. It does not advertise those IPs to external clients. For the addresses to be routable, LB IPAM is typically combined with Cilium's BGP or layer 2 announcement features, which we will cover in Chapter 10.

Summary

In this chapter we reviewed the fundamentals of service networking in Kubernetes and examined how Cilium enhances this area by leveraging eBPF. We looked at how services abstract and load-balance traffic to pod backends, and how `kube-proxy` traditionally implements this behavior using `iptables`. We then introduced Cilium's `kube-proxy` replacement, showing how eBPF maps in the kernel enable efficient load balancing, resiliency during agent downtime, and independence between the control plane and datapath.

We also explored service-specific behaviors supported by KPR, including session affinity and external and internal traffic policies, and considered their trade-offs. Finally, we discussed how external access can be provided through LoadBalancer services in environments without a cloud controller manager, using Cilium's LoadBalancer IPAM feature with BGP and layer 2 announcements (to be covered in Chapter 10) to make these addresses routable.

These features demonstrate that Cilium's KPR not only matches the functionality of `kube-proxy` but provides enhanced performance, flexibility, and operational resilience.

In the next chapter, we will build on this foundation by exploring Cilium's Ingress and Gateway API. These mechanisms handle external traffic entering the cluster while also providing fine-grained control over layer 7 traffic for advanced routing and security.

CHAPTER 7

Ingress and Gateway API

In Chapter 6, we saw how Kubernetes services enable applications to be accessible from both within and outside the cluster. While services provide a way to balance incoming traffic at layer 4, however, they lack the native ability to apply granular controls at upper layers. This means that Kubernetes services cannot perform common functions like TLS termination, application (layer 7)-level parsing, and filtering. For that, we need ingress mechanisms.

In this chapter, we'll explore how Cilium supports both Ingress and its successor, Gateway API. You will learn:

- What they are, how they differ, and when to use each
- How to publish HTTP services with Ingress, including host and path routing and TLS termination
- How Gateway API fits together with GatewayClass, Gateway, and HTTPRoute resources, and how routes attach to listeners
- How to match and route traffic at layer 7 by path, headers, method, and query parameters
- How to run progressive rollouts with traffic splitting (50/50 to 99/1) and validate the results
- How to shape traffic with header edits and HTTP redirects
- How to handle gRPC with GRPCRoute, using service and method matching
- How to route internal traffic with GAMMA (Gateway API for service mesh)

Handling External Traffic in Kubernetes

We covered how IP addresses are assigned to pods in Chapter 4, and in Chapter 5 you learned how pods communicate with one another within the cluster. But most microservices architectures will, at some point, require exposing some services outside the cluster and securely routing traffic into it.

In traditional networks, you would use tools such as reverse proxies and load balancers. In Kubernetes, Ingress has traditionally been the most commonly deployed method for routing traffic into the cluster. Ingress exposes HTTP and HTTPS routes from outside the cluster to services within the cluster. Traffic routing is controlled by rules defined on the Ingress resource.

Kubernetes doesn't provide a standard implementation for it: instead, platform engineers need to install and configure an Ingress controller, a program that will connect to the Kubernetes API server, check for Ingress resources, and implement them.

There are many Ingress controllers listed in the Kubernetes documentation (*https://oreil.ly/z6ufe*), from general-purpose reverse proxies to full API gateways. For Cilium, it's just another feature that's built in, meaning you avoid the resource and operational burdens that come with managing a separate purpose-built tool.

Let's try it.

Getting Started with Cilium Ingress

Cilium uses the standard Kubernetes Ingress resource definition, with an `ingressClassName` of `cilium`. This can be used for path-based routing and for TLS termination, as you will see shortly. You can find all the YAML manifests you will use in this chapter in the *chapter07/ingress* directory of the book's GitHub repository (*https://github.com/isovalent/cilium-up-and-running*).

Deploy a kind cluster using the *kind.yaml* config, then install Cilium with the following Helm values (*cilium-ingress-values.yaml*):

```
kubeProxyReplacement: true ❶
l2announcements: ❷
  enabled: true
ipam:
  mode: kubernetes
ingressController:
  enabled: true ❸
```

❶ Cilium Ingress requires KPR (discussed in Chapter 6).

❷ The Ingress controller creates a service of type LoadBalancer. As that service needs an IP address, we use Cilium's LB IPAM feature (also discussed in

Chapter 6). We enable the layer 2 announcement feature to make the service IP reachable from outside the cluster (we'll cover this feature in depth in Chapter 10).

3. We enable Ingress with `ingressController.enabled=true`. Ingress is disabled by default.

The application we will access from outside the cluster is called Bookinfo (*https://oreil.ly/N7kKp*). This demo set of microservices provided by the Istio project consists of several Kubernetes deployments and services. Deploy the manifest (*bookinfo.yaml*):

```
$ kubectl apply -f bookinfo.yaml
```

Then deploy the Ingress resource (*basic-ingress.yaml*):

```
apiVersion: networking.k8s.io/v1
kind: Ingress
metadata:
  name: basic-ingress
  namespace: default
spec:
  ingressClassName: cilium
  rules:
    - http:
        paths:
          - backend:
              service:
                name: details
                port:
                  number: 9080
            path: /details
            pathType: Prefix
          - backend:
              service:
                name: productpage
                port:
                  number: 9080
            path: /
            pathType: Prefix
```

Note that the `ingressClassName` field uses the value `cilium`. This instructs Kubernetes to use Cilium as the Ingress controller for this resource.

The Ingress resource contains one or more HTTP rules. Each HTTP rule contains the following information:

- An optional host. In this example, since no host is specified, the rule applies to all inbound HTTP traffic.
- A list of paths, each of which has an associated backend defined with a service name and port name (from the service) or number. A backend is a combination

of service and port names. HTTP and HTTPS requests to the Ingress resource that match the host and path of the rule are sent to the listed backend.

In our instance, we are creating an Ingress resource with two backends, each pointing to a service, based on the requested path:

- `/details` routes to the `details` service, on port 9080.
- / routes to the `productpage` service, on port 9080.

Access to the Bookinfo app with Cilium ingress is illustrated in Figure 7-1.

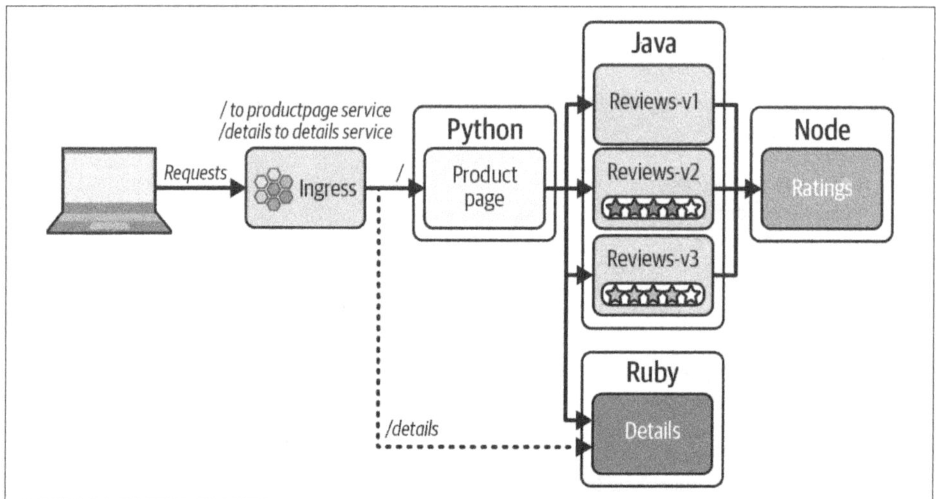

Figure 7-1. Using Cilium Ingress for HTTP traffic routing

As discussed in Chapter 2, Envoy runs as a per-node DaemonSet. When you create Ingress or Gateway API resources, Cilium's controllers translate them into CiliumEnvoyConfig (CEC) objects and program the Envoy DaemonSet accordingly. You can verify what was rendered with `kubectl get cec -A` (and `kubectl get ccec -A` for cluster-wide configs). Any change to the Ingress or Gateway API objects updates the corresponding CECs and is reconciled to Envoy.

Cilium can also program Envoy directly via CEC/CCEC without using Ingress or Gateway API. This enables custom listeners, routes, clusters, and filters for layer 7 routing and manipulation. It is a power user path with caveats (version compatibility, portability, and ownership of the config) and is outside the scope of this book.

Next, we'll deploy the Ingress manifest:

```
$ kubectl apply -f basic-ingress.yaml
ingress.networking.k8s.io/basic-ingress created
```

This creates a LoadBalancer service for the Ingress, but it won't have an external IP yet:

```
$ kubectl get svc
NAME                           TYPE           CLUSTER-IP     EXTERNAL-IP
cilium-ingress-basic-ingress   LoadBalancer   10.96.162.88   <pending>
```

As you'll recall from Chapter 6, for an IP to be assigned we need to create a CiliumLoadBalancerIPPool object (*pool.yaml*):

```
apiVersion: "cilium.io/v2"
kind: CiliumLoadBalancerIPPool
metadata:
  name: "pool"
spec:
  blocks:
  - cidr: "172.18.255.200/29"
```

Deploy the pool with `kubectl` and verify that an IP address has been assigned to the service:

```
$ kubectl get svc
NAME                           TYPE           CLUSTER-IP     EXTERNAL-IP
cilium-ingress-basic-ingress   LoadBalancer   10.96.68.40    172.18.255.200
```

You can also verify that the same external IP address is associated with the Ingress resource:

```
$ kubectl get ingress
NAME            CLASS    HOSTS   ADDRESS          PORTS   AGE
basic-ingress   cilium   *       172.18.255.200   80      13m
```

Export it as a variable (`INGRESS_IP=172.18.255.200`, for example) so that you can reuse it.

Let's now make this IP address accessible locally by deploying the following Cilium layer 2 announcement policy (*l2policy.yaml*):

```
apiVersion: "cilium.io/v2alpha1"
kind: CiliumL2AnnouncementPolicy
metadata:
  name: policy1
spec:
  loadBalancerIPs: true
  interfaces:
  - eth0
  nodeSelector:
    matchExpressions:
      - key: node-role.kubernetes.io/control-plane
        operator: DoesNotExist
```

Layer 2 announcement lets nodes advertise service IPs on the local network using the Address Resolution Protocol (ARP) for IPv4 or Neighbor Discovery (ND) for IPv6,[1] so external hosts can reach those IPs without a separate load balancer if they share a layer 2 domain. In Cilium, you enable this with a CiliumL2AnnouncementPolicy that selects which nodes and interfaces announce their IPs. You will learn how it functions in Chapter 10, but essentially the policy shown here will ensure Cilium answers ARP requests received on the worker node's `eth0` interfaces for IPs assigned to LoadBalancer services (in this case, `172.18.255.200`).

Next, we'll verify that Cilium Ingress is working as we expect by accessing the Ingress IP from our terminal.

On macOS, you will likely need to install Docker Mac Net Connect (*https://oreil.ly/ve1Ql*) to access the application running in your kind cluster over Ingress/Gateway API. This tool enables macOS users to access services running on the host network from Docker containers, working around the networking limitations of Docker Desktop on Mac. If you'd rather not install this utility, you can simply deploy another container on the same Docker network as the nodes with:

```
$ docker run -d --net kind --rm --name client \
    nicolaka/netshoot:v0.8 sleep inf
```

You can then run the following commands from the client's shell (`docker exec -it client bash`) to observe the same behavior.

From outside the cluster, let's send an HTTP request to the / path with `curl`. It takes us to the `productpage` service and returns HTTP code `200`:

```
$ curl --fail -s -o /dev/null -w "%{http_code}\n" "http://$INGRESS_IP/"
200
```

A cURL request to the `/details/1` path takes us to the book's details:

```
$ curl --fail -s "http://$INGRESS_IP/details/1"
{
  "id": 1,
  "author": "William Shakespeare",
  "year": 1595,
  "type": "paperback",
  "pages": 200,
  "publisher": "PublisherA",
  "language": "English",
  "ISBN-10": "1234567890",
```

1 Introduced in Cilium v1.19.

```
    "ISBN-13": "123-1234567890"
  }
```

However, you can't directly access other URL paths that weren't defined in *basic-ingress.yaml*. For example, you will get a `404` error if you make a request to `/ratings`, as it is not explicitly mapped in the Ingress resource:

```
$ curl --fail -so /dev/null -w "%{http_code}\n" "http://$INGRESS_IP/ratings"
404
```

In the next section we'll explore another use case for Cilium Ingress: TLS termination.

TLS Termination with Cilium Ingress

Ingress resources are commonly used as TLS termination points in Kubernetes. Because they act as the cluster's entry proxy, terminating TLS at the Ingress simplifies certificate management and provides a secure frontend for HTTP services.

In this section, we will test TLS termination using self-signed certificates generated with mkcert (*https://github.com/FiloSottile/mkcert*). While this approach is suitable for testing, it's strongly recommended to use a certificate management system such as cert-manager (*https://cert-manager.io*) in production.

We'll use the Bookinfo app again for this example, except that instead of accessing the service over HTTP (80), we will be accessing it over HTTPS (443), as illustrated in Figure 7-2.

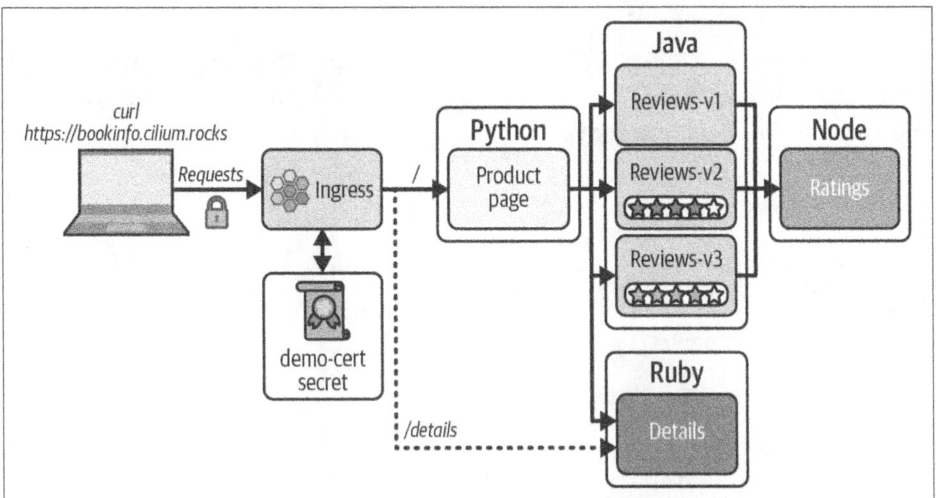

Figure 7-2. Cilium Ingress for HTTPS traffic with TLS termination

First, let's generate a wildcard certificate. Install mkcert with your package manager if you don't have it installed already, then run:

```
$ mkcert '*.cilium.rocks'
Created a new local CA 💥
Run "mkcert -install" for certificates to be trusted automatically ⚠️

Created a new certificate valid for the following names 📜
 - "*.cilium.rocks"

Reminder: X.509 wildcards only go one level deep, so this won't match
a.b.cilium.rocks ℹ️

The certificate is at "./_wildcard.cilium.rocks.pem" and the key at
"./_wildcard.cilium.rocks-key.pem" ✅

It will expire on 10 December 2027 📅
```

mkcert suggests running `mkcert -install` so the certificate becomes trusted system-wide, but we will not do that here. Installing a local certificate authority (CA) into the system trust store is unnecessary for this example and is discouraged on shared or production machines.

The previous command created a certificate and a key. We can now create a Kubernetes TLS secret using these files:

```
$ kubectl create secret tls demo-cert \
    --key=_wildcard.cilium.rocks-key.pem \
    --cert=_wildcard.cilium.rocks.pem
secret/demo-cert created
```

Once the secret is in place, define an Ingress resource that references it for TLS termination. For `bookinfo.cilium.rocks`, the following Ingress routes `/details` and `/` to two HTTP services (`details` and `productpage`):

```
apiVersion: networking.k8s.io/v1
kind: Ingress
metadata:
  name: tls-ingress
  namespace: default
spec:
  ingressClassName: cilium
  rules:
    - host: bookinfo.cilium.rocks
      http:
        paths:
          - path: /details
            pathType: Prefix
            backend:
              service:
                name: details
                port:
```

```
                number: 9080
          - path: /
            pathType: Prefix
            backend:
              service:
                name: productpage
                port:
                  number: 9080
  tls:
    - hosts:
        - bookinfo.cilium.rocks
      secretName: demo-cert
```

Once applied with `kubectl apply -f tls-ingress.yaml`, you should see the Ingress provisioned with a LoadBalancer address:

```
$ kubectl get ingress tls-ingress
NAME          CLASS    HOSTS                           ADDRESS          PORTS
tls-ingress   cilium   hipstershop.cilium.rocks,...    172.18.255.201   80, 443
```

This address can then be exported for use in cURL commands:

```
$ export TLS_INGRESS="$(kubectl get ingress tls-ingress \
    -o jsonpath='{.status.loadBalancer.ingress[0].ip}')"

$ echo "$TLS_INGRESS"
172.18.255.201
```

To avoid modifying the system trust store, we will explicitly tell cURL which CA to trust for this request. You can locate the mkcert CA directory with:

```
$ mkcert -CAROOT
~/Library/Application Support/mkcert
```

Use the CA file directly when sending the HTTPS request. The `--resolve` flag maps the hostname to the Ingress IP:

```
$ curl -s \
    --resolve "bookinfo.cilium.rocks:443:$TLS_INGRESS" \
    --cacert "$(mkcert -CAROOT)/rootCA.pem" \
    https://bookinfo.cilium.rocks/details/1 | jq
{ "id": 1, "author": "William Shakespeare", "year": 1595, ... }
```

Ingress Limitations

Ingress provides a familiar abstraction for routing external traffic into a cluster and functions well for HTTP and HTTPS routing. However, it has several limitations that become apparent in more complex environments. These are not tied to Cilium's implementation of Ingress, but apply to most Ingress implementations:

Single shared configuration role
: Ingress uses a cluster-wide controller (like NGINX or Cilium) that watches all Ingress resources and applies the same global configuration to all of them. There's no native way to delegate responsibility or apply different policies for different teams or namespaces. This means platform teams often become a bottleneck, forced to manage or approve all routing changes across the organization.

Poor multitenancy support
: Because Ingress lacks scoping and delegation, there's no built-in mechanism to enforce tenant boundaries or isolate configuration. Annotations or CRDs are often required to prevent one team's configuration from affecting another's. This limits self-service and introduces risk in shared clusters.

Nonportable annotations
: Much of Ingress's extended functionality relies on controller-specific annotations. These annotations are not standardized and are often tied to one specific Ingress implementation. As a result, workloads configured for one controller (e.g., NGINX) may not behave the same as or work well with another (e.g., HAProxy or Cilium), hurting portability.

Hard to extend
: Ingress is rigid. It covers only basic HTTP routing and offers no first-class support for TCP, gRPC, advanced traffic shaping, or custom policy enforcement. Extending functionality typically requires controller-specific annotations, which are brittle and hard to manage. Platform teams have little control over layering features or composing policies in a reusable way.

To address them, the broader SIG Network team[2] created *Gateway API*.

Introducing Gateway API

Gateway API (*https://gateway-api.sigs.k8s.io*) was created to overcome the limitations of Ingress. It provides a more expressive, extensible model for managing ingress traffic.

Gateway API offers a structured and centralized way to handle external traffic. Like Ingress, it supports HTTP(S) routing, TLS termination, traffic splitting,[3] header manipulation, and more. But whereas Ingress relies heavily on annotations for advanced features, Gateway API includes these capabilities natively. As a

2 A Special Interest Group (SIG) in Kubernetes is a group of contributors who collaborate around a particular functional area of the project, such as networking, storage, or node management. SIG Network is responsible for the components, interfaces, and APIs that expose networking capabilities to Kubernetes users and workloads.

3 Possible in some Ingress controllers with implementation-specific annotations.

result, configurations are more portable across implementations and less prone to fragmentation.

Where customization is needed, Gateway API includes clear extension points. The team behind the project continues to identify patterns shared by different implementations, promoting them into the standard API to avoid the inconsistent and vendor-specific extensions that plagued the Ingress model.

Another key design principle is role-based separation of concerns. Ingress assumed that developers managed both application and infrastructure-level networking resources. In real-world environments, however, different personas are typically involved:

- Infrastructure providers (e.g., AWS, Azure, GCP)
- Cluster operators who manage the Kubernetes platform
- Application developers focused on service configuration and delivery

By decomposing the monolithic Ingress resource into multiple Gateway API resources (the GatewayClass, Gateway, and HTTPRoute resources we will describe next), the API enables fine-grained access control. For example, developers can be granted permission to define routes in their own namespace, while operators retain control over shared infrastructure such as Gateways, as illustrated in Figure 7-3.

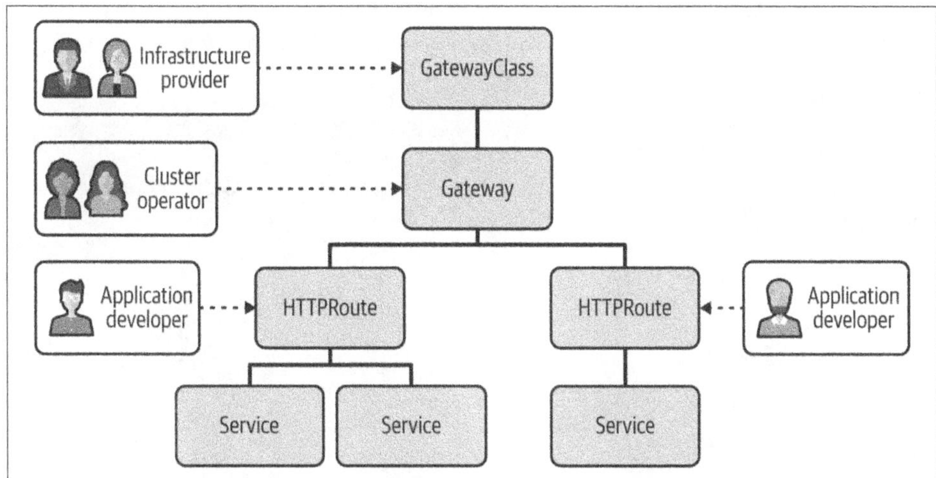

Figure 7-3. Gateway API permits role-based separation of concerns

Gateway API Objects

Gateway API introduces a set of Kubernetes resources that separate infrastructure concerns from application-level routing. This modular design helps teams manage ingress traffic more effectively across different roles.

GatewayClass

GatewayClass in Gateway API plays a role similar to IngressClass for Ingress: it declares which controller manages a class of Gateways and can carry controller defaults. When Cilium's Gateway API support is enabled, a default class named `cilium` is installed with the controller `io.cilium/gateway-controller`. Gateways that set `gatewayClassName: cilium` are reconciled by the Cilium Gateway API controller. It programs the Envoy DaemonSet, the same layer 7 proxy data plane used by Cilium Ingress.

Gateway

This resource represents an instance of a GatewayClass and acts as the entry point for external traffic. It defines one or more listeners, each specifying protocol (e.g., HTTP or HTTPS), port, hostname, and TLS settings if applicable.

All files discussed in this section are in the *chapter07/gateway* directory of the book's GitHub repository (*https://github.com/isovalent/cilium-up-and-running*).

Here is an example configuration (*basic-gateway.yaml*) for a Gateway named my-gateway:

```
apiVersion: gateway.networking.k8s.io/v1
kind: Gateway
metadata:
  name: my-gateway
spec:
  gatewayClassName: cilium
  listeners:
  - protocol: HTTP
    port: 80
    name: web-gw
    allowedRoutes:
      namespaces:
        from: Same
```

First, note that the `spec.gatewayClassName` value is `cilium`. This refers to the previously configured `cilium` GatewayClass.

The `my-gateway` Gateway will listen on port 80 for HTTP traffic coming into the cluster. The `allowedRoutes` field specifies the namespaces from which routes may be attached to this Gateway. `Same` means that only routes in the same namespace may be used. Using `All` instead of `Same` would enable this Gateway to be associated with routes in any namespace. It would also enable us to use a single Gateway across multiple namespaces that may be managed by different teams. We could specify different namespaces in the route configuration—for example, we could route traffic to *https://acme.example/payments* to a namespace where a payment app is deployed and traffic to *https://acme.example/ads* to the namespace the ads team uses for its application.

HTTPRoute

HTTPRoute is a Gateway API type for specifying routing behavior of HTTP requests from a Gateway listener to a Kubernetes service. The specification includes a set of rules that enable you to direct the traffic based on your requirements. Let's go through an example (*basic-http-route.yaml*):

```
apiVersion: gateway.networking.k8s.io/v1
kind: HTTPRoute
metadata:
  name: http-app-1
spec:
  parentRefs:
  - name: my-gateway
    namespace: default
  rules:
  - matches:
    - path:
        type: PathPrefix
        value: /details
    backendRefs:
    - name: details
      port: 9080
  - matches:
    - headers:
      - type: Exact
        name: magic
        value: foo
      queryParams:
      - type: Exact
        name: great
        value: example
      path:
        type: PathPrefix
        value: /
      method: GET
    backendRefs:
```

```
    - name: productpage
      port: 9080
```

This first rule is routing HTTP traffic with a path starting with `/details` to the `details` service over port 9080.

The second rule uses different matching criteria: if the HTTP request has an HTTP header named `magic` with a value of `foo` and a query parameter named `great` with a value of `example`, and the HTTP method is `GET`, then the traffic will be sent to the `productpage` service over port 9080.

There are other routes available with Gateway API, such as GRPCRoute (for gRPC traffic), TCPRoute, and UDPRoute. We'll see an example with GRPCRoute later in this chapter. At the time of writing, the latter two are not supported by Cilium.

Routing HTTP Traffic with Gateway API

This section will get you started with Cilium Gateway API. First, delete the existing kind cluster if it still exists and deploy a new one (*kind.yaml*).

We're deploying a new cluster for simplicity, but migrating existing clusters from Cilium Ingress to Cilium Gateway API is possible. It requires activating the Gateway API feature and migrating the configuration, either by manually creating Gateway API resources based on existing Ingress resources or by leveraging the Ingress2gateway (*https://oreil.ly/2GfH4*) tool, which reads Ingress resources from a Kubernetes cluster and outputs YAML for equivalent Gateway API objects.

Before installing Cilium with Gateway API enabled (or enabling Gateway API on an existing Cilium install), you *must* install the Gateway API CRDs. You'll find these in the Gateway API GitHub repo (*https://oreil.ly/hlyVM*).

You might wonder why this is required, since the Cilium operator typically manages CRDs. Cilium supports both *Standard* (stable, backward-compatible) and *Experimental* (feature-rich but unstable) Gateway API channels. To avoid conflicts or broken functionality, you must install the Gateway API CRDs yourself before deploying Cilium to ensure Cilium won't override a newer or Experimental version during the install or upgrade. If the Gateway API CRDs are not present at the time Helm is executed to install or upgrade Cilium, the `cilium` GatewayClass will not be created.

We'll use the Standard CRDs in our example. Cilium 1.18 conforms with Gateway API 1.3, so we will be using the 1.3 CRDs in this instance:

```
$ CRD_PATH="https://raw.githubusercontent.com/"\
    "kubernetes-sigs/gateway-api/v1.3.0/config/crd/standard/"
```

```
$ kubectl apply -f "${CRD_PATH}/gateway.networking.k8s.io_gatewayclasses.yaml"
$ kubectl apply -f "${CRD_PATH}/gateway.networking.k8s.io_gateways.yaml"
$ kubectl apply -f "${CRD_PATH}/gateway.networking.k8s.io_httproutes.yaml"
$ kubectl apply -f "${CRD_PATH}/gateway.networking.k8s.io_referencegrants.yaml"
$ kubectl apply -f "${CRD_PATH}/gateway.networking.k8s.io_grpcroutes.yaml"
```

Let's now deploy Cilium using the Helm configuration *cilium-gatewayapi-values.yaml*. Like Cilium Ingress, Cilium Gateway API requires KPR. This feature can be enabled with `gatewayAPI.enabled=true`.[4]

We'll also add a CiliumLoadBalancerIPPool object (*pool.yaml*) and a layer 2 announcement policy (*l2policy.yaml*) and deploy the sample Bookinfo application (*bookinfo.yaml*) we used in the Ingress section.

Let's now deploy the Gateway and HTTPRoute configuration we walked through earlier:

```
$ kubectl apply -f basic-gateway.yaml
gateway.gateway.networking.k8s.io/my-gateway created

$ kubectl apply -f basic-http-route.yaml
httproute.gateway.networking.k8s.io/http-app-1 created
```

First, we'll verify that a `cilium` GatewayClass has been created and that the Gateway has received an IP address and has been "programmed"—meaning that Cilium programmed the Gateway configuration into its Envoy component:

```
$ kubectl get GatewayClass
NAME     CONTROLLER                     ACCEPTED   AGE
cilium   io.cilium/gateway-controller   True       43s

$ kubectl get gateway
NAME         CLASS    ADDRESS          PROGRAMMED   AGE
my-gateway   cilium   172.18.255.200   True         27m
```

Next, we'll verify that the route was successfully attached to the Gateway. The `Accepted` HTTPRoute condition type indicates the configuration was correct and accepted:

```
$ kubectl get httproutes http-app-1 -o yaml | yq .status.parents
- conditions:
      message: Accepted HTTPRoute
      observedGeneration: 1
      reason: Accepted
  controllerName: io.cilium/gateway-controller
  parentRef:
    group: gateway.networking.k8s.io
    kind: Gateway
```

4 To activate the Gateway API feature on an existing Cilium deployment, enable it with Helm/Cilium CLI and restart the operator Deployment and agent DaemonSet.

```
    name: my-gateway
    namespace: default
```

You should now be able to access your internal Bookinfo application from outside the cluster, as illustrated in Figure 7-4. It's almost identical to Figure 7-1, the only difference being the use of the Gateway API objects instead of Ingress.

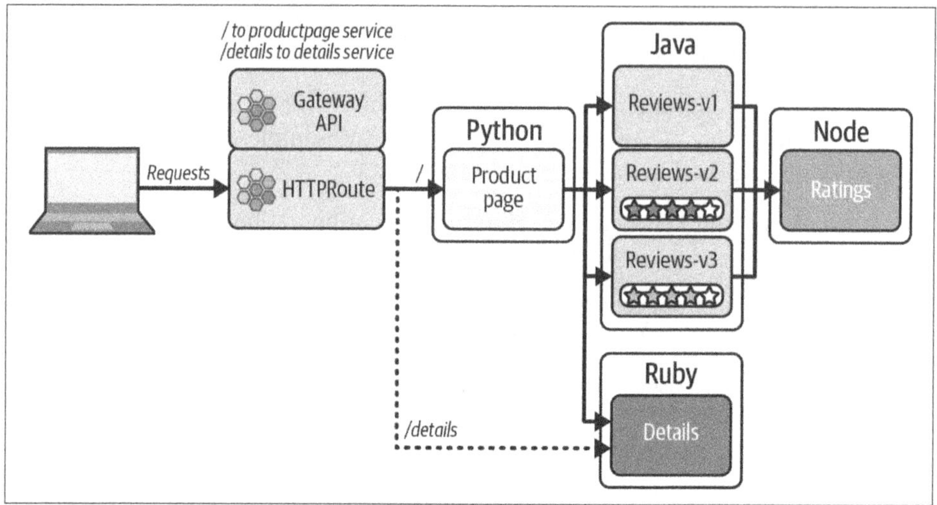

Figure 7-4. Using Cilium Gateway API for HTTP traffic routing

Save the Gateway IP as an environment variable, and then verify with cURL that HTTP path matching works as expected. Because the path starts with `/details`, this traffic matches the first rule and is proxied to the `details` service over port 9080. The cURL request should be successful:

```
$ GATEWAY="$(kubectl get gateway my-gateway -o \
    jsonpath='{.status.addresses[0].value}')"

$ echo "$GATEWAY"
172.18.255.200

$ curl --fail -s "http://$GATEWAY/details/1"
{ "id": 1, "author": "William Shakespeare", "year": 1595, ... }
```

Next, you can verify HTTP header matching. With the following `curl` command, we specify a header (`magic:foo`) and a query parameter key/value pair (`great=example`). Since cURL implicitly uses the `GET` HTTP method, traffic will be matched by the HTTPRoute rule and directed to the `productpage` backend:

```
$ curl -v -H 'magic: foo' "http://$GATEWAY?great=example"
*   Trying 172.18.255.200:80...
* Connected to 172.18.255.200 (172.18.255.200) port 80
> GET /?great=example HTTP/1.1
```

```
> User-Agent: curl/8.5.0
> Accept: */*
> magic: foo
>
< HTTP/1.1 200 OK
< server: envoy
< x-envoy-upstream-service-time: 9
<

<p>
    <h3>Hello! This is a simple bookstore application consisting of three
        services as shown below</h3>
</p>
```

We set the preceding `curl` command to verbose with the `-v` flag. It prints the HTTP data (confirming the cURL request, including the query parameters, headers, and method) for both outbound (preceded by >) and inbound (preceded by <) traffic. Notice the `x-envoy-upstream-service-time` line—it confirms that Envoy proxied the transaction and indicates that the upstream service took 9 ms to respond.

TLS Termination with Gateway API

Cilium Gateway API also supports TLS termination. The equivalent configuration to the one we saw earlier with Ingress looks like this (*tls-gateway.yaml* and *https-route.yaml*):

```
apiVersion: gateway.networking.k8s.io/v1
kind: Gateway
metadata:
  name: tls-gateway
spec:
  gatewayClassName: cilium
  listeners:
  - name: https-1
    protocol: HTTPS
    port: 443
    hostname: "bookinfo.cilium.rocks"
    tls:
      certificateRefs:
      - kind: Secret
        name: demo-cert
---
apiVersion: gateway.networking.k8s.io/v1
kind: HTTPRoute
metadata:
  name: https-app-route-1
spec:
  parentRefs:
```

```
- name: tls-gateway
hostnames:
- "bookinfo.cilium.rocks"
rules:
- matches:
  - path:
      type: PathPrefix
      value: /details
  backendRefs:
  - name: details
    port: 9080
```

Layer 7 Load Balancing Across Backends

Cilium's Gateway API implementation includes native support for HTTP traffic splitting. This feature allows you to send a percentage of traffic to different backend services without needing a separate service mesh or third-party tool. Common use cases include A/B testing, canary deployments, or blue/green rollouts where a new version of an application is gradually introduced.

In this section, we'll deploy two versions of a sample application and configure an HTTPRoute to split traffic evenly between them (50/50 weight). Later, we'll adjust the weights to simulate a more pragmatic and realistic approach to production rollouts of an application.

50/50 Load Balancing

Start by deploying a simple echo application (*echo-servers.yaml*). This YAML file deploys two internal (ClusterIP) services, `echo-1` and `echo-2`, each backed by its own set of pods and listening on different ports. This app returns the name of the pod and node handling each request, allowing us to clearly observe where the traffic is routed:

```
$ kubectl get pods,svc
NAME                                  READY   STATUS
pod/echo-1-65bf7cf9b5-6zsf6           1/1     Running
pod/echo-2-569cb769b7-zh878           1/1     Running

NAME                          CLUSTER-IP      EXTERNAL-IP   PORT(S)
service/echo-1                10.96.125.138   <none>        8080/TCP
service/echo-2                10.96.74.120    <none>        8090/TCP
```

To split incoming traffic between `echo-1` and `echo-2`, apply the HTTPRoute resource (*load-balancing-http-route.yaml*). Note the equal 50% weight under each service:

```
apiVersion: gateway.networking.k8s.io/v1
kind: HTTPRoute
metadata:
  name: load-balancing-route
spec:
```

```
  parentRefs:
  - name: my-gateway
  rules:
  - matches:
    - path:
        type: PathPrefix
        value: /echo
    backendRefs:
    - kind: Service
      name: echo-1
      port: 8080
      weight: 50
    - kind: Service
      name: echo-2
      port: 8090
      weight: 50
```

This route distributes HTTP traffic to the `/echo` path evenly between the two backend services, as illustrated in Figure 7-5.

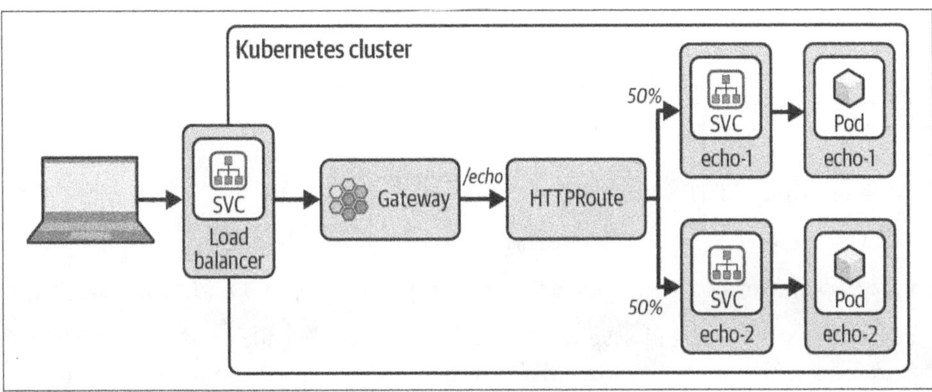

Figure 7-5. 50/50 load balancing

We can verify this by sending some requests to the `/echo` endpoint and inspecting the responses. The response body includes the pod hostname, allowing you to identify which backend received the request:

```
$ curl "http://$GATEWAY/echo"
Request served by echo-2-569cb769b7-zh878
```

Repeat the request several times. You should see responses alternating between `echo-1` and `echo-2`. To verify the distribution more precisely, run the command 1,000 times and store the output in a text file:

```
for _ in {1..1000}; do
  curl -s "http://$GATEWAY/echo" >> curlresponses.txt
done
```

With `grep`, you should see roughly equal counts for the two services:

```
$ grep -o "Request served by echo-." curlresponses.txt | sort | uniq -c
 517 Request served by echo-1
 483 Request served by echo-2
```

Adjusting Weights: 99/1 Split

Let's now simulate a canary rollout where nearly all traffic goes to one service, as shown in Figure 7-6.

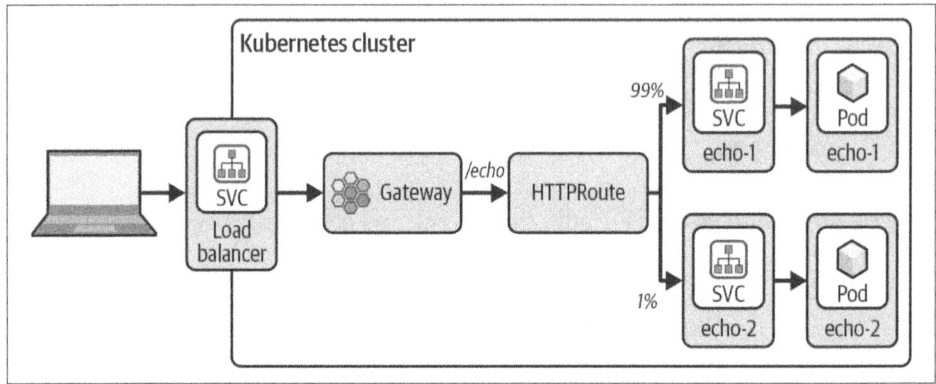

Figure 7-6. 99/1 traffic splitting with Gateway API

Edit the existing HTTPRoute resource:

```
$ kubectl edit httproute load-balancing-route
```

In the `backendRefs` section, update the weights to `99` for `echo-1` and `1` for `echo-2`.

Repeat the traffic test and save the output to another text file (*curlresponses991.txt*, for example). You should now see the vast majority of requests going to `echo-1`, with only a small fraction reaching `echo-2`:

```
$ grep -o "Request served by echo-." curlresponses991.txt | sort | uniq -c
 990 Request served by echo-1
  10 Request served by echo-2
```

Traffic Management

In addition to path-based routing and traffic splitting, Cilium Gateway API enables powerful traffic customization at layer 7 using filters in HTTPRoute resources. These filters allow you to:

- Modify both incoming request headers and outgoing response headers.
- Redirect requests by rewriting paths, hostnames, URL schemes, or status codes.
- Rewrite URL paths before forwarding requests to a backend.

- Mirror traffic to an additional backend for testing or debugging purposes.

We'll focus on the first two use cases here. See the Cilium documentation (*https://oreil.ly/USZ2l*) for more information on the many other use cases supported by Gateway API.

Modifying HTTP Headers with Gateway API

In this section, we'll explore how to add headers to HTTP requests using `RequestHeaderModifier` and how to add headers to HTTP responses using `ResponseHeaderModifier`. These techniques are useful for tasks like adding custom metadata and routing logic, A/B testing, or helping frontends adapt to different backend versions.

Modifying HTTP request headers

Start by deploying a route that matches HTTP requests to a specific path (*echo-header-http-route.yaml*):

```
apiVersion: gateway.networking.k8s.io/v1
kind: HTTPRoute
metadata:
  name: header-http-echo
spec:
  parentRefs:
    - name: my-gateway
  rules:
    - matches:
        - path:
            type: PathPrefix
            value: /cilium-add-a-request-header
      backendRefs:
        - name: echo-1
```

Send a test request and inspect the echoed request headers. You will see only the default headers (`host`, `user-agent`, etc.):

```
$ curl --fail -s "http://$GATEWAY/cilium-add-a-request-header"
Request served by echo-1-65bf7cf9b5-6zsf6

HTTP/1.1 GET /cilium-add-a-request-header

Host: 172.18.255.200
Accept: */*
User-Agent: curl/8.7.1
```

Now, update the HTTPRoute by using the `RequestHeaderModifier` filter to add a header. Deploy the *echo-header-http-route-header-modifier.yaml* file from the repo:

```
  rules:
  - matches:
```

```
  - path:
      type: PathPrefix
      value: /cilium-add-a-request-header
  filters:
  - type: RequestHeaderModifier
    requestHeaderModifier:
      add:
      - name: my-cilium-header-name
        value: my-cilium-header-value
```

The header `my-cilium-header-name` with the value `my-cilium-header-value` will be added to HTTP requests matching the path prefix. You can repeat the cURL request to verify this. The echoed headers should now include your custom header:

```
$ curl --fail -s "http://$GATEWAY/cilium-add-a-request-header"

Host: 172.18.255.200
Accept: */*
My-Cilium-Header-Name: my-cilium-header-value
User-Agent: curl/8.7.1
```

Note that you can also remove or amend an existing header by specifying the `remove` or `amend` action instead of `add`.

Modifying HTTP response headers

Now let's modify the headers in the response body. This can be useful for adding versioning information, setting custom cookies, or differentiating between beta and stable backends.

Apply the following manifest (*response-header-modifier-http-route.yaml*). Note that only the relevant portion of the manifest is being reproduced here in the book; the full code listing is available in the book's repo. The syntax is very similar to the previous example, but this time we'll use the `ResponseHeaderModifier` filter to add multiple headers to the HTTP response coming back from the server to the client. The route modifies responses to the `/multiple` path by adding three custom headers:

```
rules:
- matches:
  - path:
    type: PathPrefix
    value: /multiple
filters:
- type: ResponseHeaderModifier
  responseHeaderModifier:
    add:
    - name: X-Header-Add-1
      value: header-add-1
    - name: X-Header-Add-2
      value: header-add-2
backendRefs:
```

```
- name: echo-1
  port: 8080
```

Send a verbose cURL request to test it:

```
$ curl -v --fail -s "http://$GATEWAY/multiple"

< HTTP/1.1 200 OK
< x-header-add-1: header-add-1
< x-header-add-2: header-add-2
```

You should see that the response includes the three custom headers, confirming the `my-gateway` Gateway has added headers to the response successfully.

Alternatively, you can observe HTTP traffic behavior using Hubble (which you can enable by following the instructions in Chapter 3), for example by matching on HTTP header values:

```
$ hubble observe --http-header "X-Header-Add-1:header-add-1"
```

See Chapter 15 for more details on HTTP observability in Hubble, including how to redact sensitive headers (such as the `Authorization` header) from flow logs.

HTTP Redirects with Gateway API

Cilium Gateway API supports native HTTP redirection using filters within HTTPRoute resources. This feature allows you to modify the destination of incoming requests by changing the path, hostname, scheme, or status code. You can use redirection for a range of use cases, including application migrations, URL reorganization, and redirecting HTTP clients to HTTPS.

In this section, we'll explore four redirect scenarios, each handled by a separate rule in the same HTTPRoute manifest (*redirect-route.yaml*):

```
apiVersion: gateway.networking.k8s.io/v1
kind: HTTPRoute
metadata:
  name: redirect-path
spec:
  parentRefs:
  - name: my-gateway
  rules:
  - matches: ❶
    - path:
        type: PathPrefix
        value: /original-prefix
    filters:
    - type: RequestRedirect
      requestRedirect:
        path:
          type: ReplacePrefixMatch
          replacePrefixMatch: /replacement-prefix
```

```
- matches: ❷
  - path:
      type: PathPrefix
      value: /path-and-host
    filters:
    - type: RequestRedirect
      requestRedirect:
        hostname: example.org
        path:
          type: ReplacePrefixMatch
          replacePrefixMatch: /replacement-prefix
- matches: ❸
  - path:
      type: PathPrefix
      value: /path-and-status
    filters:
    - type: RequestRedirect
      requestRedirect:
        path:
          type: ReplacePrefixMatch
          replacePrefixMatch: /replacement-prefix
        statusCode: 301
- matches: ❹
  - path:
      type: PathPrefix
      value: /scheme-and-host
    filters:
    - type: RequestRedirect
      requestRedirect:
        hostname: example.org
        scheme: "https"
```

❶ The first rule in the manifest rewrites the path prefix while preserving the hostname and protocol.

❷ The second rule changes both the hostname and the path.

❸ The third rule demonstrates how to change the HTTP status code returned by the redirect.

❹ The final rule demonstrates how to change the scheme (protocol) to redirect from HTTP to HTTPS.

The requests are depicted in Figure 7-7.

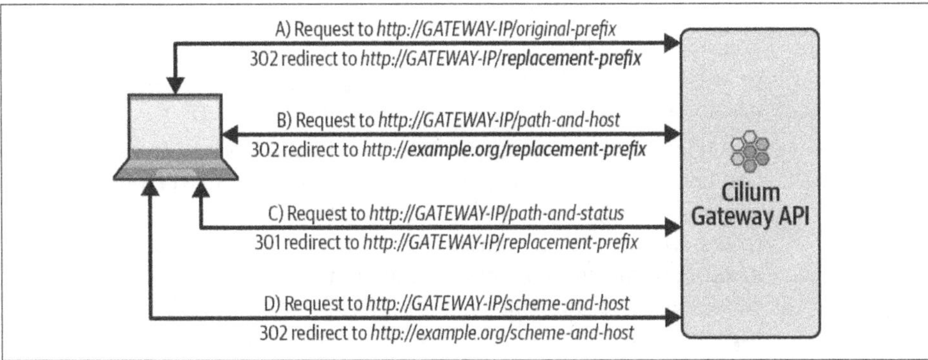

Figure 7-7. HTTP redirects with Gateway API

Let's deploy the route and verify that each rule works as expected. First, verify the path prefix redirection (Figure 7-7A). Make a request to trigger the redirect and note the `302` redirect code alongside the recommended URL:

```
$ curl -l -v "http://$GATEWAY/original-prefix"
< HTTP/1.1 302 Found
< location: http://172.18.255.200:80/replacement-prefix
```

Next, verify the redirect to a new hostname and path (Figure 7-7B). Make a request to the `/path-and-host` path:

```
$ curl -l -v "http://$GATEWAY/path-and-host"
< HTTP/1.1 302 Found
< location: http://example.org:80/replacement-prefix
```

As you can see, both the host and the prefix have been replaced.

Now verify that Cilium Gateway API can redirect you to a permanently moved URL (Figure 7-7C). Make the request and note the permanent redirection code (`301`) in the reply:

```
$ curl -l -v "http://$GATEWAY/path-and-status"
< HTTP/1.1 301 Moved Permanently
< location: http://172.18.255.200:80/replacement-prefix
```

Finally, verify the HTTP host and scheme redirect capability (Figure 7-7D). This feature can redirect users to use HTTPS instead of HTTP for a specific request.

HTTP to HTTPS redirection is best suited to URLs that are expected to be accessed by users via web browsers and should be avoided for "API" URLs that are expected to be accessed by machines.

This type of redirection can result in accidentally exposing authentication tokens. For example, machines accessing an API often attach a bearer token in the `Authorization` header of every request. If such a client is misconfigured to use an HTTP endpoint, it will send the entire request (including the token) in plain text before receiving the redirect to the HTTPS endpoint. The extra friction of not supporting HTTP at all is usually worth the security benefits of not risking credential exposure.

While you can use `curl` for this, you can also check in your browser. Assuming the IP address assigned to your Gateway is `172.18.255.200`, directly accessing *http://172.18.255.200/scheme-and-host* from your browser will redirect you to *https://example.org/scheme-and-host*.

gRPC Routing

gRPC is a high-performance remote procedure call (RPC) framework built on HTTP/2; it provides bidirectional streaming between microservices. Gateway API provides first-class support for gRPC via GRPCRoute (*https://oreil.ly/cpDa5*), which can match on host, headers, service, and method and then forward requests to the appropriate Kubernetes services.[5]

Ingress has no common standard for gRPC routing, so support is implementation-specific and often relies on controller-specific annotations. With GRPCRoute standardized in Gateway API since version 1.1.0, you get portable, annotation-free manifests that work across compliant implementations.

Let's try this out with Google Cloud's Online Boutique demo application (*https://oreil.ly/36ln-*), a web-based ecommerce app allowing users to browse items, add them to a cart, and purchase them. Online Boutique is composed of 11 microservices written in different languages that communicate using gRPC.

Deploy the app by applying the *gcp-microservices-demo.yaml* manifest, and then review the GRPCRoute manifest (*grpc-route.yaml*). It defines routes for gRPC requests targeting the `productcatalogservice` and `currencyservice` microservices on ports 3550 and 7000, respectively. The structure of GRPCRoute mirrors that of HTTPRoute:

5 A gRPC service defines a set of methods that a client can call remotely, each representing an API endpoint with a specific request and response type.

```yaml
apiVersion: gateway.networking.k8s.io/v1
kind: GRPCRoute
metadata:
  name: productcatalogservice-rule
spec:
  parentRefs:
    - namespace: default
      name: my-gateway ❶
  rules:
    - matches:
        - method:
            service: hipstershop.ProductCatalogService ❷
            method:  ListProducts ❸
      backendRefs:
        - name: productcatalogservice
          port: 3550 ❹
---
apiVersion: gateway.networking.k8s.io/v1
kind: GRPCRoute
metadata:
  name: currencyservice-rule
spec:
  parentRefs:
    - namespace: default
      name: my-gateway ❶
  rules:
    - matches:
        - method:
            service: hipstershop.CurrencyService ❷
            method:  GetSupportedCurrencies ❸
      backendRefs:
        - name: currencyservice
          port: 7000 ❹
```

❶ Attach this route to the previously deployed my-gateway entry point.

❷ Match on the fully qualified gRPC service.

❸ Match on the gRPC method.

❹ Forward to the target Kubernetes service and port.

Once you've deployed *grpc-route.yaml*, you can make gRPC requests to backend services using `grpcurl`.[6]

6 `grpcurl` is a command-line tool for interacting with gRPC services. It can be installed through your package manager (e.g., with `brew install grpcurl` on macOS).

First, access the currency service of the application, which lists the supported currencies. Note that since gRPC is binary-encoded, you also need the proto definitions[7] for the gRPC services to make gRPC requests:

```
$ grpcurl -plaintext -proto ./demo.proto "$GATEWAY:80" \
    hipstershop.CurrencyService/GetSupportedCurrencies
{ "currencyCodes": [ "EUR", "USD", "GBP", [...] ] }
```

Next, try accessing the product catalog service. You should see a collection of JSON objects describing items such as sunglasses, a tank top, and a watch in the output:

```
$ grpcurl -plaintext -proto ./demo.proto "$GATEWAY:80" \
    hipstershop.ProductCatalogService/ListProducts | jq
{"id":"OLJCESPC7Z","name":"Sunglasses","price":19.99}
{"id":"66VCHSJNUP","name":"Tank Top","price":18.99}
{"id":"1YMWWN1N4O","name":"Watch","price":109.99}
[...]
```

East–West Layer 7 Routing with GAMMA and Gateway API

While this chapter has so far focused on traffic entering the cluster (*north–south*), Gateway API can also be used to manage traffic within the cluster (*east–west*). Traditionally, Kubernetes services handle east–west traffic using layer 3/4 load balancing. For more advanced layer 7 routing (such as path-based routing, traffic splitting, or request timeouts), platform teams have relied on service meshes that introduce their own APIs and components.

The Gateway API for Mesh Management and Administration (GAMMA) initiative extends Gateway API to support these advanced routing use cases for internal traffic. GAMMA introduces no new resources, but instead allows HTTPRoute objects to bind directly to Kubernetes services instead of Gateways. In this section, you'll use Cilium's GAMMA implementation to apply Gateway API features to in-cluster traffic.

First, deploy *gamma-manifest.yaml*, which installs two `echo` services, `echo-v1` and `echo-v2`, and a client pod for internal testing. It also creates an `echo` service that acts as the frontend for routing (GAMMA refers to the combination of the cluster IP and its DNS name as the "frontend" of the service and to the collection of endpoint IPs as the "backend").

Let's look at a GAMMA route used for east–west service management (*gamma-route.yaml*). Unlike north–south Gateway API usage, the route's `parentRefs` target an internal service called `echo`:

7 Proto definitions describe the structure of gRPC services, including their methods and request and response types, using the Protocol Buffers language.

```
apiVersion: gateway.networking.k8s.io/v1
kind: HTTPRoute
metadata:
  name: gamma-route
  namespace: gamma-ns
spec:
 parentRefs:
 - kind: Service
   name: echo
  rules:
  - matches:
    - path:
        type: PathPrefix
        value: /v1
    backendRefs:
    - name: echo-v1
      port: 80
  - matches:
    - path:
        type: PathPrefix
        value: /v2
    backendRefs:
    - name: echo-v2
      port: 80
```

Deploy the route, and then test path-based routing from the internal client:

```
$ kubectl -n gamma-ns exec -it client -- curl http://echo/v1
$ kubectl -n gamma-ns exec -it client -- curl http://echo/v2
```

You should see that requests to `/v1` are routed to pods behind `echo-v1` and requests to `/v2` are routed to `echo-v2`, as illustrated in Figure 7-8.

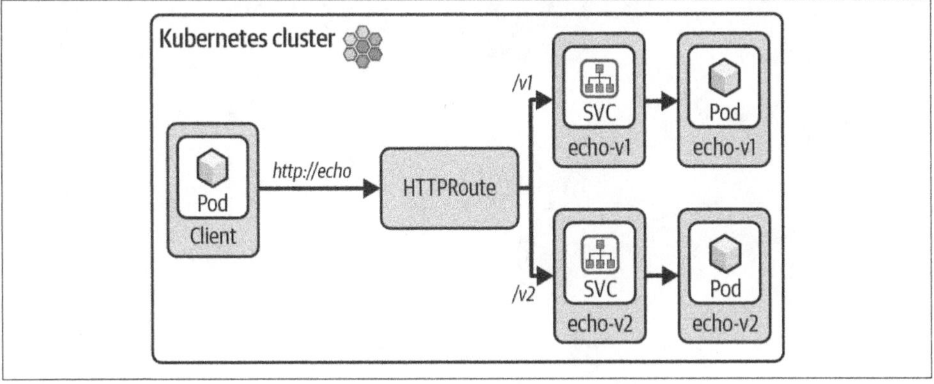

Figure 7-8. Gateway API for service mesh (GAMMA)

This demonstrates that layer 7 routing logic using HTTPRoute objects can apply to internal traffic just as it does to external traffic.

Once a route is attached to a Kubernetes service, all the other Gateway API features you've seen in this chapter (traffic splitting, request and response header modifications, path rewriting and redirects, etc.) can be applied in the same way.[8]

Summary

This chapter examined how Cilium supports layer 7 traffic management through both Ingress and Gateway API. We began with Cilium's Ingress support, showing how Cilium can route external HTTP traffic using standard Kubernetes resources and how it integrates with LoadBalancer IP address management and layer 2 announcements.

Then we shifted our focus to Gateway API, which introduces more structured and extensible routing capabilities. We walked through examples demonstrating how to route traffic based on HTTP path, headers, methods, and query parameters, and we explored how to implement TLS termination, gRPC routing, request and response header manipulation, and HTTP redirects. Finally, we saw how Gateway API can be used to manage east-west traffic through GAMMA.

The examples in this chapter showed how the same routing model can be used for both external and internal traffic, minimizing resource utilization by removing the need for a separate ingress or service mesh system. In the next chapter, you will learn about other Cilium features designed to optimize network performance and reduce latency.

8 You should also know that using GAMMA means injecting Envoy into the datapath for this flow, which comes with performance implications. You can read more about these implications in Chapter 13.

CHAPTER 8

Performance Networking and Traffic Optimization

So far we have focused on getting access and connectivity working with Cilium. Outside of the eBPF-based `kube-proxy` replacement we covered in Chapter 6, we have yet to discuss network performance.

Our goal is not just to help you run Cilium; it is to help you get as much value and performance out of it as possible. A network tool is often judged on throughput, latency, and jitter, and the same goes for Cilium.

In this chapter, we will review some of the Cilium features that enable you to optimize network performance. We will not cover them all; to avoid overwhelming the reader with too much information, we decided to leave out topics like Bottleneck Bandwidth and Round-trip propagation time (BBR), BIG TCP, and eBPF host routing.

Excluding topics is a difficult choice. To briefly summarize their value:

- BBR is a modern congestion control algorithm that improves throughput and reduces latency on long or high-bandwidth connections.
- BIG TCP increases efficiency for large-scale data transfers by allowing larger packet sizes, reducing per-packet overhead.
- eBPF host routing bypasses parts of the traditional networking stack to deliver faster packet forwarding directly within the kernel.

The Isovalent blog covers BBR (*https://oreil.ly/SolpE*) and BIG TCP (*https://oreil.ly/RjQ7j*) in numerous posts. eBPF host-routing is enabled by default if your kernel supports it, so it does not require further explanation here.

We will focus on a set of features that boost performance at the area, node, and edge levels by reducing routing hops (in the network and within the Linux stack) and by preferring nearby backends when possible:

Service Traffic Distribution [area/topology]
: Prioritizes endpoints in the same area when available, helping reduce latency and inter-area costs

Local Redirect Policy (LRP) [node]
: Prioritizes node-local backends so traffic stays on the same node, reducing cross-node hops and latency

Direct Server Return (DSR) [edge]
: Preserves the client source IP and sends responses directly from backend pods to clients, improving return path performance

eXpress Data Path (XDP) [node]
: Processes packets at the earliest possible point in the kernel to reduce per-packet overhead and lower latency

Maglev [edge]
: Provides consistent hashing so the same flow lands on the same backend, improving connection stability during node changes

Netkit [node]
: Replaces the traditional veth path with a kernel-native device model to cut overhead and bring container networking performance closer to host levels

We'll start with area-aware performance, then move to node- and edge-level techniques that reduce latency and routing hops inside and around the cluster. You can find all the YAML manifests you will use in this chapter in the *chapter08* directory of the book's GitHub repository (*https://github.com/isovalent/cilium-up-and-running*).

Service Traffic Distribution

Many Kubernetes users choose to deploy clusters across multiple zones (such as multiple availability zones in AWS, or separate physical locations for on-premises hardware), often to improve availability and resilience. However, this design can introduce trade-offs, particularly in the form of increased latency if client traffic crosses zones to reach a backend. It can also lead to higher infrastructure costs, since many cloud providers charge for interzone egress. Ideally, traffic should remain within the same zone whenever possible.

This approach is known as *topology-aware traffic engineering*: a routing strategy that takes into account the physical or logical location of both the client and the destination endpoints during forwarding decisions.

In Kubernetes, this is enabled through the Service Traffic Distribution feature.[1] By setting the `trafficDistribution` field in a service specification, you can express a preference for how traffic should be routed. At the time of writing, the only supported value is `PreferClose`, which prioritizes endpoints in the same area as the client when available.

We focus on Kubernetes v1.33 ("Octarine") in this book, but a big change was made to this feature in Kubernetes v1.34 ("Of Wind & Will"): the `PreferClose` setting was deprecated in favor of two new settings, `PreferSameZone` and `PreferSameNode`, with `PreferClose` acting as an alias of the former (*https://oreil.ly/2ExTB*). If you're following along using a newer version of Kubernetes, try using `PreferSameZone` in the following examples.

Let's try it out. While this capability is especially useful for clusters that span multiple cloud zones or datacenters, we will use a kind cluster for simplicity and cost-effectiveness. We'll deploy a four-node kind cluster and assign two nodes to `zone-a` and two nodes to `zone-b` using Kubernetes node labels, with `zone-a` and `zone-b` representing two geographically separated areas.

You will observe that, without traffic distribution enabled, the traffic to a Kubernetes service is randomly distributed across all backend pods, regardless of their location (Figure 8-1).

1 Service Traffic Distribution is considered the successor to another traffic engineering feature, Topology-Aware Routing (*https://oreil.ly/7vhzO*) (which was itself previously known as Topology-Aware Hints). While Topology-Aware Routing is also supported by Cilium, we'll only cover Service Traffic Distribution in this book.

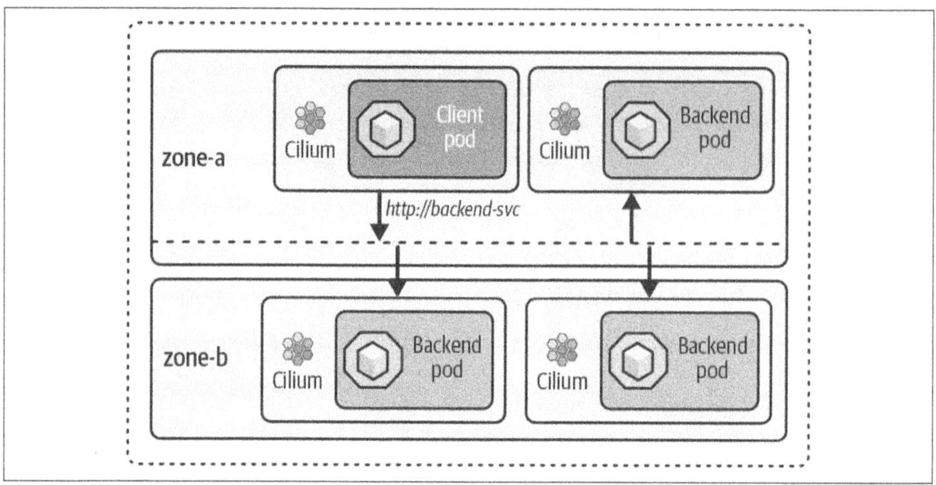

Figure 8-1. Random distribution prior to Service Traffic Distribution

Once we set `trafficDistribution: PreferClose` on a service, Kubernetes prefers sending traffic to endpoints that are in the same zone as the source, helping reduce latency and interzone data transfer costs (as illustrated in Figure 8-2).

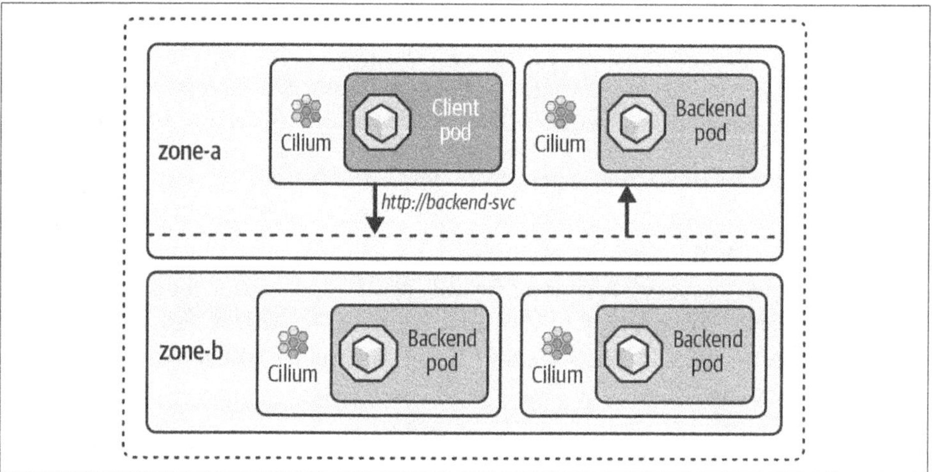

Figure 8-2. Topology-aware Service Traffic Distribution

All files discussed in this section are in the *chapter08/std* directory of the book's GitHub repository (*https://github.com/isovalent/cilium-up-and-running*).

To see this in action, deploy the cluster (*kind-cluster-config-std.yaml*) and verify where each worker is located. You should see that `kind-worker` and `kind-worker2` are both located in `zone-a`, while `kind-worker3` and `kind-worker4` are located in `zone-b`:

```
$ kubectl get nodes --show-labels
NAME            LABELS
kind-worker     topology.kubernetes.io/zone=zone-a
kind-worker2    topology.kubernetes.io/zone=zone-a
kind-worker3    topology.kubernetes.io/zone=zone-b
kind-worker4    topology.kubernetes.io/zone=zone-b
```

To enable the Service Traffic Distribution option, set the Helm value `loadBalancer.serviceTopology=true`. Note that KPR is required for Service Traffic Distribution.

Now, install Cilium (*cilium-std-values.yaml*) and create a deployment (*std-deployment.yaml*) of eight echo pods that will respond to client requests with their own name, alongside an echo service (*std-service.yaml*) to front the deployment. We will start with `trafficDistribution` disabled.

Let's now deploy three `curl` pods (*std-poller-distribution.yaml*), each continuously sending requests to the echo service and logging which backend pod responded. The list of running pods should look like this:

```
$ kubectl get pods -o wide
NAME                     READY   STATUS    IP             NODE
curl-664778b5b6-hgg5v    1/1     Running   10.244.2.76    kind-worker4
curl-664778b5b6-lhq98    1/1     Running   10.244.3.9     kind-worker3
curl-664778b5b6-zr6kt    1/1     Running   10.244.1.132   kind-worker2
echo-7f89db4f96-5h2bz    1/1     Running   10.244.2.201   kind-worker4
echo-7f89db4f96-5wshm    1/1     Running   10.244.4.66    kind-worker
echo-7f89db4f96-99g9g    1/1     Running   10.244.2.153   kind-worker4
echo-7f89db4f96-h2gv7    1/1     Running   10.244.1.90    kind-worker2
echo-7f89db4f96-h5zw4    1/1     Running   10.244.2.24    kind-worker4
echo-7f89db4f96-q66nz    1/1     Running   10.244.1.13    kind-worker2
echo-7f89db4f96-wmlkn    1/1     Running   10.244.3.223   kind-worker3
echo-7f89db4f96-xjggf    1/1     Running   10.244.4.216   kind-worker
```

Let's take a look at the logs on one of the new `curl` pods (`curl-664778b5b6-zr6kt`, located on `kind-worker2`, in `zone-a`). The following command aggregates responses by backend pod. You can see that traffic was randomly distributed across all eight echo pods, regardless of their location:

```
$ kubectl logs curl-664778b5b6-zr6kt \
   | grep "Request served by" | cut -f2 -d ':' | sort | uniq -c

  11 Request served by echo-7f89db4f96-5h2bz
   8 Request served by echo-7f89db4f96-5wshm
  12 Request served by echo-7f89db4f96-99g9g
  12 Request served by echo-7f89db4f96-h2gv7
  13 Request served by echo-7f89db4f96-h5zw4
```

```
 16 Request served by echo-7f89db4f96-q66nz
 10 Request served by echo-7f89db4f96-wmlkn
  7 Request served by echo-7f89db4f96-xjggf
```

Now, enable Service Traffic Distribution (by uncommenting the `trafficDistribution: PreferClose` line in the *std-service.yaml* manifest and reapplying it) and check the counters on the `curl-664778b5b6-zr6kt` pod again. This time, as you can see in the following output, only the stats for the NGINX pods located in the same zone increase:

```
$ kubectl logs curl-664778b5b6-zr6kt \
    | grep "Request served by" | cut -f2 -d ':' | sort | uniq -c

 48 Request served by echo-7f89db4f96-5h2bz
181 Request served by echo-7f89db4f96-5wshm ❶
 49 Request served by echo-7f89db4f96-99g9g
181 Request served by echo-7f89db4f96-h2gv7 ❶
 48 Request served by echo-7f89db4f96-h5zw4
187 Request served by echo-7f89db4f96-q66nz ❶
 46 Request served by echo-7f89db4f96-wmlkn
179 Request served by echo-7f89db4f96-xjggf ❶
```

❶ Only the counters on the pods that are in the same zone as the curl pod increase, indicating that traffic remains in the same zone.

Run the same aggregation from a `curl` pod scheduled in the other area; you should see the counts flip, with local echo pods dominating:

```
$ kubectl logs curl-664778b5b6-hgg5v \
    | grep "Request served by" | cut -f2 -d ':' | sort | uniq -c

223 Request served by echo-7f89db4f96-5h2bz
 34 Request served by echo-7f89db4f96-5wshm
259 Request served by echo-7f89db4f96-99g9g
 52 Request served by echo-7f89db4f96-h2gv7
249 Request served by echo-7f89db4f96-h5zw4
 52 Request served by echo-7f89db4f96-q66nz
231 Request served by echo-7f89db4f96-wmlkn
 38 Request served by echo-7f89db4f96-xjggf
```

Note that when no local backend is available, traffic is forwarded to backends outside the local zone. As a bonus exercise, you can test this yourself by destroying the echo servers and verifying that the client accesses backends in the other zone.

Keep in mind these constraints around topology-aware features:

- For a given service, if `externalTrafficPolicy` or `internalTrafficPolicy` is set to `Local`, that policy takes precedence over `trafficDistribution` for the corresponding traffic type. Refer back to Chapter 6 for an explanation of traffic policies.

- If those policy fields are set to `Cluster` (the default) or are not set, `trafficDistribution` guides routing for that traffic type and will attempt to send traffic to an endpoint in the same area as the client.
- These mechanisms work best when incoming traffic is roughly evenly distributed across areas. If a large proportion of traffic originates from a single zone, the endpoints allocated to that zone can be overloaded; this approach is not recommended when most traffic is expected to come from one zone.

Local Redirect Policy

While Service Traffic Distribution helps direct traffic within the same zone, reducing cross-zone charges and latency, you may want to avoid even internode traffic by directing service requests to a local backend. To achieve this, Cilium offers an eBPF-based feature called Local Redirect Policy (LRP). LRP enables traffic destined for a particular IP address and port/protocol tuple or Kubernetes service to be redirected locally to backend pods within a node, using eBPF.

There are many scenarios where an application runs on every node, typically using a DaemonSet. Examples include logging agents, monitoring sidecars, or DNS forwarders. While this ensures high availability, pods do not always connect to the local instance. Without LRP, traffic may be routed to an instance on another node, leading to unnecessary cross-node traffic and added latency (Figure 8-3).

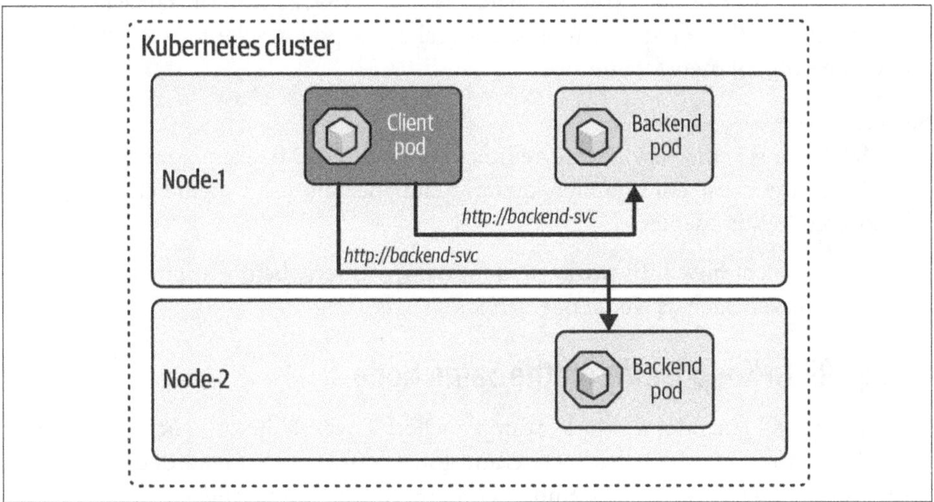

Figure 8-3. Without LRP

LRP ensures service-bound traffic is redirected locally (Figure 8-4). The most evident use case is with NodeLocal DNSCache, an architecture that can reduce DNS lookup latency in your clusters.

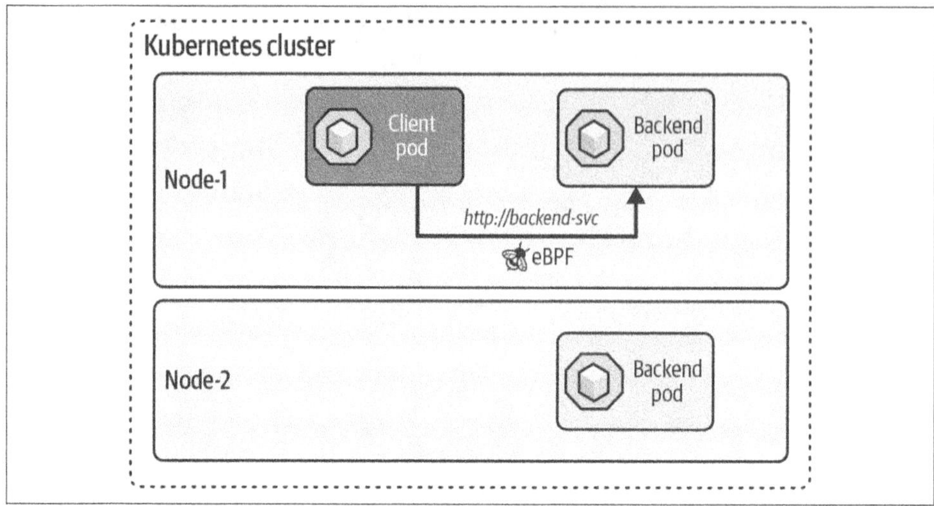

Figure 8-4. With LRP

There are two policy types:

`AddressMatcher`
: Matches an *`IP:port`* destination and redirects locally. `AddressMatcher` is handy for node-local metadata caches on managed Kubernetes platforms such as EKS and GKE. For example, you can match `169.254.169.254:80` (instance metadata) and redirect those requests to a node-local cache pod. Cache misses will then go to the external metadata service.

`ServiceMatcher`
: Matches a specific service and redirects to node-local backends for that service. This is the most common policy type and the one used in the two examples covered in this chapter.

Let's take a look at how LRP works on a fundamental level before applying it to more specific use cases, such as NodeLocal DNS.

Using LRP to Keep Traffic on the Same Node

To start, we will consider a simple example where Local Redirect Policy will redirect traffic bound for a Kubernetes service and force traffic to be forwarded only to the local backends (i.e., on the same Kubernetes node as the source client).

All files discussed in this section are in the *chapter08/lrp* directory of the book's GitHub repository (*https://github.com/isovalent/cilium-up-and-running*).

Deploy a kind cluster (*kind-cluster-config-lrp.yaml*) and install Cilium (*cilium-lrp-values.yaml*). Note the flag required to activate this feature (`localRedirectPolicies.enabled=true`).[2]

Next, deploy the Kubernetes pod and service for which traffic needs to be redirected (*lrp-deployment.yaml*). Once again, we're using a deployment of two echo servers to show which pod receives the client request, with a service named `echo-server` fronting the backend pods.

The two replicas are scheduled on two different nodes. Let's first see how, prior to using LRP, requests to the service are load-balanced across the two backends. Deploy the client (*netshoot-client.yaml*), then check with `kubectl` where each pod is scheduled:

```
$ kubectl get pods -o wide
NAME                            READY   STATUS    IP           NODE
echo-server-78fbb56cc7-phmpq    1/1     Running   10.0.0.209   kind-worker
echo-server-78fbb56cc7-pvkgf    1/1     Running   10.0.2.27    kind-worker2
netshoot-client                 1/1     Running   10.0.2.226   kind-worker2
```

Now, test access from the client to the service:

```
$ kubectl exec -it netshoot-client -- curl echo-server:8080
Request served by echo-server-78fbb56cc7-phmpq

$ kubectl exec -it netshoot-client -- curl echo-server:8080
Request served by echo-server-78fbb56cc7-pvkgf
```

The response includes the pod name, and we can see that requests are being distributed to both pods—the one on the same node as the client and the one on a different node.

Verify that Cilium created a ClusterIP service entry pointing to backends located on both nodes:

```
$ kubectl get svc echo-server
NAME          TYPE        CLUSTER-IP      EXTERNAL-IP   PORT(S)    AGE
echo-server   ClusterIP   10.96.219.113   <none>        8080/TCP   2m37s

$ kubectl exec -it -n kube-system ds/cilium -- cilium-dbg service list
ID  Frontend                Service Type  Backend
6   10.96.219.113:8080/TCP  ClusterIP     1 => 10.0.0.209:8080/TCP (active)
                                          2 => 10.0.2.27:8080/TCP (active)
```

Then deploy the Local Redirect Policy (*svc-lrp.yaml*):

```
apiVersion: "cilium.io/v2"
kind: CiliumLocalRedirectPolicy
```

2 While enabling KPR is not strictly required for LRP, it is recommended. See the Cilium documentation (*https://oreil.ly/_xw_h*) on LRP for more information on the prerequisites.

```
metadata:
  name: "echo-server-lrp"
spec:
  redirectFrontend: ❶
    serviceMatcher:
      serviceName: echo-server
      namespace: default
  redirectBackend: ❷
    localEndpointSelector:
      matchLabels:
        app.kubernetes.io/name: echo-server
    toPorts:
      - port: "8080"
        protocol: TCP
```

❶ Identifies the Kubernetes service for which traffic should be intercepted. Cilium matches this service by name and namespace to determine which frontend requests are eligible for local redirection.

❷ Specifies the set of local pods (based on labels) and destination port to which frontend traffic should be redirected, if a matching pod exists on the same node.

When a policy of this type is applied, the existing service entry created by Cilium will be replaced with a new service entry of type `LocalRedirect`. This entry can only have node-local backend pods.

Let's verify the behavior by executing `cilium-dbg service list` on the Cilium agent running on the same node as our client pod. The following output confirms that Cilium will forward traffic to the `echo-server` service only to the local backend (`echo-server-78fbb56cc7-pvkgf`, with IP `10.0.2.27`):

```
$ kubectl -n kube-system exec -it cilium-5d5jq -- cilium-dbg service list
7    10.96.219.113:8080/TCP   LocalRedirect   1 => 10.0.2.27:8080/TCP (active)
```

By running the `curl` command several times in a loop, we can see that only the pod colocated on the same node as the client receives the request:

```
$ for i in {1..20}; do
  echo -n "Req $i -> "
  kubectl exec netshoot-client -- curl -s echo-server:8080 \
    | grep "Request served by" \
    | awk '{print $4}'
done

Request 1 -> echo-server-78fbb56cc7-pvkgf
Request 2 -> echo-server-78fbb56cc7-pvkgf
[...]
Request 19 -> echo-server-78fbb56cc7-pvkgf
Request 20 -> echo-server-78fbb56cc7-pvkgf
```

The Local Redirect Policy ensured traffic stayed on the same node.

Using LRP to Redirect DNS Traffic Locally

The most common use case for LRP is to optimize DNS performance, alongside the NodeLocal DNSCache Kubernetes architecture. This architecture relies on a DNS caching agent running on each cluster node as a DaemonSet. With LRP you can be sure that DNS traffic from a pod goes to the DNS cache running on the same node as the pod, reducing latency, among other benefits (*https://oreil.ly/_JAwL*).

Before using LRP to redirect DNS traffic and optimize latency, we first need to create a local DNS node-cache (*node-local-dns.yaml*). The manifest is rather long, so let's summarize some of the core components:

- The service account named `node-local-dns` will be used by the DaemonSet to run with specific permissions in the cluster.
- The service named `kube-dns-upstream` exposes port 53 for DNS queries over both UDP and TCP and forwards them to a target port on the DNS pods selected by the `k8s-app: kube-dns` label (the `coreDNS` pods). This service is used to handle upstream DNS queries when the node-local DNS cache is not able to resolve a request.
- The ConfigMap defines the CoreDNS configuration (Corefile) for DNS caching on the node level:
  - It defines behavior for DNS requests in the `cluster.local` domain (Kubernetes service discovery) and external DNS queries (outside `cluster.local`).
  - Caching is configured with success and denial limits for both `cluster.local` and reverse lookup zones (`in-addr.arpa` and `ip6.arpa`).
  - Metrics are exposed on port 9253 for Prometheus and health checks are enabled.
- The DaemonSet named `node-local-dns` runs a `node-cache` container on every node in the cluster:
  - Each node will have a local DNS caching service, which significantly reduces DNS lookup times for workloads on the node.
  - The DaemonSet doesn't use the cluster's default DNS settings but instead relies on its own DNS configuration.
  - The `args` define the local IP addresses for the cache (`169.254.20.10` and `10.96.0.10`), which are the node-local IPs used by this service.
  - It exposes ports 53 for DNS (both TCP and UDP) and port 9253 for metrics.

Health checks are configured via the `/health` endpoint.

Once this is deployed, you will see a DNS agent running on each node:

```
$ kubectl get pods -n kube-system -o wide
NAME                   READY   STATUS    IP           NODE
node-local-dns-h5hgx   1/1     Running   10.0.1.252   kind-control-plane
node-local-dns-kvvmk   1/1     Running   10.0.2.20    kind-worker2
node-local-dns-xrwvl   1/1     Running   10.0.0.172   kind-worker
```

Next, deploy the following Local Redirect Policy (*dns-lrp.yaml*). The policy will redirect traffic bound to the CoreDNS servers, forwarding it to the node-local DNS cache agents:

```
apiVersion: "cilium.io/v2"
kind: CiliumLocalRedirectPolicy
metadata:
  name: "nodelocaldns"
  namespace: kube-system
spec:
  redirectFrontend:
    serviceMatcher:
      serviceName: kube-dns
      namespace: kube-system
  redirectBackend:
    localEndpointSelector:
      matchLabels:
        k8s-app: node-local-dns
    toPorts:
      - port: "53"
        name: dns
        protocol: UDP
      - port: "53"
        name: dns-tcp
        protocol: TCP
```

Look on any of the Cilium agents and you will now see `LocalRedirect` entries for the DNS service, over TCP and UDP ports:

```
$ kubectl exec -it ds/cilium -n kube-system -- cilium-dbg service list
ID   Frontend               Service Type    Backend
3    10.96.0.10:53/UDP      LocalRedirect   1 => 10.244.2.46:53/UDP (active)
4    10.96.0.10:53/TCP      LocalRedirect   1 => 10.244.2.46:53/TCP (active)
```

You can verify that the redirects are working by checking the DNS caches' metrics. First, let's get the IP of the DNS cache pod on the `kind-worker` node (where our client was deployed):

```
$ DNS_LOCAL="$(kubectl -n kube-system get po \
    -l k8s-app=node-local-dns \
    --field-selector spec.nodeName=kind-worker \
    -o jsonpath='{.items[].status.podIP}')"

$ echo "$DNS_LOCAL"
10.0.0.172
```

Let's also get the IP of the "non-local" DNS cache pod:

```
$ DNS_NON_LOCAL="$(kubectl -n kube-system get po \
    -l k8s-app=node-local-dns \
    --field-selector spec.nodeName=kind-worker2 \
    -o jsonpath='{.items[].status.podIP}')"

$ echo "$DNS_NON_LOCAL"
10.0.2.20
```

We can now make DNS requests from the client pod and check the DNS request counts on the local DNS cache pod and the one running on the other worker node:

```
$ kubectl exec netshoot-client -- curl "$DNS_LOCAL:9253/metrics" | \
    grep 'coredns_dns_request_size_bytes_count'
coredns_dns_request_count_total{zone="cluster.local."} 1  # local

$ kubectl exec netshoot-client -- curl "$DNS_NON_LOCAL:9253/metrics" | \
    grep 'coredns_dns_request_size_bytes_count'
coredns_dns_request_count_total{zone="cluster.local."} 1  # non-local
```

The values here indicate that only one request has been made to each DNS cache. Let's run a few DNS requests, and then check the counts again:

```
$ kubectl exec netshoot-client -- nslookup oreilly.com
$ kubectl exec netshoot-client -- nslookup isovalent.com
$ kubectl exec netshoot-client -- nslookup cilium.io

$ kubectl exec netshoot-client -- curl "$DNS_LOCAL:9253/metrics" | \
    grep 'coredns_dns_request_size_bytes_count'
coredns_dns_request_count_total{zone="cluster.local."} 14  # local

$ kubectl exec netshoot-client -- curl "$DNS_NON_LOCAL:9253/metrics" \
    | grep 'coredns_dns_request_size_bytes_count'
coredns_dns_request_count_total{zone="cluster.local."} 1   # non-local
```

As expected, it increases for the local DNS cache, while the number for the other cache stays the same.

Direct Server Return

We'll discuss controlling traffic entering the cluster from external sources and leaving the cluster (ingress and egress) in Chapters 10 and 11, respectively. For traffic returning to the client, an optional feature that can help improve performance is Direct Server Return (DSR).

Consider a situation where a service is exposed externally (through NodePort or LoadBalancer) and the service endpoint runs on a different node (`Node-2`) from the node the client connects to (`Node-1`), as illustrated in Figure 8-5.

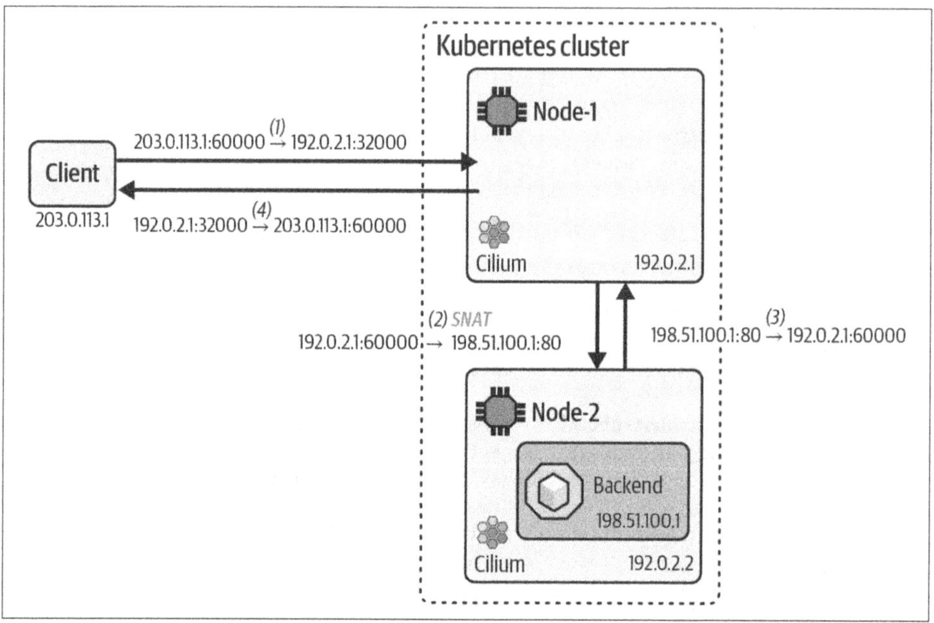

Figure 8-5. Without DSR

When `Node-1` forwards client requests to `Node-2`, it will source-NAT the traffic, replacing the client's IP address with its internal IP from its own PodCIDR. This has two negative implications:

Loss of observability
: The backend receiving the traffic sees the packet as originating from `Node-1` instead of the actual client.

Indirect return path
: The backend traffic is sent to `Node-1` and then on to the client, instead of directly to the client.

Cilium's DSR feature leverages eBPF to preserve the source IP address and to ensure traffic is returned directly to the client, as illustrated in Figure 8-6.

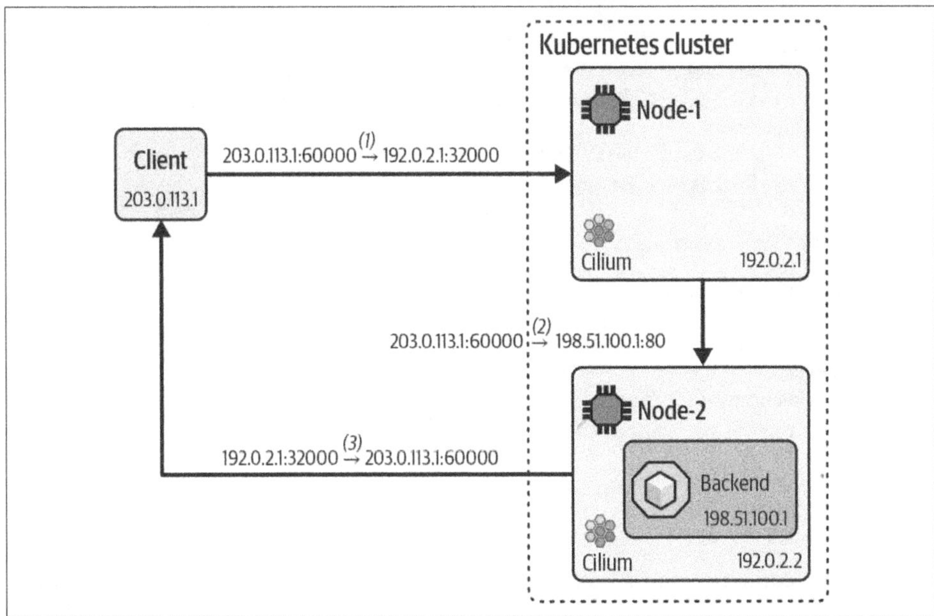

Figure 8-6. Node port access with Direct Server Return

All files discussed in this section are in the *chapter08/dsr* directory of the book's GitHub repository (*https://github.com/isovalent/cilium-up-and-running*).

Before trying out DSR, let's see what happens without it, which is Cilium's default behavior. In a generic kind cluster (`kind create cluster --config kind.yaml`) with a default Cilium installation, deploy the following manifests (*dsr-deployment.yaml* and *dsr-service.yaml*). It's a deployment of two replicas running a simple "What's My IP?" application and an associated NodePort service:

```
apiVersion: apps/v1
kind: Deployment
metadata:
  name: echo
spec:
  replicas: 2
  selector:
    matchLabels:
      app.kubernetes.io/name: echo
  template:
```

```
    metadata:
      labels:
        app.kubernetes.io/name: echo
    spec:
      containers:
        - name: echo
          image: quay.io/isovalent-dev/egressgw-whatismyip:latest
          ports:
            - containerPort: 8000
---
apiVersion: v1
kind: Service
metadata:
  name: echo-nodeport
spec:
  type: NodePort
  selector:
    app.kubernetes.io/name: echo
  ports:
    - port: 80
      targetPort: 8000
      protocol: TCP
      nodePort: 30080
```

Start a client container on the same Docker network, with the following command:

```
$ docker run -d --network kind --rm --name client nicolaka/netshoot:v0.8 \
    sleep infinity
```

Its IP is `172.18.0.5`—let's check if this is the IP returned by the "What's My IP?" service:

```
$ docker exec -it client ip -4 -o a show eth0 | awk '{print $4}'
172.18.0.5/16
```

Now, access the service over the `kind-control-plane` node from the client container using the allocated node port of the service (30080 in our example):

```
$ kubectl get svc
NAME            TYPE        CLUSTER-IP     EXTERNAL-IP   PORT(S)        AGE
echo-nodeport   NodePort    10.96.40.253   <none>        80:30080/TCP   10m
kubernetes      ClusterIP   10.96.0.1      <none>        443/TCP        46m

$ kubectl get nodes -o wide
NAME                 STATUS   ROLES           AGE   VERSION   INTERNAL-IP
kind-control-plane   Ready    control-plane   46m   v1.33.0   172.18.0.4
kind-worker          Ready    <none>          46m   v1.33.0   172.18.0.3
kind-worker2         Ready    <none>          46m   v1.33.0   172.18.0.2

$ docker exec -it client curl 172.18.0.4:30080
10.244.0.232
```

The response shows the client's IP address—however, it is not the client's source IP address but an internal pod IP address (10.244.0.232) assigned to the `kind-control-plane` node:

```
$ docker exec kind-control-plane ip a
[...]
13: cilium_host@cilium_net: <BROADCAST,MULTICAST,NOARP,UP,LOWER_UP> mtu 65520 qdisc
noqueue state UP group default qlen 1000
    link/ether 7e:48:5d:5d:f4:c4 brd ff:ff:ff:ff:ff:ff
    inet 10.244.0.232/32 scope global cilium_host
```

This confirms that, when forwarding packets to the worker nodes where the backends reside, `kind-control-plane` changes the source IP to its own.

Let's now try this with DSR. Use the following Helm values (*cilium-dsr-values.yaml*). Set the `loadBalancer.mode=dsr` flag to enable DSR. Note that DSR requires KPR and is only supported in native routing mode or with Geneve (it is not currently supported with VXLAN encapsulation):

```
kubeProxyReplacement: true
routingMode: native
ipv4NativeRoutingCIDR: "172.18.0.0/16"
autoDirectNodeRoutes: true
k8sServiceHost: "kind-control-plane"
k8sServicePort: 6443
loadBalancer:
  mode: "dsr"
```

After installation, verify that DSR is enabled:

```
$ kubectl -n kube-system exec ds/cilium -- cilium-dbg status --verbose
KubeProxyReplacement:   True
  Mode:                 DSR
    DSR Dispatch Mode: IP Option/Extension
```

Apply the deployment (*dsr-deployment.yaml*) and service (*dsr-service.yaml*) once more before accessing the "What's My IP?" service over NodePort again:

```
$ docker exec -it client curl 172.18.0.4:30080
172.18.0.5
```

With DSR enabled, the address the service returns is the IP of the client. This confirms the source IP was preserved and the server replied directly back to the client.

You can verify that the service entry in the eBPF map is set to `dsr` with:

```
$ kubectl -n kube-system exec -it ds/cilium -- cilium-dbg bpf lb list
[...]
SERVICE ADDRESS             BACKEND ADDRESS (REVNAT_ID) (SLOT)
172.18.0.4:30080/TCP (0)   0.0.0.0:0 (7) (0) [NodePort, dsr]
```

As a final note on DSR, you might recall that in Chapter 6 we introduced `externalTrafficPolicy: Local` as a way to preserve source IPs when services are accessed from outside the cluster. DSR achieves the same goal using a different mechanism. The key differences are:

- The `Local` external traffic policy is configured per service. It preserves the source IP by ensuring traffic is only routed to nodes that host a backend pod. Return traffic is sent via the host network stack.
- DSR is enabled at the cluster level in Cilium's configuration. It allows external traffic to be received by any node, even if it does not host a backend.

eXpress Data Path

The eXpress Data Path (XDP) feature allows for eBPF code to be executed in hardware directly on the physical network interface, processing packets before they even transit to the CPU and the kernel.

The main use cases for XDP are protection against distributed denial-of-service (DDoS) attacks and firewalling, since XDP enables packets to be dropped early with minimal overhead. XDP also supports load balancing and forwarding, including redirection to other network interfaces or CPU cores, and it can be used for pre-stack filtering, such as dropping unwanted protocols like UDP or Stream Control Transmission Protocol (SCTP) before they reach the kernel's networking stack.

Unlike user space frameworks such as Data Plane Development Kit (DPDK), XDP still works in cooperation with the kernel. This means you can offload the fast path to XDP while leaving the kernel to handle more complex processing, such as full TCP connection tracking or policy enforcement.

XDP applies only to packets that arrive through a physical network interface. Traffic between pods on the same node, for example, does not pass through the network interface controller (NIC) and will not benefit. However, for ingress traffic from external clients or LoadBalancer services, XDP can reduce per-packet latency and CPU usage by processing traffic earlier in the stack.

To enable XDP with Cilium, set `loadBalancer.acceleration=native`. This enables native XDP mode if supported by the NIC driver. Most modern drivers support XDP, but if the hardware does not, the setting may be ignored or fall back to a safer configuration. You can also use `best-effort` to allow automatic fallback.

XDP is not enabled by default because not all NIC drivers support native XDP mode. Enabling it unconditionally could lead to errors or degraded performance. Use `loadBalancer.acceleration=native` to enable XDP explicitly, or `best-effort` to allow fallback on unsupported hardware.

If you want to understand XDP in more detail, we recommend *Learning eBPF* by Liz Rice (O'Reilly), which offers a clear and accessible explanation of how XDP fits into the broader eBPF ecosystem.

Maglev Consistent Hashing

By default, Cilium load-balances service-bound traffic randomly across backends. This can be verified in a cluster with Cilium's default settings:

```
$ kubectl -n kube-system exec -it ds/cilium -- cilium-dbg status --verbose
[...]
  Backend Selection:       Random
```

The problem with this approach is that, if the node handling a connection fails, the next request may land on another node that has no knowledge of which backend pod was previously selected.

As a result, connection-oriented protocols like TCP may experience unexpected disruptions, because the backend selected by the new external node has no knowledge of the original connection and responds by rejecting it.

Figure 8-7 illustrates random load balancing:

1. A client connects to an external-facing node (Node 1).
2. Node 1 randomly selects a backend (for example, Node 3) and forwards the traffic.
3. If Node 1 fails, the client's next packet reaches a different external node (Node 2).
4. Node 2 also performs random load balancing and might select a different node (such as Node 4).
5. Node 4 has no state for the original connection and responds by resetting it.[3]

3 When a TCP packet reaches a backend pod that did not see the initial handshake, it has no session context and treats the packet as invalid. It responds with a TCP RST (reset), which instructs the client to immediately terminate the connection.

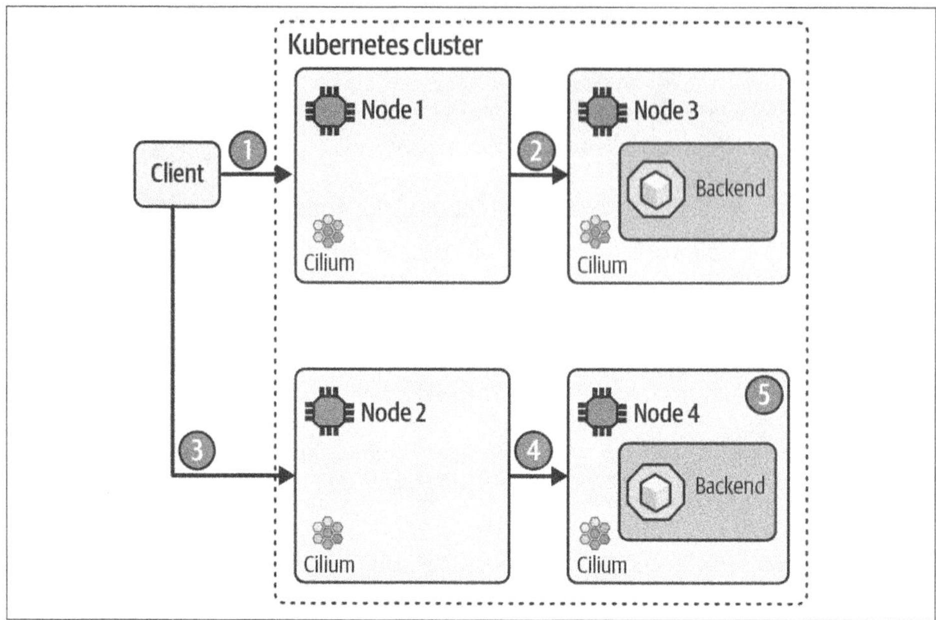

Figure 8-7. Random load balancing (default)

To address this, Maglev provides *consistent hashing*, ensuring that client connections identified by the same 5-tuple—source IP address, source port, destination IP address, destination port, and transport protocol—are routed to the same backend, regardless of which external node handles the request. This helps avoid connection drops during node failures or load balancer changes. Operators should consider enabling it when session stickiness and stability are critical, especially for TCP-based workloads.

Maglev,[4] originally created by Google, provides consistent hashing to minimize disruption during node or backend changes. Each load-balancing node hashes the packet's 5-tuple against a shared lookup table. As a result, all nodes independently arrive at the same backend selection without needing to share state.

This approach improves resilience and ensures stable load balancing, even as nodes or backends are added or removed. However, Maglev is not enabled by default in Cilium because it introduces a fixed-size lookup table and may slightly increase memory usage. Most users will not need it unless their workloads require strong session affinity or must gracefully handle node-level disruptions.

For a deeper dive, see the Maglev whitepaper (*https://oreil.ly/2OHvH*).

Figure 8-8 illustrates Maglev load balancing with Cilium:

1. A client connects to an external-facing node (Node 1).
2. Node 1 uses Maglev to deterministically select backend Node 3, based on the connection's 5-tuple.
3. If Node 1 fails, the client retries via Node 2.
4. Node 2 uses the same Maglev hash and also selects Node 3.
5. Node 3 continues handling the session without interruption.

4 The name "Maglev" refers to *magnetic levitation*, the technology used in high-speed trains such as the Japanese Shinkansen. The original paper described the load balancer as fast, highly available, and easily scalable, much like its namesake.

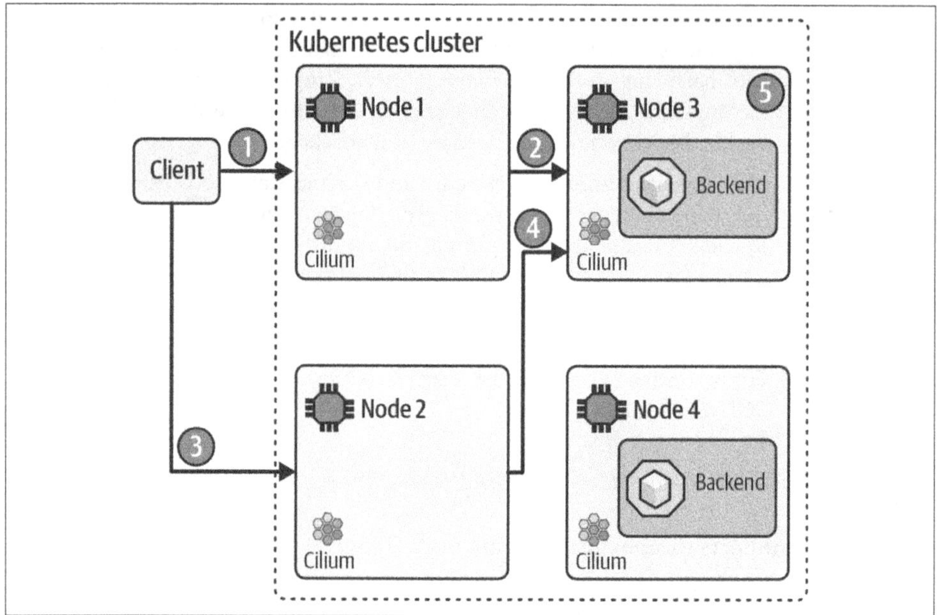

Figure 8-8. Maglev load balancing

All files discussed in this section are in the *chapter08/maglev* directory of the book's GitHub repository (*https://github.com/isovalent/cilium-up-and-running*).

To illustrate how Maglev load balancing using Cilium with BGP and DSR works in practice, we've provided a script (*setup-maglev.sh*) that automates the setup of a suitable environment. It builds a kind cluster with one control plane and four worker nodes. Two of the worker nodes are configured to act as external-facing BGP speakers, while the remaining two host backend workloads. The script also deploys and configures the BGP peer. The topology is illustrated in Figure 8-9.

The script installs Cilium with KPR enabled (a requirement for Maglev) and configured for native routing, DSR, and the Maglev load balancing algorithm:

```
kubeProxyReplacement: true
loadBalancer:
  mode: "dsr"
  algorithm: "maglev"
bgpControlPlane:
  enabled: true
```

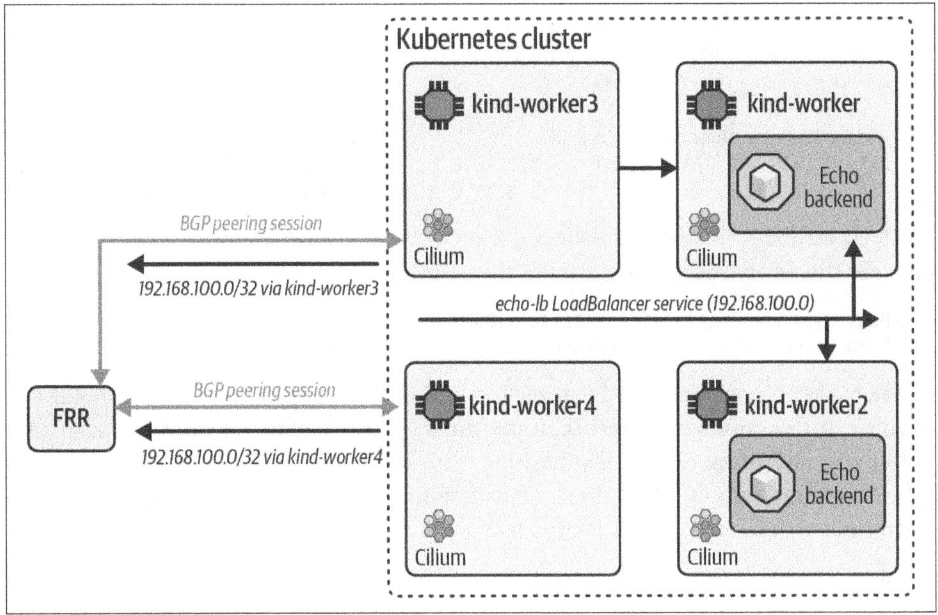

Figure 8-9. Maglev topology

To demonstrate Maglev behavior, the script deploys an echo server with two backend pods across the `kind-worker` and `kind-worker2` nodes. It also creates a LoadBalancer service with the IP `192.168.100.0`:

```
$ kubectl get deployment echo
NAME   READY   UP-TO-DATE   AVAILABLE   AGE
echo   2/2     2            2           94s

$ kubectl get svc echo-lb
NAME      TYPE           CLUSTER-IP     EXTERNAL-IP     PORT(S)          AGE
echo-lb   LoadBalancer   10.96.67.194   192.168.100.0   8080:31024/TCP   88s
```

When the cluster is ready, verify that Cilium is healthy with `cilium-dbg status` and that Maglev is chosen as the load balancing algorithm:

```
$ kubectl -n kube-system exec -it ds/cilium -- cilium-dbg status --verbose
KubeProxyReplacement Details:
[...]
  Backend Selection:      Maglev (Table Size: 16381)
```

BGP peering sessions should be established between the cluster and the BGP peers:

```
$ cilium bgp peers
Node           Peer         State         Uptime   Family         Recv   Adv
kind-worker3   172.18.0.8   established   28s      ipv4/unicast   0      1
kind-worker4   172.18.0.8   established   29s      ipv4/unicast   0      1
```

Access the FRRouting (FFR) device with `docker exec -it frr vtysh`, and then check the routing table to verify that the device has received the route to the service IP `192.168.100.0/32`:

```
75ea0285c9ea# show ip route bgp
B>* 192.168.100.0/32 [20/0] via 172.18.0.2, eth0, weight 1, 00:01:34
  *                         via 172.18.0.3, eth0, weight 1, 00:01:34
```

Next, access the FRR shell with `docker exec -it frr bash` and install `curl` with `apk add curl` to verify successful access to the service:

```
bash-5.1# curl http://192.168.100.0:8080
Request served by echo-f69bb6cf9-4sm72
```

In the backend's response, you can see the pod name (here, `echo-f69bb6cf9-4sm72`). If you run the same command multiple times, you will see responses coming from both pods, indicating *inconsistent* hashing. This is because the hashing is based on the 5-tuple, and by default, the source port will automatically change. You need to fix the source port, with a command like the following:

```
$ curl --local-port 6000 http://192.168.100.0:8080
```

If you repeat this command every minute or so, you will now see the same backend pod answering, confirming consistent hashing.

If you run the same command too quickly, you're likely to see an error message like `curl: (45) bind failed with errno 98: Address in use`. This happens because the source port specified with `--local-port` is still in use. The operating system prevents rebinding to the same local port too soon, to avoid ambiguity in connection tracking. This can be particularly problematic when trying to demonstrate connection consistency (e.g., with Maglev) where fixed source ports are required for deterministic load balancing behavior. A simple workaround is to introduce a delay (e.g., `sleep 5`) between connection attempts or cycle through a range of source ports.

The *simple-maglev-test.sh* script located in the book's GitHub repository verifies that Maglev consistently maps a given 5-tuple to the same backend pod across repeated requests. It sends traffic from the FRR client across 10 consecutive ports and prints the selected backends:

```
$ ./simple-maglev-test.sh
 Simple Maglev consistency test from FRR container
 Target: 192.168.100.0:8080
 Testing 10 requests with fixed source ports
 Testing Maglev consistency:
Format: SourcePort -> Backend

Port 60001 -> echo-f69bb6cf9-42hmc
Port 60002 -> echo-f69bb6cf9-42hmc
Port 60003 -> echo-f69bb6cf9-nscx5
Port 60004 -> echo-f69bb6cf9-nscx5
```

```
Port 60005 -> echo-f69bb6cf9-nscx5
Port 60006 -> echo-f69bb6cf9-nscx5
Port 60007 -> echo-f69bb6cf9-42hmc
Port 60008 -> echo-f69bb6cf9-42hmc
Port 60009 -> echo-f69bb6cf9-42hmc
Port 60010 -> echo-f69bb6cf9-nscx5

✅ Test complete!
```

If you repeat the same command (after waiting a few minutes, to avoid the port rebinding issue), it will generate another set of results. Compare these with the previous output. The result should be the same, confirming consistent hashing:

```
$ ./simple-maglev-test.sh
🌐 Simple Maglev consistency test from FRR container
📍 Target: 192.168.100.0:8080
🔄 Testing 10 requests with fixed source ports
OK: 136 MiB in 60 packages

📊 Testing Maglev consistency:
Format: SourcePort -> Backend

Port 60001 -> echo-f69bb6cf9-42hmc
Port 60002 -> echo-f69bb6cf9-42hmc
Port 60003 -> echo-f69bb6cf9-nscx5
Port 60004 -> echo-f69bb6cf9-nscx5
Port 60005 -> echo-f69bb6cf9-nscx5
Port 60006 -> echo-f69bb6cf9-nscx5
Port 60007 -> echo-f69bb6cf9-42hmc
Port 60008 -> echo-f69bb6cf9-42hmc
Port 60009 -> echo-f69bb6cf9-42hmc
Port 60010 -> echo-f69bb6cf9-nscx5

✅Test complete!
```

Netkit

Most CNI plugins attach a Kubernetes pod to its node by a virtual Ethernet (veth) pair. The pod's `eth0` interface sits in the pod network namespace and is paired with a peer in the host network namespace. This arrangement allows pods to reach other pods and external workloads through the host (refer back to Chapter 5 for a refresher on Linux and container networking primitives).

If you want to confirm the pairing, a single check from within a pod is enough:

```
netshoot-client:~# ip a show eth0
22: eth0@if23: <BROADCAST,MULTICAST,UP,LOWER_UP> mtu 65520 qdisc noqueue state UP
  group default qlen 1000
```

The `@if`*`N`* suffix indicates a veth peer. While veth pairs are widely adopted as the standard Linux container networking mechanism, the technology dates back over 15 years to Linux kernel 2.6.24 and carries several drawbacks. First, veth relies on layer 2 communication and uses ARP for a container to reach the peer end of the veth pair. This is unnecessary overhead: pods shouldn't need to perform ARP resolution to reach a directly connected peer.

More importantly, veth introduces performance costs. When traffic exits a pod or enters it from an external node, packets must traverse multiple layers: from the container's network stack to the host namespace, and then through the host's networking stack to the physical interface. This path includes transitions between namespaces and use of per-CPU backlog queues, all of which add latency and consume CPU cycles, especially under load.

Netkit was introduced to the Linux kernel in version 6.7 by Daniel Borkmann and Nikolay Aleksandrov. The idea is simple: move the eBPF hook points into the pod network namespace so decisions can be made earlier, then steer packets to their next hop without incurring the extra transitions typical of the veth path. For egress traffic, that can mean forwarding directly to the physical device, avoiding parts of the host stack such as the per-CPU backlog queue (Figure 8-10).

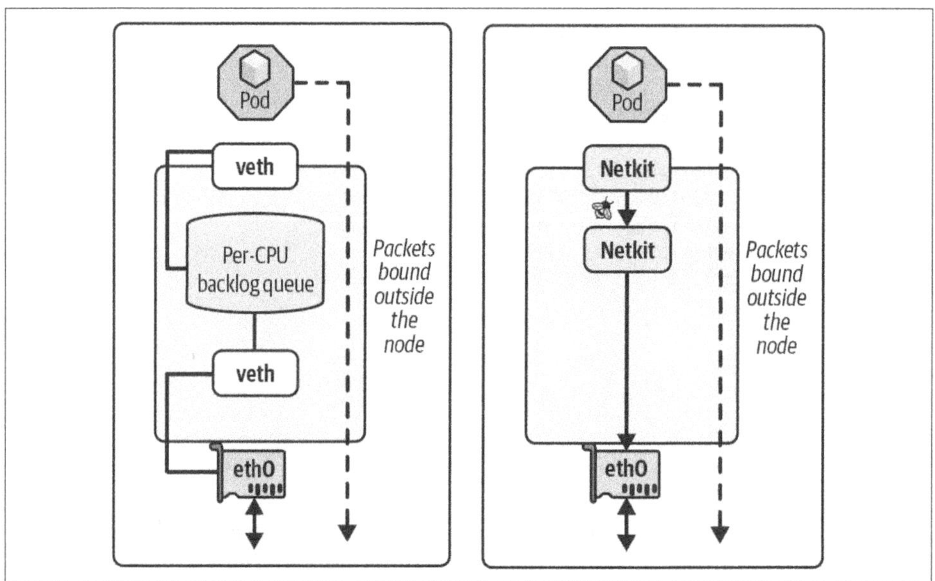

Figure 8-10. Veth versus netkit

In its initial implementation, netkit creates network devices as a pair: a primary device in the host namespace and a peer in the pod's namespace. BPF program management is handled solely by the primary device, preventing pods from modifying or removing attached programs. This design avoids conflicts between competing eBPF applications and ensures consistent control by Cilium.

Cilium integrates with netkit and can configure netkit devices in place of traditional veth pairs. By default, Cilium netkit operates at layer 3, which avoids ARP for local next-hop resolution. Layer 2 support is also available.

Early adopters have noticed significant performance improvements, with Bytedance experiencing a 10% improvement in throughput, as documented in a case study (*https://oreil.ly/RYVyn*).

For more information on netkit, consult Nico's Isovalent blog post (*https://oreil.ly/wh-p2*) and Jonathan Corbet's article "The BPF-Programmable Network Device" (*https://oreil.ly/n5wXk*) on LWN.net.

Summary

In this chapter, we explored several Cilium features designed to improve network performance across a variety of scenarios. We began with Service Traffic Distribution, which prioritizes sending traffic to local or nearby endpoints. We then looked at LRP, which keeps traffic node-local to avoid unnecessary latency and CPU overhead.

We introduced DSR as a way to preserve source IPs and optimize return-path performance and explored XDP for early packet processing at the driver level. We also discussed Maglev for consistent hashing and connection stability and netkit for removing the legacy veth bottleneck by moving eBPF logic closer to the application.

This chapter is not intended to be exhaustive. Cilium includes many other performance features that were not covered here, such as BIG TCP, BBR congestion control, advanced queue management, and integration with hardware acceleration. The aim was to provide a practical tour of some of the more widely used and impactful capabilities.

In the next chapter, we'll turn our attention to multicluster networking and explore how Cilium enables seamless connectivity and identity-aware policy enforcement across Kubernetes clusters.

CHAPTER 9

Multicluster Networking

As organizations grow, they often move beyond a single Kubernetes cluster. This jump from one to multiple environments presents a challenge for network security and observability.

Cilium's features are normally confined to the context of a single cluster. Identity is not represented across multiple clusters, so a policy to allow a pod in another cluster by its labels will not function, nor will observability features (see Chapter 15).

One solution is to treat the clusters as truly independent, exposing services using load balancer services, Ingress, or Gateway API (see Chapters 6 and 7) and treating the remote cluster as no different from any other external endpoint. If only a few well-defined services are shared between clusters this can work well, but as the environment grows more complex it becomes unsustainable, requiring encoding specific CIDR ranges for services in the remote cluster across policies using `toCIDRSet` (see Chapter 12), using Egress Gateway (see Chapter 11), or incorporating additional tools for observability.

Cilium Cluster Mesh exists to solve these problems. Meshed clusters share networking and identity information and avoid the need to expose services beyond the cluster altogether. In this chapter we will explore the use cases for Cluster Mesh and walk through how to configure and administrate meshed clusters. You can find all the YAML manifests you will need in the *chapter09* directory of the book's GitHub repository (*https://github.com/isovalent/cilium-up-and-running*).

Multicluster Kubernetes

Organizations deploy multiple Kubernetes clusters for many reasons. A few common ones include:

Organizational structure
: Organizations may find it easier to manage clusters inside the organizational units where they will be used (for example, a business unit or accounting cost center).

Resilience
: With on-premise deployments, deploying clusters at multiple sites enables business continuity in the case of a datacenter failure at one site and "stretching" clusters across multiple regions is complex and discouraged,[1] leading to multiple clusters instead.

Scale limitations
: Beyond a certain point (usually around the 10,000-node mark), Kubernetes itself hits limitations.

Multicloud setups
: This is often a regulatory mandate in industries such as finance or healthcare, to avoid becoming dependent on a single vendor.

Regardless of the rationale, workloads will still need to communicate between clusters. If the goal is redundancy, then services will need to be deployed across multiple clusters, and client workloads will need a way of communicating across cluster boundaries. As mentioned previously, the service discovery, security, and observability features we've discussed so far depend on context from the cluster and don't work outside of it. Users can treat these services as external, but this introduces significant operational complexity. Cilium Cluster Mesh offers a handy solution, extending those features across multiple clusters.

Note that when we talk about operating multiple clusters, we don't usually mean different environments where separate clusters are used to represent different stages of a deployment cycle (e.g., production, preproduction, staging, testing, and development). These environments are generally not interconnected.

1 As Josh Rosso et al. note in *Production Kubernetes* (O'Reilly), "The default settings in etcd are designed for the latency in a single datacenter...We strongly discourage the use of etcd clusters distributed across different regions."

What Cluster Mesh Solves

We first introduced Cluster Mesh back in Chapter 1. This feature extends Cilium's functionality in two specific ways:

Multicluster service discovery
: This change is transparent to applications, which can still use local cluster IP services as normal, with no change to how they interact with them. Cilium can perform advanced routing in the eBPF datapath, including preferring same-cluster endpoints if available but transparently failing over to endpoints in meshed clusters in the event of a local service failure.

Multicluster network policy
: Network policy can be applied across clusters, and a policy can be written to target the cluster's name as a security label. See Chapter 12 for an in-depth discussion of Cilium's network policies.

Cluster Mesh doesn't provide connectivity between clusters (you need to implement that yourself), and it doesn't handle routing packets between pods in different clusters beyond service discovery and encapsulation if using tunnel routing mode. We'll discuss this more when we talk about cluster requirements later in this chapter.

Use Cases

Let's consider an application hosted in a cluster in London, which must access a backend service replicated across two clusters in two different regions: Paris and Zurich. We'll explore a few possible solutions without using Cluster Mesh, and then compare them to a solution using Cluster Mesh.

The first option, shown in Figure 9-1, is to expose a LoadBalancer service (see Chapter 6) from each cluster and announce the routes over BGP to a BGP-capable network fabric (see Chapter 10). Using ExternalDNS (*https://oreil.ly/EIHcH*) and an internally hosted DNS server outside the cluster, a DNS name could be chosen for these services, such as `backend-service.example.com`, and the DNS server will then serve multiple `A` records for this domain name—one per cluster.

This approach is relatively simple. BGP support is ubiquitous in on-premises enterprise-grade networking hardware, and most cloud providers have similar implementations in their networks (for example, Amazon Network Load Balancers). Any of the provided IP addresses will successfully route to one of the backend services over the fabric.

However, this approach has several limitations. First and foremost, it depends on the clients correctly performing their own load balancing and failover. For some architectures this may be entirely acceptable, but often applications have an implicit assumption that there is a single IP address for a given destination. Improperly configured clients may simply select the first IP in the list when given multiple addresses and not correctly "fail over" to the other instances.

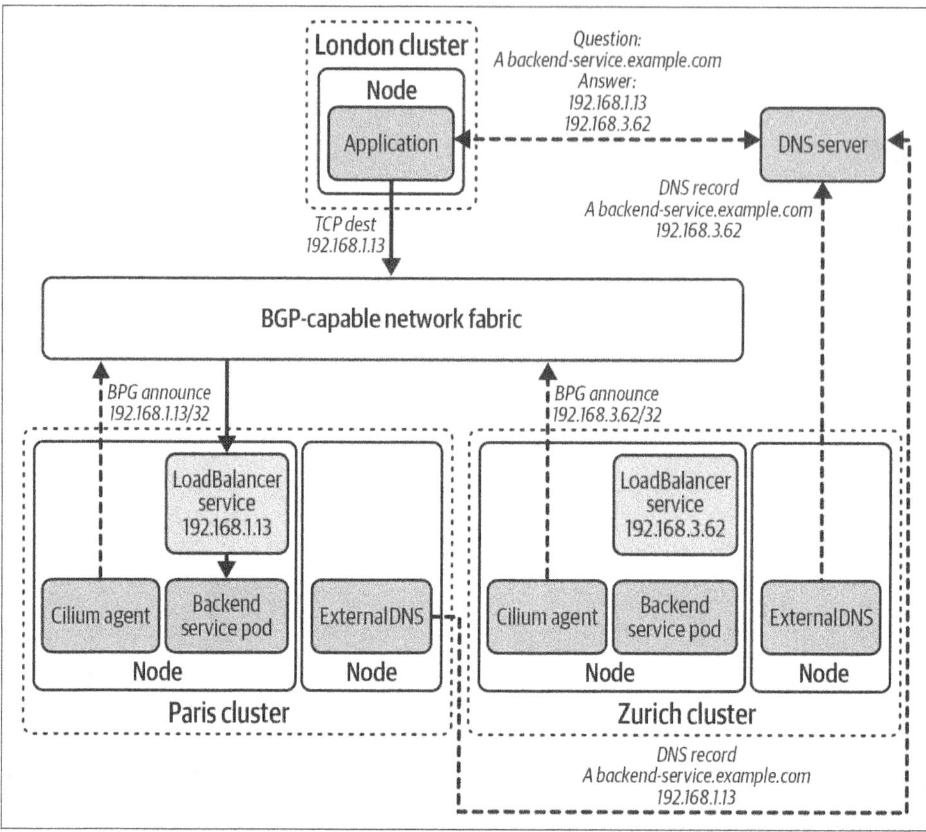

Figure 9-1. Multicluster services without Cluster Mesh using BGP with DNS and client-side load balancing

Another issue is that it's difficult to control traffic flow. For example, if administrators wish to remove a service or a cluster from operation for maintenance, they must remove the DNS records and wait for the DNS time-to-live (TTL) to expire to ensure that no clients with stale DNS records are still connected. Failing over long-lived HTTP connections, such as WebSockets, which do not refresh DNS once a long-lived TCP session is established, is not supported. It also requires management of multiple additional components, including a DNS server visible to the London cluster and ExternalDNS in the Paris and Zurich clusters.

If we wanted a single IP address for the distributed application instead, a traditional solution is to deploy an external load balancer appliance, as shown in Figure 9-2—often a physical device or hosted cloud service—and use that to map the IP to the different possible backends. These load balancers are not usually aware of the internals of the clusters, so the backends configured in the appliance must themselves be externally advertised Kubernetes LoadBalancer services.

Some load balancers are aware of Kubernetes internals and can resolve target IP addresses to pod IPs without using services, but this requires natively routed clusters. This approach is also possible using more advanced network fabrics with equal-cost multi-path (ECMP) routing.

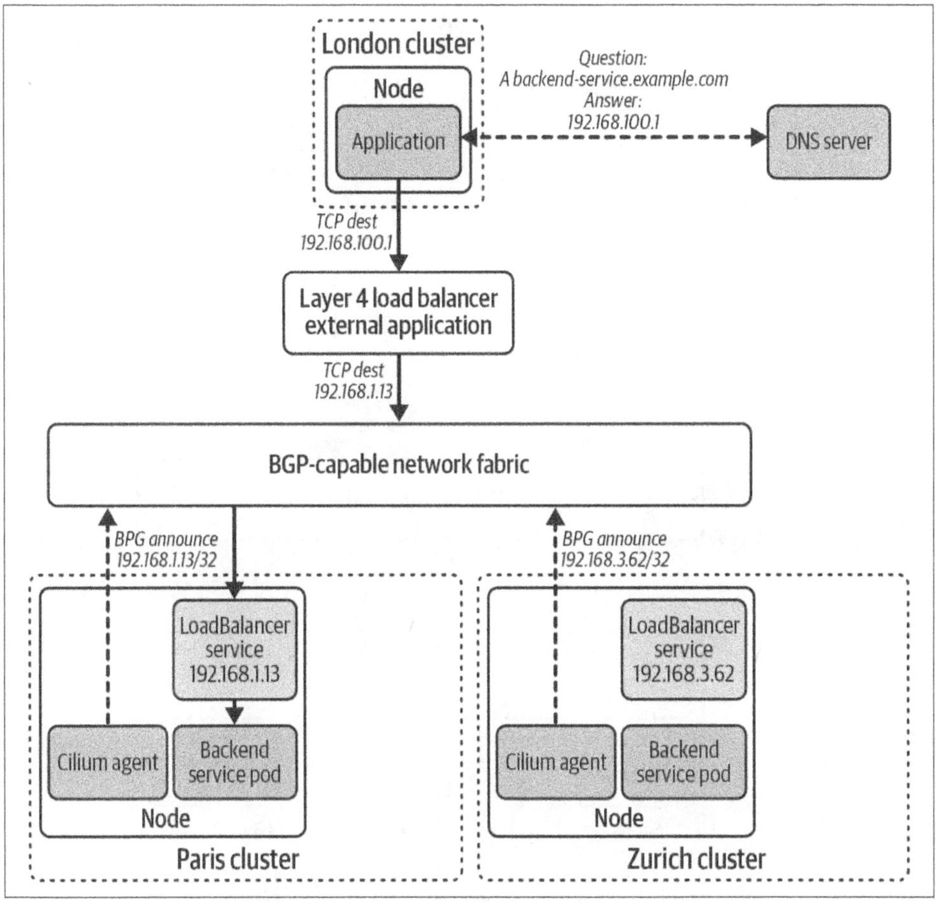

Figure 9-2. Multicluster services using an external load balancer appliance

This removes the responsibility for load-balancing decisions from the clients, as well as the need to use ExternalDNS, but it still requires deploying and configuring an external appliance. It also still requires using a DNS server, externally managing the mapping from IP address to DNS name for all clusters, and using a BGP-capable network fabric.

Now let's see how we can approach this problem using Cilium Cluster Mesh and global services. As shown in Figure 9-3, the external coordination of the IP address and service name are gone, and all the fabric needs to do is provide reachability. The application resolves the global service the same way as a local service, using a normal `<service>.<namespace>.svc` DNS record served by the in-cluster DNS service. The coordination to identify the remote cluster endpoints for the service and the resolution from the cluster IP service to a remote backend pod are handled entirely by Cilium.

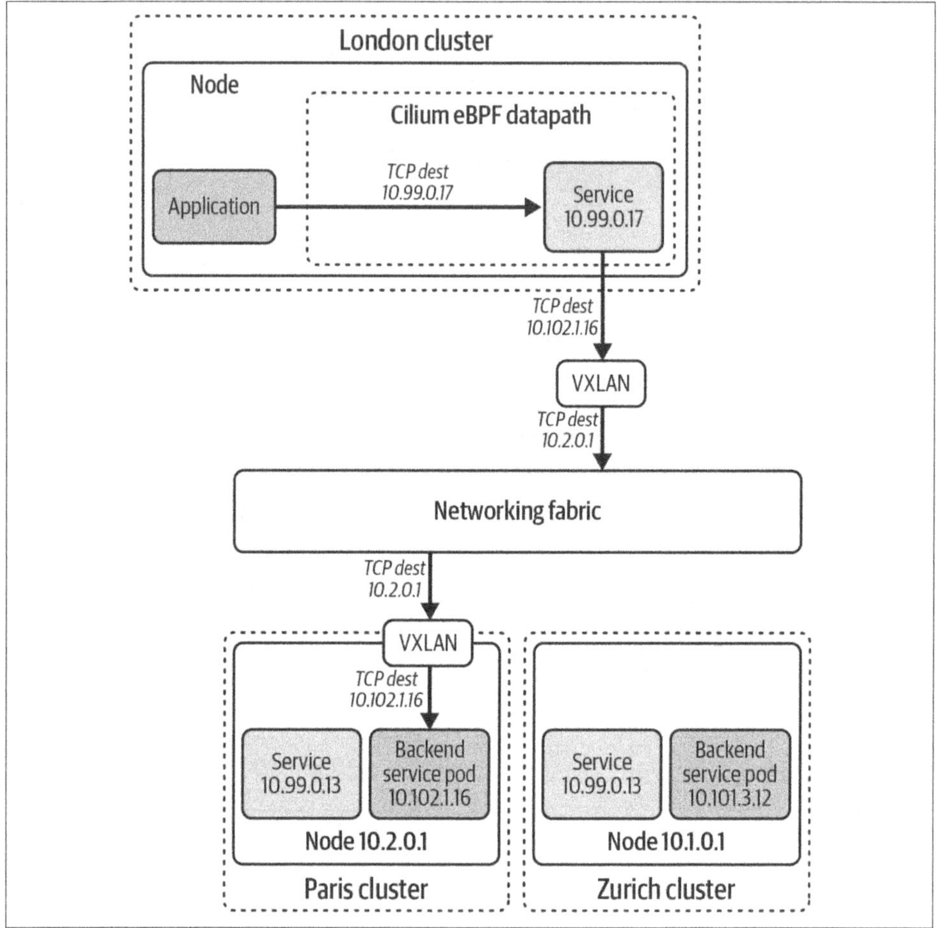

Figure 9-3. Multicluster services with Cluster Mesh and VXLAN tunneling

With this approach, we also require much less of the underlying fabric—only that all nodes (for overlay routing mode clusters) or all pods (for natively routed clusters) have layer 3 connectivity. We may still use BGP, for example to advertise pod IP ranges, and BGP LoadBalancer services may still be desired for services exposed outside of the mesh, but the hard requirements on the underlying network are significantly reduced using Cluster Mesh.

Cluster Mesh Architecture

Now that you have an idea of what Cluster Mesh offers, let's take a look at how it works. Cilium Cluster Mesh is designed to avoid a single point of failure. There is no coordinator cluster or centralized control plane. Instead, each cluster is aware of a path to each other cluster and is able to communicate with it directly.

Metadata is passed between clusters using a Cluster Mesh–specific component called the Cluster Mesh API Server. This pulls information about endpoints, identities, and other settings from the Kubernetes API of its local cluster and presents an API to remote clusters to use to retrieve that information.

Cluster Mesh also includes a component called KVStoreMesh[2] that serves a cache of remote cluster information to Cilium agents in the local cluster. Agents then use this information to understand remote cluster identities for policy and endpoints for routing decisions.

An overview of this design is shown in Figure 9-4. This architecture results in more overall connections[3] but means there are no single points of failure. Cluster Mesh can continue to operate even in complex failure modes where the mesh is disconnected into groups that still have connectivity between each other, without needing any kind of leader/follower or consensus-based coordination.

---

2 KVStoreMesh is enabled by default in Cilium v1.16+. It's possible to disable it, but we can't think of a good reason to do so.

3 $n(n - 1) / 2$ total connections across a mesh of n clusters.

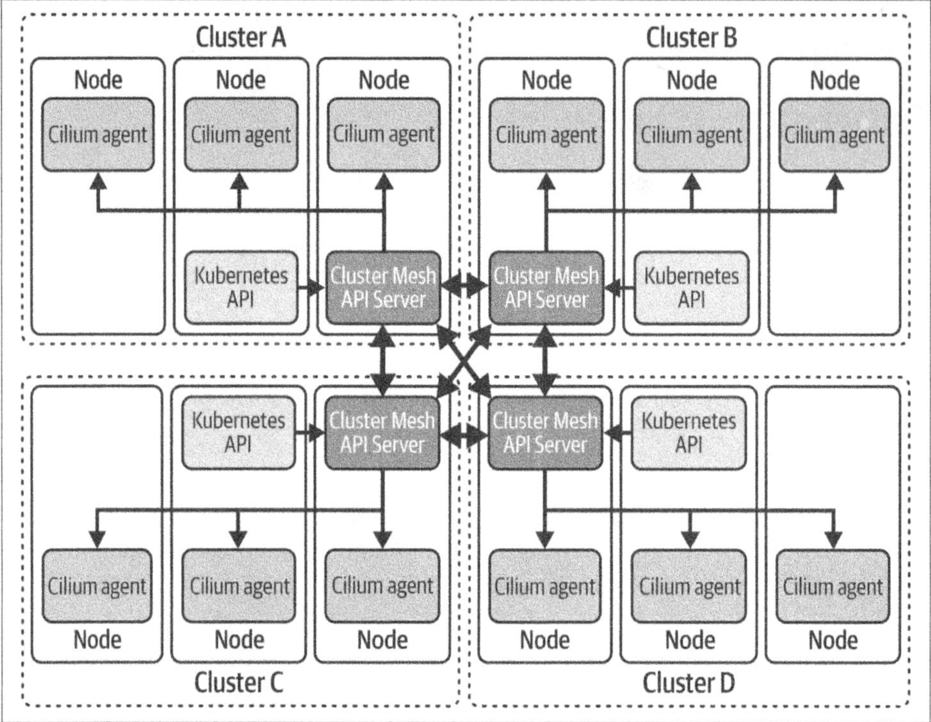

Figure 9-4. Metadata propagation in Cluster Mesh

Application Datapath

Application data does not flow through the Cluster Mesh API Server. Cilium Cluster Mesh requires that all nodes in all clusters in the mesh have IP connectivity to each other on the announced node IP addresses. Clusters do not have to share a layer 2 domain. A common way to accomplish this is by using tunnels, VPNs, or other networking setups between clusters. Since the implementation details are strongly dependent on the network environment, this chapter assumes this property of the underlying network without describing how to configure it.

For example, in Figure 9-5 each cluster has a `/16` CIDR block, each node is allocated a `/24` PodCIDR within that block, and all clusters use `10.0.0.0/8` as their native routing subnet.[4] In this example, all pods have layer 3 connectivity to all other pods,[5] and cluster C's cluster IP service range is `192.0.2.0/22`.

4 See Chapter 4 for a discussion of IPAM in Cilium.

5 This could be accomplished by announcing the pod IP ranges over BGP or various other mechanisms.

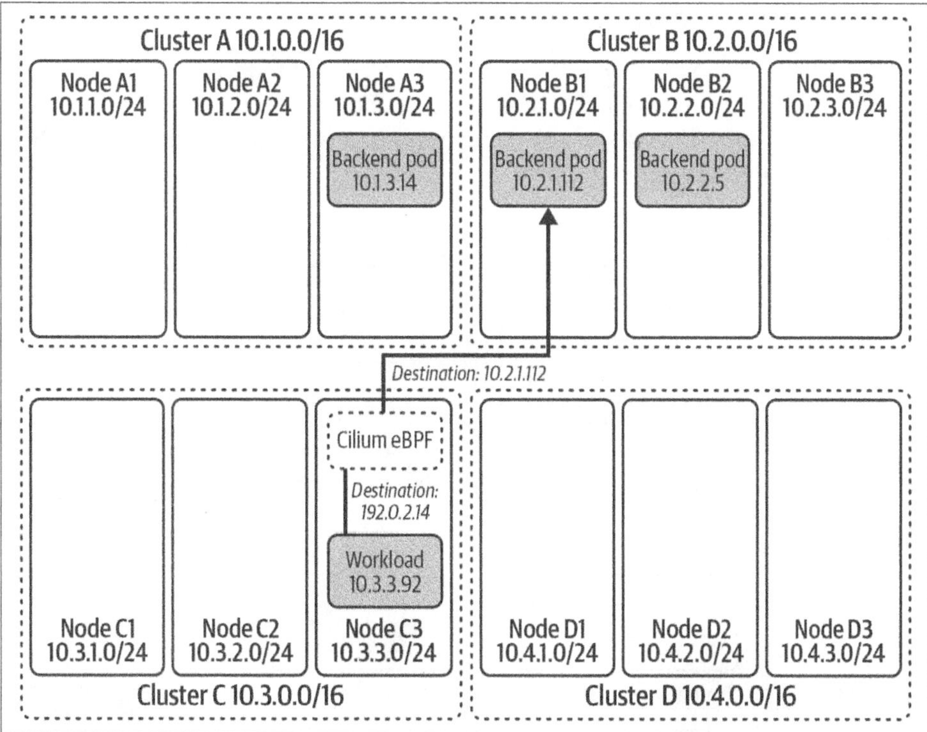

Figure 9-5. Datapath connectivity with a cluster IP service and native routing

If a workload pod on node C3 wishes to resolve a local service that is configured as a global service, backed by pods in other nodes, it will see no difference between that one and any other service. We'll explain how to configure a global service in "Global Services" on page 187.

There are three backends in two other clusters, so Cilium's eBPF cluster IP service resolution translates the destination IP to the destination pod's IP before sending it on. This is possible because the Cilium agent on node C3 is aware of the global nature of the service and, through the Cluster Mesh API Server, is aware of the service's backends in remote clusters.

If you enable the `kube-proxy` replacement (discussed in Chapter 6) for a cluster, then all services, including NodePort and LoadBalancer services, will work with global services. It doesn't have to be enabled for all clusters in the mesh; however, for clusters that don't have KPR enabled, cross-cluster service resolution will only work with ClusterIP services (since Cilium always uses eBPF for this type of service, whether KPR is enabled or not).

Cluster Mesh API Server

While often viewed as a single component, the Cluster Mesh API Server itself has several components deployed as a single pod, as shown in Figure 9-6. This diagram shows two Cluster Mesh API Server pods running in two different clusters and how metadata is propagated between them.

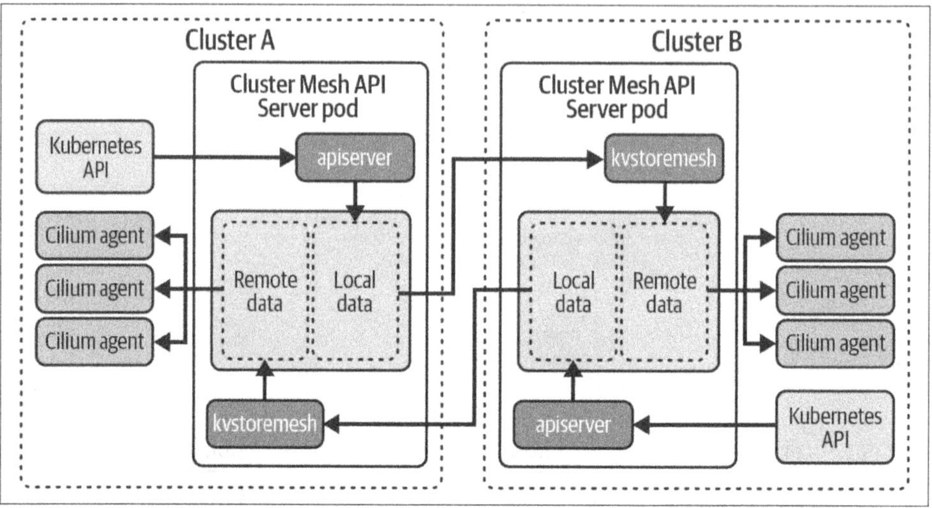

Figure 9-6. Cluster Mesh API Server internals and metadata propagation

The Cluster Mesh API Server runs as a container alongside an instance of etcd. This etcd is managed entirely by Cilium and is distinct from the etcd cluster that underpins the Kubernetes API. It runs in memory as a single instance with no replication, as it stores no canonical data; it serves only as a cache for data and an API surface. When clusters are meshed together, it's this etcd API that is exposed to other clusters.

The Cluster Mesh API Server reads local state from the local Kubernetes API and writes a copy into its local etcd. Remote Cluster Mesh API Servers can then connect to that etcd instance, read the data from there, and replicate it into their local etcd instances. Finally, local Cilium agents can read the state of remote endpoints propagated into the etcd instance and program the eBPF datapath accordingly.

Meshing Clusters

In this section, we'll step through an example of meshing three Kubernetes clusters. We'll be using kind in our example, but the general approach is the same with any cluster. Once we've established our mesh, we'll use it for the rest of this chapter to demonstrate Cluster Mesh features.

Preparing Clusters

There are a number of requirements for the clusters to be meshed:

- All the clusters have to be running Cilium as the CNI, although this can be in a chaining mode.
- All the clusters must have the same routing mode (encapsulation or native).
- The PodCIDR ranges cannot overlap.
- All nodes in all clusters must have layer 3 connectivity to each other. In native routing mode, this must be true of pods too.
- All clusters must use the same maximum mesh size, either 255 or 511 clusters. The default is 255, and using 511 enforces identity limitations.[6]

We'll also assume that all clusters are running the same version of Cilium. In a real environment, you should limit version skew between clusters in a mesh as much as possible. In general, as long as all clusters are within a minor version of each other it's considered a supported configuration. For example, a mesh of v1.15.8, v1.16.4, and v1.16.1 is acceptable, but a mesh of v1.15.8, v1.16.4, and v1.17.2 is not.

You'll also need to pick a domain name that will have each cluster as a subdomain, used for the TLS certificates that will identify the clusters. The default is `mesh.cilium.io`, but it's possible to use your own. You can set the domain name with the Helm value `clustermesh.config.domain`. It must be the same on every cluster in the mesh.

Finally, each cluster in the mesh will require a unique numeric ID and human-readable name. This is configured in Helm with `cluster.id` and `cluster.name`. For example, if the mesh domain name is `example.com` and the cluster's name is `test`, then the cluster's domain name for the mesh is `test.example.com`. This domain name doesn't have to resolve to anything via DNS; it is only referred to internally.

6 Allowing 511 clusters halves the number of possible identities per cluster from 65,535 to 32,767. Unless you're managing an extremely large estate, we recommend sticking with the default of 255.

In this chapter, we're going to mesh three clusters named `red`, `green`, and `blue`. Details on these clusters are given in Table 9-1.[7]

Table 9-1. Configuration details for our three test clusters

cluster.name	cluster.id	PodCIDR
red	1	10.1.0.0/16
green	2	10.2.0.0/16
blue	3	10.3.0.0/16

Use the provided kind configuration (*kind.yaml*) to deploy the three clusters. Make sure that they're correctly named, as we'll use the names later in the kind context:

```
for cluster in red green blue; do
  kind create cluster --config kind.yaml --name "$cluster"
done
```

Once the deployment is complete, you can access the clusters with `kubectl` using `--context kind-`*`name`*.

Configuring Cilium for Cluster Mesh

Before we can write our Cilium configuration, we need to know the IP addresses of the nodes. Normally you'd want to deploy a load balancer (discussed in Chapter 10) to provide a stable IP for the Cluster Mesh API Servers, but in this simple example we're going to make use of a NodePort service and set the communication IP to be the IP of the control-plane nodes. We'll get these IPs with a short script (*02-generate-cilium-config.sh*):

```
for cluster in red green blue; do
  echo "$cluster: $(kubectl --context "kind-$cluster" \
    get node "$cluster-control-plane" \
    -ojsonpath='{.status.addresses[?(@.type=="InternalIP")].address}')"
done
```

Running this will produce output like the following:

```
red: 10.89.0.14
green: 10.89.0.16
blue: 10.89.0.20
```

To deploy Cilium, we'll write a single Helm template values file (*cilium.template.yaml*) with all of the shared configuration options, then use Helm's `--set` syntax to configure the per-cluster flags differently for each cluster:

7 We've assigned each cluster a pod IP range that includes its cluster ID to make it easier for you to keep track of which IP addresses belong to each cluster. As long as each cluster has a unique ID and a unique nonoverlapping pod IP range, there is no requirement that there be any relation between the two.

```yaml
clustermesh:
  useAPIServer: true
  config:
    enabled: true
    clusters:
      - name: red
        port: 32379
        id: 1
        ips:
          - 10.89.0.14
      - name: green
        port: 32379
        ips:
          - 10.89.0.16
      - name: blue
        port: 32379
        ips:
          - 10.89.0.20
  apiserver:
    tls:
      authMode: cluster
      auto:
        enabled: true
        method: cronJob
        schedule: "0 0 1 */4 *"
```

We've enabled Cluster Mesh by setting `clustermesh.config.enabled=true`, enabled the Cluster Mesh API Server with `clustermesh.useAPIServer=true`, and configured each cluster in the mesh as an entry under `clustermesh.config.clusters`. We also specified the `cronJob` TLS generation method for TLS certificates, which we will explain in the next section.

While it's possible to mesh clusters *imperatively* using the Cilium CLI, and some documentation does so for illustrative purposes, it's almost always preferable to do so *declaratively* using Helm configuration.

The previous script generates a *cilium.yaml* file from this template automatically. Once we have that file, we can use Helm to install Cilium. For each cluster, we'll need to set the `cluster.id`, `cluster.name`, and `ipam.operator.clusterPoolIPv4CIDRList` Helm values using the information in Table 9-1. We can do this using a short bash script to address each cluster in turn (*03-deploy-cilium.sh*):

```bash
clusters=(red green blue)
for i in "${!clusters[@]}"; do
  name="${clusters[$i]}"
  id="$((i + 1))"
  helm upgrade --install \
    --kube-context "kind-$name" \
```

```
    cilium cilium/cilium \
    --namespace kube-system \
    --version "1.18.3" \
    --values cilium.yaml \
    --set "cluster.id=$id" \
    --set "cluster.name=$name" \
    --set "ipam.operator.clusterPoolIPv4PodCIDRList=10.$id.0.0/16"
done
```

After running this script, all the clusters should be active with Cilium running. However, the mesh will not be in a healthy state yet.

Propagating TLS Trust

The final step is to make the clusters trust each other. For now, although Cluster Mesh is configured, each cluster has a unique root of trust, and they will reject each other's access attempts. We can check this by looking at the Cluster Mesh status in one of the clusters (note that the Cilium CLI supports the `--context` flag to specify the cluster, just like `kubectl` does):

```
$ cilium --context kind-blue clustermesh status

⚠️ 3/3 nodes are not connected to all clusters [min:0 / avg:0.0 / max:0]

❌ cilium-pq95v is not connected to cluster green: remote cluster
configuration required but not found
💡 This is likely caused by KVStoreMesh not being connected to
the given cluster

💡 Run 'kubectl exec -it -n kube-system clustermesh-apiserver-79fbd6596f-gxv2w
-c kvstoremesh -- /usr/bin/clustermesh-apiserver kvstoremesh-dbg
troubleshoot green' to investigate the cause
```

We've shortened the output here, but we can see that our `blue` cluster is unable to access either of the others. Helpfully, the output gives us an additional debugging command to try. After running it, we get this output, again shortened for clarity:

```
Cluster "green":

🔌 Endpoints:
   - https://green.mesh.cilium.io:32379
     ✅ Hostname resolved to: 10.89.0.16
     ✅ TCP connection successfully established to 10.89.0.16:32379
     ❌Cannot establish TLS connection to green.mesh.cilium.io:32379:
tls: failed to verify certificate: x509: certificate signed by unknown
authority (possibly because of "crypto/rsa: verification error" while
trying to verify candidate authority certificate "Cilium CA")
```

The TLS certificate for the remote cluster is not being accepted. We'll discuss models of distributing trust in "TLS Certificates in Cluster Mesh" on page 196, but for now we're going to make each cluster trust every other cluster.

Recall that when we installed Cilium, we specified the `cronJob` method of certificate generation. This caused Cilium to automatically generate a certificate authority when it was first installed, but it doesn't regenerate the CA if it's reinstalled using `helm upgrade`.

To fix this issue, download the generated CA certificates for each cluster and combine them into a single trust bundle using the following script (*04-write-ca-bundle.sh*):

```
ca_bundle="ca-bundle.crt"
rm -f "$ca_bundle"
for name in red green blue; do
  kubectl \
  --context "kind-$name" \
  --namespace kube-system \
  get secret \
  cilium-ca \
  -o jsonpath="{.data['ca\.crt']}" | base64 --decode >> "$ca_bundle"
done
```

Then append them to the Cilium configuration as a shared trust bundle:

```
$ yq -i \
    ".tls.caBundle.content=\"$(cat ca-bundle.crt)\", \
    .tls.caBundle.enabled=true" \
    cilium.yaml
```

Versions of Cilium prior to v1.18.5 require an additional step to make this method of TLS distribution work, due to a bug. You can find the necessary script in the book's GitHub repository (*chapter09/05-patch-sever-cert.sh*).

Reapply the Cilium configuration using the same `helm` command we used in the script at the end of the previous section and restart the Cluster Mesh API Server to pick up the new settings:

```
for name in red green blue; do
  kubectl rollout restart \
  --context "kind-$name" \
  --namespace kube-system \
  deploy/clustermesh-apiserver
done
```

We can then confirm that Cluster Mesh is healthy using the same command as before:

```
$ cilium --context kind-blue clustermesh status

✅ All 3 nodes are connected to all clusters [min:2 / avg:2.0 / max:2]
✅ All 1 KVStoreMesh replicas are connected to all clusters [min:2 / avg:2.0 /
max:2]
```

```
🔌 Cluster Connections:
  - green: 3/3 configured, 3/3 connected - KVStoreMesh: 1/1 configured, 1/1
connected
  - red: 3/3 configured, 3/3 connected - KVStoreMesh: 1/1 configured, 1/1
connected
```

With our clusters meshed, nothing changes at first. All clusters continue to operate as they were before—but this set of changes enables us to use Cluster Mesh's features.

Testing Cluster Mesh

We can use Cilium's built-in connectivity test to verify Cluster Mesh behavior between any two clusters in our mesh (here, the `red` and `green` clusters):

```
$ cilium connectivity test --context kind-red --multi-cluster kind-green
```

The `--context` and `--multi-cluster` flags both take Kubernetes context names, like the `--context` and `--kube-context` flags in previous commands, not cluster names as configured in Helm as `cluster.name`.

One of the tests performed by `cilium connectivity test` verifies that no errors exist in the Cilium logs. If you've been following this chapter verbatim, there will be errors from when we first set up Cluster Mesh without the shared certificate authorities. You can run the test anyway to verify that there are no other errors, or you can skip that test with the extra flag `--test '!check-log-errors/no-errors-in-logs'`.

These tests only test connectivity between a given pair of clusters. You can iterate through every pair using this script (*06-connectivity-test.sh*):

```
clusters=(red green blue)
for i in "${!clusters[@]}"; do
  for j in "${!clusters[@]}"; do
    if [ "$j" -gt "$i" ]; then
      cluster_a="${clusters[$i]}"
      cluster_b="${clusters[$j]}"
      echo "Testing $cluster_a and $cluster_b"
      cilium connectivity test \
        --context "kind-$cluster_a" \
        --multi-cluster "kind-$cluster_b" \
        --test '!check-log-errors/no-errors-in-logs'
    fi
  done
done
```

The script runs for each pair of clusters in the `clusters` array, meaning $n(n - 1) / 2$ tests, where each test can take several minutes. We don't recommend this approach for larger meshes, as it will take a long time.

Global Services

Now that we have our meshed clusters configured, we can begin to use Cilium's features across the mesh. The first feature we'll look at is cross-cluster services. In Kubernetes, a service is a networking abstraction over a group of backend pods, providing a stable network identity in an environment where pods may be created, removed, or replaced at any moment. Using a *global service*, we can accomplish the same service indirection for backends in other clusters in the mesh.

Configuring Global Services

Cilium implements cluster IP services using the eBPF datapath. Figure 9-7 provides an overview of this process (see Chapter 6 for details). The translation from a service IP to a backend pod IP occurs in eBPF as the packet exits the pod.

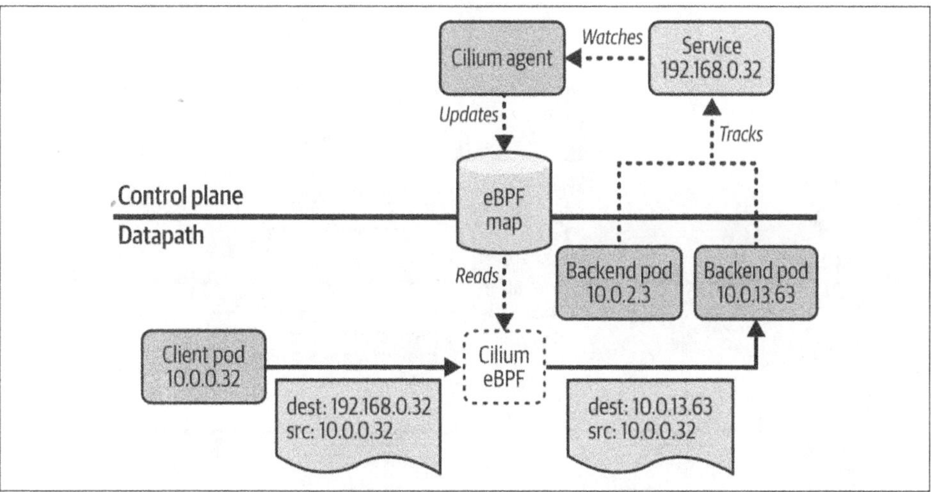

Figure 9-7. A typical Kubernetes cluster IP service in Cilium

By creating two services with the same name and namespace in two different clusters and annotating them with `service.cilium.io/global: "true"`,[8] we can make Cilium import information about endpoints in other clusters across the mesh. Cilium's eBPF datapath can then select the endpoints in other clusters the same way as local ones.

8 This is an annotation, not a label.

The quotes around `"true"` are required. If you put `service.cilium.io/global: true` in your YAML without quotes, this will be interpreted as a string key to a Boolean value, and Kubernetes expects annotations to be a map of strings to strings, not strings to Booleans. If you try it, you'll get an error like `json: cannot unmarshal bool into Go struct field ObjectMeta.metadata.annotations of type string`.

It's important to note that the services only need to have the same name and namespace in each cluster. It doesn't matter if the cluster IP service range isn't the same, and the two services will not synchronize their service IPs. In Figure 9-8 you can see the two services have different IPs in the two clusters, but both clusters can view all endpoints in either cluster. This is an important consequence of the decentralized design of Cluster Mesh: there is no single canonical view of a service across all clusters; it only ensures that global services in different clusters can use each other's endpoints.

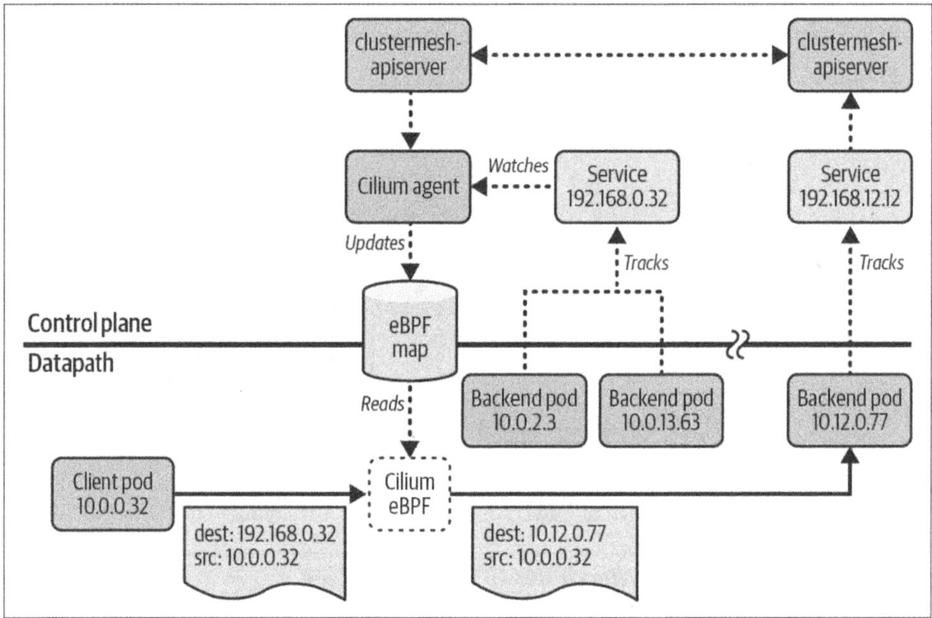

Figure 9-8. A global service across meshed clusters

Let's configure a service in our example clusters to show this feature in action. We'll deploy a service to every cluster that responds with the current node name. Because our nodes are named after the clusters, we can use this to understand which cluster the response is coming from. Here's the service portion of the manifest (*global-service.yaml*):

```
apiVersion: v1
kind: Service
metadata:
  name: nginx
  annotations:
    service.cilium.io/global: "true"
spec:
  selector:
    app.kubernetes.io/name: nginx
  ports:
  - port: 80
    targetPort: 8080
    protocol: TCP
```

Using a short script (*07-deploy-global-service.sh*), we can quickly apply it to all of our clusters:

```
for cluster in red green blue; do
  kubectl apply \
    --context "kind-$cluster" \
    --filename global-service.yaml
done
```

Then we can test the service's behavior with a test pod:

```
$ kubectl run test \
    --context kind-green -it --rm \
    --image nicolaka/netshoot -- bash

test:~# curl nginx
<html><body><p>Hello from blue-worker</p></body></html>

test:~# curl nginx
<html><body><p>Hello from red-worker</p></body></html>

test:~# curl nginx
<html><body><p>Hello from blue-worker</p></body></html>

test:~# curl nginx
<html><body><p>Hello from red-worker</p></body></html>

test:~# curl nginx
<html><body><p>Hello from blue-worker</p></body></html>

test:~# curl nginx
<html><body><p>Hello from blue-worker</p></body></html>

test:~# curl nginx
<html><body><p>Hello from green-worker2</p></body></html>

test:~# curl nginx
<html><body><p>Hello from red-worker</p></body></html>
```

We can see that we're getting a random backend responding each time since Cilium balances our requests across the possible backends of the global service.

Endpoint Affinity

At the moment, our global service allows routing from a source in any of the configured clusters to an endpoint in any other cluster, and the flow is chosen randomly for each connection. We can, however, use other annotations to control the preference between local and remote endpoints. This is useful when you'd prefer to use a local version of a service but want to transparently fail over to a remote copy when the local version isn't available. This sort of affinity is shown in Figure 9-9.

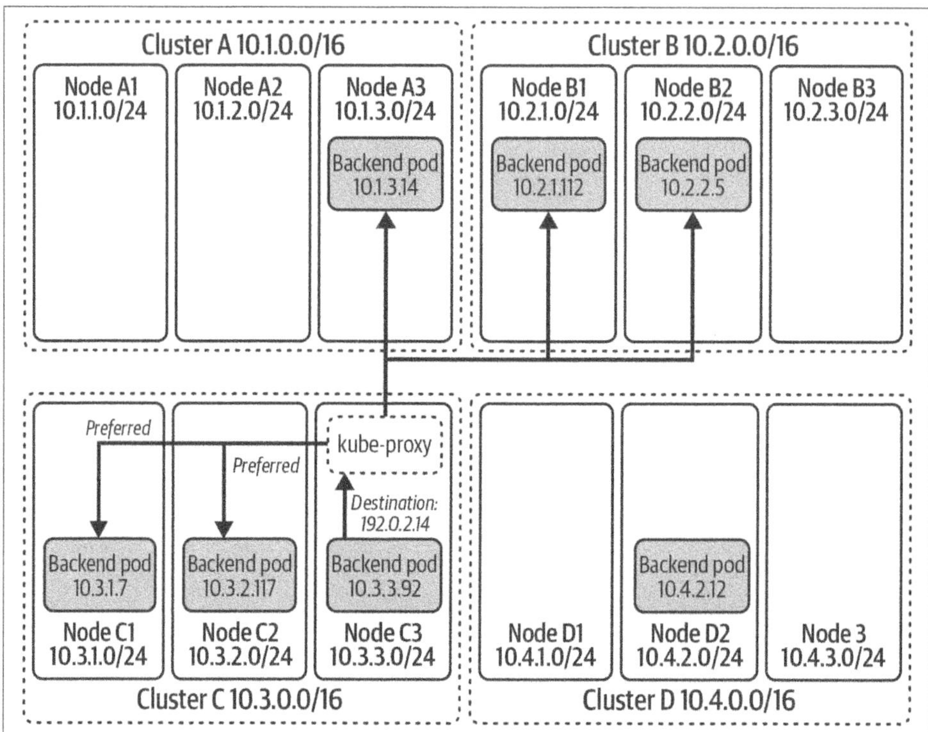

Figure 9-9. Local service affinity for a global service

This kind of cross-region transparent failover can lead to issues in some cases. Cilium will dutifully fail over to remote endpoints, but if the remote clusters have a much higher latency, and the workloads cannot handle higher latencies from cross-cluster traffic, then such a failover can contribute to cascading failures.

It's impossible to predict this in isolation, so you should always perform regular tests of failover mechanisms—including Cluster Mesh—in non-production environments to test how your application and particular networking and cluster setup will behave during a cross-region failover.

To show endpoint affinity in action, let's start by annotating one of our services to use local affinity. We'll use the one in the `green` cluster as an example:

```
$ kubectl \
    --context kind-green \
    annotate service nginx \
    'service.cilium.io/affinity=local'
service/nginx annotated
```

Using the same test pod as before, we can see the change in behavior:

```
$ kubectl run test --context kind-green -it --rm \
    --image nicolaka/netshoot -- bash

test:~# curl nginx
<html><body><p>Hello from green-worker</p></body></html>

test:~# curl nginx
<html><body><p>Hello from green-worker</p></body></html>

test:~# curl nginx
<html><body><p>Hello from green-worker</p></body></html>
```

The endpoint in the local cluster now always responds. If we remove that backend pod, however, the service will still use remote endpoints:

```
$ kubectl \
    --context kind-green \
    scale deployment nginx \
    --replicas=0
deployment.apps/nginx scaled
```

Pods don't need to be restarted to pick up this change, as it's performed in the eBPF datapath. We're only showing the test pod being launched every time for clarity. You can leave a single test pod running during all of this configuration if you prefer.

Let's see what happens when we run our test now:

```
$ kubectl run test \
    --context kind-green \
    -it \
    --rm \
    --image nicolaka/netshoot \
    -- bash

test:~# curl nginx
<html><body><p>Hello from blue-worker2</p></body></html>

test:~# curl nginx
<html><body><p>Hello from red-worker2</p></body></html>

test:~# curl nginx
<html><body><p>Hello from blue-worker2</p></body></html>
```

Once again, a random backend responds to each request.

Note that service affinity only affects the cluster in which it's set on the service. For example, if we repeat the same test on the `blue` cluster, it won't show service affinity:

```
$ kubectl \
    --context kind-green \
    scale deployment nginx \
    --replicas=1
deployment.apps/nginx scaled

$ kubectl run test \
    --context kind-blue \
    -it \
    --rm \
    --image nicolaka/netshoot -- bash

test:~# curl nginx
<html><body><p>Hello from green-worker2</p></body></html>

test:~# curl nginx
<html><body><p>Hello from green-worker2</p></body></html>

test:~# curl nginx
<html><body><p>Hello from red-worker2</p></body></html>

test:~# curl nginx
<html><body><p>Hello from blue-worker2</p></body></html>
```

This is a consequence of Cluster Mesh's distributed design. Because there is no global coordinated view of a service—only services that can communicate with each other across the mesh—the settings that affect routing behavior are local to the cluster using that service.

Global Policy

Cilium's network policy engine (discussed in Chapter 12) assigns every endpoint an *identity*. Identities for pods derive their labels from the pod's labels, which means that you can write a network policy to target other pods by their labels—for example, allowing only pods with `role: backend` to access a database.

These identities are also shared across the mesh, meaning that a network policy can select endpoints from other clusters using the same `fromEndpoints` and `toEndpoints` statements used for local policy.

Without Cluster Mesh, when services are exposed to other clusters using load balancers of some kind (see "Use Cases" on page 173), egress policy is possible—if error prone—by applying policy to the CIDR ranges corresponding to services exposed in other clusters or by using FQDN policy (see Chapter 13). Ingress policy is much harder, since traffic from an unmeshed external cluster will use the same IP range for all nodes (and for pods, for a natively routed cluster), so different workloads cannot be differentiated. The only mechanism at layer 3 is to use Cilium's Egress Gateway (discussed in Chapter 11) to assign external IP addresses for egress traffic that are then used as part of `fromCIDR` statements in the other cluster.

All of these approaches are error prone and add complexity. Using Cluster Mesh, we can rely on Cilium to automatically share endpoint identity information between clusters and write policy in largely the same way as we do with one cluster.

This behavior changed in Cilium v1.19. In Cilium v1.18, which we're using here, and in earlier versions, Cilium policy automatically selected endpoints from any cluster in the mesh unless the cluster name was specified. From Cilium v1.19, policy only selects endpoints from the *local* cluster by default.

Much like with services, while Cluster Mesh allows policy in meshed clusters to refer to endpoints in other clusters using security labels, it does not automatically synchronize policy. For example, a `CiliumClusterwideNetworkPolicy` with an `endpointSelector` set to select all endpoints will apply only to endpoints in the cluster in which it is installed.

We can use our existing `red`, `green`, and `blue` clusters as an example. The `red` cluster will contain our client application, while the `green` and `blue` clusters will contain copies of the server. We already have a global service and backend pods deployed in each, so we'll reuse that deployment here. It's important to keep the global service in the `red` cluster, but we want to remove the pods that could be a part of it locally:

```
$ kubectl delete --context kind-red deployment nginx
deployment.apps "nginx" deleted
```

We see the result of this in Figure 9-10, where the `red` cluster does not have any backends for the `nginx` service but can still refer to the remote endpoints in the `green` and `blue` clusters.

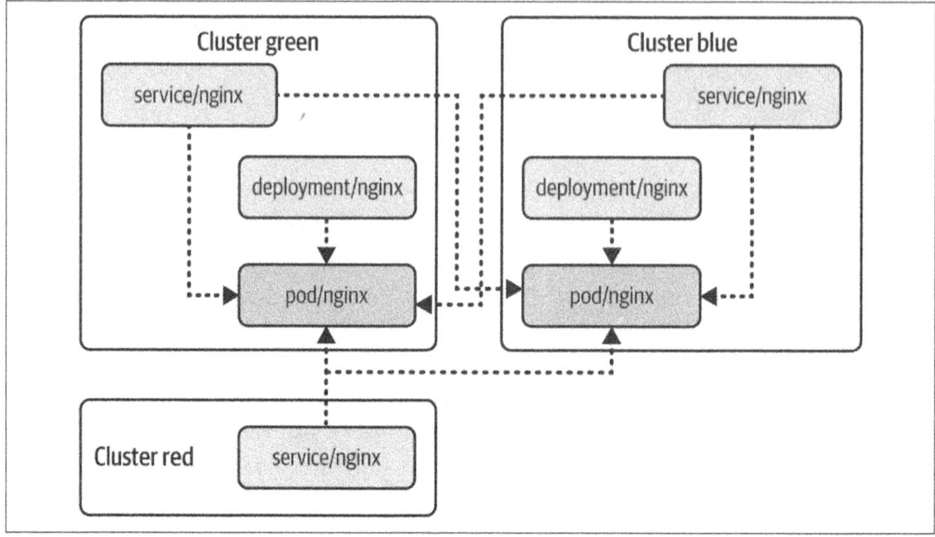

Figure 9-10. Global services where the `red` cluster only has remote endpoints

We'll secure the NGINX pods on the `blue` and `green` clusters first (*nginx-policy.yaml*), using the identity label `io.cilium.k8s.policy.cluster` to refer to endpoints specifically in other clusters:

```
apiVersion: "cilium.io/v2"
kind: CiliumNetworkPolicy
metadata:
  name: nginx
spec:
  endpointSelector:
    matchLabels:
      app.kubernetes.io/name: nginx
  ingress:
  - fromEndpoints:
    - matchLabels:
        app.kubernetes.io/name: frontend
        io.cilium.k8s.policy.cluster: red
    toPorts:
    - ports:
      - port: "8080"
        protocol: TCP
```

We need to apply this policy only to the `blue` and `green` clusters, as the `red` cluster has no NGINX pods anymore:

```
$ kubectl apply --context kind-blue --filename nginx-policy.yaml
ciliumnetworkpolicy.cilium.io/nginx created

$ kubectl apply --context kind-green --filename nginx-policy.yaml
ciliumnetworkpolicy.cilium.io/nginx created
```

We can then apply the egress policy (*frontend-policy.yaml*) in the `red` cluster and select our test pod by specifying the required label `app.kubernetes.io/name: frontend`:

```
apiVersion: "cilium.io/v2"
kind: CiliumNetworkPolicy
metadata:
  name: frontend
spec:
  endpointSelector:
    matchLabels:
      app.kubernetes.io/name: frontend
  egress:
  - toEndpoints:
    - matchLabels:
        "k8s:io.kubernetes.pod.namespace": kube-system
        "k8s:k8s-app": kube-dns
    toPorts:
    - ports:
      - port: "53"
        protocol: ANY
      rules:
        dns:
        - matchPattern: "nginx.default.svc.cluster.local."
  - toEndpoints:
    - matchLabels:
        app.kubernetes.io/name: nginx
      matchExpressions:
      - key: io.cilium.k8s.policy.cluster
        operator: In
        values:
        - green
        - blue
    toPorts:
    - ports:
      - port: "8080"
        protocol: TCP
```

The details of this policy are covered in Chapter 12, but it constrains the egress traffic of pods with the `app.kubernetes.io/name: frontend` label in the clusters where it is applied. Egress traffic has to match one of two egress rules to be permitted: either DNS requests to CoreDNS for the NGINX service, or port 8080 TCP connections to NGINX backends in the green or blue clusters. After applying this policy we can again test it with our test pod, noting that we have to add the frontend label:

```
$ kubectl apply --context kind-red --filename frontend-policy.yaml
ciliumnetworkpolicy.cilium.io/frontend created

$ kubectl run test --context kind-red \
  -it --rm --image nicolaka/netshoot \
  --labels 'app.kubernetes.io/name=frontend' -- bash

test:~# curl nginx
<html><body><p>Hello from blue-worker2</p></body></html>

test:~# curl nginx
<html><body><p>Hello from blue-worker2</p></body></html>

test:~# curl nginx
<html><body><p>Hello from green-worker2</p></body></html>
```

Using a different pod, we can test the permissions. If we relaunch our test pod without the app.kubernetes.io/name label we can verify that the ingress permissions are working:

```
$ kubectl run test --context kind-red -it --rm \
    --image nicolaka/netshoot -- bash

test:~# curl nginx -m2
curl: (28) Connection timed out after 2002 milliseconds
```

This use of cross-cluster policy allows applications to apply the same fine-grained security controls as they can in-cluster. Finally, we'll tear down the environment by deleting the clusters:

```
for cluster in red green blue; do
  kind delete cluster --name "$cluster"
done
```

TLS Certificates in Cluster Mesh

The internals of Cluster Mesh use TLS certificates to secure components as they communicate. These not only encrypt the metadata of the cluster as it is in transit, but also prevent attackers from pulling metadata from a cluster with Cluster Mesh enabled or imitating another cluster in the mesh.

Figure 9-11 illustrates our previous example, in which each cluster autogenerated a self-signed certificate authority and used that to sign the various certificates for internal usage. When we needed to mesh clusters, we distributed the certificate authorities between clusters to allow the remote connections to trust each other.

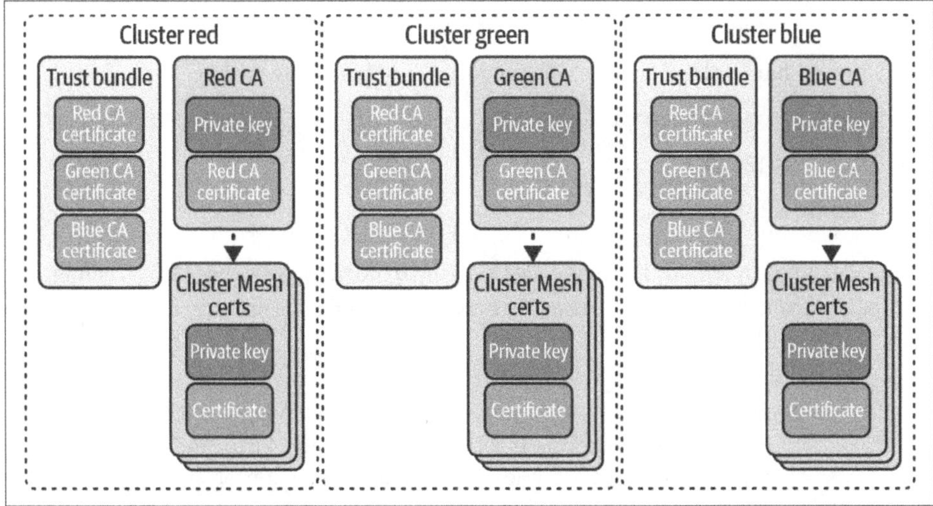

Figure 9-11. Shared CA bundle setup

Each cluster has its own CA to sign certificates. With Cluster Mesh enabled, each cluster will trust certificates signed by any of the CAs in the trust bundle.

While we avoided transferring private key material, this isn't a very sustainable option. Any time we needed to add a new cluster, or change the CA on a cluster, we'd have to update the trust bundles on every other cluster in the mesh. A better approach is to use a single certificate authority.

There are four certificates used in Cluster Mesh, stored as Kubernetes secrets. One of them is a server certificate, and the other three are client certificates. The client certificates have a common name derived from the cluster's defined name (see Table 9-2).

Table 9-2. Cluster Mesh client certificates

Certificate	Common name	Purpose
`clustermesh-apiserver-admin-cert`	`admin-${cluster.name}`	The Cluster Mesh API Server presents this to its sidecar etcd.
`clustermesh-apiserver-remote-cert`	`remote-${cluster.name}`	The Cluster Mesh API Server presents this to other etcd instances in remote clusters.
`clustermesh-apiserver-local-cert`	`local-${cluster.name}`	Cilium agents present this to their local Cluster Mesh API Server's etcd.

The server certificate is stored in the secret `clustermesh-apiserver-server-cert` and is served by etcd from connections using all of the client certificates. This server TLS certificate needs to, between its common name and Subject Alternative Names, be signed for:

- Domain name `${cluster.name}.${clustermesh.config.domain}`
- Domain name `clustermesh-apiserver.${cilium-namespace}.svc`
- Domain name `localhost`
- IP address `127.0.0.1`
- IP address `::1`

where `cluster.name` and `clustermesh.config.domain` are the Helm values set for that cluster, and `cilium-namespace` is the Kubernetes namespace Cilium was installed in for that cluster.

If not using IPv6, the certificate does not need to be signed for `::1`. It's harmless to include it if IPv6 is not enabled, but omitting it in a dual-stack cluster can lead to difficult-to-debug problems where Cluster Mesh functioning depends on whether IPv4 or IPv6 is used. Therefore, we recommend including it even in certificates intended for IPv4-only clusters, to make any future IPv6 migration easier. See Chapter 4 for more on dual-stack configuration.

Figure 9-12 illustrates how the Cilium agent and the Cluster Mesh API server authenticate and communicate using the four certificates described in the text (one server certificate and three client certificates).

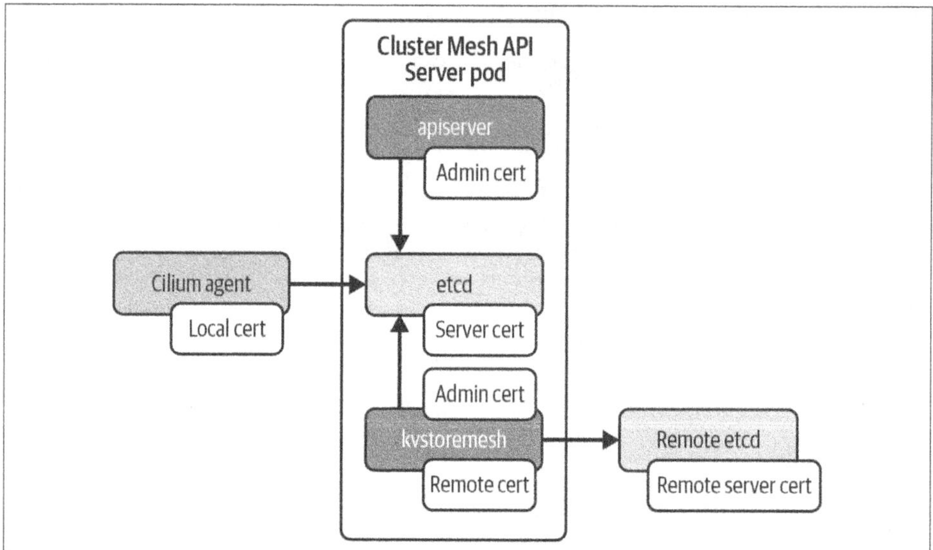

Figure 9-12. Cluster Mesh API Server certificate usage

Building a Cluster Mesh deployment with a custom certificate authority is complex and beyond the scope of this book. See the Cilium documentation (*https://oreil.ly/Vxink*) for the full details.

Summary

Most users will never enable Cluster Mesh. It implies both an architecture that requires multiple intracomponent flows and a compelling use case for multicluster Kubernetes. Individual Kubernetes clusters can scale to thousands of nodes and accommodate all but the very largest applications. Multiregion or multicloud mandates are rare outside of regulated industries such as healthcare or finance, and going multicluster for extra redundancy is often overshadowed by easier ways to accomplish the same goal.

For some, Cluster Mesh is a feature for contingency planning. You don't need it now, but you don't know if you will in the future, and if you do, you don't want to have to rearchitect your entire application to fix it. With Cilium, you keep the option to use it later open, without needing to change anything else.

If cluster mesh is on your future roadmap at all, our parting advice is to always pick a unique pod IP range for each cluster, even if you think you may never mesh them. This makes it easy to do so in the future without having to perform an IPAM migration.

For those few who do find themselves truly needing multicluster Kubernetes, Cluster Mesh can replace an entire category of load balancers, switches, DNS servers, and complex network infrastructure with a handful of lines of YAML. In some cases, a desired architecture might not be possible any other way. For those users, Cluster Mesh might be Cilium's greatest feature.

CHAPTER 10

Cluster Access

Accessing applications inside a Kubernetes cluster from the outside world is a common requirement. An external client, whether it's a user's laptop, an upstream router, or another application, needs a stable way to reach a service inside the cluster.

In Chapter 7, we introduced Cilium's support for Kubernetes Ingress and Gateway API as mechanisms to load-balance and manipulate traffic once it reaches the cluster. However, we have not yet explained how external clients become aware of the cluster's external-facing IP address. That is the focus of this chapter.

The most straightforward option provided by Kubernetes is a service of type NodePort. With a NodePort service, Kubernetes opens the same port number on every node in the cluster and forwards traffic from that port to the service's backend pods. This works without additional setup and is often used in simple clusters where clients know the node IPs directly.

NodePort introduces two layers of selection. At the first layer, the client chooses which node to contact. At the second layer, the node that receives the traffic forwards it to one of the healthy backend pods, as explained in Chapter 6. The second layer works consistently because Kubernetes tracks pod health and removes failing backends. The first layer is where problems appear.

If the client chooses a node that later becomes unavailable, there is no mechanism in Kubernetes that automatically redirects the connection to another node. The client must detect the failure and retry a different node IP. This creates a fragile dependency on client behavior and the surrounding network environment, where firewalls or upstream systems may expect a single stable destination IP rather than a list of node addresses and port numbers.

Figure 10-1 illustrates both layers of behavior. On the left, the client selects a node and the cluster forwards the request to a random healthy backend pod. On the right, the chosen node has failed. Although other nodes and pods remain available, the path is broken because the client keeps sending packets to the originally selected node. It's only when the client realizes the node is down (via an intermediary load balancer tracking the node health, for example) that traffic can be routed to an alternate, healthy node.

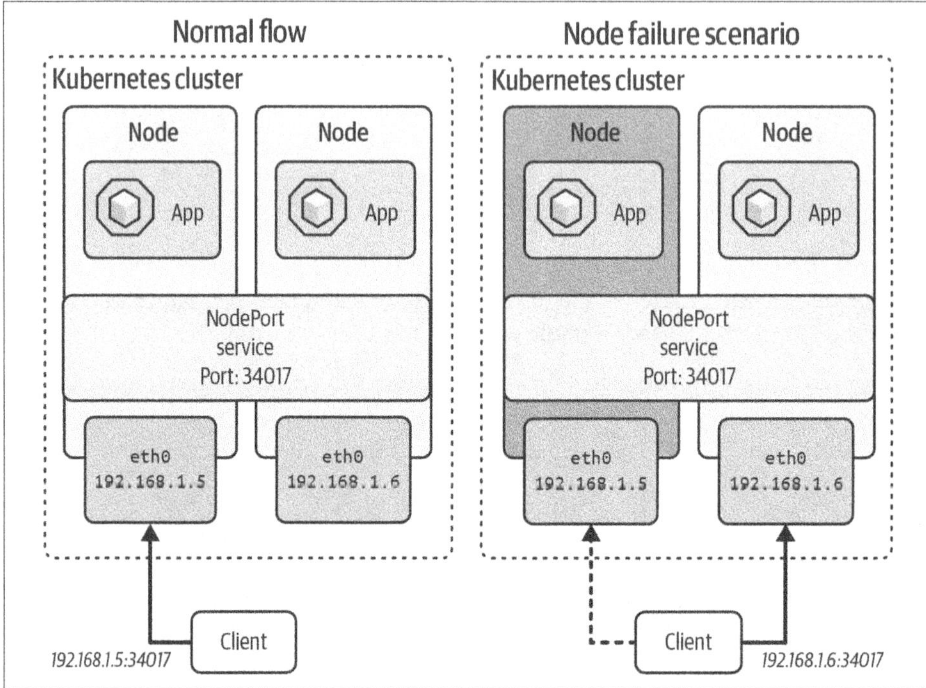

Figure 10-1. NodePort client connectivity during normal behavior and during node failure conditions

To overcome these issues, Cilium introduces two mechanisms that make external access seamless:

- *L2 Announcements*, which make services appear as directly connected IPs on the local network
- *BGP*, which advertises service IPs into the routing fabric for scalable and resilient connectivity

In this chapter, we will explore both approaches, step through their configuration, and highlight their strengths and trade-offs.

L2 Announcements

Cilium's *L2 Announcements* feature, sometimes called *L2 Aware LB*, makes Kubernetes services visible and reachable on the local area network. This approach is especially useful in environments that lack BGP support or where running BGP is considered too complex.

When this feature is enabled, Cilium responds to ARP queries for external IPs and/or LoadBalancer IPs. These IPs are virtual; they do not belong to any specific network interface. Instead, one node is elected as the announcer for each virtual IP (VIP). That node replies to ARP requests using its own MAC address.[1] From the client's perspective, the VIP looks like a directly attached IP, and traffic is forwarded through the elected node, which then load-balances it to the service's backend pods.

In contrast, NodePort places the burden on the client to select and track node IPs. If the chosen node fails, the IP and port combination becomes unusable. L2 Announcements mitigate this by allowing the VIP to move automatically to another node.

You can find all the YAML manifests used in this section in the *chapter10/l2* directory of the book's GitHub repository (*https://github.com/isovalent/cilium-up-and-running*).

Setting Up the Environment

To test L2 Announcements, we will create a kind cluster without `kube-proxy`. The only requirement for this feature is KPR, which we introduced in Chapter 6.

Create the cluster (*kind-cluster-config.yaml*) and install Cilium using Helm with values defined in *cilium-l2-values.yaml*:

```
kubeProxyReplacement: true
k8sServiceHost: kind-control-plane
k8sServicePort: 6443
l2announcements:
  enabled: true
```

Next, start a client container on the same Docker network so that it can send traffic directly to the cluster:

```
$ docker run -d --network kind --rm --name client \
    nicolaka/netshoot:v0.8 sleep infinity
```

1 This book is based on Cilium 1.18. IPv6 support for L2 Announcements was added in Cilium 1.19. IPv6 relies on the Neighbor Discovery (ND) protocol (*https://oreil.ly/6Y2pw*) rather than ARP.

Configuring L2 Announcements

Before creating the service, verify that all cluster nodes and the client are on the same network. In this example, the network is `172.18.0.0/16`. From within the client container, run the following command to display its IP configuration:

```
$ docker exec -it client ip -4 a show eth0
11: eth0@if34: <BROADCAST,MULTICAST,UP,LOWER_UP> mtu 65535 qdisc
    noqueue state UP group default link-netnsid 0
    inet 172.18.0.5/16 brd 172.18.255.255 scope global eth0
       valid_lft forever preferred_lft forever
```

It's important that the service IP you assign comes from the same network range, so the client can reach it directly. In the next step we will create a CiliumLoadBalancerIPPool that allocates addresses from the block `172.18.255.200/29` (we covered LB IPAM pools in Chapter 6). This block lies within the client's `172.18.0.0/16` network, ensuring that traffic is delivered without requiring any routing changes.

You can assign a VIP from another subnet, but the client's routing table must be configured accordingly. Otherwise, the client assumes the IP is outside the local network and sends the traffic to the default gateway instead.

Deploy the IP pool (*pool.yaml*) and the simple httpd application with its associated LoadBalancer service (*app.yaml*). The service is labeled `announcement: l2` so it matches the L2 Announcement policy we will deploy next:

```
apiVersion: apps/v1
kind: Deployment
metadata:
  name: httpd
spec:
  replicas: 2
  selector:
    matchLabels:
      app.kubernetes.io/name: httpd
  template:
    metadata:
      labels:
        app.kubernetes.io/name: httpd
    spec:
      containers:
      - name: httpd
        image: httpd:2.4
        ports:
        - containerPort: 80
---
apiVersion: v1
kind: Service
```

```
metadata:
  name: httpd
  labels:
    announcement: l2
spec:
  type: LoadBalancer
  selector:
    app.kubernetes.io/name: httpd
  ports:
  - port: 80
```

Check the service to confirm that it has been assigned an IP from the pool:

```
$ kubectl get svc httpd
NAME    TYPE           CLUSTER-IP    EXTERNAL-IP      PORT(S)        AGE
httpd   LoadBalancer   10.96.84.34   172.18.255.200   80:32179/TCP   20m
```

At this point, the service has an external IP, but clients still cannot reach it. No node is yet responding to ARP queries for that address. In the next step, we will apply the L2 Announcement policy to make the service accessible.

Applying the L2 Announcement Policy

To make the service reachable, we need to tell Cilium which services to announce and on which nodes. This is done with a CiliumL2AnnouncementPolicy. Apply the manifest (*l2policy.yaml*):

```
apiVersion: "cilium.io/v2alpha1"
kind: CiliumL2AnnouncementPolicy
metadata:
  name: l2-policy
spec:
  serviceSelector:
    matchLabels:
      announcement: l2 ❶
  nodeSelector:
    matchExpressions:
      - key: node-role.kubernetes.io/control-plane ❷
        operator: DoesNotExist
  interfaces:
  - ^eth0 ❸
  loadBalancerIPs: true ❹
```

❶ Selects services that carry the label `announcement: l2` (such as the httpd service we just created)

❷ Excludes nodes with the control-plane role, so only worker nodes can become announcers[2]

❸ Restricts announcements to the `eth0` interface (by default, Cilium announces services on all node interfaces)[3]

❹ Enables announcements for LoadBalancer IPs

This interface selector is not a security feature. Services may still be reachable through unadvertised interfaces, for example if ARP entries are manually configured.

Once the policy is applied, Cilium will elect one of the worker nodes as the announcer for the service external IP. You can identify the current leader (in this case, `kind-worker2`) by inspecting the Kubernetes leases:

```
$ kubectl -n kube-system get lease | grep l2announce
cilium-l2announce-default-httpd         kind-worker2
```

Inspecting ARP Traffic

Now that the service has been assigned an external IP and an announcer node has been elected, let's inspect what happens on the wire when the client tries to reach it.

Our objective is to capture the ARP request sent by the client for the service IP (`172.18.255.200` in this example), to observe how the elected node responds with its MAC address and to show the TCP handshake and the first HTTP response. First, check the MAC address on the `kind-worker2` node:

```
$ docker exec -it kind-worker2 ip link show dev eth0
11: eth0@if32: <BROADCAST,MULTICAST,UP,LOWER_UP> mtu 65535 qdisc
    noqueue state UP mode DEFAULT group default
    link/ether ea:f5:fb:51:a1:17 brd ff:ff:ff:ff:ff:ff link-netnsid 0
```

2 By default, Cilium considers all nodes to be potential announcers, but in most clusters the control-plane nodes are reserved for system components and are not used for forwarding application traffic. Restricting announcements to workers avoids putting datapath responsibilities on the control plane.

3 Selectors in Cilium CRDs support RE2-compatible regular expressions. RE2 is a regular expression engine implemented by Google that is considered a fast, safe, thread-friendly alternative to backtracking regular expression engines.

Next, open two terminal windows side by side:

- In the first window, run `tcpdump` inside the client container to capture ARP traffic.
- In the second window, generate traffic from the client to the service IP.

In the first terminal, first check the ARP cache. There should be no entry for the service IP as the client has yet to try to access it and has not made an ARP request yet:

```
$ docker exec -it client ip neigh
```

Start `tcpdump` to observe ARP and HTTP traffic:

```
$ docker exec -it client tcpdump -i eth0 -n
```

In the second terminal, access the service IP. The request triggers ARP resolution and completes successfully:

```
$ docker exec -it client curl http://172.18.255.200
<html><body><h1>It works!</h1></body></html>
```

In the `tcpdump` output, you will see a broadcast ARP request from the client asking "`who-has >172.18.255.200`." Immediately after, the elected node responds with its own MAC address:

```
ARP, Request who-has 172.18.255.200 tell 172.18.0.5, length 28
ARP, Reply 172.18.255.200 is-at ea:f5:fb:51:a1:17, length 28
```

Figure 10-2 shows both sides of the ARP process. The client sends a broadcast ARP request for the service IP, which is received by all nodes. The elected announcer node responds with an ARP reply containing its MAC address. Once the client learns this MAC address, it can send traffic directly to the node that currently holds the announcement lease.

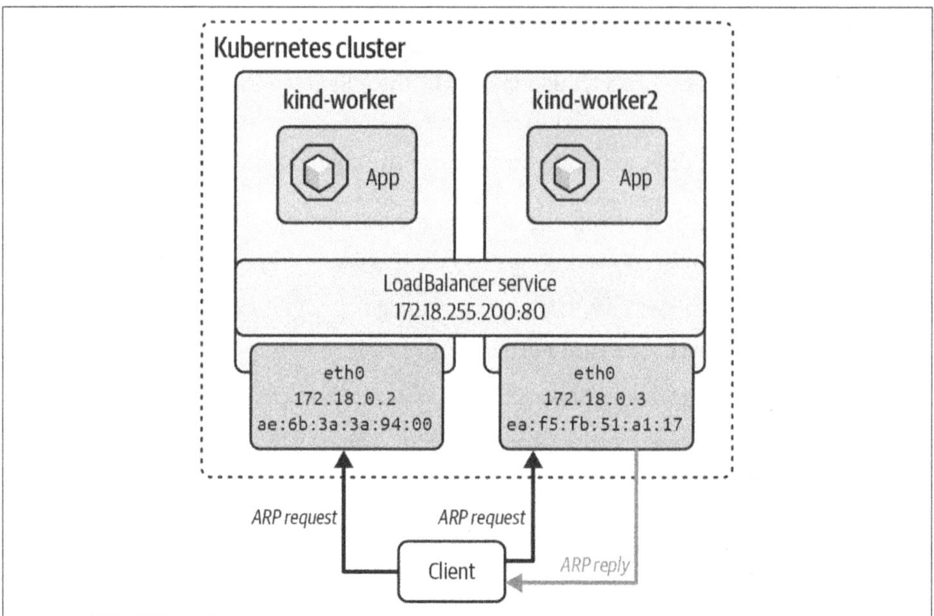

Figure 10-2. ARP request and reply with Cilium L2 Announcements

That ARP information is now saved in the client's ARP table:

```
$ docker exec -it client ip neigh
172.18.255.200 dev eth0 lladdr ea:f5:fb:51:a1:17 REACHABLE
```

Immediately after this, the client establishes a TCP connection. The complete `tcpdump` output will look like this:

```
ARP, Request who-has 172.18.255.200 tell 172.18.0.5, length 28         ❶
ARP, Reply 172.18.255.200 is-at ea:f5:fb:51:a1:17, length 28           ❷
IP 172.18.0.5.45300 > 172.18.255.200.80: Flags [S], ...                ❸
ARP, Request who-has 172.18.0.5 tell 172.18.0.3, length 28             ❹
ARP, Reply 172.18.0.5 is-at 76:0f:e0:c7:27:fe, length 28               ❺
IP 172.18.255.200.80 > 172.18.0.5.45300: Flags [S.], ...               ❻
IP 172.18.0.5.45300 > 172.18.255.200.80: Flags [.], ...                ❼
IP 172.18.0.5.45300 > 172.18.255.200.80: Flags [P.], ... HTTP GET      ❽
IP 172.18.255.200.80 > 172.18.0.5.45300: Flags [.], ...                ❾
IP 172.18.255.200.80 > 172.18.0.5.45300: Flags [P.], ... HTTP 200 OK ❿
IP 172.18.0.5.45300 > 172.18.255.200.80: Flags [.], ...                ⓫
IP 172.18.0.5.45300 > 172.18.255.200.80: Flags [F.], ...               ⓬
IP 172.18.255.200.80 > 172.18.0.5.45300: Flags [F.], ...               ⓭
IP 172.18.0.5.45300 > 172.18.255.200.80: Flags [.], ...                ⓮
```

❶ Client asks "`who-has 172.18.255.200`" (ARP request)

❷ Elected announcer node replies with its MAC address (ARP reply)

❸ Client sends SYN to initiate connection ([S])

❹ Announcer node asks "who-has 172.18.0.5" (ARP request)

❺ Client replies with its MAC address (ARP reply)

❻ Announcer node responds to SYN with SYN-ACK ([S.])

❼ Client sends ACK, completing the three-way TCP handshake ([.])

❽ Client sends HTTP request (GET) as a PSH+ACK ([P.])

❾ Server acknowledges the request ([.])

❿ One of the httpd pods responds with HTTP 200 OK ([P.])

⓫ Client acknowledges the HTTP response ([.])

⓬ Client sends FIN to close the connection ([F.])

⓭ Server responds with its own FIN ([F.])

⓮ Client acknowledges, completing the TCP termination ([.])

Note that the announcer node performs its own ARP lookup for the client's IP (172.18.0.5) and learns its MAC address.

Once ARP resolution has completed, the elected node receives all traffic for the service IP, forwards each request to one of the httpd pods, and returns the pod's response to the client.

Simulating a Node Failure

With the service now reachable through the elected announcer node, we can explore what happens when the node becomes unavailable. The objective of this exercise is to show how the lease is transferred to another node and how connectivity is restored, but it will also reveal some of the inner limitations of L2 Announcement.

Let's simulate a node failure by stopping the elected announcer node:

```
$ docker stop kind-worker2
```

At this point, the client's ARP cache still maps the service IP (`172.18.255.200`) to the MAC address of the stopped node, so until the cache expires, packets are sent into a black hole:

```
$ docker exec -it client curl -m 5 172.18.255.200
curl: (28) Connection timed out after 5001 milliseconds
```

Meanwhile, Cilium's leader election process continues in the background. Nodes that participate in announcements monitor the lease, and if the current holder does not renew it within the configured lease duration, they request ownership from the API server. The first request that succeeds becomes the new leader and begins advertising the service IP. When a node takes over, it sends a gratuitous ARP[4] so that clients can update their neighbor tables without waiting for their ARP entries to expire.

If the client accepts the gratuitous ARP, failover happens almost immediately because the new leader's announcement updates the client's neighbor table at once. However, many clients and network devices ignore these messages because they can be used for ARP spoofing. Clients that ignore the gratuitous ARP will continue using the stale ARP entry until it expires. When that happens, the client sends a fresh ARP request, learns the MAC address of the new leader, and connectivity is restored:

```
$ docker exec -it client curl -m 5 172.18.255.200
<html><body><h1>It works!</h1></body></html>
```

You can verify the lease has been transferred to `kind-worker` with this command:

```
$ kubectl -n kube-system get lease | grep l2announce
cilium-l2announce-default-httpd        kind-worker
```

It is possible to use L2 Announcements for pod IPs rather than service IPs. This can be enabled by setting the Helm value `l2podAnnouncements.enabled=true`. However, this is generally discouraged since pods are ephemeral and advertising pod IPs directly bypasses the service abstraction and its load-balancing behavior.

4 A gratuitous ARP (gARP) is an ARP reply sent without an initial request, used to refresh ARP tables on other devices.

As this discussion has illustrated, while Cilium's L2 Announcements feature is useful in simpler environments, it has some notable limitations:

- Only one node handles traffic for each VIP, so there is no load balancing between nodes.
- Failover depends on ARP cache expiry, which can be slow.
- Faster failover relies on gratuitous ARP, but many clients ignore these messages for security reasons.

Because of these drawbacks, this feature is better suited for development or constrained environments than for production systems where failover speed and security are critical. For those systems, it's generally preferable to use the other mechanism Cilium provides for exposing services to external clients: BGP.

BGP

Cilium's BGP functionality provides a more flexible and robust alternative to L2 Announcements. Rather than depending on ARP, BGP enables routing of service IPs at layer 3, making it suitable for larger or more complex environments—especially those already running routing protocols and infrastructure. The BGP functionality we cover in this book is referred to as *Cilium BGP Control Plane*.

BGP is particularly useful in production environments where high availability, fast failover, and load balancing across nodes are important requirements. It does introduce operational overhead because it must be configured and maintained, and it requires BGP-capable devices or software. However, BGP is widely used across datacenter networks, so many environments already provide the necessary routing infrastructure.

Figure 10-3 illustrates how Cilium BGP Control Plane functions. With BGP enabled, Cilium selects which services to advertise using label selectors. It determines which nodes should act as BGP speakers, and then initiates route announcements to configured peers. The BGP peers learn the routes and may redistribute them further into the network. External clients can then reach these services using standard IP routing.

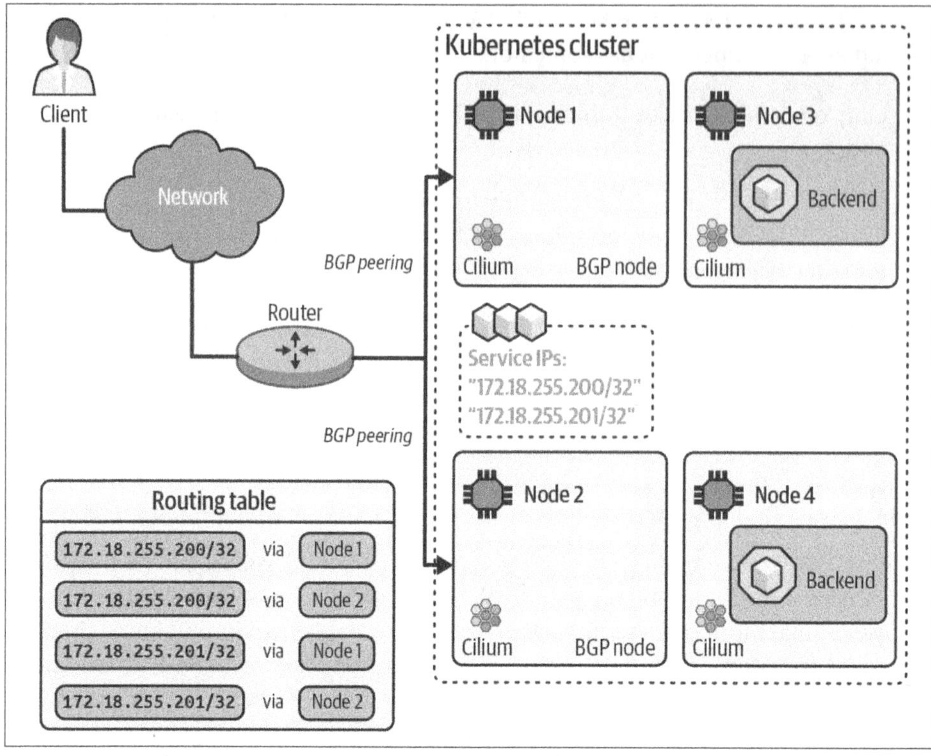

Figure 10-3. Cilium BGP Control Plane overview

You can find all the YAML manifests used in this section in the *chapter10/l3* directory of the book's GitHub repository (*https://github.com/isovalent/cilium-up-and-running*).

Setting Up the Environment

Start by deploying your cluster using the same *kind-cluster-config.yaml* we used previously. Next, install Cilium using Helm with the values defined in *cilium-bgp-values.yaml*. `bgpControlPlane.enabled=true` enables BGP in Cilium. BGP peerings and Autonomous System Numbers (ASN) configurations are then defined via custom resources.

To see the Cilium BGP feature in action, we need a BGP-capable device to peer with. For this example, we'll deploy a Free Range Routing (FRR) instance outside of the cluster but connected to the same Docker network. FRR (*https://oreil.ly/BQuz8*) is an open source routing suite supporting BGP, Open Shortest Path First (OSPF), and other protocols on Linux and other UNIX-like systems.

The configuration for FRR in this section is available in the *chapter10/l3/frr* directory of the book's GitHub repository. It contains three files:

- *frr.conf.template* is the template configuration file.
- *daemons* enables the BGP daemon (bgpd=yes).
- *vtysh.conf* contains minimal configuration for the vtysh CLI.

You only need to generate *frr.conf* from the template.

First, capture the IP addresses of the worker nodes:

```
$ kubectl get nodes -o wide
NAME                STATUS   ROLES           INTERNAL-IP
kind-worker         Ready    <none>          172.18.0.2
kind-worker2        Ready    <none>          172.18.0.3

$ WORKER_IP=172.18.0.2

$ WORKER2_IP=172.18.0.3
```

Next, generate an FRR configuration file from the provided template and use the UNIX utility sed to modify the template values with the IP addresses of the worker nodes:

```
$ sed -e "s/NEIGHBOR1/${WORKER_IP}/" \
    -e "s/NEIGHBOR2/${WORKER2_IP}/" \
    frr.conf.template | tee frr.conf

frr version 10.3.1
frr defaults traditional
hostname frr
log syslog
service integrated-vtysh-config

router bgp 64512 ❶
  bgp router-id 172.18.255.254 ❷
  neighbor 172.18.0.2 remote-as 64512 ❸
  neighbor 172.18.0.3 remote-as 64512 ❸
  !
  address-family ipv4 unicast
    neighbor 172.18.0.2 activate ❹
    neighbor 172.18.0.3 activate ❹
  exit-address-family
```

❶ Runs BGP with local ASN 64512

❷ Defines a router ID (172.18.255.254)

❸ Configures the worker nodes as internal BGP (iBGP) peers

❹ Activates IPv4 unicast routing for those peers

Finally, start the FRR container on the same Docker network as the kind cluster, using the newly created configuration file:

```
$ docker run -d --privileged --rm --net kind \
    -v "$PWD/frr.conf:/etc/frr/frr.conf" \
    -v "$PWD/vtysh.conf:/etc/frr/vtysh.conf" \
    -v "$PWD/daemons:/etc/frr/daemons" \
    --name frr quay.io/frrouting/frr:10.3.1
```

At this point FRR is running, but no routes have been exchanged yet. You can check its status with:

```
$ docker exec -it frr vtysh -c "show bgp summary wide"
IPv4 Unicast Summary:
BGP router identifier 172.18.255.254, local AS number 64512

Neighbor      V   AS      MsgRcvd  MsgSent  Up/Down  State/PfxRcd
172.18.0.2    4   64512   0        0        never    Active
172.18.0.3    4   64512   0        0        never    Active

Total number of neighbors 2
```

For users familiar with working with BGP on traditional network operating systems like Cisco IOS, this output should look familiar. Still, let's walk through some of the key details to understand what we're seeing. The command displays the current BGP status on the FRR router. It shows two BGP neighbors: `172.18.0.2` and `172.18.0.3`, which correspond to our Kubernetes worker nodes. The output also includes both the local and remote ASNs. In this case, both are set to `64512`, meaning the sessions are using iBGP, where peers reside within the same autonomous system (AS).[5]

Looking at the `State/PfxRcd` column, we can see that the sessions are in the `Active` state. In BGP terms, `Active` means the session configuration is present and the router is attempting to establish a TCP connection with the peer, but it hasn't succeeded yet. This is expected behavior at this stage: although the FRR router is configured and attempting to peer, we haven't yet configured Cilium to act as a BGP peer. Once that configuration is applied, we should see these sessions move from `Active` to `Established`.

Before we can observe Cilium's BGP functionality in action, we need to deploy an application that will be reachable from outside the Kubernetes cluster. We will deploy a simple httpd application (*l3/app-l3.yaml*), just as we did in the L2 Announcements section. We will also use a CiliumLoadBalancerIPPool (*l3/pool.yaml*) to allocate IPs from the `172.18.255.200/29` subnet. Once the manifests are applied, the service will once again be assigned an IP address:

5 While this example uses iBGP, Cilium also fully supports external BGP (eBGP) with the same configuration model.

```
$ kubectl get svc httpd
NAME    TYPE           CLUSTER-IP     EXTERNAL-IP      PORT(S)        AGE
httpd   LoadBalancer   10.96.64.189   172.18.255.200   80:31789/TCP   3m35s
```

Enabling Cilium BGP Control Plane

Now that FRR is running and ready to peer with the cluster, let's look at how Cilium advertises service IPs via BGP. Cilium's BGP Control Plane is driven by a set of Kubernetes custom resources that offer a flexible and declarative way to configure BGP peers, policies, and route advertisements. These resources allow you to fine-tune how BGP is configured across the cluster nodes and how routes are shared with external peers.

The key resources involved in managing BGP Control Plane are:

CiliumBGPClusterConfig
: Defines one or more BGP instances and associated peer configurations that can be applied to nodes in the cluster

CiliumBGPPeerConfig
: Specifies peer configuration settings that can be reused across multiple peers

CiliumBGPAdvertisement
: Declares which prefixes (e.g., service IPs or PodCIDRs) should be advertised to the BGP routing table and under what conditions

BGP Control Plane v2 was introduced in Cilium 1.16. Before this release, configuring BGP required the use of the CiliumBGPPeeringPolicy custom resource to define peers, advertisements, and policies. CiliumBGPPeeringPolicy still exists for backward compatibility and can be used in legacy setups. However, it is now deprecated and should no longer be used in new deployments.

CiliumBGPClusterConfig

We'll begin by examining the CiliumBGPClusterConfig custom resource, which defines the BGP behavior for a group of nodes. A simple example follows (*cilium-bgp-cluster-config.yaml*):

```
apiVersion: cilium.io/v2
kind: CiliumBGPClusterConfig
metadata:
  name: frr
spec:
  nodeSelector: ❶
    matchExpressions:
    - key: node-role.kubernetes.io/control-plane
      operator: DoesNotExist
```

```
bgpInstances:
- name: instance-64512
  localASN: 64512 ❷
  localPort: 179 ❸
  peers:
  - name: peer-64512-frr
    peerASN: 64512 ❹
    peerAddress: 172.18.0.6 <4>
    peerConfigRef: ❺
      name: peer-config
```

❶ `nodeSelector` selects all nodes except the control plane, meaning the configuration will apply only to worker nodes.

❷ `localASN` specifies the ASN that the selected nodes will use to identify themselves in BGP communications.

❸ `localPort` defines the local port used for BGP sessions.

❹ `peerASN` and `peerAddress` define the ASN and IP address of the external BGP peer (in this case, the FRR router). Note that the IP address might be different if you've deployed other clients on the kind network.

❺ `peerConfigRef` references a separate CiliumBGPPeerConfig resource that holds reusable peer-specific settings.

By default, BGP Control Plane only initiates outbound connections to peers and does not listen for inbound ones. This avoids port conflicts with other BGP daemons, like BIRD. To enable listening, set the `localPort` field. If using port 179, ensure Cilium has the `CAP_NET_BIND_SERVICE` capability.

CiliumBGPPeerConfig

The CiliumBGPPeerConfig resource defines the configuration applied to individual BGP peers. This allows you to separate common peer settings from the cluster-wide configuration, making them reusable across multiple BGP instances. Typical parameters include timers, supported address families, and optional features such as Graceful Restart and authentication. Here is an example (*cilium-bgp-peer-config.yaml*):

```
apiVersion: cilium.io/v2
kind: CiliumBGPPeerConfig
metadata:
  name: peer-config
spec:
  timers:
    connectRetryTimeSeconds: 30 ❶
```

```
    keepAliveTimeSeconds: 20 ❷
    holdTimeSeconds: 60 ❸
  families: ❹
    - afi: ipv4
      safi: unicast
      advertisements:
        matchLabels:
          advertise: "bgp"
  gracefulRestart: ❺
    enabled: true
    restartTimeSeconds: 15
```

❶ `connectRetryTimeSeconds` determines how long Cilium waits before retrying a failed TCP connection to a peer. A lower value allows faster recovery in case of transient network issues.

❷ `keepAliveTimeSeconds` sets the interval for sending BGP keepalive messages, which let the peer know the session is still alive. This value must be less than `holdTimeSeconds`.

❸ `holdTimeSeconds` specifies the maximum time Cilium will wait without hearing from the peer before declaring the session dead. If no BGP message (such as a keepalive) is received during this interval, the peer is considered unreachable. A typical configuration is 3x the keepalive interval.[6]

❹ The `families` section defines the types of routes that Cilium will exchange with the peer. Currently, two address family identifiers (AFIs) are supported: `ipv4` and `ipv6`. For both of these, the only currently supported subsequent address family identifier (SAFI) is `unicast`. This is the mechanism that links peers to specific advertisement policies. Within this block, `advertisements.matchLabels` selects which CiliumBGPAdvertisement resources apply to this peer. In this example, only advertisements labeled `advertise: bgp` will be considered.

❺ Setting `gracefulRestart` to `true` enables the BGP Graceful Restart mechanism (RFC 8538 (*https://oreil.ly/MhNG8*)). When BGP is terminated, even gracefully, it typically results in the immediate withdrawal of all routes by the peer. This can cause traffic black holes or disruptions, even if the node's workloads are still operational and able to serve traffic. Cilium's BGP Control Plane runs inside the Cilium agent. When the agent is restarted, such as during an upgrade, it tears down the BGP session. The peer will then remove all previously advertised

6 BGP peers negotiate the actual timer values during session establishment. The lower of the two values (between Cilium and the peer) is what will be used. If Cilium sets a `holdTimeSeconds` of `60` but the peer uses `30`, then `30` will be applied.

routes from that node. To avoid this, Cilium supports Graceful Restart. When it's enabled, Cilium signals to the peer that it intends to restart the session and will reconnect within `restartTimeSeconds`. During this time, the peer retains the routes previously learned from Cilium, assuming the node is still reachable. If the session is reestablished within that window, routing continues without interruption. If not, the peer eventually withdraws those routes. This mechanism ensures better resilience during expected restarts or upgrades by avoiding unnecessary route flaps or traffic loss.

By default, BGP does not use authentication. In production environments, it is strongly recommended to enable MD5 authentication to secure BGP sessions. In Cilium, this can be configured using the `authSecretRef` field in the CiliumBGPPeerConfig resource. You'll also need to configure the corresponding authentication on the peer router.

CiliumBGPAdvertisement

The CiliumBGPAdvertisement resource defines which prefixes Cilium should announce via BGP. These prefixes can include service IPs, PodCIDRs, and pod IP pools (when using Multi-Pool IPAM mode, discussed in Chapter 4). You can also control conditions under which advertisements are made. Here's an example (*cilium-bgp-advertisement.yaml*):

```
apiVersion: cilium.io/v2
kind: CiliumBGPAdvertisement
metadata:
  name: bgp-advertisement
  labels: ❶
    advertise: bgp
spec:
  advertisements:
    - advertisementType: "Service" ❷
      service:
        addresses: ❸
        - LoadBalancerIP
      selector:
        matchLabels:
          announcement: bgp
      attributes: ❹
        localPreference: 200
        communities:
          standard:
          - "64512:99"
```

❶ The `labels` section includes `advertise: bgp`. This is crucial: it must match the `advertisements.matchLabels` defined in the CiliumBGPPeerConfig. This is how Cilium links advertisements to peers.

❷ In the `advertisementType` field we specify `"Service"`, which tells Cilium to advertise Kubernetes services. Other available advertisement types are `"PodCIDR"` and `"CiliumPodIPPool"`. As mentioned in "Dynamic routing with BGP" on page 84, there are situations where advertising PodCIDRs makes sense, particularly when using native routing to ensure routing entries are properly populated across the cluster. However, letting clients establish connections to workloads directly via PodCIDR or CiliumPodIPPool can introduce problems—clients would need to be aware of ever-changing pod IPs, and there's no built-in mechanism for load balancing or failure detection, increasing complexity for the client. For these reasons, advertising services is the preferred approach when exposing workloads outside the cluster.

❸ Within `service.addresses`, we choose which type of service IP to advertise. Valid options include `LoadBalancerIP`, `ClusterIP`, or `ExternalIP`. In our case, we are advertising the `LoadBalancerIPs` of services that are labeled with `announcement: bgp`. As this example shows, this allows us to fine-tune which services are advertised via BGP simply by applying labels.

❹ You can also attach optional BGP `attributes` to the advertisement. `localPreference` is a BGP attribute used in iBGP (within the same AS) to influence route selection. Higher values are preferred. The default is `100`, but here we've set it to `200`, making these routes preferable over others with lower local preference. BGP `communities` are optional metadata that can be attached to BGP routes. They act like tags, allowing network operators to apply policies or influence routing decisions further downstream. In our example, we attach the community `64512:99` to advertised service IPs. The first part, `64512`, is the ASN. The second part, `99`, is an arbitrary identifier. This means the community has no predefined meaning. Unless the upstream peers (for example, our FRR device) are explicitly configured with a policy to interpret `64512:99`, this setting will not affect routing behavior.[7]

7 There are also well-known communities defined by the BGP specification. For example, `no-advertise` indicates that the peer should not advertise this route to any peer, and `no-export` specifies that the peer should not advertise this route outside the local AS.

Applying the Policies and Verifying Route Advertisements

Let's apply our BGP configuration:

```
$ kubectl apply -f cilium-bgp-cluster-config.yaml
ciliumbgpclusterconfig.cilium.io/frr created

$ kubectl apply -f cilium-bgp-advertisement.yaml
ciliumbgpadvertisement.cilium.io/bgp-advertisement configured

$ kubectl apply -f cilium-bgp-peer-config.yaml
ciliumbgppeerconfig.cilium.io/peer-config configured
```

Cilium should now be successfully establishing BGP connections with the FRR router. We can inspect the BGP session status on the FRR side using the following command:

```
$ docker exec -it frr vtysh -c "show bgp summary"

Neighbor        V   AS      MsgRcvd   MsgSent   Up/Down    State/PfxRcd
172.18.0.2      4   64512   205       203       01:06:53   1
172.18.0.3      4   64512   205       203       01:06:53   1
```

The output confirms that BGP sessions with both worker nodes, `172.18.0.2` and `172.18.0.3`, have been established. The `State/PfxRcd` column shows that one prefix has been received from each peer. This tells us that our service, advertised through Cilium BGP Control Plane, is being successfully propagated and accepted by the FRR router.

You can also use the Cilium CLI to inspect the BGP peering status across all BGP-speaking nodes and check which routes are being advertised to peers:

```
$ cilium bgp peers
Node           Peer         State         Uptime    Family          Adv
kind-worker    172.18.0.6   established   1h8m      ipv4/unicast    2
kind-worker2   172.18.0.6   established   1h8m      ipv4/unicast    2

$ cilium bgp routes advertised ipv4 unicast peer 172.18.0.6
Node           Prefix               NextHop
kind-worker    172.18.255.200/32    172.18.0.2
kind-worker2   172.18.255.200/32    172.18.0.3
```

The same commands are available with the `cilium-dbg` CLI tool on the Cilium agent itself:

```
$ kubectl exec -n kube-system -it cilium-mckp9 -- cilium-dbg bgp peers
Local AS   Peer AS   Peer Address      Session       Uptime     Advertised
64512      64512     172.18.0.6:179    established   1h11m46s   2

$ kubectl exec -n kube-system -it cilium-mckp9 -- cilium-dbg bgp routes
VRouter   Prefix              NextHop   Age      Attrs
64512     172.18.255.200/32   0.0.0.0   39m20s   [{Origin: i} {Nexthop: 0.0.0.0}]
```

Next, let's check the routing table inside the FRR container to confirm that the advertised service IP is routable via both worker nodes:

```
$ docker exec -it frr ip route
default via 172.18.0.1 dev eth0
172.18.0.0/16 dev eth0 proto kernel scope link src 172.18.0.6
172.18.255.200 nhid 13 proto bgp metric 20
        nexthop via 172.18.0.2 dev eth0 weight 1
        nexthop via 172.18.0.3 dev eth0 weight 1
```

The table now includes an entry for the service IP `172.18.255.200`. This prefix is associated with two next hops: one via `172.18.0.2` (`kind-worker`) and another via `172.18.0.3` (`kind-worker2`). Both next hops are given equal weight, which makes sense since the worker nodes are identically configured and equally reachable.

Because the two routes have the same cost, the Linux kernel uses ECMP routing to distribute traffic between them. With ECMP, traffic destined for the service IP is load-balanced across both worker nodes. The exact distribution depends on the kernel's ECMP hash policy, which typically uses a combination of source and destination IP addresses, ports, and protocol fields.

This confirms that BGP peering is functioning correctly: routes are exchanged, the service IP is known to FRR, and traffic will be distributed across the nodes able to serve it.

Finally, we can verify end-to-end connectivity by requesting the service IP from inside the FRR container. Since the FRR image does not include `curl`, we use `wget`:

```
$ docker exec -it frr wget -qO- 172.18.255.200
<html><body><h1>It works!</h1></body></html>
```

This confirms that traffic is reaching the application inside the Kubernetes cluster via BGP.

Summary

Cilium provides two primary options for exposing applications within the cluster to external clients: L2 Announcements and BGP.

L2 Announcements is a simple and accessible method that uses ARP to announce IP addresses at layer 2. Because ARP is a basic and widely supported network protocol, this approach works out of the box in almost any environment without requiring BGP knowledge or network devices with BGP support. It is especially suitable for smaller or simpler network setups, where clients and cluster nodes reside in the same subnet. However, this simplicity comes at a cost:

No built-in load balancing
: Traffic is directed to a single node at a time, and balancing load between nodes is not supported.

Slow failover
: If the active node becomes unavailable, failover depends on ARP cache expiration and client behavior, which can introduce significant delay.

BGP, in contrast, operates at layer 3 and advertises IPs via routing updates to upstream routers. This allows external clients to reach services through standard IP routing, without being in the same subnet as the cluster. While more powerful, BGP does have some additional requirements. Notably:

- Peering requires routers or routing software (such as FRR) that supports BGP, which may introduce operational overhead or cost.
- Some familiarity with routing concepts and BGP configuration is needed.

That said, once BGP is in place, it brings the following significant advantages:

Excellent scalability
: BGP is designed to scale across large networks and complex topologies.

Fast failover
: Route updates can reflect node availability more quickly than ARP-based mechanisms.

Cross-network support
: Clients can be in entirely different networks from the cluster.

Flexible IP allocation
: Any routable IP can be advertised, not just ones that are in the cluster's subnet.

Built-in load balancing
: BGP combined with ECMP allows traffic to be balanced across multiple nodes without additional components.

With both approaches, it is recommended to advertise services rather than pods. Services provide a stable abstraction that is designed to handle things like lifecycle management, failover, and load balancing—advertising individual pods bypasses the native service model of Kubernetes and introduces significant operational complexity for the client. Take these points into consideration when choosing your approach. The best choice depends on your network architecture, scale, and operational maturity.

In the next chapter, we will turn our attention to egress traffic and explore how Cilium provides control over outbound connections from your workloads.

CHAPTER 11

Cluster Egress

Now that you know how to direct traffic inside your cluster, let's focus on how to control packets as they leave.

The nature of containerized applications and Kubernetes networking can lead to a lack of visibility for engineers and operators needing to understand the origins of a packet. Indeed, by default, when a packet leaves the cluster, Cilium replaces the source IP address of the originating pod with the IP address of the node it runs on.

This feature, known as *masquerading*, is where we'll start the chapter. We'll explain why masquerading is needed, the two modes that are available (eBPF and `iptables`), and how to customize it. We'll spend most of the chapter on Egress Gateway, a feature that provides a deterministic way to assign egress IP addresses and interfaces to traffic leaving the cluster. Finally, we'll look at Cilium's Bandwidth Manager, a lesser-known egress traffic control feature that allows you to rate-limit traffic from bandwidth-hungry pods.

You can find all the YAML manifests you will use in this chapter in the *chapter11* directory of the book's GitHub repository (*https://github.com/isovalent/cilium-up-and-running*).

Let's dig in!

Masquerading

One of the design principles of Kubernetes is to provide isolation for workloads across a shared infrastructure. But applications within a cluster don't use the underlying network for this; instead, they use the internal pod network.

PodCIDR networks are typically allocated from RFC 1918 private address blocks and thus not routable (as you know from the previous chapters, access to internal applications is usually via external-facing services rather than to the pod IPs directly). External entities that need to send traffic back to the originating pod will, in most cases, not know how to reach pod networks. However, they should be able to access Kubernetes nodes, as the node IP range will be routable. For this reason, Cilium will, by default, automatically *masquerade* the source IP address of all traffic leaving the cluster to the node's IPv4/IPv6 address.

Masquerading is a form of source NAT (SNAT) used to perform a many-to-one address translation, where multiple source IP addresses are masked behind a single address. In Kubernetes, this is the node's IP address.

Figure 11-1 illustrates an example of a packet emitted by a pod with the IP address `10.244.1.3`. Cilium masquerades it and sets the source IP to `172.18.0.3`, the IP of the node.

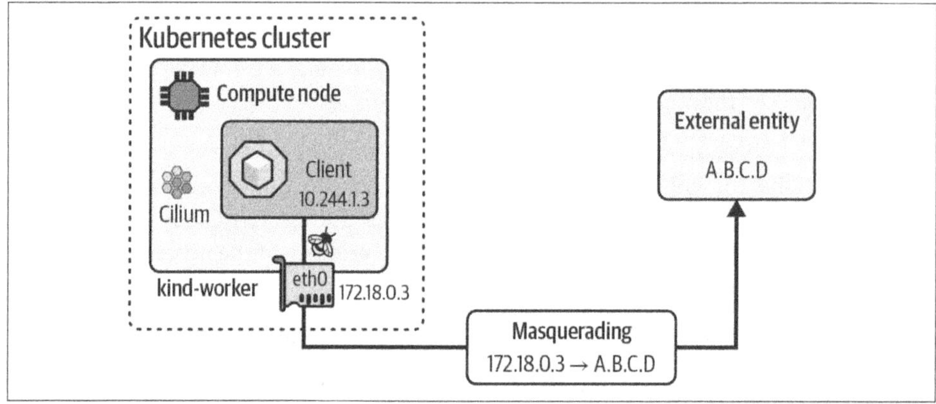

Figure 11-1. Masquerading

This default Cilium masquerading behavior can be disabled with the option `enable-ipv4-masquerade: false` for IPv4 or `enable-ipv6-masquerade: false` for IPv6 traffic leaving the host.

Configuring Masquerading

To see how masquerading works in practice, let's deploy a kind cluster (*kind.yaml*) and install Cilium with the default values. We can verify the default masquerading behavior by checking the status of the Cilium agent:

```
$ kubectl exec -it -n kube-system -c cilium-agent ds/cilium -- \
    cilium-dbg status | grep Masquerading
Masquerading:            IPTables [IPv4: Enabled, IPv6: Disabled]
```

All files discussed in this section are in the *chapter11/masquerade* directory of the book's GitHub repository (*https://github.com/isovalent/cilium-up-and-running*).

Next, we'll deploy a client pod (*netshoot-client-pod.yaml*). The pod receives an IP address from the `10.244.X.0/24` range, as we observed when using kind and Cilium in the default Cluster Scope IPAM mode in Chapter 4. Note the IP address of the node the pod runs on (`172.18.0.2` in our example):

```
$ kubectl get pod netshoot-client -o wide
NAME              IP             NODE
netshoot-client   10.244.1.252   kind-worker

$ kubectl get node kind-worker -o wide
NAME          INTERNAL-IP
kind-worker   172.18.0.2
```

Let's now deploy an external system as a Docker container and attach it to the kind Docker network. We'll use the same `echo-server` image we used in Chapter 8. Since the server logs the requester's source IP, we will be able to see whether masquerading takes place:

```
$ docker run -d \
    --platform=linux/amd64 \
    --name kind-echo-server \
    --network kind \
    kicbase/echo-server:1.0
```

If we get the IP address of the `echo-server` container, we'll see that, as expected, it's on the same network:

```
$ docker inspect -f '' \
    kind-echo-server
172.18.0.7
```

We can also confirm that access from the client to the external echo server is successful:

```
$ kubectl exec -it netshoot-client -- curl 172.18.0.7:8080
Request served by add431403996

HTTP/1.1 GET /

Host: 172.18.0.7:8080
Accept: */*
User-Agent: curl/8.14.1
```

The server logs the source IP address of the incoming connection to its standard output, which you can see using `docker logs`:

```
$ docker logs kind-echo-server
Echo server listening on port 8080.
172.18.0.2:43490 | GET /
```

The source IP is that of the node the pod resides on, not the pod's own IP—the traffic was masqueraded as it left the node.

By default, Cilium does not masquerade traffic destined for IPs within the PodCIDR of the local node. For example, in the earlier scenario, traffic from the `netshoot-client` pod to the `10.244.1.0/24` subnet (assigned to `kind-worker`) would be sent with its original source IP intact. This makes sense: the traffic never leaves the node and can be delivered directly, so rewriting the source IP is unnecessary.

If pod IPs are routable across a broader network, you can extend this behavior by configuring Cilium with the `ipv4-native-routing-cidr` (or `ipv6-native-routing-cidr` for IPv6) parameter. Any destination within the specified CIDR will bypass masquerading. This ties directly back to the native routing mode we explored in Chapter 5: when the underlying network already has routes to pod IPs, masquerading adds no value and in fact obscures the original source identity.

Masquerading Modes

Cilium supports two masquerading modes: one based on `iptables`, and another using eBPF. By default, `iptables` is used, as it works with all kernel versions. However, modern kernels (4.19 and later) support eBPF-based masquerading, which is more efficient and provides greater flexibility over which traffic is subject to SNAT. We recommend enabling it by setting `bpf.masquerade=true` in your Helm values, especially if you're using the Egress Gateway feature, which depends on it.

In advanced scenarios—such as when using Multi-Pool IPAM (covered in Chapter 4), where pod IPs are allocated from separate, nonoverlapping CIDRs—you may need to explicitly define which CIDRs should bypass masquerading. Cilium supports this via the `ip-masq-agent` feature, which you can enable by setting `ipMasqAgent.enabled=true`.

Let's try it. First, deploy Cilium in a generic kind cluster (*kind.yaml*), using the following Helm values (*cilium-masquerade-values.yaml*) to enable eBPF-based masquerading (instead of `iptables`) and the `ip-masq-agent` feature:

```
kubeProxyReplacement: true
bpf:
  masquerade: true
ipMasqAgent:
  enabled: true
```

You can verify that they're enabled by checking the Cilium agent:

```
$ kubectl exec -it -n kube-system ds/cilium -- cilium-dbg status
Masquerading:    BPF (ip-masq-agent)    [eth0]    10.244.0.0/24
```

By default, the agent automatically provisions a default set of non-masquerade CIDRs, covering well-known private and reserved IP ranges:

```
$ kubectl exec -it ds/cilium -n kube-system -- cilium-dbg bpf ipmasq list
IP PREFIX/ADDRESS
198.18.0.0/15
198.51.100.0/24
203.0.113.0/24
100.64.0.0/10
169.254.0.0/16
172.16.0.0/12
192.0.2.0/24
192.88.99.0/24
192.168.0.0/16
240.0.0.0/4
10.0.0.0/8
192.0.0.0/24
```

You can customize it by creating a ConfigMap to define the CIDRs that should be excluded from masquerading. For example, the following configuration (*ip-masq-agent-cm.yaml*) disables masquerading for RFC 1918 address ranges:

```
apiVersion: v1
kind: ConfigMap
metadata:
  name: ip-masq-agent
data:
  config: |
    nonMasqueradeCIDRs:
    - 10.0.0.0/8
    - 172.16.0.0/12
    - 192.168.0.0/16
    masqLinkLocal: true
```

Deploy the *ip-masq-agent-cm.yaml* file in the `kube-system` namespace and verify, after a minute or so, that the changes are reflected correctly. You should see that the default set of non-masquerade CIDRs has been replaced by the ones specified in the ConfigMap:

```
$ kubectl exec -it ds/cilium -n kube-system -- cilium-dbg bpf ipmasq list
IP PREFIX/ADDRESS
10.0.0.0/8
172.16.0.0/12
192.168.0.0/16
```

Now, redeploy your client pod (*netshoot-client-pod.yaml*) and set up two terminals. In one, run a debugger container attached to the echo server to observe incoming traffic over port 8080 with `tcpdump`:

```
$ docker run --rm -it --network container:kind-echo-server \
  nicolaka/netshoot \
  tcpdump -i eth0 port 8080 -nnn -A
```

In the other terminal, attempt another connection from the client pod:

```
$ kubectl exec -it netshoot-client -- curl -v 172.18.0.7:8080
*   Trying 172.18.0.7:8080...
```

In the `tcpdump` output in the first terminal, you should see packets arriving with the client pod's source IP, confirming that masquerading was disabled for traffic bound to `172.18.0.7`:

```
13:26:18.143095 IP 10.244.1.252.46382 > 172.18.0.7.8080: Flags [S]
13:26:18.143166 IP 172.18.0.7.8080 > 10.244.1.252.46382: Flags [S.]
```

However, the connection hangs. The echo server responds, but the return packet never reaches the client pod. Since the pod IP isn't masqueraded, and the echo server has no route to the pod network, the response is dropped (Figure 11-2).

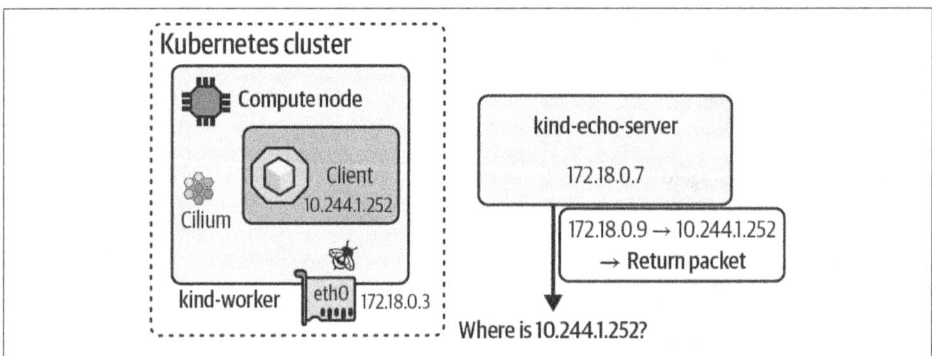

Figure 11-2. Disabling masquerading can cause connectivity issues, for example when the PodCIDR is unknown to systems outside the cluster

This highlights a key trade-off. In some scenarios, disabling masquerading is desirable—for example, when pod IPs are routable across the underlying network, or when you want external systems such as firewalls or monitoring tools to see the original pod IP for auditing or security purposes. In most environments, however, masquerading is necessary to ensure return traffic can find its way back into the cluster. Without it, external systems often have no route to the pod network, and responses are dropped.

The key point here is that while masquerading is necessary for connectivity in many cases, it also introduces a loss of source identity. From the perspective of an external system such as a firewall, the packet appears to come from the node itself. This has implications for security and observability:

- The firewall cannot identify which specific pod or namespace originated the request.
- Fine-grained policies based on workload identity become difficult to enforce at the network edge.

To address this limitation and preserve source identity while still enabling return traffic, Cilium offers the Egress Gateway feature, which we'll explore next.

Egress Gateway

Cilium's Egress Gateway feature provides a way to assign deterministic and predictable IP addresses to traffic leaving the cluster, based on characteristics such as pod labels and namespaces. It enables you to route pod traffic connections destined for specific cluster-external CIDRs through particular *egress gateway nodes*. Matching packets leaving the cluster are masqueraded with selected, predictable IPs associated with those gateway nodes, instead of the IP addresses of the pods themselves or the nodes on which they are running.

For example, Figure 11-3 shows a pod with IP `10.1.2.106` running on a node with IP `172.18.0.3`. Traffic from this pod is routed through an egress gateway node using the dedicated egress IP `10.0.3.42`, which is assigned specifically to that pod (or its namespace). When the pod connects to an external service at `10.0.4.2`, the service sees the source as `10.0.3.42`, allowing the connection to be traced back to the originating tenant. By contrast, with standard masquerading the same connection would appear as `172.18.0.3 > 10.0.4.2`, making it impossible to distinguish which pod generated the traffic.

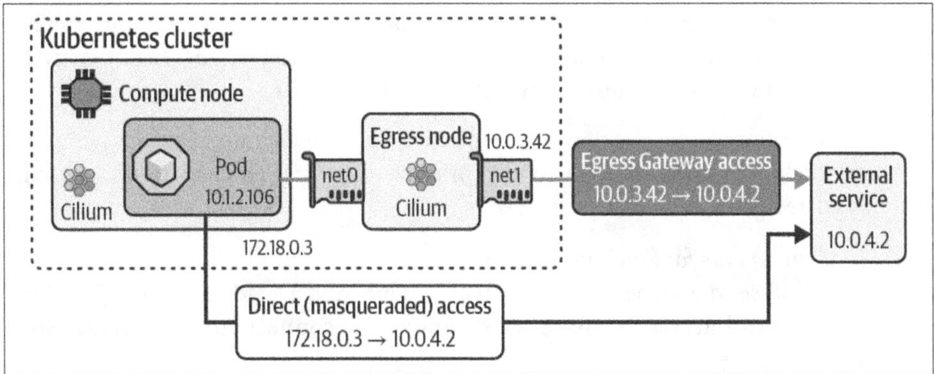

Figure 11-3. Egress Gateway overview

Let's consider some of the common scenarios where using Egress Gateway is beneficial.

Egress Gateway Use Cases

The following are some of the most common use cases for this feature. For each, we first present the operational need and then show how Egress Gateway provides a solution:

Tenant-specific egress IPs

In multitenant clusters, different teams or business units share the same infrastructure. To meet compliance and auditing requirements, you often need to identify which tenant accessed an external system based on its source IP. By default, node masquerading hides this information.

With Egress Gateway, each tenant can be assigned a static egress IP. This makes audit logs easier to interpret and simplifies firewall rules, since traffic from a given tenant always exits with the same predictable address. We will explore this particular use case (the most common one) in the example walk-through in the next section.

Restricting egress to trusted destinations

Some workloads must be limited to a defined set of external systems. For example, applications in a payments namespace may only be allowed to connect to a payment gateway or internal API.

Egress Gateway allows you to enforce such restrictions with egress policies that explicitly define which destinations workloads can reach. Attempts to connect elsewhere are blocked.

Environment-based egress controls

Clusters often run multiple environments, such as development, staging, and production. These environments typically have different network requirements: development workloads may need broad internet access, for example, while production workloads must follow stricter routing paths.

Egress Gateway enables environment-specific policies, such as allowing dev workloads to egress directly to the internet but forcing prod traffic through designated gateway nodes.

Static IP requirements for SaaS integrations

Many SaaS services, such as Snowflake, GitHub, and Datadog, require IP allowlists to control access. Without fixed source IPs, connectivity may break when node IPs change.

Egress Gateway provides a solution by routing traffic through stable, predefined egress IPs. These IPs can then be added to SaaS allowlists, ensuring consistent and reliable access.

Now that you have an idea of why you might want to use this feature, let's see how it works in practice.

Cilium Egress Gateway Example Walk-Through

Consider a scenario with two tenants: `hr` and `sales`. They share the same Kubernetes cluster, each in their own namespace, and both need to access a third-party directory system. For compliance reasons, that system must be able to audit which tenant initiated the connection, based on the source IP address.

As we saw earlier, the default masquerading behavior hides the original pod IPs behind the node IP. This means the directory system will see all access as coming from the same source, making it impossible to distinguish between tenants, as illustrated in Figure 11-4.

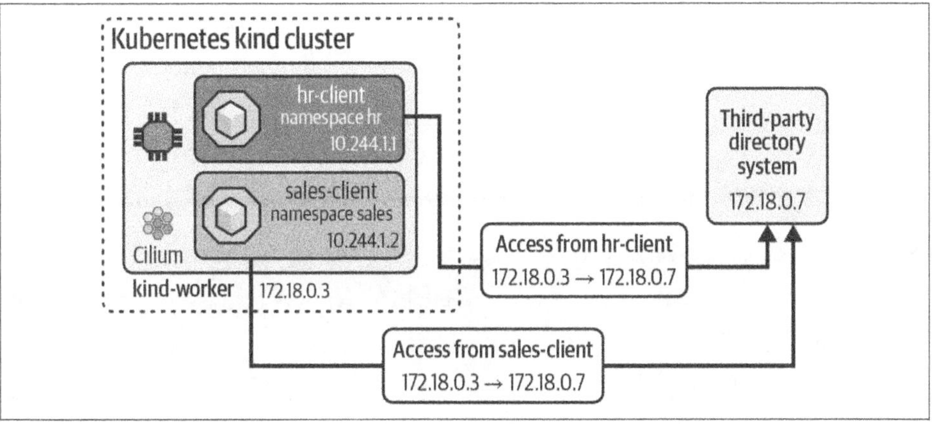

Figure 11-4. Default masquerading hides tenant identity

Cilium's Egress Gateway feature solves this problem by enabling us to assign tenant-specific egress IPs. With this approach, packets leaving the cluster carry an address that reflects the originating tenant, allowing the directory system to reliably trace who accessed it.

To see how to implement this feature, let's deploy a new kind cluster using the following configuration (*egress-gateway/kind-egress.yaml*):

```
kind: cluster
apiVersion: kind.x-k8s.io/v1alpha4
networking:
  disableDefaultCNI: true
nodes:
```

```
- role: control-plane
- role: worker ❶
- role: worker ❶
- role: worker ❷
  kubeadmConfigPatches:
  - |
    kind: InitConfiguration
    nodeRegistration:
      kubeletExtraArgs:
        register-with-taints: "egress-gw:NoSchedule" ❸
 - role: worker ❷
  kubeadmConfigPatches:
  - |
    kind: InitConfiguration
    nodeRegistration:
      kubeletExtraArgs:
        register-with-taints: "egress-gw:NoSchedule" ❸
```

❶ We use two worker nodes to run our applications.

❷ And we create two dedicated egress nodes.

❸ While not required, we decide not to run pods on the egress nodes themselves.

Let's add a couple of additional IP addresses on both egress nodes. These are secondary IP addresses attached to the `eth0` interface on `kind-worker3` and `kind-worker4`:

```
$ docker exec kind-worker3 ip addr add 172.18.0.100/16 dev eth0

$ docker exec kind-worker4 ip addr add 172.18.0.101/16 dev eth0
```

We'll install Cilium with Egress Gateway enabled (*cilium-egress-values.yaml*). This feature requires both KPR and eBPF-based masquerading to be enabled:

```
kubeProxyReplacement: true
egressGateway:
  enabled: true
devices:
  - eth0
bpf:
  masquerade: true
```

Next, we'll define an Egress Gateway policy. We do this using the CiliumEgressGatewayPolicy (CEGP) custom resource.[1] When designing such a policy, we must consider three core areas:

1 You can use the command `kubectl explain cegp` to describe the fields and structure of the CEGP resource.

- Which pods should be subject to the policy?
- Which traffic should be subject to the policy?
- Which egress node, interface, and source IP should be used to exit the cluster?

We'll start by specifying the pods that will fall under the scope of the policy. We can match based on labels, names, namespaces, and/or traffic from a particular set of nodes:

```
apiVersion: cilium.io/v2
kind: CiliumEgressGatewayPolicy
metadata:
  name: egress-sample
spec:
[...]
  selectors:
  - podSelector:
      matchLabels:
        env: prod
    namespaceSelector:
      matchLabels:
        name: hr
    nodeSelector: ❶
      matchLabels:
        node.kubernetes.io/name: kind-worker
[...]
```

❶ This field is optional; if not specified, the policy applies to all nodes.

Next, we'll define the list of destination CIDRs that the policy applies to. We can also optionally exclude some subset networks from consideration. In this example, traffic to all IPs within `192.168.0.0/16` will be matched by the policy, except traffic bound for the `192.168.100.0/24` subnet:

```
apiVersion: cilium.io/v2
kind: CiliumEgressGatewayPolicy
metadata:
  name: egress-sample
spec:
  [...]
  destinationCIDRs:
  - "192.168.0.0/16"
  excludeCIDRs:
  - "192.168.100.0/24"
```

Finally, using a `nodeSelector`, we select the nodes that will act as a gateway for the policy, based on their labels. We can also select which IP address will be used, specifying either the IP address itself or the network interface on which the egress IP address is configured:

```
apiVersion: cilium.io/v2
kind: CiliumEgressGatewayPolicy
metadata:
  name: egress-sample
spec:
  egressGateway:
    nodeSelector:
      matchLabels:
        node.kubernetes.io/name: node2
    egressIP: 10.168.60.100
    # Or ❶
    # interface: eth0
```

❶ The `egressIP` and `interface` properties cannot both be specified in the `egress Gateway` spec. Cilium will ignore Egress Gateway policies that contain both of these properties.

When neither the `egressIP` nor the `interface` field is specified, the policy will use the first IP assigned to the interface with the default route.

The *chapter11/egress-gateway* directory in the GitHub repository contains Egress Gateway policies for our two tenants, based on the template we've just shown (*egress-gw-policy-hr.yaml* and *egress-gw-policy-sales.yaml*):

```
apiVersion: cilium.io/v2
kind: CiliumEgressGatewayPolicy
metadata:
  name: hr-egress
spec:
  destinationCIDRs:
  - "172.18.0.0/16"
  selectors:
  - namespaceSelector:
      matchLabels:
        name: hr
  egressGateway:
    nodeSelector:
      matchLabels:
        egress-gw : "hr"
    egressIP: 172.18.0.100
---
apiVersion: cilium.io/v2
kind: CiliumEgressGatewayPolicy
metadata:
  name: sales-egress
spec:
  destinationCIDRs:
  - "172.18.0.0/16"
  selectors:
  - namespaceSelector:
      matchLabels:
```

```
        name: sales
  egressGateway:
    nodeSelector:
      matchLabels:
        egress-gw : "sales"
    egressIP: 172.18.0.101
```

To put them to use, let's first deploy and label the two tenant namespaces:

```
$ kubectl create ns hr && kubectl create ns sales

$ kubectl label ns hr name=hr && kubectl label ns sales name=sales
```

We'll also label our nodes—the `hr` tenant will exit the cluster via `kind-worker3`'s interface (using its secondary interface) while the `sales` tenant will use `kind-worker4`:

```
$ kubectl label nodes kind-worker3 egress-gw=hr

$ kubectl label nodes kind-worker4 egress-gw=sales
```

Next, we'll deploy two client pods, one for each namespace:

```
$ kubectl apply -n sales -f netshoot-client-pod.yaml

$ kubectl apply -n hr -f netshoot-client-pod.yaml
```

We can now deploy the two policies. The topology can be seen in Figure 11-5.

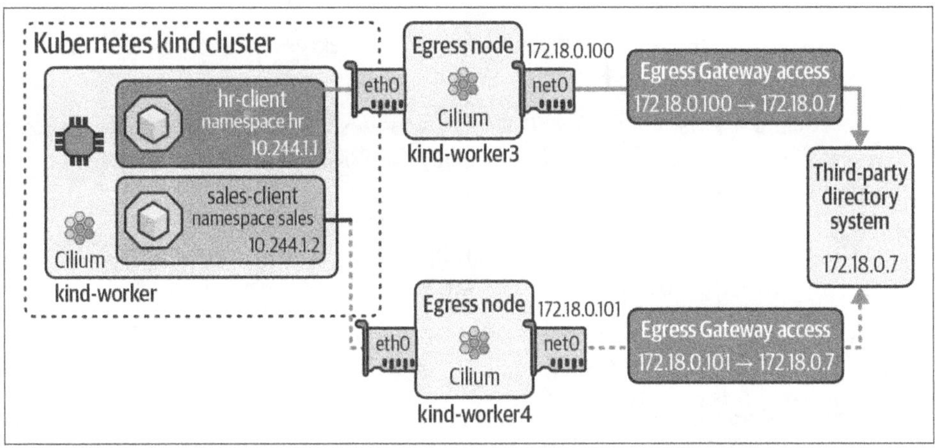

Figure 11-5. Egress Gateway policy example

Let's now confirm that both policies have taken effect. For our third-party directory system, we'll use the echo server once again to verify that SNAT is taking place. Since its IP falls within the policies' destination CIDR and the pods are selected based on their namespace, the *hr* and *sales* egress policies should apply to their respective namespaces.

Access from both pods is successful:

```
$ kubectl exec -n sales -it netshoot-client -- curl 172.18.0.7:8080
Request served by add431403996

$ kubectl exec -n hr -it netshoot-client -- curl 172.18.0.7:8080
Request served by add431403996
```

The logs on the echo server confirm the source IP was changed to `172.18.0.100`, the secondary IP we added on `kind-worker3`:

```
$ docker logs kind-echo-server
Echo server listening on port 8080.
172.18.0.101:57060 | GET /
172.18.0.100:50318 | GET /
```

This can also be verified by checking on the Cilium agent itself, with the `cilium-dbg bpf egress list` command:

```
$ kubectl exec -it -n kube-system cilium-89vx2 -- cilium-dbg bpf egress list
Source IP     Destination CIDR    Egress IP       Gateway IP
10.0.2.194    172.18.0.0/16       172.18.0.101    172.18.0.3
10.0.2.251    172.18.0.0/16       0.0.0.0         172.18.0.4
```

As we can see here:

- The `Source IP` corresponds to the IP of each pod selected by the policy's `podSelector`.
- The `Gateway IP` is the internal IP of the egress node selected by the `nodeSelector`.
- The `Egress IP` is set to `0.0.0.0` on all nodes except the designated egress gateway. On that node, the egress IP from the policy is applied and used for the outbound traffic.

We can also verify that access from a client in the default namespace to the server is masqueraded with the pod's node IP (`172.18.0.3`):

```
$ kubectl apply -f netshoot-client-pod.yaml
pod/netshoot-client created

$ kubectl get nodes kind-worker -o wide
NAME          STATUS   ROLES    AGE   VERSION   INTERNAL-IP
kind-worker   Ready    <none>   43h   v1.33.1   172.18.0.3

$ kubectl exec -it netshoot-client -- curl 172.18.0.7:8080
Request served by add431403996

$ docker logs kind-echo-server
Echo server listening on port 8080.
172.18.0.3:58858 | GET /
```

It's important to note that traffic from the pod's node to the egress node always travels over VXLAN, regardless of whether the cluster is running in native routing or encapsulation mode. This internal use of VXLAN can be confusing to some users, as they may expect native routing to avoid tunneling altogether. In this case, VXLAN is used only between the source node and the egress node to preserve the pod's identity and ensure consistent policy enforcement. The source identity is encoded in the VNI field of the VXLAN header, just as we saw in Chapter 5.

The */pcaps* folder in the book's GitHub repository includes a sample capture file, *egress_vxlan.pcap*, showing egress traffic. You can explore this capture directly using `tcpdump`:

```
$ tcpdump -r egress_vxlan.pcap
IP 172.18.0.2.38007 > 172.18.0.4.8472: OTV, flags [I]
IP 10.244.1.52.47312 > 172.18.0.7.8080: Flags [S], seq 3065752045, length 0
```

This confirms that traffic was sent encapsulated over VXLAN (UDP port 8472), with the outer IP header using the pod's node IP (`172.18.0.2`) as the source and the egress node's IP (`172.18.0.4`) as the destination. The capture also shows the original pod-to-pod packet preserved inside (`10.244.1.52 > 172.18.0.7`).

Once an Egress Gateway policy is applied and a node is selected, that node will always be used for matching traffic. There is no built-in load balancing or failover. This is the main limitation of Cilium's Egress Gateway feature today: if the chosen egress node becomes unavailable, traffic will be dropped. High-availability support is available in Isovalent's enterprise distribution of Cilium.

Note that traffic from the `hr` and `sales` clients to IP addresses outside the destination CIDR specified in the Egress Gateway policies will not exit via the egress nodes. Instead, it will follow the standard masquerading logic. You can verify this by running additional tests to nonmatching destinations if you'd like to observe the difference in behavior.

Bandwidth Manager

Controlling egress traffic is about more than preserving source IP addresses or setting predictable IPs: it's also about ensuring the traffic doesn't saturate the available bandwidth. Left unmanaged, it's easy for a handful of high-throughput pods to quickly consume the network capacity, leading to throttling or packet loss.

All files discussed in this section are in the *chapter11/bandwidth-manager* directory of the book's GitHub repository (*https://github.com/isovalent/cilium-up-and-running*).

Cilium includes an optional feature called *Bandwidth Manager* that can apply bandwidth limits to pods. Unlike Egress Gateway, which operates at the cluster level, bandwidth restrictions are enforced at the node level.

Bandwidth Manager uses Kubernetes annotations to ensure fair usage and to prevent accidental overconsumption. In clusters shared by multiple tenants, it works particularly well in conjunction with Egress Gateway. Configuring Egress Gateway ensures that traffic leaves the cluster with a deterministic source IP, while using Bandwidth Manager prevents noisy neighbor problems.

This example won't work in local environments like kind. Bandwidth enforcement depends on access to global `sysctl` settings (such as `/proc/sys/net/core`), which are not available inside nested network namespaces like those used by kind. As a result, to see this feature in action, you'll need to run on bare metal or virtual machines with full kernel access, or use a managed Kubernetes platform such as Azure Kubernetes Service.

To try it out, we'll use AKS. Follow the instructions from "Encapsulation mode with Geneve" on page 88 to create a cluster in BYOCNI mode before installing Cilium with the following Helm values (*cilium-bm-values.yaml*). Note that Bandwidth Manager is disabled by default and therefore needs to be explicitly enabled:

```
aksbyocni:
  enabled: true
azure:
  resourceGroup: bandwidth-rg
cluster:
  name: bandwidth-rg
nodeinit:
  enabled: true
operator:
  replicas: 1
bandwidthManager:
  enabled: true
```

Again, we can verify that it's enabled by checking the Cilium agent:

```
$ kubectl -n kube-system exec ds/cilium -- \
    cilium-dbg status | grep BandwidthManager
BandwidthManager:         EDT with BPF [CUBIC] [eth0]
```

With Cilium installed, we'll begin by benchmarking network performance using the `netperf` tool. The goal is to establish a baseline measurement before enabling egress bandwidth enforcement, so we can clearly see the difference once limits are applied.

To do this, we'll deploy a pair of `netperf` pods (*bandwidth-manager-pods.yaml*), one to act as a server and the other as a client:

```
apiVersion: v1
kind: Pod
metadata:
  labels:
    app.kubernetes.io/name: netperf-server ❶
  name: netperf-server
spec:
  containers:
  - name: netperf
    image: cilium/netperf
    ports:
    - containerPort: 12865
---
apiVersion: v1
kind: Pod
metadata:
  name: netperf-client ❷
spec:
  affinity:
    podAntiAffinity: ❸
      requiredDuringSchedulingIgnoredDuringExecution:
      - labelSelector:
          matchExpressions:
          - key: app.kubernetes.io/name
            operator: In
            values:
            - netperf-server
        topologyKey: kubernetes.io/hostname
  containers:
  - name: netperf
    args:
    - sleep
    - infinity
    image: cilium/netperf
```

❶ This pod will act as the server. It will generate the outbound traffic during the performance test.

❷ This pod will act as the client. It will initiate the test and receive the data stream.

❸ This pod anti-affinity rule ensures that the client is not scheduled on the same node as the server, allowing us to observe cross-node traffic control.

The pods will allow us to measure throughput and demonstrate the impact of bandwidth enforcement.

Now, let's start running network throughput tests with `netperf`:

```
$ kubectl get pods -o wide
NAME             IP           NODE
netperf-client   10.0.2.156   aks-nodepool1-…000002
netperf-server   10.0.1.14    aks-nodepool1-…000001

$ NETPERF_SERVER_IP=10.0.1.14

$ kubectl exec netperf-client -- netperf -t TCP_MAERTS -H \
    "${NETPERF_SERVER_IP}"
Recv   Send    Send
Socket Socket  Message  Elapsed
Size   Size    Size     Time     Throughput
bytes  bytes   bytes    secs.    10^6bits/sec

131072  16384  16384    10.00    8827.69
```

This `netperf` command performs a one-way throughput test. In our environment, the benchmark exceeds 8 Gbps!

A typical `netperf` test is called `TCP_STREAM` and goes from the `netperf` client to the `netperf` server. Therefore, a stream from the `netperf` server to the client will be `STREAM` backwards: `MAERTS`. This is how servers typically operate, with larger data flows going from server to client.

Let's now rate-limit traffic leaving the `netperf` server pod. Bandwidth Manager is configured via a specific pod annotation, `kubernetes.io/egress-bandwidth`. When Bandwidth Manager is enabled and the Cilium agent detects that the annotation is set for a particular pod, the agent pushes the bandwidth requirements into the eBPF datapath, enforcing traffic limits on the physical interface. We can demonstrate this by adding the following annotation:

```
$ kubectl annotate pod/netperf-server kubernetes.io/egress-bandwidth="10M"
pod/netperf-server annotated
```

When you run the same tests again, you will see that traffic was limited to just under 10 Mbps, as desired:

```
Recv   Send    Send
Socket Socket  Message  Elapsed
Size   Size    Size     Time     Throughput
bytes  bytes   bytes    secs.    10^6bits/sec

131072  16384  16384    10.00       9.54
```

Note that traffic can also be limited in the opposite direction, as it enters the pod, by using the `kubernetes.io/ingress-bandwidth` annotation. However, by the time ingress rate limiting is enforced, the traffic will already have hit the wire and hogged bandwidth. Limiting egress bandwidth is more effective as it works as closely as possible to the emitting pod, preventing a high volume of traffic from leaving the node's interface.

If you created a cloud-hosted cluster to test this feature, remember to delete it to avoid further costs.

Summary

In this chapter, you learned how Cilium gives you fine-grained control over how traffic exits your cluster. We looked at three key features that shape egress behavior:

- Masquerading, which controls how pod source IPs are preserved or rewritten
- Egress Gateway, which enables deterministic, policy-driven SNAT with fixed egress IPs
- Bandwidth Manager, which prevents noisy neighbors from exhausting node-level bandwidth

Together, these features help you build more predictable, secure, and scalable egress paths.

In the next chapter, we'll shift our focus from access to and from the cluster to what traffic is allowed between workloads. We'll begin our deep dive into Cilium's security capabilities with an exploration of network policy.

CHAPTER 12
Network Policy

Network security controls are used to protect workloads by preventing unintended access, halting lateral movement, and enforcing organizational policy. All of this can be done at the network level, reducing the need to coordinate policy across disparate teams and third-party applications. Traditional approaches are difficult to implement in a cloud native environment. Pod and service IPs can change without warning, and all pods usually occupy the same CIDR range, so external network security appliances cannot differentiate traffic from different workloads.[1]

Cilium's network policy feature, an extension of the Kubernetes NetworkPolicy, is an in-cluster replacement for these traditional controls that is deeply integrated into existing Kubernetes concepts such as namespaces, workload labels, and services.

All the manifests for this chapter are in the *chapter12* directory of the book's GitHub repository (*https://github.com/isovalent/cilium-up-and-running*). We'll call out the filenames you need as we refer to them, and only show the important bits here.

Creating a Basic Policy

Let's start by creating a cluster and deploying Cilium. We don't need any special configuration to use network policy, but see previous chapters for examples of deploying using kind.

We'll deploy a simple web server (*webserver.yaml*) and protect it with network policy. As in previous chapters, we'll use NGINX, but configured to serve text on port 8080 and metrics on port 9113. We'll label the pod with `app.kubernetes.io/name:`

1 As we saw in Chapter 11, Cilium's default behavior is to masquerade the source IP of all traffic leaving the cluster to the node's IP address. The Egress Gateway feature enables you to assign fixed IPs for egress traffic, making it possible to distinguish which tenant it originated from.

webserver, which we'll use later to refer to it in our policy. We'll also deploy two services: a ClusterIP service called webserver to map port 80 to port 8080 and a headless service called webserver-metrics to map to port 9113. Deploying them into a test cluster and using a test pod, we can see what it responds with when no network policy is in place:

```
$ kubectl apply --filename chapter12/webserver.yaml
deployment.apps/webserver created
configmap/nginx-config created
service/webserver created
service/webserver-metrics created

$ kubectl run test -it --rm --image nicolaka/netshoot -- bash

test:~# curl -sm1 webserver
Hello from Cilium Up and Running!

test:~# curl -s webserver-metrics:9113/metrics | grep ^nginx_http_requests_total
nginx_http_requests_total 1
```

From now on, when we mention a *test pod* we mean one deployed as shown in this example, by running kubectl run. Later, we'll need to apply labels to our test pod to be captured, which you can do with the --labels flag. We're going to be running in lots of different containers in this chapter; we'll prefix commands with just $ if they're intended to be run from a remote machine and with test:~# if they're intended to be run inside a test pod, as shown in this example.

Restricting Traffic by Port

Let's now apply a simple policy (*webserver-8080-only.yaml*) that allows only TCP ingress on port 8080, blocking all other traffic. We'll show the full policy and step through it so you can get an idea of what it looks like:

```
apiVersion: cilium.io/v2
kind: CiliumNetworkPolicy ❶
metadata:
  name: webserver ❷
  namespace: default
spec:
  endpointSelector: ❸
    matchLabels:
      app.kubernetes.io/name: webserver
  ingress: ❹
    - toPorts: ❺
      - ports:
        - port: "8080"
          protocol: TCP
```

❶ This is a CiliumNetworkPolicy. It's a namespaced policy and not a CiliumClusterwideNetworkPolicy, so the endpoint selector only applies to endpoints in the same namespace.

❷ Like any Kubernetes object, it needs metadata, but the metadata does not affect how the policy works. We use the name `webserver`.

❸ The `spec.endpointSelector` field is a label selector, just like `spec.selector` on Kubernetes deployments and services. For now you can think of this as selecting pod labels, but technically it selects the security labels of Cilium identities. We'll cover what those are and the implications of this later. In our case, the `app.kubernetes.io/name: webserver` label is on the web server we deployed earlier.

❹ Policies can have both ingress rules and egress rules. We're only specifying a list of ingress rules.

❺ We have a single ingress rule with a single statement, `toPorts`. This rule is applied to traffic attempting to enter the endpoint; if the traffic matches the rule, it's accepted. Rules can have multiple statements to filter on different properties of the traffic. Ours only includes `toPorts`, so it matches only TCP traffic destined for port 8080. If it had additional rules, traffic matching any of those rules would be permitted. Cilium's service resolution is always performed before network policy is applied, so even though the `webserver` service maps port 80 to port 8080 and the client pod communicates on port 80, the policy needs to be for port 8080.

The `port` in a network policy is always enclosed in quotes. It can be a number or a name (e.g., `"http"` instead of `"80"`), and it can refer to a declared container port if the workload has one. In our case, the container exposed no specific ports, and Cilium doesn't require workloads to do so.

Let's apply this policy to our cluster and repeat our test:

```
$ kubectl apply -f webserver-8080-only.yaml
ciliumnetworkpolicy.cilium.io/webserver created

$ kubectl run test -it --rm --image nicolaka/netshoot -- bash

test:~# curl -sm1 webserver
Hello from Cilium Up and Running!
```

```
test:~# curl -m1 webserver-metrics:9113/metrics
curl: (28) Connection timed out after 1001 milliseconds
```

The HTTP connection on port 8080 works, but attempting to reach the metrics service on port 9113 fails with a timeout. Network policy is applied in eBPF at layer 3 and blocked traffic is dropped with no response. The TCP `SYN` packet from cURL is ignored, and the backend pod never sees any traffic on port 9113.

Endpoints and Policy Enforcement

We've informally used the term *endpoint* to refer to "something on a network." In the context of network policy, we mean specifically a CiliumEndpoint. Cilium generates an endpoint for any pod it manages. We can view these by inspecting the CiliumEndpoint resource:

```
$ kubectl get ciliumendpoint
NAME                          SECURITY IDENTITY   ENDPOINT STATE   IPV4
webserver-ff7cc8f4c-69hbs     11866               ready            10.0.0.131
webserver-ff7cc8f4c-lxlwc     11866               ready            10.0.0.215
webserver-ff7cc8f4c-z64mk     11866               ready            10.0.0.163
```

When you write a network policy, the `endpointSelector` is used to *select* these endpoints. The Cilium agent will determine which ones are selected and program the Cilium eBPF datapath for those pods to enforce the policy. This updating, called "policy regeneration," occurs when you launch a pod or update a policy, not while processing packets.

Network policy is applied in the endpoint datapath immediately after traffic exits the pod on egress and immediately before it enters on ingress. This means policy enforcement can't be done on pods that run in the host network (i.e., with `spec.hostNetwork=true`).

Default Deny

If an endpoint is not selected by *any* policy, all traffic to and from that endpoint is permitted. This is known as a *default allow* model. However, if even a single network policy selects an endpoint with at least one rule for a given direction of traffic (ingress or egress), then all traffic for that endpoint in that direction must match a rule to be permitted. In other words, once a policy applies to an endpoint for a given traffic direction, the behavior switches to *default deny*.

This is how traffic to port 9113 is being blocked. We only added a rule for port 8080; because we didn't also allow port 9113, it's blocked by Cilium. This is only true for the endpoints selected by the policy—other endpoints are unaffected. Similarly, because our policy only restricted *ingress* and not *egress*, traffic can still leave our NGINX pods freely.

We can test this by running cURL from inside one of those pods. The NGINX pods don't contain cURL, but we can launch an ephemeral container to execute testing tools from within the pod's network namespace, as if the NGINX container was doing it:

```
$ pod_name="$(kubectl get po \
    -l app.kubernetes.io/name=webserver \
    -o=jsonpath='{.items[0].metadata.name}')"

$ kubectl debug \
    --image nicolaka/netshoot \
    --profile=general \
    -it "${pod_name}" -- bash

webserver-ff7cc8f4c-4wvtw:~# curl -sI https://cilium.io | head -n1
HTTP/2 200
```

Network policy also doesn't apply between processes within a pod. Even though port 9113 is blocked, because the test container we launched with `kubectl debug` is inside the NGINX pod, we can still access it on `localhost`.

Sometimes you don't want a policy to impact other traffic. We can control this using the `spec.enableDefaultDeny` setting. The `ingress` and `egress` keys can be set independently for a given policy. They default to `true` if not set. Setting one or both to `false` exempts the policy from triggering the default deny behavior for traffic in that direction:

```
spec:
  enableDefaultDeny:
    ingress: false
    egress: false
```

This setting applies only for the policy in which it is specified. If an endpoint is selected by *any* policy that has default deny enabled, the default deny behavior will apply.

Egress Rules

Maybe we don't want to allow our NGINX pods to egress to all destinations. Perhaps we're concerned about one of them becoming compromised and want to restrict lateral movement. We can protect against this too by adding a new policy (*webserver-no-egress.yaml*) with an egress rule:

```
spec:
  egress:
    - {}
```

This policy has no ingress rules and a single egress rule that is blank with no statements. Because there is a rule at all, Cilium enforces the default deny behavior on egress, but this rule does not match any traffic, so all egress will be blocked.

Applying *webserver-no-egress.yaml* and testing again from our debug ephemeral container in the NGINX pod, we can see that outbound traffic is blocked:

```
webserver-ff7cc8f4c-4wvtw:~# curl -m1 https://cilium.io
curl: (28) Resolving timed out after 1002 milliseconds
```

An important observation, however, is that this restriction does *not* apply to responses to incoming traffic that is permitted. If we launch a test pod like before, we can still get a response to our HTTP request even though all egress traffic is blocked:

```
test:~# curl -s webserver
Hello from Cilium Up and Running!
```

Note also that we could have added this rule to the existing policy instead of creating a new one—it makes no difference to the policy engine if rules are located together in a single policy or split across several different ones.[2]

Identity

Policy based on ports has uses for blanket restrictions, but it's only part of the story. The core of any network security solution is *identity*. To apply rules that allow or block certain traffic, you must know the identities of the endpoints that are communicating.

The Foundations of Security

Broadly speaking, solutions determine identity either at layer 3, based on IP addresses, or at layer 7, based on authentication data contained in the traffic itself.

Layer 3 security doesn't place restrictions on the type of traffic, which could be TCP or UDP. It usually requires little to no coordination with the applications themselves and is often implemented in extremely efficient network appliances. With the exception of "stateful" layer 4 firewalls,[3] layer 3 enforcement is typically entirely stateless, so load can be shared across multiple appliances without requiring state coordination. However, this approach relies on ascribing meaning to an IP address.

2 That said, as we'll see in "Combining Statements" on page 261, if any rule in a policy is *invalid*, the whole policy is not applied. For this reason, it can sometimes be preferable to break them up.

3 Layer 4 firewalls track expected responses to UDP traffic or allow TCP responses on the same port, but identity is still derived from IP address.

Sysadmins of eld may have assigned specific IP addresses or ranges to different types of physical or virtual machines by their function. For example, assigning the subnet `198.51.100.0/24` to application servers means that a firewall can enforce the rule "only application servers may access the database servers" by allowing only TCP traffic on port 5432 from `198.51.100.0/24`.[4]

This assignment is brittle. If done by convention, a future misconfiguration may invalidate security assumptions. For instance, if an entire `/24` subnet of 255 addresses is used for five application servers, a future administrator might shrink the CIDR range for the servers to consume only `198.51.100.104/29` and reallocate the other addresses to other functions. But if the firewalls are not updated, these other servers will have unintended database access. Even if the allocations and any changes are adequately documented, this approach makes policy hard to read and requires referencing a separate IP address mapping document. It also requires that devices cannot spoof IP addresses on the network fabric, for example by issuing gratuitous ARP (IPv4) or ND (IPv6) packets to confuse the network into incorrectly assigning IP addresses to unexpected devices.[5]

Layer 7 security mechanisms, such as bearer tokens or mutual TLS (mTLS) in HTTP, embed identity in the application protocol. This approach can make use of advanced cryptography such as SPIFFE identity documents, but it is dependent on the protocol supporting it and must be implemented in the application itself or reverse proxies.

Identity in Cilium

Cilium's policy engine ascribes identity at layer 3 based on the source or destination IP address of the packet, but it uses Kubernetes's knowledge of the entire cluster to accurately and automatically map in-cluster IP addresses to concrete identities. Because Cilium is a CNI, it must be consulted before any pods can be started or stopped. This means a Cilium agent always has an up-to-date view of which IPs are used for which identities.

Cilium doesn't maintain a direct mapping of IP addresses to policy decisions. Such a mapping, even if updated automatically, would need to change every time a pod launched or was terminated. Instead, Cilium has a layer of indirection called a *Cilium identity*. Each pod has exactly one Cilium identity, and every IP address that the Cilium datapath might encounter, be it internal or external, maps to exactly one identity. This mapping is stored in a per-node eBPF map called the *IP cache*.

An example of an IP cache map is shown in Table 12-1. In a dual-stack cluster (see Chapter 4) the same map contains both IPv4 and IPv6 entries. You can consult the IP

4 This is the default port used by the popular open source database PostgreSQL.

5 Enterprise-grade switches often have protections for this.

cache on your node with the command `cilium-dbg bpf ipcache list` from within the agent's container.

Table 12-1. An example IP cache map

IP range	Identity	Explanation
`192.0.2.33/32`	30525	A pod's IPv4 address
`0.0.0.0/0`	2	A "catch-all" IPv4 rule for the `world` identity
`::/0`	10	A "catch-all" IPv6 rule for the `world` identity
`233.252.0.17/32`	1	The host's IPv4 address
`203.0.113.0/24`	16777218	A defined IPv4 CIDR range from a policy
`2001:db8:aa::e8/128`	1	The host's IPv6 address
`2001:db8::34c9/128`	30525	A pod's IPv6 address
`2001:db8:ffff::/48`	16777219	A defined IPv6 CIDR range from a policy

Each entry associates a CIDR with a single identity. The map operates with longest prefix match (LPM) semantics: if multiple entries match a single IP, the one with the longest prefix—the "most specific" one—is used. For example, `192.0.2.33` matches both `192.0.2.33/32` and `0.0.0.0/0`, but the former is more specific, so it's the one that is chosen.

For individual resources such as pods, we use a `/32` (IPv4) or `/128` (IPv6) CIDR to select only a single IP, but wider ranges can be used when implementing CIDR network policies (see "Beyond the Cluster" on page 263). Notice also the `/0` entries used for the "catch-all" `world` identity; we'll talk more about that later in the chapter.

Cilium doesn't iterate over all of the IP cache entries to find the most specific one for every packet. Instead, the IP cache is implemented as an LPM trie,[6] a type of data structure called a *radix tree.* With this implementation, the time it takes to find the match is proportional to the length of an IP address, which is fixed, and not the number of entries in the map. For more information, see Chapter 12 of Thomas Cormen et al.'s *Introduction to Algorithms*, 3rd edition (MIT Press).

Note also that if Cilium is already aware of a source's identity via other means, it does not need to consult the IP cache. When applying ingress policy to traffic from a pod on the same node, for example, no lookup is necessary. And as we discussed in Chapter 5, when Cilium is running in encapsulation mode, the source identity

6 This isn't a typo of "tree," although a trie is a type of tree.

of traffic that passes between nodes is encoded in the VNI field in the VXLAN or Geneve header, which avoids the need for an identity lookup.

Cilium stores metadata about cluster identities in the cluster itself using the CiliumIdentity custom resource. We can see the identities for the pods we've already created by viewing this resource:

```
$ kubectl get ciliumidentity -o yaml /
    -l 'io.kubernetes.pod.namespace=default'

items:
- apiVersion: cilium.io/v2
  kind: CiliumIdentity
  metadata:
    name: "22727"
  security-labels:
    k8s:io.kubernetes.pod.namespace: default
    k8s:run: test
- apiVersion: cilium.io/v2
  kind: CiliumIdentity
  metadata:
    name: "24505"
  security-labels:
    k8s:io.kubernetes.pod.namespace: default
    k8s:app.kubernetes.io/name: webserver
```

The CiliumIdentity resource isn't namespaced, even though the identities themselves usually are. This means that to limit our listing to only identities for pods in the `default` namespace, we can't use `--namespace` in the command like we normally would. Instead, we use a label filter for `io.kubernetes.pod.namespace`, as shown here. Somewhat confusingly, this filter applies to the label on the CiliumIdentity object, *not* to the security labels associated with that identity (which are listed under the `security-labels` key).

That brings us to the last important property of identities: we never refer to them directly, and instead select them using security labels. The primary source of these labels is the labels on the pod. For example, we can see that one of our identities has the security label `k8s:app.kubernetes.io/name: webserver`, from the label on our NGINX pod.

If multiple pods have the same labels, Cilium will assign them the same identity. This is useful if you have multiple replicas of a single service that are, from a policy perspective, the same. Our `webserver` pods were a good example of this, as they shared the same identity even though there were multiple pods.

Limiting Identity-Relevant Labels

One of the most important optimizations for large clusters is to restrict the number of *identity-relevant* labels. By default Cilium considers almost any label on a pod to be identity relevant, and all of them will be used as security labels on the identity. However, this can have unintended consequences where labels have high cardinality that isn't used in policy.

For example, batch processing systems often apply a "task identifier" label to pods they create. This can mean that every task launched will have a unique value for this label and will therefore create a new identity. Creating new identities causes every agent in the cluster to recalculate the policy maps for every single endpoint on the local node. On high-churn clusters, or clusters with large numbers of pods, this can cause maps to become exhausted (see Chapter 16), or the amount of policy regeneration may lead to degraded performance.

The solution is to limit the identity-relevant labels so that these labels are ignored for identity generation, often meaning that new pods will not require new identities. The flipside of this is that if labels are not on security identities, they cannot be used in `fromEntities` statements in policy and they cannot be used to select endpoints with `endpointSelector`.

You can configure identity-relevant labels using the `labels` Helm value, either selecting labels to include or excluding labels by placing a `!` before the label name.

The Policy Datapath

After the identity is determined, Cilium has to decide what to do with the packet. Each endpoint has its own policy map, computed ahead of time by the Cilium agent. It encodes the action to take for each unique mapping of identity, direction (ingress/egress), protocol, and port.[7]

Figure 12-1 shows a simplified example of the policy flow for a natively routed cluster. First, it uses the IP cache to determine the source identity, mapping 10.0.0.68/32 to resolve identity 22727. It can then use this identity along with other information about the packet, such as the protocol and port, to check the policy map and decide what to do with the packet. In this case, it will match the policy rule for (22727, Ingress, TCP, 8080) → ALLOW. The purpose of identity in Cilium is to provide indirection between an IP address and a policy decision. All policy decisions are precomputed ahead of time by the Cilium agent and encoded into the datapath as

7 This is why there is no `fromPorts` policy in Cilium: the datapath can't encode a source port requirement.

these simple lookups of *IP → identity* and then *identity, direction, protocol, port → decision*.

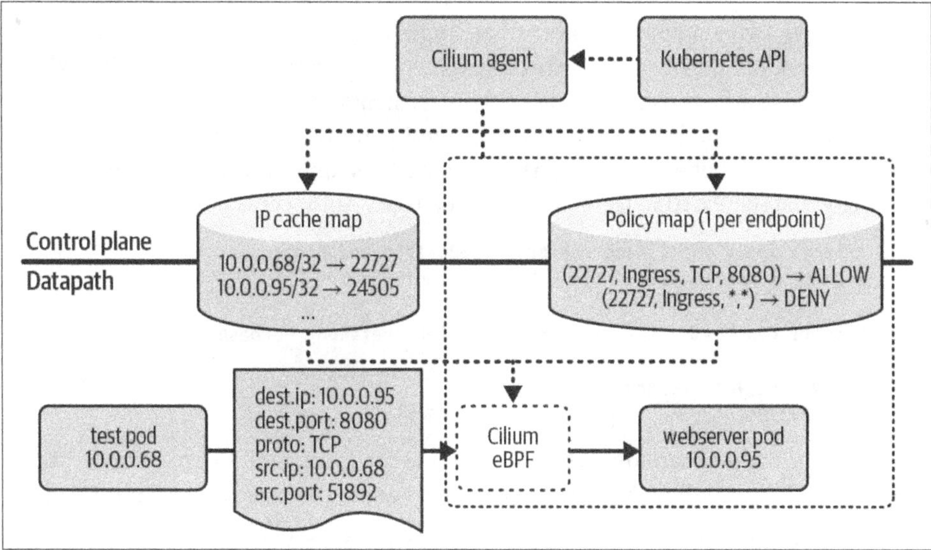

Figure 12-1. A packet transiting the eBPF datapath and being evaluated against policy

The possible policy outcomes are that the packet is accepted and forwarded to the container, dropped with no response sent, or sent to a user space proxy for further processing. We'll discuss the role of proxies in layer 7 policy in Chapter 13, but even in a layer 7 case, it's the eBPF datapath that is programmed to send traffic to a proxy.

Selecting Identities with Policy

Now that we understand how identities and policy outcomes are determined, let's turn our attention to how to define policies to control which identities may communicate.

From Endpoints

Let's rewrite our policy for the web server to use the `fromEndpoints` statement. This is the first of the "identity-limiting" policy statements we'll cover, and it allows us to apply our policies to any identities that match certain security labels. The list of ingress rules in the policy will look like this (*webserver-8080-from-endpoints.yaml*):

```
ingress:
  - fromEndpoints:
    - matchLabels:
        app.kubernetes.io/name: test
    toPorts:
```

```
    - ports:
      - port: "8080"
        protocol: TCP
```

We now have two statements within that single ingress rule: the `toPorts` statement from before and a new `fromEndpoints` statement. When multiple statements exist in the same rule, traffic must match *all* of the statements to match the rule. Here, traffic must be both destined for TCP port 8080 *and* coming from an endpoint with the security label `app.kubernetes.io/name: test`. Let's apply this policy to our cluster and verify that our existing test pod, without a label, can't access port 8080:

```
$ kubectl apply --filename webserver-8080-from-endpoints.yaml
ciliumnetworkpolicy.cilium.io/webserver configured

$ kubectl run test -it --rm --image nicolaka/netshoot -- bash

test:~# curl -m1 webserver
curl: (28) Connection timed out after 1004 milliseconds
```

At this point, the pod cannot access the server at all. Next, we'll re-create our test pod with the label expected by the policy, `app.kubernetes.io/name: test`, and try again:

```
$ kubectl run test -it --rm --image nicolaka/netshoot \
    --labels "app.kubernetes.io/name=test" -- bash

test:~# curl -sm1 webserver
Hello from Cilium Up and Running!

test:~# curl -m1 webserver-metrics:9113/metrics
curl: (28) Connection timed out after 1002 milliseconds
```

Once we relaunch the test pod with the correct label, we are able to access the server. However, we're still not able to access the metrics service.

Policy with Multiple Rules

We can take this a step further by introducing a second ingress rule authorizing a different identity to scrape the web server's metrics. The new rule looks like this (*webserver-ingress-all.yaml*):

```
  - fromEndpoints:
    - matchLabels:
        io.kubernetes.pod.namespace: metrics
        app.kubernetes.io/name: metrics-collector
    toPorts:
    - ports:
      - port: "9113"
        protocol: TCP
```

Instead of adding an additional statement to our existing rule, we've added a second rule to our policy. This one permits access to TCP port 9113 from identities with the security labels `io.kubernetes.pod.namespace: metrics` and `app.kubernetes.io/name: metrics-collector`. As with a normal label selector in Kubernetes, when we have multiple labels, an identity needs to match *all* of them to be selected.

The `io.kubernetes.pod.namespace` label is a special one populated by Cilium: it contains the name of the namespace the pod associated with the identity belongs to.[8] Taken together, this new ingress rule permits TCP access to port 9113 from pods that have the label `app.kubernetes.io/name: metrics-collector` *and* are in the `metrics` namespace.

While the statements and selectors inside a rule are additive, rules themselves are not. Figure 12-2 shows a graphical representation of the updated policy.

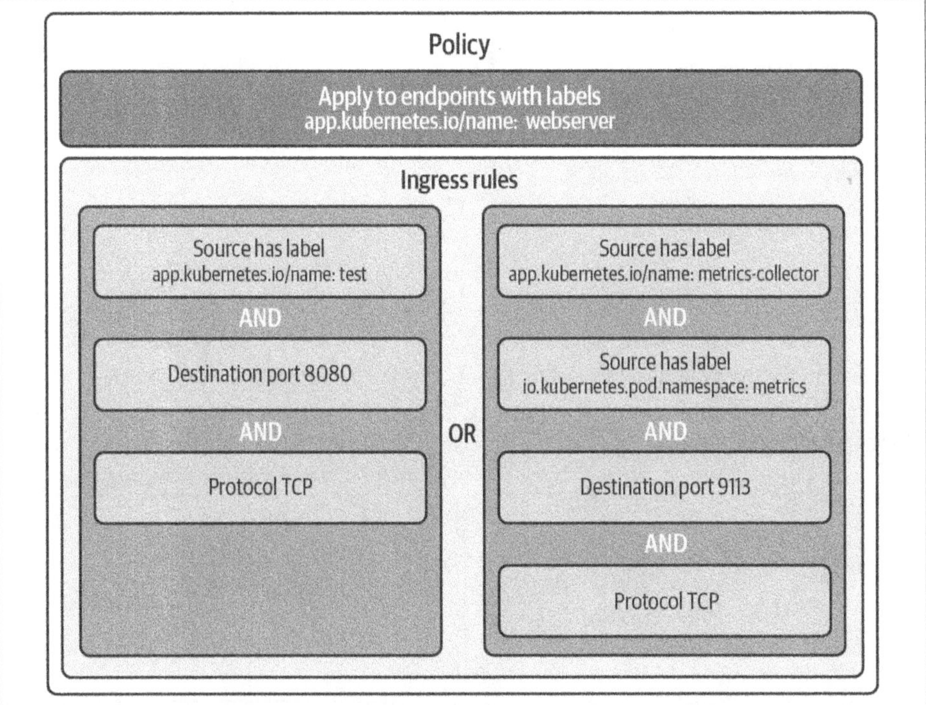

Figure 12-2. A graphical representation of a Cilium network policy

Traffic must match at least one rule, making each rule an "or," but to match a rule traffic must match all statements, making statements within a rule "and."

8 You can't "trick" the policy engine by setting a pod label literally named `io.kubernetes.pod.namespace`. Cilium will ignore labels on pods that would overlap with the special labels.

Multiple Statements Versus Multiple Rules

There's a subtlety we glossed over when talking about rules with multiple statements and then multiple rules in a policy. Consider the two following fragments of policies, listing only the ingress rules:

```
  ingress:
    - fromEndpoints:
      - matchLabels:
          app.kubernetes.io/name: test
      toPorts:
      - ports:
        - port: "8080"
          protocol: TCP
---
  ingress:
    - fromEndpoints:
      - matchLabels:
          app.kubernetes.io/name: test
    - toPorts:
      - ports:
        - port: "8080"
          protocol: TCP
```

Can you see the difference? The first policy fragment has no dash before `toPorts`. It defines a single rule with a `fromEndpoints` and a `toPorts` statement. The second policy fragment has a dash at the start of that line, which splits the list into two ingress rules: one that contains the `fromEndpoints` statement and another ingress rule that contains the `toPorts` statement. Figure 12-3 shows these two policy fragments graphically.

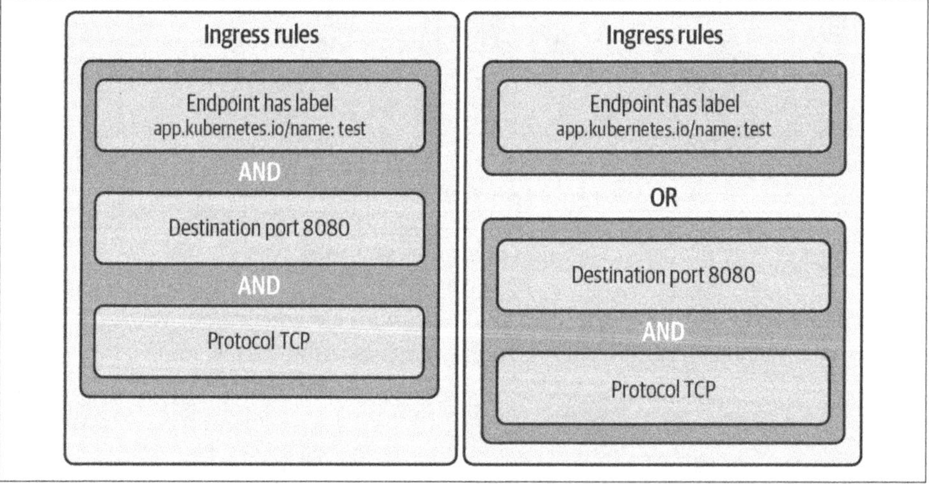

Figure 12-3. A graphical representation of the two lists of ingress rules

Applying the second policy fragment would mean that endpoints with the label `app.kubernetes.io/name: test` could reach *any* port on our workload, including any sensitive ports, and *any* identity—including ones external to the cluster—could access TCP port 8080. Depending on the nature of the misconfiguration, this small difference can lead to a significant security risk.

Cluster-wide Policy

Normally, a CiliumNetworkPolicy is only able to select endpoints in the same namespace as the policy. The rules in that policy may refer to endpoints in other namespaces, as we've seen, but the policy itself can't affect endpoints outside that namespace. This is an important property of Kubernetes namespace isolation, and it means that in a multitenant cluster where namespaces are used for tenant isolation, a user creating a network policy in one namespace can't impact pods in other namespaces. However, sometimes we do want to apply policy to every endpoint in every namespace at the same time.

In our previous example, we added an ingress rule to allow the metrics collector to reach the metrics endpoint. We'd rather not have to specify in every single endpoint's policy that it should permit access from the collector. For that, we can use a CiliumClusterwideNetworkPolicy. The cluster-wide policy supports all the same features as a namespaced one, and the implementation is the same. The only difference is that the object isn't namespaced, so the `endpointSelector` can select endpoints in any namespace in the cluster.

Cluster-wide policy is a powerful tool, but that capability comes with risk when you can impact the entire cluster at once. If you select all endpoints (using `endpointSelector: {}`) with a cluster-wide policy and don't disable default deny, as we described earlier in this chapter, you can easily "lock out" access to a cluster by accident, preventing any pods from communicating.

Let's write a new cluster-wide policy (*clusterwide-metrics.yaml*) to select all endpoints so that the metrics collector can access them on port 9113:

```
apiVersion: cilium.io/v2
kind: CiliumClusterwideNetworkPolicy
metadata:
  name: clusterwide-metrics
spec:
  endpointSelector: {}
  enableDefaultDeny:
    ingress: false
  ingress:
    - fromEndpoints:
```

```
- matchLabels:
    io.kubernetes.pod.namespace: metrics
    app.kubernetes.io/name: metrics-collector
toPorts:
- ports:
  - port: "9113"
    protocol: TCP
```

This way, we don't need a policy for every endpoint to allow the metrics service to scrape them. You can repeat the test from the previous section (after adjusting the namespaced policy to not mention port 9113) to see this in action.

Reserved Labels, Reserved Identities, and Entities

We've seen that Cilium dynamically creates identities for workloads and attaches security labels to those identities. This forms the foundation of Cilium's identity and security model, letting us apply policy to endpoints by selecting their identities using a policy's `endpointSelector` and refer to other identities with `fromEndpoints` and `toEndpoints` statements in our policy rules.

Cilium also has a number of hardcoded labels and identities, along with a mechanism to make use of common groupings of label selectors called *entities*. Reserved labels, reserved identities, and entities are closely entwined in their behavior and often referred to interchangeably, but it's important to understand the differences between them:

- A *reserved label* uses the `reserved:` prefix. Cilium has special handling for how it applies each reserved label to identities, and they can't be sourced from pod or namespace labels.
- A *reserved identity* is a special hardcoded identity for a particular purpose, usually with at least one reserved label applied to it. Some of these are listed in Table 12-2; for the full list, see the Cilium documentation (*https://oreil.ly/_3ltP*).
- An *entity* is a built-in shorthand for a set of label selectors. You can write policy using `toEntities`/`fromEntities` with these instead of using `toEndpoints`/`fromEndpoints`. Some of these are listed in Table 12-3, and again, you can find a full list in the Cilium documentation (*https://oreil.ly/Wrpps*).

Sometimes there is a clear correspondence between all three—for example, the `ingress` entity selects the `reserved:ingress` label, which is only present on the `ingress` reserved identity. On the other hand, the `world` entity selects the `reserved:world`, `reserved:world-ipv4`, and `reserved:world-ipv6` labels, each of which has a corresponding reserved identity, but Cilium also places the `reserved:world` label on other identities, such as CIDR and FQDN identities that we'll cover later in this chapter and in Chapter 13, respectively. This can make it a little unclear what we're talking about if we simply use a term like "`world` identity"—do we really mean the `world` reserved identity, or do we mean the `reserved:world` security label? Often this is obvious in context, but when debugging issues or handling corner cases, it's useful to remember that they are not the same.

Table 12-2. Some of the reserved identities in Cilium

ID	Identity name	Security labels	Description
1	`host`	`reserved:host`	The current host
2	`world`	`reserved:world`	Any endpoint outside of the cluster
6	`remote-node`	`reserved:remote-node`	Any other node in the cluster
7	`kube-apiserver`	`reserved:kube-apiserver` `reserved:remote-node`	The Kubernetes API server
8	`ingress`	`reserved:ingress`	Traffic to a pod in the cluster that has passed through Cilium's Ingress or Gateway API implementation (discussed in Chapter 7)
10	`world-ipv6`	`reserved:world-ipv6`	External IPv6 traffic

The entities map closely to the reserved identities, with most having a 1:1 correspondence via the `reserved` label. The `cluster` entity is an unusual one, selecting a large number of the `reserved` labels and also the security label for endpoints on this cluster.

Table 12-3. Some of the entities in Cilium

Entity name	Selector
`all`	Special wildcard selector

`world`	`reserved:world`
	`reserved:world-ipv4`
	`reserved:world-ipv6`

`host`	`reserved:host`
`ingress`	`reserved:ingress`
`remote-node`	`reserved:remote-node`
`kube-apiserver`	`reserved:kube-apiserver`

`cluster`	`reserved:host`
	`reserved:remote-note`
	`reserved:init`
	`reserved:ingress`
	`reserved:health`
	`reserved:unmanaged`
	`reserved:kube-apiserver`
	`k8s:io.cilium.k8s.policy.cluster` matching the cluster name

The `cluster` and `world` entities may seem like opposites, but that's not always the case. For example, if the Kubernetes API server is outside the cluster, its identity can have both the `reserved:kube-apiserver` and `reserved:world` labels and be included in both of those entities.

The reserved identities can be given other labels in some cases. For example, on a control-plane node—a Kubernetes node that runs control-plane components such as the `kube-apiserver`—the `host` identity will also have the `reserved:kube-apiserver` label.

Let's put this into practice and write a policy for CoreDNS. We want it to only be able to make and accept the connections we expect it to. We can start by writing out the flows we expect:

- Other pods and nodes in the cluster should be able to make DNS requests. DNS always uses port 53, but it can run over UDP or TCP.
- CoreDNS needs to communicate with the `kube-apiserver` to retrieve information about locations inside the cluster that it should provide DNS names for.
- CoreDNS needs to be able to make DNS queries to upstream DNS servers.

Each flow is represented by a rule in our policy (*coredns.yaml*):

```
apiVersion: cilium.io/v2
kind: CiliumNetworkPolicy
metadata:
  name: coredns
  namespace: kube-system
spec:
  endpointSelector:
    matchLabels:
      k8s-app: kube-dns
  ingress:
    - toPorts:
        - ports:
          - port: "53"
            protocol: ANY
      fromEntities:
        - cluster
  egress:
    - toPorts:
        - ports:
          - port: "6443"
            protocol: TCP
      toEntities:
        - kube-apiserver
    - toPorts:
        - ports:
          - port: "53"
            protocol: ANY
```

```
        toEntities:
          - world
```

This policy doesn't select which pods are able to send traffic to CoreDNS, but it ensures that traffic from pods that are able to do so will be accepted.

Combining Statements

We've introduced two different ways of filtering destinations by identity, and we'll cover a few more later in this chapter and in Chapter 13. However, these statements cannot be combined in the same rule. For example, this egress rule is invalid:

```
egress:
  - toEndpoints:
      - matchLabels:
          externally-exposed: "true"
    toEntities:
      - world
    toPorts:
      - ports:
          - port: "80"
            protocol: TCP
```

Cilium will not reject policy with invalid rules, but the entire policy will be marked as invalid. This means no rules in the policy will be applied, even if some would be valid independently.

We can check the validity of an applied policy with `kubectl`. For example, for the previous policy (assuming it's named `invalid-policy`), we would see:

```
$ kubectl get cnp invalid-policy
NAME             AGE   VALID
invalid-policy   48s   False

$ kubectl describe cnp invalid-policy
[...]
Status:
  Conditions:
    Message: combining ToEndpoints and ToEntities is not supported yet
```

In this case, we could fix the problem by rewriting the policy to use two different rules—one for endpoints and one for entities.

It's not always obvious which statements in a rule can be combined and which cannot. For example, both `toEndpoints` and `toEntities` can be combined with `toPorts`, but they can't be combined with each other. You can see a summary of the different possible statements in egress and ingress rules in Figures 12-4 and 12-5. These are nonexhaustive and only list the most commonly used policy statements.

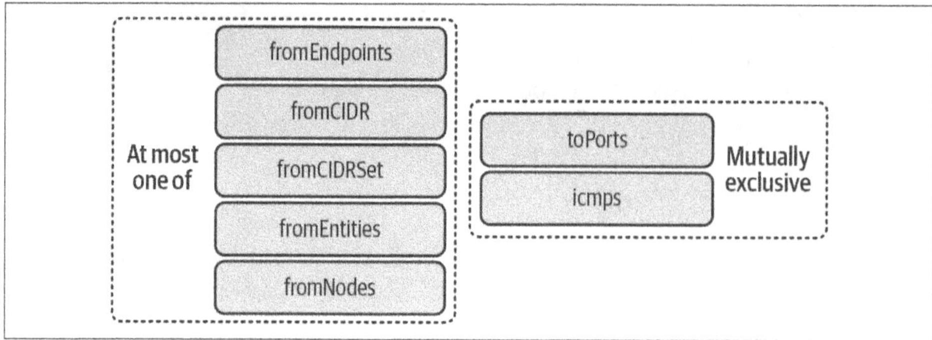

Figure 12-4. Ingress rule statements

We haven't introduced all the concepts in Figure 12-4 yet. We'll cover `fromCIDR` and `fromCIDRSet` in the next section. We don't cover `icmps` in this book as ICMP policies are only useful if all of your nodes are in the same layer 2 domain, but they can be used to restrict traffic at layer 2, such as for ICMP ping. The important point for now is that in general, you can have one statement that selects the source's identity and another that selects something about the traffic.

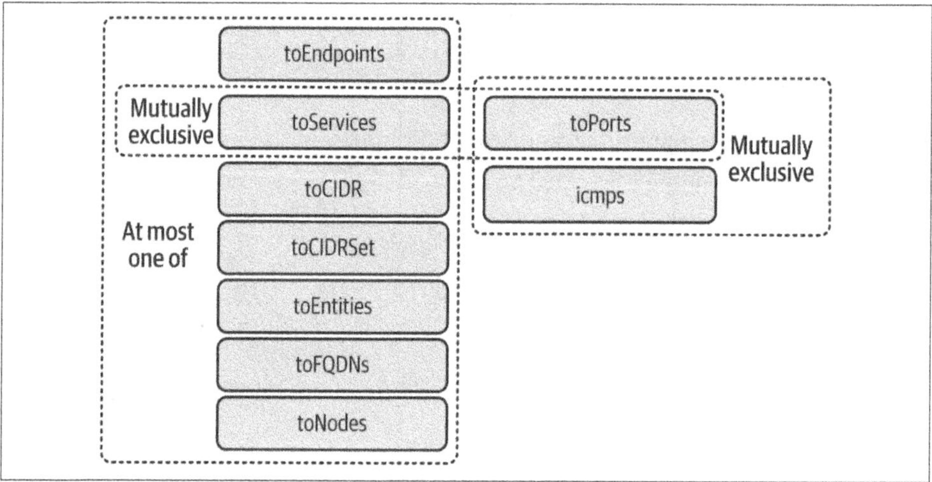

Figure 12-5. Egress rule statements

The common statements in egress rules are very similar, with most having an equivalence. `toFQDNs` is used for a special type of rule called an FQDN rule that we'll cover in Chapter 13. `toServices` can be used to select identities by entities that are themselves selected by a particular Kubernetes service. It can't be combined with `toPorts` because `toServices` inherits the port information from the service in question.

Beyond the Cluster

So far we've taken advantage of Cilium's ability as the CNI to be aware of every pod and node in the cluster, but we can extend this concept of identity beyond the cluster. We've already seen the `world` identity and entity, which can be used to describe endpoints outside of the cluster but not inside it. We can take this a step further using a CIDR range policy.

CIDR Ranges

As indicated in Figures 12-4 and 12-5, we can use `toCIDR`/`fromCIDR` and `toCIDRSet`/`fromCIDRSet` statements in our policies. Like the corresponding statements for endpoints and entities, these allow us to define traffic sources and destinations, and they can be used anywhere you'd expect in policy. Using `toCIDR`/`fromCIDR` is a simpler way of specifying a CIDR identity, while using `toCIDRSet`/`fromCIDRSet` allows you to "carve out" exceptions from otherwise continuous CIDR ranges.

A new identity is created for each CIDR range specified, and the IP caches on each node are updated to map the given range to that identity. Note that CIDR ranges in network policies do *not* apply to IP addresses that already have an identity, such as those used for pods or cluster services. For example, if you have a pod with IP `233.252.0.17`, adding an ingress rule on another pod to permit `233.252.0.0/24` would *not* permit traffic from that pod. Always use `fromEndpoints` or `fromEntities` to select traffic from locations inside the cluster.

CIDR Policy

Let's add a CIDR egress policy to our workload (*tocidr.yaml*). This time we'll apply the policy to our test pod, and we'll restrict egress traffic to only be possible to `1.1.1.1`:

```
apiVersion: cilium.io/v2
kind: CiliumNetworkPolicy
metadata:
  name: client
spec:
  endpointSelector:
    matchLabels:
      app.kubernetes.io/name: test
  egress:
    - toCIDR:
        - "1.1.1.1/32"
```

After applying this policy, we can verify the behavior in our test pod. Remember that for it to be selected by the policy, you must launch your test pod with `--labels "app.kubernetes.io/name=test"`:

```
$ kubectl apply -f tocidr.yaml
ciliumnetworkpolicy.cilium.io/client configured

$ kubectl run test -it --rm \
    --image nicolaka/netshoot \
    --labels "app.kubernetes.io/name=test" -- bash

test:~# curl -m1 https://1.1.1.2
curl: (28) Connection timed out after 1003 milliseconds

test:~# curl -sI https://1.1.1.1 | head -n1
HTTP/2 301
```

The first request times out because traffic to `1.1.1.2` is not allowed by the policy. The second request succeeds with an HTTP `301` response, which indicates that the connection was permitted.

Identity with Ingress and Gateway API

When Cilium is acting as an Ingress controller or Gateway API implementation (see Chapter 7), traffic to the Ingress or Gateway IP is passed to Cilium's Envoy proxy. After it's forwarded to the backend pod, it no longer has the original client IP as its origin; this is replaced by an IP that is used internally for this ingress traffic. This is shown in Figure 12-6, with `10.0.0.207` being used as the internal ingress IP. This IP is allocated by Cilium automatically from the node's pod IP range.

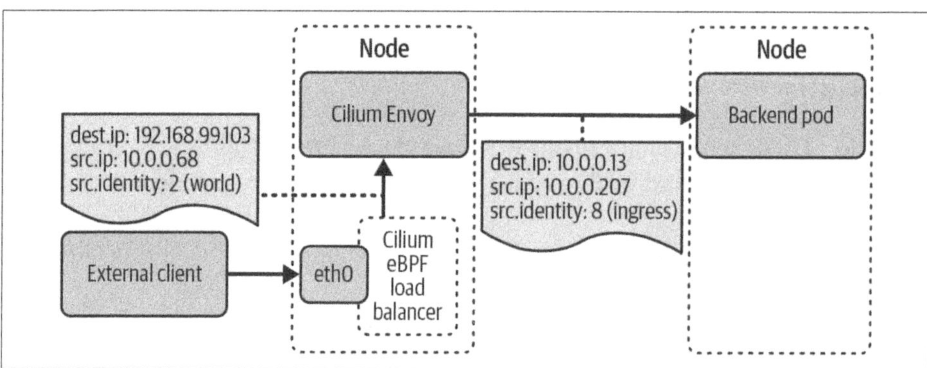

Figure 12-6. Traffic flow with `ingress` identity

Where pods are expected to be backends for Ingress or Gateway API, they must permit access from the `ingress` identity, typically by using a `fromEntities` rule permitting the `ingress` entity.

Deny Rules

Just as we can allow traffic with an ingress or egress rule and rely on default deny behavior to block unspecified traffic, we can use an `ingressDeny` or `egressDeny` rule to do the opposite and explicitly block certain traffic. Perhaps we want to prevent services from accessing the Kubernetes API at all. The API server will block access to unauthenticated clients, but you may still wish to restrict access anyway to protect against authentication bugs in the Kubernetes API server.

Deny rules count as rules for deciding if default deny should apply to an endpoint, so if we only block traffic and don't disable default deny we'll block everything by accident. Putting this all together, we can write a cluster-wide policy (*kube-api-deny.yaml*) to block any pod that isn't in the `kube-system` namespace from accessing the Kubernetes API. Note that other services, such as cert-manager and Argo CD, commonly deploy into their own namespaces and also require Kubernetes API access, so the namespace exclusion list may need to be expanded for your environment:

```
apiVersion: cilium.io/v2
kind: CiliumClusterwideNetworkPolicy
metadata:
  name: kube-api-deny
spec:
  endpointSelector:
    matchExpressions:
      - key: io.kubernetes.pod.namespace
        operator: NotIn
        values:
          - kube-system
  enableDefaultDeny:
    egress: false
  egressDeny:
    - toEntities:
        - kube-apiserver
```

A detail we've left implicit until now is that Cilium policy is *unordered*. The ordering of statements within a rule doesn't matter, nor does the ordering of rules within a policy, or even if they're in different policies. The datapath is fundamentally unordered too, with per-identity policy decisions being generated ahead of time.

So far, this hasn't mattered: traffic was allowed if a policy allowed it, and if an endpoint was selected by any policy that didn't have `enableDefaultDeny` turned off, then all other traffic was dropped. With the addition of deny rules, however, we are left with a question: What happens if traffic is both denied and allowed by different policies?

In Cilium's case, deny *always* takes priority over allow, no matter what. It doesn't matter if one is cluster-wide and the other is a namespaced policy, or if one is "broader" than another. This is very useful for setting cluster-wide baseline policy that can't be overridden even if individual teams can write their own network policy, but it makes deny policy a bit of a blunt instrument. Once you've denied a particular flow, you can't make exceptions without modifying the policy.

Summary

Policy is a powerful part of Cilium's toolset. The mapping from IP to identity allows the datapath to be simultaneously expressive and performant. We've seen how policy can be used to protect workloads on the cluster, prevent lateral movement, and stop pods from egressing unexpectedly. In the next chapter, we'll cover advanced use cases of Cilium's policy engine that go beyond simple layer 3 filtering.

CHAPTER 13
Layer 7 and FQDN Policy

In this chapter, we'll cover a number of advanced use cases for network policy that build on the foundation of network policy we established in Chapter 12. If you haven't read that chapter, you should at least be familiar with how rules are structured and how the policy datapath works. Our focus here will be on layer 7 policy for HTTP, HTTPS, DNS, and FQDN policy. All the manifests for this chapter are in the *chapter13* directory of the book's GitHub repository (*https://github.com/isovalent/cilium-up-and-running*).

Layer 7 Policy

In the previous chapter, we applied policy purely at layer 3. We used various ways of understanding the identity of the traffic, such as `toEndpoints`, `toEntities`, and `toCIDR` egress rule statements and their ingress equivalents, but ultimately all of the policy we've applied has acted based on the IP address and port information in the packet.

If we can uniquely identify all of the resources we want to secure purely based on these factors, that's great—but often we need to go further. For example, what if we want a workload's access to an external service to be read-only? If it's a service over HTTP, we can limit egress to only the relevant IP address or identity and only TCP port 80, but our policy will apply equally to `GET` and `POST` requests. Similarly, such a policy will not allow us to restrict access to only some URL paths, such as `/api`. What if we wanted to secure an HTTP server where we expect different clients to use different paths? Or what if multiple virtual servers are hosted at the same IP address and traffic to them is filtered and routed based on the HTTP `Host` header or TLS Server Name Indication (SNI) header? This is especially important for external services that might be hosted on content delivery networks (CDNs) or managed services where the same IP address may be used to serve several different services.

For example, if we wanted to allow our pods to access an API on *api.weather.example*, we might know a specific IP range is used for that site and use a `toCIDR` rule to permit access to that range on port 443 or port 80. But if the range in question is owned by a CDN, other sites—say, a file hosting site *filehost.example*—may be using it too. This would inadvertently allow the pods we permitted to access *api.weather.example* to also access *filehost.example*. In isolation, this may not be an issue, but an attacker could potentially exploit this flaw to exfiltrate sensitive data from a compromised pod or implement a "command and control" mechanism for malware. These examples may be abstract, involving lots of "ifs" and "coulds," but they are indicative of a very real limitation in IP-based identity when used with HTTP and HTTPS services with virtual servers or CDNs.

Securing HTTP

To improve upon the layer 3 policies and provide greater flexibility for securing HTTP services, Cilium network policies support layer 7 policy rules. To illustrate, we'll deploy a test cluster, Cilium, and the same web server we used in Chapter 12 to demonstrate layer 3 network policy, but with a slightly different configuration (*webserver.yaml*) to provide different responses on different HTTP paths: "API" from `/api` and "Admin" from `/admin`. We'll also apply the same ingress security policy, using `fromEndpoints`. This will allow only endpoints with the label `app.kubernetes.io/name: test` to access TCP port 8080 on the web server.

After deploying a test pod, we can see that we're able to access all paths and that we get different responses on different paths:

```
$ kubectl apply --filename webserver.yaml
deployment.apps/webserver created
configmap/nginx-config created
service/webserver created
service/webserver-metrics created

$ kubectl apply -f webserver-8080-from-endpoints.yaml
ciliumnetworkpolicy.cilium.io/webserver created

$ kubectl run test -it --rm \
    --labels "app.kubernetes.io/name=test" \
    --image nicolaka/netshoot -- bash

test:~# curl -s webserver
Hello from Cilium Up and Running!

test:~# curl -s webserver/api
API

test:~# curl -s webserver/admin
Admin
```

```
test:~# curl -m1 webserver-metrics:9113/metrics
curl: (28) Connection timed out after 1003 milliseconds
```

Layer 7 policy builds upon the port definition of a layer 3 policy by adding a `rules` block to a `toPorts` statement as part of an ingress or egress rule. Let's update our network policy to include a layer 7 rule:

```
toPorts:
  - ports:
      - port: "8080"
        protocol: TCP
    rules:
      http:
        - method: GET
          path: "/api"
```

The new rule allows HTTP `GET` requests on the `/api` path. After applying the policy (*webserver-http-rule.yaml*), let's run the tests from our test pod again:

```
test:~# curl -s webserver
Access denied

test:~# curl -s webserver/api
API

test:~# curl -s webserver/admin
Access denied

test:~# curl -m1 webserver-metrics:9113/metrics
curl: (28) Connection timed out after 1004 milliseconds
```

We can access our `webserver` pod on `/api`, and the connection to the metrics server still times out, but connection attempts to other paths result in an "Access denied" response If we check the headers on the response, we can learn a little more:

```
test:~# curl -D - webserver
HTTP/1.1 403 Forbidden
content-length: 15
content-type: text/plain
date: Thu, 23 Oct 2025 20:25:41 GMT
server: envoy

Access denied
```

We can now see that the response code is `403 Forbidden`. We can also see there is a `server` header that reports as Envoy, not NGINX. It's useful to remember that the behavior of blocked traffic is different on layer 3 and layer 7. The connection to port 9113 times out, but the blocked connections to port 8080 are established and then responded to with a `403`.

The `path` in a layer 7 HTTP rule is a regular expression (regex). This means that `/api` matches `/api` *exactly* and will not allow access to `/api/` or sub-URLs like `/api/v1/`

posts. To allow access to an entire subtree, you would need to use a wildcard match such as `path: /api/.*`. (Note that `path: /api.*` would likely be wrong, as it would permit access to other directories in the path whose names begin with `api`, such as `/api-beta/v1`.)

The Envoy Datapath

When evaluating ingress traffic, the Cilium eBPF datapath follows the same identity resolution and policy lookup flow described in "The Policy Datapath" on page 252. The datapath resolves the identity of the source based on the source IP, determines whether the packet belongs to an existing connection, and then inspects the endpoint's policy map using the source identity, protocol, and destination port.

Layer 7 policy builds on this same foundation. When traffic targets a port with layer 7 rules attached, the datapath redirects the packet to Envoy for layer 7 processing.

As you may recall from Chapter 2, Envoy is not deployed as a sidecar container and injected into the `webserver` pod; it's deployed as a DaemonSet, so each node has its own dedicated instance that Cilium communicates with locally. Because Cilium decides whether layer 7 enforcement is required on a per-port and per-protocol basis, traffic that does not require it is not redirected to Envoy. Figure 13-1 illustrates the layer 7 packet flow for a client accessing the web server.

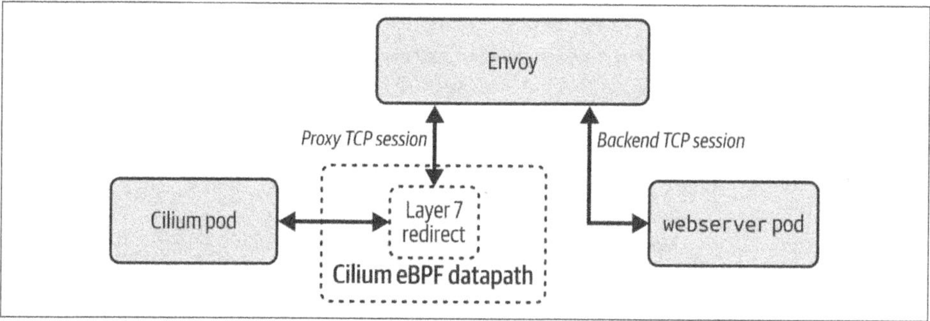

Figure 13-1. Data flow on a layer 7 port

The TCP handshake between the client and the service is performed by Envoy. Only once the HTTP request has been fully sent and Envoy has evaluated it against the configured rules does it decide whether to respond with a `403` or to proxy the request to the backend. In the latter case, Envoy acts as a user space proxy, forming its own TCP connection to the backend and performing an equivalent HTTP request. We can see this by inspecting the access logs on the web server. Let's scale our deployment down to one pod so we can know which web server served our request and view its access logs:

```
$ kubectl scale deploy/webserver --replicas=1
deployment.apps/webserver scaled

$ kubectl rollout restart deploy/webserver
deployment.apps/webserver restarted
```

Then, in our test pod, we'll perform some requests:

```
test:~# curl -s webserver
Access denied

test:~# curl -s webserver/api
API
```

Finally, we can check the IP of the test pod and view the logs on the `webserver` pod:

```
$ kubectl get po test -o jsonpath='{.status.podIP}'
10.0.0.212

$ kubectl logs deploy/webserver -c nginx | grep "curl"
10.0.0.196 <truncated> "GET /api HTTP/1.1" 200 4 "-" "curl/8.14.1" "-"
```

There are two useful things to notice here. First, the request that was denied by policy didn't make it to the backend pod because it was blocked by Envoy. Second, although we can see that the IP of the test pod is `10.0.0.212`, NGINX is reporting the source IP of the request as `10.0.0.196`. This special IP is reserved out of the node's pod IP range for use by Envoy when communicating with the local pods. It's referred to by Cilium as the CiliumInternalIP, and we can see it on the CiliumNode object:

```
$ kubectl get ciliumnode -o yaml | yq '.items[].spec.addresses'
- ip: 10.89.0.3
  type: InternalIP
- ip: 10.0.0.196
  type: CiliumInternalIP
```

Performance

Envoy is a high-performance layer 7 proxy, and it was chosen by the Cilium project to form its layer 7 datapath in part because of this performance. However, it can never be as fast as eBPF. Although it may be minimal, there will always be some latency added to connections that use layer 7 policy. There may also be decreased throughput or increased requirements on the node's CPU and memory resources, depending on the configuration. Most services will not be impacted, but if your application is particularly latency-sensitive or if you have a deep microservices architecture where a single user request can result in many chained HTTP requests within your cluster, the increased latency may become problematic.

The per-node Envoy instance discussed here is the same as the one that handles connections for Gateway API and Ingress. The configurations are independent, but there are cases where traffic can flow into Envoy multiple times. For example, traffic to a pod with a layer 7 ingress rule that applies to the `ingress` identity that is behind a Gateway API gateway will transit Envoy twice: once on the ingress node to resolve the gateway and any HTTP rules, and then a second time on the backend pod's node (which may be the same node) to apply layer 7 policy.

In general, we don't recommend applying layer 7 policy to the `ingress` identity, as most filtering you would want to do can be accomplished on the gateway level instead. If you're applying layer 7 policy to in-cluster (or meshed cluster) endpoints and also have a gateway, you can add a rule to allow all traffic on the HTTP port from the gateway using `fromEntities: [ingress]` while still keeping the layer 7 rules on other in-cluster sources using `fromEndpoints`.

There's nothing *wrong* with introducing a proxy for layer 7 security, but it does introduce extra hops and latency. We can test this using some network performance tools. These aren't available in the debug image we've been using, so we're going to use a different container for this purpose. Because we'll need to do some setup, we'll leave this one running. We'll launch a Kali Linux container, install a performance testing application called Siege, and disable verbose output by editing the config file with *sed*:

```
$ kubectl run perf --labels "app.kubernetes.io/name=test" \
    --image kalilinux/kali-rolling -- sleep infinity
pod/perf created

$ kubectl exec -it perf -- bash

┌──(root㉿perf)-[/]
└─# apt update && apt install -y siege
[output omitted]

┌──(root㉿perf)-[/]
└─# siege --config
[output omitted]

┌──(root㉿perf)-[/]
└─# sed -i 's/verbose = true/verbose = false/g' ~/.siege/siege.conf
```

Siege (*https://oreil.ly/Jydol*) is a benchmarking tool capable of performing large load tests on web servers. As with all security and testing tools, we don't advise running them on servers you don't control. You're not likely to be able to cause enough traffic by yourself for a large website to be adversely affected, but you might get blocked by automated protection systems. Running these tests on your company's internal servers may also get you an annoyed email from your IT department.

This testing was performed on a kind cluster inside a Linux virtual machine running on a Mac. This is *far* from an ideal case for Cilium's deployment and performance. The results here, including the scale of the difference, will be much worse than in real deployments. The key point is that there is a difference in performance when using layer 7 policy, not the absolute numbers.

We're going to keep our single replica on a single node. First we'll reset the network policy to be the pure layer 3 approach from Chapter 12 (*webserver-8080-from-endpoints.yaml*) and perform a simple test by using `kubectl exec` in our performance testing pod:

```
$ kubectl apply --filename webserver-8080-from-endpoints.yaml
ciliumnetworkpolicy.cilium.io/webserver configured

$ kubectl exec perf -- siege --benchmark --concurrent 25 --reps 100 \
    webserver/api
** SIEGE 4.1.6
** Preparing 25 concurrent users for battle.
The server is now under siege...
Transactions:                   2500 hits
Availability:                 100.00 %
Elapsed time:                  10.21 secs
Data transferred:               0.01 MB
Response time:                  0.03 secs
Transaction rate:             244.86 trans/sec
Throughput:                     0.00 MB/sec
Concurrency:                    6.25
Successful transactions:        2500
Failed transactions:               0
Longest transaction:            5.01
Shortest transaction:           0.00
```

We've gotten some pretty useful information out of this test. We told it to use 25 concurrent connections with 100 attempts each, meaning 2,500 total connections. From this we see 244.86 transactions per second with a response time of around 30 ms. Now let's apply our layer 7 policy (*webserver-http-rule.yaml*) and retry:

```
$ kubectl apply -f webserver-http-rule.yaml
ciliumnetworkpolicy.cilium.io/webserver configured

$ kubectl exec perf -- siege --benchmark --concurrent 25 --reps 100 \
    webserver/api
** SIEGE 4.1.6
** Preparing 25 concurrent users for battle.
The server is now under siege...
```

```
Transactions:                   2500 hits
Availability:                 100.00 %
Elapsed time:                  20.35 secs
Data transferred:               0.01 MB
Response time:                  0.02 secs
Transaction rate:             122.85 trans/sec
Throughput:                     0.00 MB/sec
Concurrency:                    2.75
Successful transactions:        2500
Failed transactions:               0
Longest transaction:            5.01
Shortest transaction:           0.00
```

We can see a big difference, with our transaction rate being cut in half, although the individual response time is still around 20 ms.

Again, these numbers are not representative of real workloads, and it's not generally true that adding layer 7 policy reduces performance by 50%. You'll need to test throughput in your particular environment, and the results are highly dependent on the hardware configuration used. However, we did want to illustrate that there is a performance cost to using layer 7 policy.

DNS Policy

Cilium can also intercept and handle other types of layer 7 traffic, including DNS traffic. DNS rules allow us to restrict the kinds of DNS queries that a client can make. Let's rewrite our policy (*dns-policy.yaml*) to allow egress traffic on ports 80 and 443 to any destination, but restrict DNS requests (on port 53) to only *cilium.io*:

```
apiVersion: cilium.io/v2
kind: CiliumNetworkPolicy
metadata:
  name: http-egress
spec:
  endpointSelector:
    matchLabels:
      app.kubernetes.io/name: test
  egress:
    - toPorts:
        - ports:
            - port: "80"
              protocol: TCP
            - port: "443"
              protocol: TCP
      toEntities:
        - world
    - toPorts:
        - ports:
            - port: "53"
              protocol: ANY
          rules:
```

```
          dns:
            - matchPattern: "cilium.io"
      toEndpoints:
        - matchLabels:
            k8s-app: kube-dns
            io.kubernetes.pod.namespace: kube-system
```

As in our CoreDNS policy in Chapter 12, we've set the protocol for port 53 to `ANY` to allow both TCP and UDP traffic.

Let's apply this policy, deploy a test pod, and run a few tests:

```
$ kubectl apply --filename dns-policy.yaml
ciliumnetworkpolicy.cilium.io/http-egress created

$ kubectl run test -it --rm --labels "app.kubernetes.io/name=test" \
    --image nicolaka/netshoot -- bash

test:~# curl -sI https://cilium.io. | head -n1
HTTP/2 200

test:~# curl -m1 https://example.com
curl: (6) Could not resolve host: example.com
```

We're able to connect to *cilium.io*, but not *example.com*. Note that we use `cilium.io.` in the `curl` command, with a trailing dot. Without the dot, the pod will first attempt to resolve `cilium.io` using its configured search domains, which will fail.

Note that this blocking is *only* at the DNS level. Because egress is enabled via port 443, we can actually "smuggle" a DNS request out another way, bypassing this policy. For example, in our pod we can use DNS over HTTPS with a known HTTPS resolver at `1.1.1.1`, and then use the IP we're given to directly communicate with our intended host with no DNS request:

```
test:~# curl -s -H 'accept: application/dns-json' \
    'https://1.1.1.1/dns-query?name=example.com&type=A' | jq -r \
    '.Answer[0].data'
23.220.75.245

test:~# curl -s --resolve example.com:443:23.220.75.245 https://example.com
[...]
<head><title>Example Domain</title>
```

Coincidentally, many content filtering systems operate using only DNS blocking. Please follow the rules of common sense when it comes to bypassing security tooling, and if you get an uncomfortable visit from your corporate IT department, don't blame us.

FQDN Policy

Cilium has an alternative to pushing all egress traffic through a layer 7 proxy to check the host field—one that works even for non-HTTP traffic. It ties back to Cilium's understanding of identity, discussed in Chapter 12. If we want pods to be able to reach *cilium.io* but we don't want to allow other egress, we can look up the IP address for that domain and use a CIDR policy to allow only access to it. If all we want is host-based security, not filtering based on other factors of the HTTP request, such as the path or method, then this approach is fine. There's no Envoy interception, so it's more performant and reliable, and we don't need to intercept *every* port 80 or port 443 egress connection to make it work.

The only problem is the static IPs in such policies. We have to know somehow that those IPs are the correct ones, and we must remember to update them if things change. If the cluster is dual stack, we need to handle IPv6 addresses too. If only we could somehow automate that synchronization, we could make this approach much more robust. Enter FQDN policy.

Writing FQDN Policy

A fully qualified domain name (FQDN) is a complete and unambiguous domain name that uniquely identifies a host in the Domain Name System—something like `cilium.io.` or `webserver.default.svc.cluster.local.`. You'll notice that the FQDNs used in this section all end with a dot. This is what distinguishes a "fully qualified" domain name (like `cilium.io.`) from a regular one (like `cilium.io`). The dot represents the root of the DNS hierarchy and is usually implicit, so in practice we often omit it. However, the presence or absence of the dot matters in the context of FQDN policy.

Non-FQDNs and Search Domains

A non-fully qualified domain name (without a trailing dot) can be resolved using DNS search domains, where the resolver appends configured suffixes to the name until a match is found. We can see this behavior in action by using `dig`, a command-line tool for querying DNS servers, on a test pod. Note that the pod we're using here doesn't have the `app.kubernetes.io/name` label, so it won't be selected by our DNS policy from the previous section (*dns-policy.yaml*):

```
$ kubectl run dnstest -it --rm --image nicolaka/netshoot -- bash

dnstest:~# cat /etc/resolv.conf
search default.svc.cluster.local svc.cluster.local cluster.local
nameserver 10.96.0.10
options ndots:5
```

```
dnstest:~# dig example +showsearch | grep "IN\tA"
;example.default.svc.cluster.local. IN  A
;example.svc.cluster.local.     IN      A
;example.cluster.local.         IN      A
;example.                       IN      A

dnstest:~# dig example. +showsearch | grep "IN\tA"
;example.                       IN      A
```

By including the `+showsearch` query option, we instruct `dig` to display the sequence of domain names the resolver tries during resolution. When we request `example.` instead of `example`, the name is treated as fully qualified and no suffixes are appended to the domain name.

Using FQDNs (including the trailing dot) becomes important when considering DNS caching behavior or building DNS-based tooling, as we're about to.

When a client attempts to reach a server, it will query its configured DNS server to resolve the requested domain name to an IP address and will then use that IP address to request the content. Cilium allows us to automate the connection between an FQDN lookup and a CIDR policy using a `toFQDN` rule. This is implemented using the built-in DNS proxy we introduced in Chapter 2. Let's try it out (*fqdn-policy.yaml*):

```
apiVersion: cilium.io/v2
kind: CiliumNetworkPolicy
metadata:
  name: fqdn-egress
spec:
  endpointSelector:
    matchLabels:
      app.kubernetes.io/name: test
  egress:
    - toFQDNs:
        - matchName: "cilium.io"
      toPorts:
        - ports:
            - port: "80"
              protocol: TCP
            - port: "443"
              protocol: TCP
    - toEndpoints:
        - matchLabels:
            k8s-app: kube-dns
            io.kubernetes.pod.namespace: kube-system
      toPorts:
        - ports:
            - port: "53"
              protocol: ANY
          rules:
```

```
            dns:
              - matchPattern: "*"
```

We once again have two egress rules. The first is our FQDN rule, where we're allowing the same two ports as before. The DNS rule is a bit different: we're using a match pattern of * to allow all DNS requests. From the pod's perspective this is functionally the same as not intercepting DNS requests at all, but this is a critical part of how FQDN policy functions.

After applying this policy, we can test again. Remember to remove any leftover network policy from previous steps:

```
$ kubectl apply --filename fqdn-policy.yaml
ciliumnetworkpolicy.cilium.io/fqdn-egress created

$ kubectl run test -it --rm --labels "app.kubernetes.io/name=test" \
    --image nicolaka/netshoot -- bash

test:~# curl -sI https://cilium.io | head -n1
HTTP/2 200

test:~# curl -m1 https://example.com
curl: (28) Connection timed out after 1001 milliseconds
```

Our request to the allowed domain worked, while our request to *example.com* was rejected. We also can test that the technique we used earlier to bypass DNS policy doesn't work here:

```
test:~# curl -m1 -H 'accept: application/dns-json' \
    'https://1.1.1.1/dns-query?name=example.com&type=A'
curl: (28) Connection timed out after 1000 milliseconds

test:~# curl -m1 --resolve example.com:443:23.220.75.245 https://example.com
curl: (28) Connection timed out after 1001 milliseconds
```

We can't access our DNS server, and even if we could, or if we got the IP through some other mechanism, we wouldn't be able to access it.

FQDN Identity

Functionally, FQDN policy works much like a CIDR policy that auto-updates based on the response to the DNS request that's being proxied by the node. In Figure 13-2, we walk through the expected flow of a request and see how Cilium updates itself to track these details.

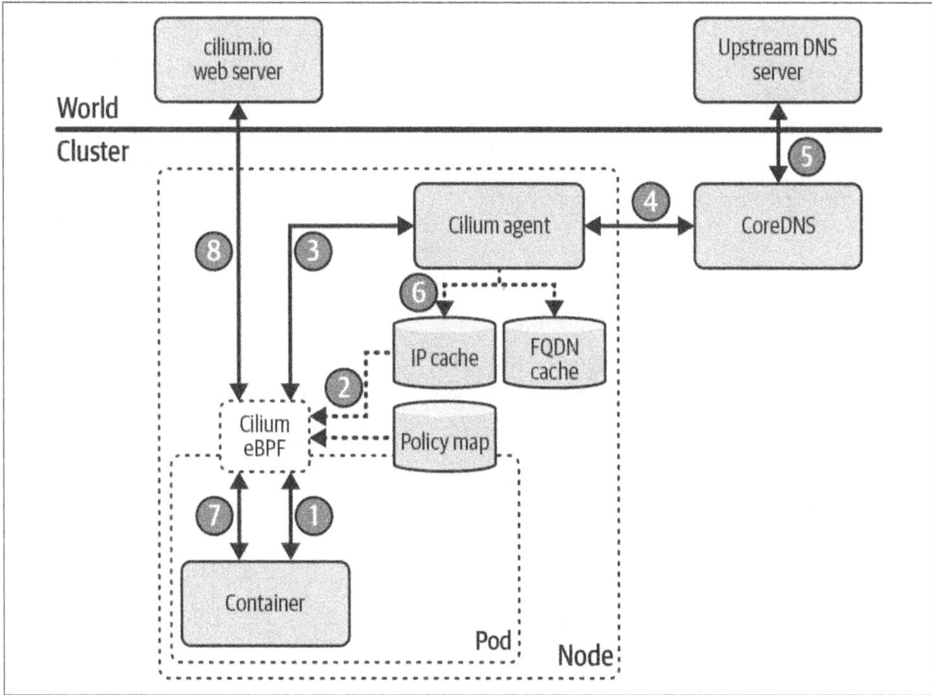

Figure 13-2. Packet and information flow using Cilium's FQDN policy

Let's go through this step by step:

❶ The container makes a DNS request for an `A` record for `cilium.io.`. This leaves the pod via a UDP packet destined for the CoreDNS service IP.

❷ The eBPF datapath translates the CoreDNS service IP to the CoreDNS pod's IP, then applies policy. It uses the IP cache (discussed in Chapter 12) to map that IP to the pod's identity, and uses the policy map for the pod to determine what to do with the packet.

❸ Because of our DNS filtering rule, the eBPF datapath forwards the packet to the node's Cilium agent.

❹ The Cilium agent checks the DNS request against its internal policy map to determine if the DNS name is permitted, and if it is, it proxies the request on to the destination DNS server.

❺ The cluster's DNS server responds, as it's not a local endpoint it has an entry for, and if it doesn't have the name cached, it reaches out to its configured upstream resolver to get the public IP hosting `cilium.io.`.

❻ The agent reads the response from CoreDNS and updates the FQDN cache with the mapping of the returned IP to `cilium.io.`. If an identity already exists for the FQDN, it will update the IP cache to map this IP to that identity. Otherwise, it will create a new identity and map the IP to it before responding. This may trigger a policy regeneration on the node, for example if the new identity needs to be inserted into the pod's policy map.

❼ The pod gets its response to the DNS request and immediately makes a TCP connection to the IP.

❽ The packet once again transits the eBPF datapath. This time, the IP resolves to the FQDN identity and the policy map allows the traffic out to the external endpoint.

We can see from this how Cilium intercepts the DNS traffic and uses it to build automatically updating mappings from special FQDN identities to IP addresses. A side effect of this FQDN identity mapping is that the resulting traffic is evaluated based on layer 3 rules. Therefore, this method works even for traffic that is not HTTP, including FTP, SSH, and other protocols.

FQDN Cache Poisoning

When using this kind of DNS interception with FQDN policy, you should take care to restrict it only to trusted DNS servers. If you allow DNS interception to any DNS servers, an attacker could use a poisoned DNS server to inject arbitrary IP addresses into the FQDN→IP mapping, allowing for policy bypass.

For example, if a compromised client is only allowed to egress to `api.example` but the attacker controls a DNS server, they could make a DNS request for `api.example` to their poisoned server and associate any IP with that address, thereby allowing the workload to make a request to any location via CIDR. This won't allow bypassing egress policy to in-cluster endpoints because they can't overlap with FQDN identities.

This is particularly bad if you're using `toFQDN` rules in an egress *deny* policy. If the pods backing a service are not permitted to access `api.example` but can access `metrics.example`, then a malicious pod on the same node could use this technique to make a mapping for `api.example` that resolves to the same IP as `metrics.example`, and because these mappings are node-wide, the first pod would have its access blocked at layer 3.

These are edge cases, and they can be avoided by restricting DNS queries to the cluster's standard CoreDNS proxy—a good practice anyway, as arbitrary DNS requests could be used for data exfiltration.

Content Delivery Networks

In the modern era, many websites are hosted on third-party content delivery networks (CDNs) such as Cloudflare, Amazon Cloudfront, or Netlify. These products provide a range of services, including acting as distributed global caches to reduce load on backend services, caching content geographically closer to users for lower latency, implementing geo-blocks, and providing DDoS protection. All of these ultimately rely on the CDN provider terminating TCP and TLS connections on their content network and the customer updating their DNS names to resolve to the CDN's endpoints. This can pose a problem for `toFQDN` policy, as the IP address for a particular FQDN may be shared by many sites.

CDN collisions are difficult to demonstrate since they're dependent on the DNS setup, but the following example works at the time of writing.

For example, it just so happens that *cilium.io* and *isovalent.com* are hosted on the same CDN. Let's see what happens if we deploy a test pod in our cluster with the same FQDN policy from earlier (*fqdn-policy.yaml*) and attempt to access both of these domains:

```
$ kubectl run test -it --rm --labels "app.kubernetes.io/name=test" \
    --image nicolaka/netshoot -- bash

test:~# curl -sI https://cilium.io | head -n1
HTTP/2 200

test:~# curl -m1 https://isovalent.com
curl: (28) Connection timed out after 1001 milliseconds

test:~# curl -s --resolve "isovalent.com:443:$(dig +short cilium.io)" \
    https://isovalent.com | \
    grep -Eo 'Isovalent was founded[[:alnum:][:space:]]*' | head -n1
Isovalent was founded by the creators and maintainers of Cilium and eBPF
```

The first request to `cilium.io` succeeds because it matches the allowed FQDN policy. The direct request to `isovalent.com` fails, as expected, because that domain is not permitted. However, by forcing cURL to resolve `isovalent.com` using the IP for `cilium.io`, we bypass the FQDN policy. Because both sites share a CDN, the CDN can serve traffic for *isovalent.com* from either IP address. In practice, this kind of bypass is only possible in cases where domains share CDN IPs and the client deliberately overrides DNS resolution. It's also dependent on CDN behavior. If you need to be absolutely sure that clients are accessing the correct domain, you'll have to use a layer 7 HTTP policy that filters on the host field and proxies through Envoy.

This issue can also occur if you're intercepting external traffic through a non-Cilium layer 7 egress proxy outside of the cluster, as that may cause all external addresses to resolve to the same IP address from the perspective of workloads in the cluster.

TLS Interception

TLS interception[1] is when Cilium's Envoy proxy terminates outbound TLS connections from workloads (using certificates signed by an internal CA), inspects the decrypted traffic for layer 7 policy enforcement, and then establishes a separate TLS connection to forward the request to the external destination. In this example, we're going to restrict a pod's egress traffic to an external HTTPS API. Figure 13-3 shows the certificates and trust bundles we'll need to configure to:

- Provide Cilium with a set of public CA certificates to trust for the upstream connection. Without this trust bundle, Cilium won't be able to verify the identity of the upstream provider.
- Provide Cilium with a certificate to present for the proxied connection.
- Override the client pod's trust bundle with the CA for the provided certificate.

1 Sometimes anachronistically referred to as "man-in-the-middle."

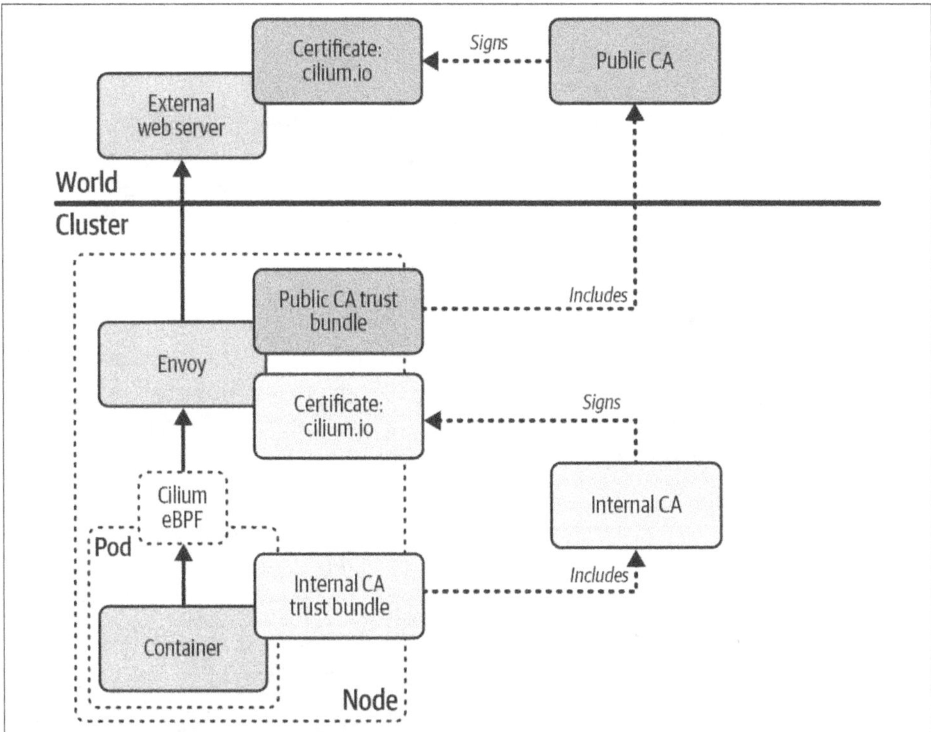

Figure 13-3. Trust bundle and certificate distribution for TLS interception

A *trust bundle* is a group of certificate authorities that a given client trusts to issue certificates for a TLS connection. Most containers are built with a trust bundle of commonly trusted public certificate authorities, provided by the underlying Linux distribution used to build them.

Secrets and Security in Cilium

As you know, Cilium deploys a single Envoy instance per node that performs all layer 7 filtering for workloads on that node, configured by the Cilium agent on the node. All Cilium agent instances use the same Kubernetes service account, so they share the same Kubernetes permissions. Because any node could, in theory, host any workload, all Envoy instances need to include any secrets used by any TLS policy.

This presents a problem, as permission to read secrets in Kubernetes is a very broad permission that carries a high risk of exposing sensitive data. To mitigate this risk, Cilium does not grant the agent access to all secrets by default. Instead, it's granted read access to all secrets in a special namespace, usually `cilium-secrets`. We can either write our secrets into that namespace for Cilium to use or make use of Cilium's secret sync feature to copy relevant secrets into the namespace. (This requires that the

Cilium operator has the ability to read all secrets, but since the operator isn't directly exposed to any external connections, this presents a smaller "attack surface.")

You can still grant Envoy permissions to read from all namespaces if you want, by setting the Helm value `tls.readSecretsOnlyFromSecretsNamespace=false`. It's not a recommended approach, but if it's preferable to copying the secrets you can configure Cilium in this way.

In this example we have full control of the certificates, so we're going to disable secret sync and populate our secrets directly into the `cilium-secrets` namespace. The eventual approach will be as seen in Figure 13-4. Note that this diagram includes only trust bundles and certificates that will be read by Cilium, not the trust bundle for the internal issuer that will be mounted into the client pod.

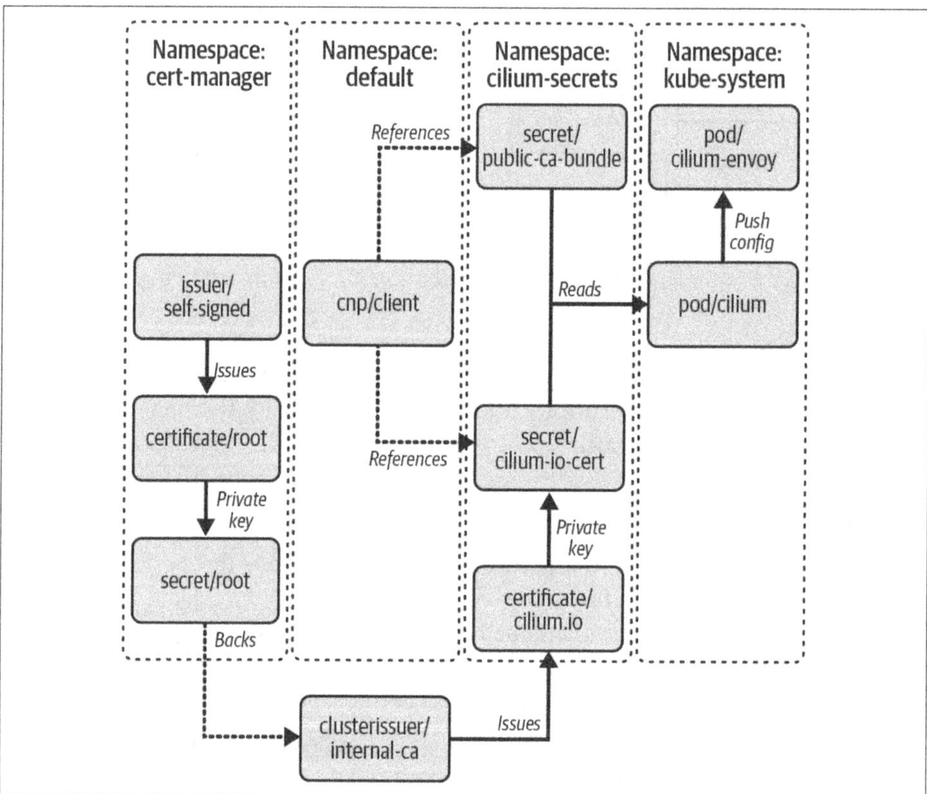

Figure 13-4. Issuers, certificates, and trust bundles in an HTTPS layer 7 policy

Writing HTTPS Policy

We can use the cert-manager and trust-manager projects to create our internal CA, sign certificates, and distribute the trust bundles. Set up a test cluster with kind and configure Cilium with `tls.secretSync.enabled: false`. Once Cilium is installed, install cert-manager and trust-manager. We're installing them using the `oci://` paths instead of using a Helm repo (the recommended method from the cert-manager documentation (*https://oreil.ly/fV_1D*)), so no `helm repo add` command is required:

```
$ helm upgrade --install \
    cert-manager oci://quay.io/jetstack/charts/cert-manager \
    --version v1.19.0 \
    --namespace cert-manager \
    --create-namespace \
    --set crds.enabled=true

$ helm upgrade --install \
    trust-manager oci://quay.io/jetstack/charts/trust-manager \
    --version v0.20.2 \
    --namespace cert-manager \
    --set secretTargets.enabled=true \
    --set "secretTargets.authorizedSecrets[0]=public-ca-bundle"
```

We're setting options on trust-manager to allow it to write to secrets. In this case, it's only allowed to write a secret named `public-ca-bundle` in all namespaces. This is because the trust bundle that Cilium loads to verify the external TLS connection must be in a secret, not in a config map.

Public Trust

Getting a public trust bundle is the easiest step. We'll use trust-manager's default public CA bundle (*tls/public-ca-bundle.yaml*) and have it inject the certificates from the bundle into a secret in the `cilium-secrets` namespace:[2]

```
apiVersion: trust.cert-manager.io/v1alpha1
kind: Bundle
metadata:
  name: public-ca-bundle
spec:
  sources:
  - useDefaultCAs: true
  target:
    secret:
      key: "trust-bundle.pem"
    namespaceSelector:
```

2 See the trust-manager documentation (*https://oreil.ly/JOgx3*) for details on how the `useDefaultCAs` source is populated and how to keep it updated.

```
        matchLabels:
          secrets-namespace: "true"
```

We'll apply a custom label to the namespace so that trust-manager can find it. After creating the namespace and applying this bundle, we can see that the bundle and secret have been created:

```
$ kubectl label --context kind-tls namespace cilium-secrets \
    secrets-namespace="true"
namespace/cilium-secrets labeled

$ kubectl apply --context kind-tls --filename public-ca-bundle.yaml
bundle.trust.cert-manager.io/public-ca-bundle created

$ kubectl get --context kind-tls bundle
NAME               CONFIGMAP TARGET   SECRET TARGET   SYNCED   REASON   AGE
public-ca-bundle   trust-bundle.pem                   True     Synced   8m41s

$ kubectl get secrets --context kind-tls --namespace cilium-secrets
NAME               TYPE     DATA   AGE
public-ca-bundle   Opaque   1      39s
```

We've chosen to include a standard bundle of public CAs, instead of only the ones for our targeted site. If you're writing TLS policy for just one site, you could elect to include only the public CA for that site. However, this can be quite brittle as sites may change their public CA at any time without warning, and they won't expect this change to affect users. If you control the external site as well, you might consider this option, but for a third-party public site, it's best to use a standard bundle.

Internal CA

Now we need to create an internal certificate authority (*tls/internal-ca.yaml*), which we'll use to sign certificates for outgoing connections. We can use cert-manager to create a self-signed issuer:

```
apiVersion: cert-manager.io/v1
kind: Issuer
metadata:
  name: selfsigned
  namespace: cert-manager
spec:
  selfSigned: {}
```

Then, we can use this self-signed issuer to create a root certificate, and finally create a certificate authority from this root:

```
apiVersion: cert-manager.io/v1
kind: Certificate
metadata:
  name: root
  namespace: cert-manager
```

```yaml
spec:
  isCA: true
  commonName: internal-ca
  secretName: root
  privateKey:
    algorithm: ECDSA
    size: 256
    rotationPolicy: never
  issuerRef:
    name: selfsigned
    kind: Issuer
    group: cert-manager.io
---
apiVersion: cert-manager.io/v1
kind: ClusterIssuer
metadata:
  name: internal-ca
spec:
  ca:
    secretName: root
```

We can now sign certificates for our intercepted TLS connections with this issuer. As we're connecting to *cilium.io*, we'll sign a certificate for that domain using our new internal certificate authority (*tls/cilium-io-cert.yaml*):

```yaml
apiVersion: cert-manager.io/v1
kind: Certificate
metadata:
  name: cilium-io-cert
  namespace: kube-system
spec:
  commonName: cilium.io
  secretName: cilium-io-cert
  privateKey:
    algorithm: ECDSA
    size: 256
  issuerRef:
    name: internal-ca
    kind: Issuer
    group: cert-manager.io
```

We now have a root certificate, a CA for that root certificate, and a certificate issued by that CA for `cilium.io`, just as we described in Figure 13-3.

Overriding Pod CA Certificates

For our test pod to trust the internal CA, we'll need to mount the CA certificate. We'll use trust-manager again to populate a ConfigMap with the internal CA in it (*tls/internal-ca-bundle.yaml*). This will create the ConfigMap in every namespace, so any pod can mount it:

```
apiVersion: trust.cert-manager.io/v1alpha1
kind: Bundle
metadata:
  name: internal-ca-bundle
spec:
  sources:
    - secret:
        name: root
        key: "ca.crt"
  target:
    configMap:
      key: "ca.crt"
```

We don't have to tell trust-manager which namespace the "root" secret for the internal CA is in—trust-manager can only read secrets from the "trust namespace," which is the `cert-manager` namespace by default. See the trust-manager documentation for details.

Next, we'll create a pod and mount this ConfigMap (*tls/test-pod.yaml*). In netshoot's case it's a Debian-based image, and the trust bundle is expected to be at */etc/ssl/certs/ca-certificates.crt*. By using a volume mount over this path, we can overwrite whatever TLS certificates are already in the container image with our new bundle:

```
apiVersion: v1
kind: Pod
metadata:
  labels:
    app.kubernetes.io/name: test
  name: test
spec:
  containers:
    - name: netshoot
      image: nicolaka/netshoot
      args:
        - sleep
        - infinity
      volumeMounts:
        - name: ca-certs
          mountPath: /etc/ssl/certs/
  volumes:
    - name: ca-certs
      configMap:
        name: internal-ca-bundle
        items:
          - key: ca.crt
            path: ca-certificates.crt
```

Because we need to mount a volume, we can't shortcut this with `kubectl run`, so create the pod manually and use `kubectl exec` instead.

Note that we've fully replaced the container's provided certificates. Because our internal bundle didn't *also* contain the public certificates, this container will be unable to establish TLS connections to any public endpoints. To trust both internal and public endpoints, include the default CAs in the internal bundle.

TLS Policy

We've got our pod running with an internal certificate authority present. We also have a certificate for `cilium.io` issued by that CA. We now have everything we need to intercept TLS and enforce policy at layer 7 for this pod.

Suppose we want to only allow access to the Cilium blog on the `/blog/` path. We'll write our network policy just like a normal HTTP policy, but with two new statements, `originatingTLS` and `terminatingTLS` (*tls/policy.yaml*):

```
apiVersion: cilium.io/v2
kind: CiliumNetworkPolicy
metadata:
  name: client
spec:
  endpointSelector:
    matchLabels:
      app.kubernetes.io/name: test
  egress:
    - toPorts:
        - ports:
            - port: "443"
              protocol: TCP
          originatingTLS:
            secret:
              namespace: cilium-secrets
              name: public-ca-bundle
              key: trust-bundle.pem
          terminatingTLS:
            secret:
              namespace: cilium-secrets
              name: cilium-io-cert
          rules:
            http:
              - host: cilium.io
                path: /blog/.*
    - toPorts:
        - ports:
            - port: "53"
              protocol: ANY
      toEndpoints:
        - matchLabels:
            k8s-app: kube-dns
            io.kubernetes.pod.namespace: kube-system
```

If we apply this policy and exec into our test pod, we can view it all working as expected:

```
$ kubectl exec test -it -- bash

test:~# curl -sI https://cilium.io/blog/ | head -n1
HTTP/1.1 200 OK

test:~# curl -sI https://cilium.io/blog/2025/05/20/cilium-l7-policies/ | \
    head -n1
HTTP/1.1 200 OK

test:~# curl -sI https://cilium.io | head -n1
HTTP/1.1 403 Forbidden
```

Note that the URL scheme here was `https://`, cURL provided no certificate errors, and we didn't ignore certificate errors in cURL with `-k`. As far as the client application was concerned, this was a perfectly normal TLS connection, intercepted by Cilium.

With TLS connections, this kind of path-based policy isn't possible without interception as the path being requested is part of the encrypted communication, and without terminating and re-originating TLS using a proxy the path cannot be observed in transit.

Limitations

There are a number of limitations and drawbacks to TLS interception in Cilium. The major one is the intermediate certificate itself. While wildcard certificates are possible, most TLS clients will not accept multiple levels of wildcard for all possible combinations of subdomains. This means that you can't use a single certificate for all TLS connections and instead have to use a certificate per domain. In the setup we used here, the certificate for `cilium.io` is presented for any connections to port 443. Here's what will happen if we attempt to reach `example.com`:

```
test:~# curl https://example.com
curl: (60) SSL: certificate subject name 'cilium.io' does not match target
hostname 'example.com'
More details here: https://curl.se/docs/sslcerts.html

curl failed to verify the legitimacy of the server and therefore could not
establish a secure connection to it. To learn more about this situation and
how to fix it, please visit the webpage mentioned above.
```

Even though we connected to `example.com`, Cilium presented the configured certificate for `cilium.io`. If we ignore the certificate error we can get as far as Envoy denying the access:

```
test:~# curl -k https://example.com
Access denied
```

This means that TLS certificate management can become difficult. It's possible to combine layer 7 filtering with `toFQDN` rules to serve the correct TLS certificate, but there's no SNI header capability in layer 7 policy to handle multiple certificates for different domain names. In general, TLS interception isn't well suited to being a blanket policy, where all TLS traffic is intercepted. Instead, it's best used for targeted policy where layer 3 or layer 4 policy isn't enough.

Summary

In this chapter we've covered a large number of advanced use cases for Cilium's network policy. We've also expanded the identity model and filtering beyond the eBPF datapath and into the realm of layer 7 proxies. Both of these represent an expansion of Cilium's scope, from a "simple" CNI to a fully fledged network appliance and a core part of modern cloud native networking infrastructure.

CHAPTER 14

Transparent Encryption

Cilium's Transparent Encryption feature is capable of encrypting traffic as it transits between Cilium managed endpoints. It's called *transparent* because it is not visible to the pods on each end and requires no coordination from the workloads themselves. Cilium encrypts packets as they leave the source node and decrypts them as they enter the destination node. It handles all aspects of the process, including key distribution and management.

Transparent Encryption can use either WireGuard or IPsec as the underlying encryption technology. Both of these are industry-standard encapsulation methods. We'll use WireGuard in this chapter, but IPsec (*https://oreil.ly/s5a0O*) has similar concepts and the same flows are encrypted with both. IPsec mode takes more work to set up, requiring the administrator to create shared secrets and configure encryption algorithms, but if you have regulatory reasons to require specific algorithms or key lengths it may be an attractive alternative to WireGuard's automatic configuration.

You can find all the YAML manifests you will use in this chapter, along with several convenient scripts, in the *chapter14* directory of the book's GitHub repository (*https://github.com/isovalent/cilium-up-and-running*).

Use Cases

The two primary use cases for Transparent Encryption are to meet a compliance requirement for in-flight encryption or as part of an overall security posture. The two motivations often coexist. We recommend keeping focused on what you are specifically protecting against instead of enabling encryption simply because of a vague sense that it is "more secure."

In this section, we will briefly discuss compliance and threat modeling and highlight how Cilium can help. However, these are complex topics, and this book will not go into great detail on them. We recommend consulting additional resources for further information, such as *Threat Modeling* by Izar Tarandach and Matthew J. Coles (O'Reilly).

Compliance

Compliance frameworks are lists of requirements and controls, usually maintained by a third-party organization and often enforced by external auditors. They are common in many countries for regulated industries such as healthcare and finance, where failure to comply can have a significant impact on an organization's ability to do business. They can also be transitive, such that if your organization provides services to a regulated organization, you may need to follow the same rules as a condition of doing business with them.

Compliance frameworks often mandate exact technical details or architectures, such as listing cryptographic ciphers or key lengths that are acceptable. When assessing Transparent Encryption against a compliance framework, it's important to open a discussion with your auditors to understand exactly what the requirements are and how Cilium can be configured to meet them.

Transparent Encryption is often useful in situations where a *platform team* that manages the cluster is distinct from *application teams* that manage the workloads. In this model, the platform team can enforce an "encryption in flight" requirement across the whole cluster without having to coordinate with each individual application team to ensure that they are correctly implementing encryption in their applications.

Threat Models

As part of a larger security approach, Transparent Encryption can be used to preserve the confidentiality and integrity of data as it transits the underlying network infrastructure between Cilium nodes. This is useful for protecting against an attacker who may have gained the ability to observe or modify data in transit, as shown in Figure 14-1, but who doesn't have elevated permissions on the nodes themselves.

> From Cilium's perspective, the nature of the underlying network fabric doesn't matter. All that matters is that it provides layer 2 or layer 3 connectivity between nodes. It could be as simple as a single switch that connects each node together in a single layer 2 domain, or a complex leaf/spine setup with bonded connections to each node. Some features, such as BGP announcement and native routing, may require other features of the underlying fabric.

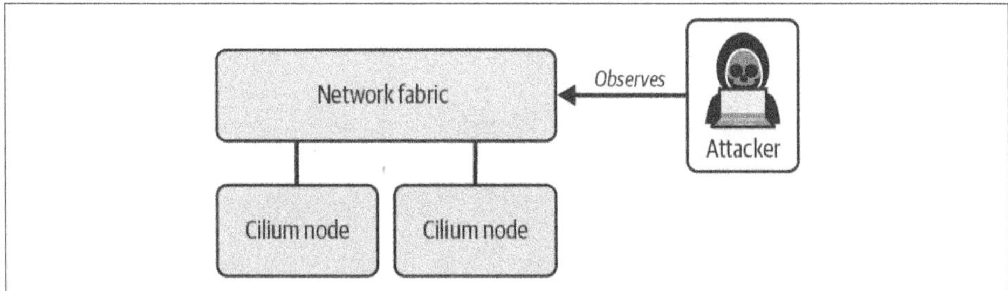

Figure 14-1. An attacker observing network traffic between nodes

If the Cilium nodes are virtual machines, it might matter how those virtual machines are attached to the physical network. As shown in Figure 14-2, if the hypervisor provides networking and acts as a switch,[1] an attacker could observe packets here instead.

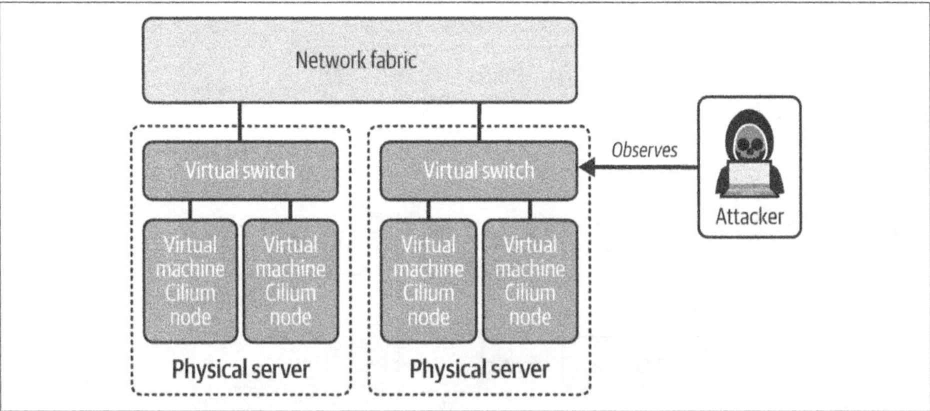

Figure 14-2. An attacker observing network traffic on a virtual switch on a hypervisor

Traffic Flow

Transparent Encryption does not use mutual TLS (mTLS) and does not require a layer 7 proxy to establish a TCP session with the workload. When a packet is sent between managed pods on two different nodes, Cilium encrypts the original packet and encapsulates it in a new WireGuard packet. This new packet is sent to the remote node, and the content is decapsulated and decrypted before being delivered to the target pod.

1 In some hypervisor setups, individual virtual machines are exposed directly to the underlying network using technologies such as SR-IOV. This is highly implementation-specific and depends on the hardware, network interfaces, hypervisor, and underlying network design.

It's important to note that packets are only encrypted if they are traveling between two Cilium-managed pods and those pods are on different nodes. Packets are *not* encrypted if they are traveling between:

- Pods on the same node
- A pod and a host process or host network namespace pod
- Two host processes or host network namespace pods
- Any process and a destination outside of the cluster
- Any communication that does not use the network, such as HTTP over UNIX socket
- Processes within the same pod

Figure 14-3 shows these flows with only the cross-node communication between pods in a cluster passing through the encrypted WireGuard tunnel.

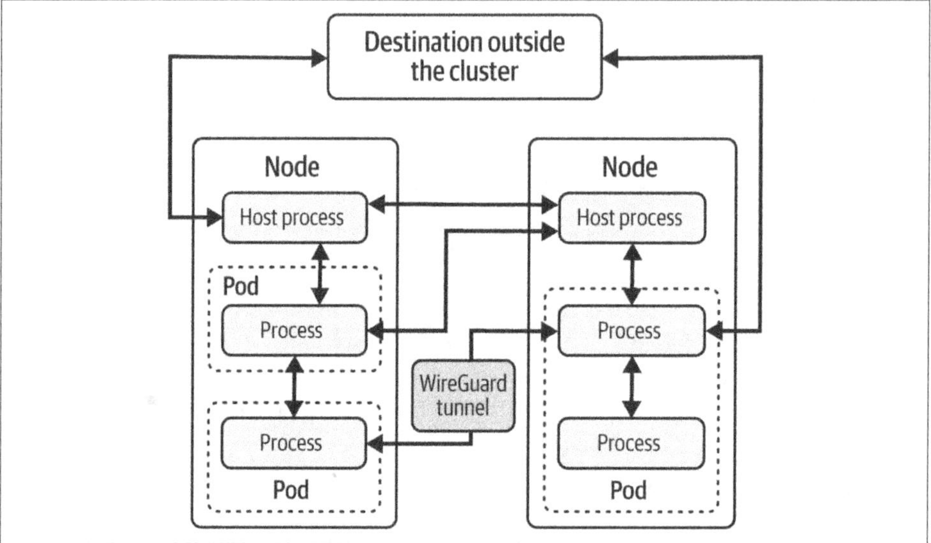

Figure 14-3. Encryption cases

A common question is why Cilium does not encrypt traffic between pods on the same node. It may seem like a strange omission, but the rationale is simple: when packets travel between pods on the same node, Cilium's eBPF datapath moves them directly from one pod's network interface to the other pod's, in kernel. There is no Linux bridge, virtual switch, or other networking system between the pods. If Cilium did perform encryption here, it would encrypt traffic only to immediately decrypt it again, so it would provide no benefit. (See Chapter 5 for details of the intranode datapath.)

Transparent Encryption is performed after any resolution of ClusterIP services, so packets bound for a service's virtual IP will be encrypted only if the selected backend is on another node. Similarly, with layer 7 network policy, the packets are encrypted only after leaving the per-node Envoy proxy on egress and are decrypted on ingress just before entering the Envoy proxy on the remote node.

The encryption and encapsulation in the datapath are performed entirely using the kernel's implementation of WireGuard.[2] Cilium is responsible for key distribution, configuring the WireGuard tunnels, and steering packets into those tunnels.

Encapsulation

WireGuard uses a layer 3 encapsulation method—the packet up to the IP header (including TCP/UDP headers and any layer 7 headers) is encrypted unaltered and sent as a payload in a WireGuard UDP packet on port 51871, which is the default WireGuard port used in Cilium. On the remote node, the encapsulated packet is unwrapped and the original packet decrypted before being delivered to the target pod.

As shown in Figure 14-4, for clusters using tunneling routing modes such as VXLAN, the encryption occurs *after* the tunnel encapsulation is performed. Because VXLAN encapsulates at layer 2, a packet on the wire between nodes has an encrypted payload containing the application payload,[3] inner TCP header, inner IP header, inner Ethernet frame, VXLAN header, outer UDP header, and outer IP header. The encrypted payload has a WireGuard header, UDP header, IPv4 header, and Ethernet frame header, along with a WireGuard footer.

2 This requires Linux kernel 5.6 or later, but nearly all modern distributions meet this requirement (with the exception of older long-term support releases such as Ubuntu 20.04 LTS).

3 VXLAN encapsulation can occur after packet fragmentation, so a single VXLAN packet may not contain a complete layer 3 packet.

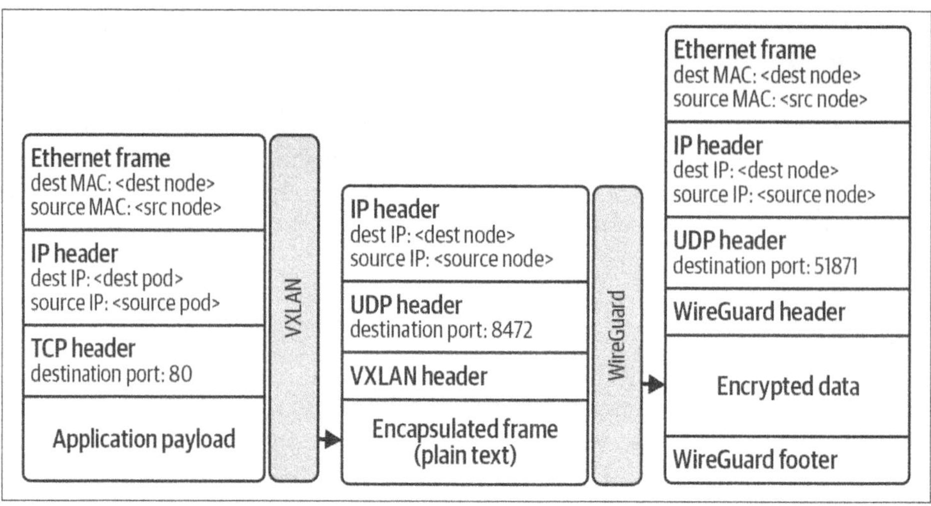

Figure 14-4. Encryption and encapsulation of a packet using VXLAN tunneling

For clusters in native routing mode, there is no double encapsulation from VXLAN, but pod-to-pod packets are still encapsulated in a WireGuard packet before being sent between nodes, as shown in Figure 14-5.

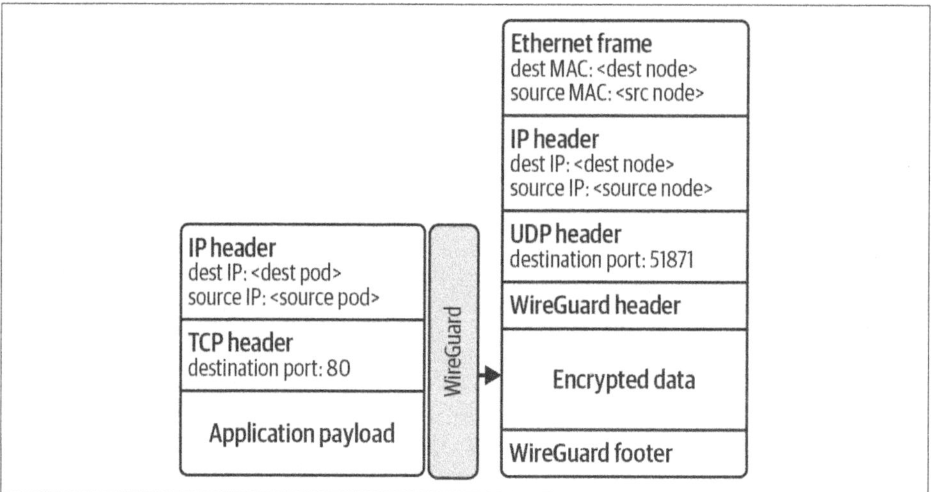

Figure 14-5. Encryption and encapsulation of a packet in a natively routed cluster

Even in a natively routed cluster using Transparent Encryption, it's still recommended to make your pod CIDR ranges routable to the underlying network (see Chapters 5 and 10 for details) to handle node-to-pod, pod-to-node, and north–south traffic from pods.

Encryption and Authentication

WireGuard prevents observers on the network from observing the contents of the packets, or even directly observing which pods are communicating, by encrypting traffic. However, they can still see that communication is taking place. For example, an attacker could observe which nodes are communicating, how big the packets are, and how regular they are. This information could be used to infer the difference between streaming content (regular packets of similar size) and request/response interactions (a small set of packets in one direction followed by a larger burst of packets in the opposite direction), or to "map" an application topology between nodes. If this kind of implied data is sensitive in your application, then evaluating Transparent Encryption for your use case is beyond the scope of this book.

WireGuard is also responsible for authentication between nodes. When the Cilium agent starts with WireGuard encryption enabled, it generates a public/private key pair and attaches the public key to its CiliumNode object as an annotation named `network.cilium.io/wg-pub-key`. Other nodes then use these annotations to discover the public keys of their peers in the cluster. The WireGuard tunnels are configured to only accept traffic signed with the expected key pair. This effectively protects traffic in transit from tampering or spoofing, because key distribution is done entirely via the Kubernetes API, and the security of the WireGuard encryption is predicated on the security of the Kubernetes API plane.

Configuring and Validating Transparent Encryption

Encryption is enabled in Cilium using the following Helm values:

```
encryption:
  enabled: true
  type: wireguard
```

If you are enabling encryption on an existing cluster, you must restart the Cilium agents and the operator to see the changes apply. You should expect to see traffic drops and disruptions during this process.

In this example, we'll be using a local cluster with kind. To be able to demonstrate routing between nodes, we're going to create a cluster with one control-plane node and two worker nodes. We'll use native routing and enable the `kube-proxy` replacement to simplify the datapath and let us concentrate on observing the encryption mode.

Launch the test cluster (*kind.yaml*) with `kind create cluster --config chapter14/kind.yaml --name ch14`, taking care to name it `ch14`, and install Cilium with Helm using the provided values file (*cilium.yaml*).

Once the cluster is running and Cilium is installed and ready, we can test that Transparent Encryption is enabled by checking the output of `cilium status`. Run the following command from the Cilium CLI. The encryption status isn't visible in the normal output, but it is in the extended JSON output:

```
$ cilium status -o json \
    | jq '.cilium_status[].encryption.wireguard.interfaces'
[
  {
    "listen-port": 51871,
    "name": "cilium_wg0",
    "peer-count": 3,
    "peers": null,
    "public-key": "itVM9s3GXsjJa9xwNlwSxfT1VKGdyOaomN7wDE7mqwE="
  }
],
[...]
```

This shows us the public key for the node, and the fact that WireGuard is enabled. We can also view the public keys in the CiliumNode object in Kubernetes as an annotation:

```
$ kubectl get ciliumnode -o json | jq "$(cat <<EOF
.items[] | {
  "name": .metadata.name,
  "wg-pub-key": .metadata.annotations["network.cilium.io/wg-pub-key"]
}
EOF
)"

{
  "name": "ch14-control-plane",
  "wg-pub-key": "qkCH1M3cYPFUzd/lyMRIGFMQxJ9bAPVwn6MrKakNGnw="
}
{
  "name": "ch14-worker",
  "wg-pub-key": "itVM9s3GXsjJa9xwNlwSxfT1VKGdyOaomN7wDE7mqwE="
}
{
  "name": "ch14-worker2",
  "wg-pub-key": "ZLCwOShY+Vj67R9yu4oQJwEshD9NAdeAtPT666wMb1k="
}
```

These public keys are exchanged using the Kubernetes API, meaning that the authentication to the Kubernetes API itself is the root of trust for Transparent Encryption.

Testing Encryption

We can test that Transparent Encryption is working by observing network traffic between nodes, just as our hypothetical attacker in Figure 14-1 would do.

The testing we're doing here isn't enough to conclusively prove the strength of the encryption, only that the expected traffic is being passed through a WireGuard tunnel and is not transmitted in plain text. Comprehensive cryptanalysis is beyond the scope of this book.

Viewing Unencrypted Traffic

To begin with, we'll get an idea of what unencrypted traffic looks like. Disable encryption by setting `encryption.enabled=false` and restarting the Cilium agent and operator:

```
$ helm upgrade --install \
    cilium cilium/cilium \
    --kube-context kind-ch14 \
    --namespace kube-system \
    --reuse-values \
    --set "encryption.enabled=false"

$ helm rollout restart \
    --context kind-ch14 \
    --namespace kube-system \
    deployment/cilium-operator \
    daemonset/cilium
```

We can view intranode traffic on our kind cluster by observing network flows on the host running our kind container images. How you access this host will depend on your personal setup, but once you have access, you can observe traffic using `tcpdump`. In our case, because we're using kind containers on a virtual machine, the nodes are connected together using a network bridge in the VM. We can access it directly and observe traffic on the bridge.

First, we'll deploy our test pods—one for an NGINX web server and another for a client—along with a service for the web server (*testbed.yaml*). We use Kubernetes anti-affinity rules to force the two pods to be deployed on different nodes.[4] If we didn't do this, they could end up on the same node, and we wouldn't be able to see the communication in this example.

Once the pods are deployed and running, in another terminal we can begin to capture packets. By running a container directly on the Docker host with `--network host` and `--privileged`, we can access the network bridge used by kind. We can use

4 See the Kubernetes documentation (*https://oreil.ly/2bnQn*) for more information on affinity and anti-affinity.

docker network list to get the details on which bridge this is and dump packets from it in text using -A, with -i "*<interface>*" to select the bridge and -l to flush to stdout so we can filter in real time using grep. We're looking for exposed bearer tokens in plain text:

```
$ bridge_name="$(docker network list \
    --format json \
    | jq -r '.[] | select(.name == "kind") | .network_interface')"

$ docker run \
    --network host \
    --privileged \
    -it \
    nicolaka/netshoot \
    tcpdump -lAi "$bridge_name" \
    | grep "Bearer"
```

With this running, we can issue a curl request from our test pod to our web server, which due to our anti-affinity rules we know will transit through the bridge:

```
$ kubectl exec deploy/client \
    -- curl -sIH "Authorization: Bearer MYSECRETTOKEN" \
    webserver | head -n1
HTTP/1.1 200 OK
```

Our NGINX server isn't actually configured to require a bearer token, but this form of token in the header mechanism is common in HTTP services. Regardless, we can still see it in the output from our packet capture. You should see MYSECRETTOKEN output in your packet capture logs in your other terminal as you perform this test.

Viewing Encrypted Traffic

Let's turn encryption back on and see what effect that has on our capture:

```
$ helm upgrade --install \
    cilium cilium/cilium \
    --kube-context kind-ch14 \
    --namespace kube-system \
    --reuse-values \
    --set "encryption.enabled=true"

$ helm rollout restart \
    --context kind-ch14 \
    --namespace kube-system \
    deployment/cilium-operator \
    daemonset/cilium
```

Now when we run the same curl command, we won't see the token exposed in the output. If we search for different terms, we won't see any plain-text HTTP content at all. Instead, all traffic is encrypted and sent over a WireGuard tunnel on port 51871; the underlying network fabric only sees UDP traffic.

If we capture traffic on the WireGuard tunnel port instead, we can see the encrypted data. We won't use the plain-text output this time, but instead will get the hex output with `-XX` and verbose header information with `-v`. Instead of using `grep`, we'll pass a PCAP filter directly to `tcpdump` for `udp and port 51871`:

```
$ docker run \
    --network host \
    --privileged \
    -it \
    nicolaka/netshoot \
    tcpdump -vlXXi "$bridge_name" udp and port 51871
```

Once the capture is running, try issuing the `curl` command again in another terminal. You should see output like the following in the first terminal:

```
tcpdump: listening on docker1, link-type EN10MB (Ethernet), snapshot length
262144 bytes
02:55:16.978847 IP (tos 0x0, ttl 64, id 28877, offset 0, flags [none], proto
UDP (17), length 172)
    10.89.0.22.51871 > 10.89.0.21.51871: UDP, length 144
        0x0000:  eabb ef9a 623c 8a8d 46bf 99b8 0800 4500  ....b<..F.....E.
        0x0010:  00ac 70cd 0000 4011 f497 0a59 0016 0a59  ..p...@....Y...Y
        0x0020:  0015 ca9f ca9f 0098 1586 0400 0000 0fee  ................
        0x0030:  8e1a 1c00 0000 0000 0000 ce32 aab0 b7ff  ..........2....
        0x0040:  b693 e50b d0bf 9956 8f71 d15d d9fa 4b4a  .......V.q.]..KJ
        0x0050:  6165 3c1c bece 4f1d 5d08 52ad 2167 521e  ae<...O.].R.!gR.
        0x0060:  461f c82e f1cb fc3b eaec 226a 5b12 baad  F......;.."j[...
        0x0070:  8727 3fa9 4748 c742 5e64 8b72 a5c1 8122  .'?.GH.B^d.r..."
        0x0080:  9c52 0417 e932 aac3 d587 4779 ea56 7650  .R...2....Gy.VvP
        0x0090:  ef4d 086c d744 6390 5be3 4daa f5d7 6514  .M.l.Dc.[.M...e.
        0x00a0:  f79b e90b ae13 46c8 3780 8a74 5333 c30f  ......F.7..tS3..
        0x00b0:  3de8 9295 1193 edf8 09d1                 =.........
[...]
```

From this, we can see that otherwise unencrypted traffic is correctly encrypted and that this change is invisible to the underlying pods.

Viewing Unencrypted Flows

Finally, as a counterexample, we can investigate what happens for traffic between a node and a pod. We'll patch the client test deployment to use the host network namespace instead:

```
$ kubectl patch \
    --context kind-ch14 \
    deploy client \
    --type json \
    --patch-file /dev/stdin <<EOF
[
  {
    "op": "replace",
```

```
    "path": "/spec/template/spec/hostNetwork",
    "value": true
  },
  {
    "op": "replace",
    "path": "/spec/template/spec/dnsPolicy",
    "value": "ClusterFirstWithHostNet"
  }
]
EOF

deployment.apps/client patched
```

Once the deployment has completed, we can reissue our `curl` command. This time, we'll see that even with Transparent Encryption enabled, traffic from a node—in this case, a pod in the host's network namespace—to a pod on another node is not encrypted.

Summary

Transparent Encryption covers a common service mesh use case by enforcing encryption of data in transit between nodes across the network. Cilium accomplishes this without using mTLS, allowing it to function on application traffic that is not HTTP, including UDP traffic. The encryption is completely transparent to the applications and requires no changes from them to be compatible.

CHAPTER 15
Observability with Hubble

Hubble is built on top of Cilium and eBPF, providing deep visibility into how applications communicate and behave. It focuses primarily on networking observability, helping operators understand dependencies between services and identify performance or security issues.

What makes Hubble particularly valuable is that it provides visibility not only at layers 3 and 4, where most flow tools operate, but also at layer 7. This means it can reveal application-level information such as HTTP methods or DNS queries, giving you a more complete picture of traffic behavior. Hubble also surfaces security-related context, such as blocked connections and the policies that caused them, allowing you to refine network policies based on observed flows.

All of this happens transparently, without requiring any modification to the applications themselves. In addition to live flow visibility, Hubble exposes Prometheus metrics, enabling integration with common observability tools such as Prometheus and Grafana for monitoring and alerting.

Hubble Architecture

Before we start using Hubble, it is worth taking a moment to understand how its main components fit together. Hubble collects information by tapping into Cilium's eBPF datapath. A Hubble agent runs on every node as part of the Cilium DaemonSet; it is not a separate pod. Each agent reports flow data from its own node only, which means querying a single agent provides a limited view of cluster-wide activity.

To gain a more holistic picture of flows across the cluster, Hubble introduces an aggregation layer called *Hubble Relay*. Relay runs as a deployment and aggregates data from all node-local agents, gathering their flow data and exposing it through a single

API endpoint. Most users interact with Relay rather than with the agents directly, since it provides a unified cluster-wide view of network flows.

Figure 15-1 illustrates that architecture.

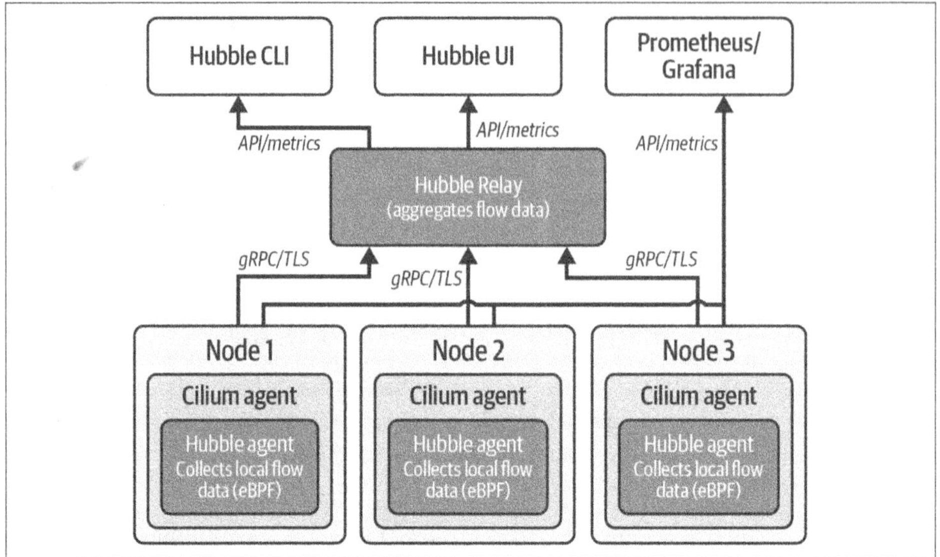

Figure 15-1. Hubble architecture

You can find the YAML manifests you will use in this chapter in the *chapter15* directory of the book's GitHub repository (*https://github.com/isovalent/cilium-up-and-running*).

When Cilium is installed, the Hubble agent is automatically enabled by default. You can validate this on any Cilium-enabled cluster—for example, a generic kind cluster (*kind.yaml*) with a default Cilium installation (`cilium install`). You can then verify it from inside the Cilium agent, since the Hubble agent runs as part of that:

```
$ kubectl exec -n kube-system ds/cilium -c cilium-agent -- hubble status
Healthcheck (via unix:///var/run/cilium/hubble.sock): Ok
Current/Max Flows: 4,095/4,095 (100.00%)
Flows/s: 11.72
```

The output confirms the Hubble agent is running and healthy. You can then query Hubble directly by connecting to the agent using `kubectl exec`. This method allows you to view current flows (from the current node only) by executing the following `hubble observe` command:

```
$ kubectl exec -n kube-system ds/cilium -c cilium-agent -- hubble observe
```

```
10.244.0.10:33666 (host) ->
  kube-system/coredns-674b8bbfcf-6wl44:8181 (ID:8159)
  to-endpoint FORWARDED (TCP Flags: ACK, PSH)

10.244.0.10:59786 (host) ->
  kube-system/coredns-674b8bbfcf-hjd28:8181 (ID:8159)
  to-endpoint FORWARDED (TCP Flags: SYN)

10.244.0.10:59786 (host) <-
  kube-system/coredns-674b8bbfcf-hjd28:8181 (ID:8159)
  to-stack FORWARDED (TCP Flags: SYN, ACK)
```

Each line represents a flow record that includes direction, source and destination information, and TCP flags.

You can think of this as a context-aware version of `tcpdump`: it provides packet-level visibility but enriches it with Kubernetes metadata. In the example output shown here, the source is identified as the host, while the destination is one of the CoreDNS pods in the `kube-system` namespace.[1]

Each record also includes a numeric ID, which represents the endpoint's identity within Cilium. You encountered these identities earlier in Chapter 12, where you saw how they are used to apply network policy and track flows.

Be cautious about who is granted access to any of the Hubble data. Flow logs can include potentially sensitive information, such as source and destination addresses or HTTP headers. It's best to limit access to only those who truly need it.

By default, `hubble observe` only shows flows from the node where you run it, which may not be particularly helpful in a real-world scenario with numerous applications spread across multiple nodes. To aggregate flows from all nodes, you will need to use Hubble Relay.

Hubble Relay

Hubble Relay is not enabled by default. To enable it, you will need to add the following to the Cilium Helm values file (or, as shown in Chapter 3, simply use `cilium hubble enable`):

1 In case you are wondering why CoreDNS is being accessed on ports 8181 and 8080 instead of the default port 53 for DNS, it's because these ports are configured for readiness and liveness probes in the CoreDNS deployment.

```
hubble:
  relay:
    enabled: true
```

You should then see a separate deployment in the kube-system namespace:

```
$ kubectl get deployment -n kube-system hubble-relay
NAME           READY   UP-TO-DATE   AVAILABLE   AGE
hubble-relay   1/1     1            1           38m
```

There are other ways to access Hubble besides using kubectl exec on the agent pod. This matters because kubectl exec grants broad privileges, given that the agent runs as a privileged pod. If you want to limit access to network observability only, use kubectl port-forward to connect to Hubble Relay instead:

```
$ kubectl port-forward -n kube-system deploy/hubble-relay 4245
Forwarding from 127.0.0.1:4245 -> 4245
Forwarding from [::1]:4245 -> 4245
```

Using kubectl port-forward allows you to access Hubble Relay without exposing the entire node, making it a safer alternative for monitoring network traffic. You can then use the Hubble CLI[2] to target Hubble Relay at 127.0.0.1:4245 without shell access to a privileged container.

Hubble CLI

In the CLI, start by checking the status of the Hubble deployment with hubble status:

```
$ hubble status
Healthcheck (via localhost:4245): Ok
Current/Max Flows: 12,285/12,285 (100.00%)
Flows/s: 17.55
Connected Nodes: 3/3
```

Through Relay, you can visualize flows across the whole cluster, rather than on a per-node basis:

```
$ hubble observe
Aug 23 21:15:59.253: kube-system/hubble-relay-db5c57949-2lv5g:59492 (ID:57594) ->
  192.168.97.2:4244 (kube-apiserver)
  to-stack FORWARDED (TCP Flags: ACK, PSH)

Aug 23 21:15:59.253: kube-system/hubble-relay-db5c57949-2lv5g:35740 (ID:57594) ->
  192.168.97.3:4244 (host)
  to-stack FORWARDED (TCP Flags: ACK, PSH)

Aug 23 21:15:59.253: 192.168.97.3:59492 (host) ->
```

2 We covered installing the Hubble CLI in Chapter 3.

```
  192.168.97.2:4244 (kube-apiserver)
  to-network FORWARDED (TCP Flags: ACK, PSH)

Aug 23 21:15:59.254: kube-system/hubble-relay-db5c57949-2lv5g:47428 (ID:57594) ->
  192.168.97.4:4244 (remote-node)
  to-stack FORWARDED (TCP Flags: ACK, PSH)

Aug 23 21:15:59.254: 192.168.97.3:47428 (host) ->
  192.168.97.4:4244 (remote-node)
  to-network FORWARDED (TCP Flags: ACK, PSH)

Aug 23 21:15:59.255: kube-system/hubble-relay-db5c57949-2lv5g:47428 (ID:57594) <-
  192.168.97.4:4244 (remote-node)
  to-endpoint FORWARDED (TCP Flags: ACK, PSH)

Aug 23 21:15:59.255: kube-system/hubble-relay-db5c57949-2lv5g:59492 (ID:57594) <-
  192.168.97.2:4244 (kube-apiserver)
  to-endpoint FORWARDED (TCP Flags: ACK, PSH)
```

Keep in mind that the Hubble agent must be accessible to view flows. Since the Hubble agent is part of the Cilium agent, any time the Cilium agent is down (e.g., during updates), you will not be able to fetch Hubble flows from that node until it is back up again.

To demonstrate the Hubble functionality, let's deploy, in a dedicated `webshop` namespace, the Online Boutique demo application we previously used in "gRPC Routing" on page 138 and inspect its traffic flows:

```
$ kubectl create ns webshop
namespace/webshop created

$ kubectl apply -n webshop -f gcp-microservices-demo.yaml
deployment.apps/emailservice created
[....]
service/adservice created
serviceaccount/adservice created
```

This setup reflects a common scenario for Kubernetes administrators: someone has deployed a collection of services into the cluster without providing much context or documentation. Hubble can be used to gain visibility into how these services interact.

To start, we can filter flows to only those within the `webshop` namespace:

```
$ hubble observe -n webshop
```

Suppose we identify the frontend service as one of particular interest. We can then filter flows even further by limiting output to only those involving pods with the label `app=frontend`:

```
$ hubble observe -n webshop --label app=frontend
```

Hubble offers many filters to help narrow down flows. Run the following command to list all the supported options:

```
$ hubble observe --help
```

Table 15-1 shows some of the most commonly used flags.

Table 15-1. Common Hubble flags

Flag	Description
`-n <namespace>`	Filter by Kubernetes namespace
`-t <type>`	Filter by event type (drop, trace, etc.)
`--label <label>`	Filter by Kubernetes label
`--from-pod <pod-name>`	Show flows originating from a specific pod
`--http-status <status-code>`	Filter HTTP flows by response status code
`--output json`	Format output as structured JSON

These filters can be combined to focus on specific patterns or security events.[3]

Let's now assume that we have mistakenly deployed the following aggressive `CiliumNetworkPolicy` (*deny-all-ingress.yaml*), which blocks all ingress traffic within the `webshop` namespace:

```
apiVersion: "cilium.io/v2"
kind: CiliumNetworkPolicy
metadata:
  name: "deny-all-ingress"
  namespace: webshop
spec:
  endpointSelector: {}
  ingress:
  - {}
```

This configuration blocks all ingress traffic because it includes an empty ingress rule (`ingress: - {}`) combined with a wildcard selector (`endpointSelector: {}`). This means that for every pod in the `webshop` namespace, no ingress traffic is explicitly allowed—and as you will remember from Chapter 12, by default, Cilium denies all traffic not explicitly permitted. The result is that no service-to-service communication is possible within the namespace.

Using Hubble, we can analyze the dropped traffic, using the `-n` filter to focus on the `webshop` namespace only and the `-t` filter to show only dropped packets:

3 A handy cheat sheet listing many of the Hubble CLI flags and filters is available on the Isovalent website (*https://oreil.ly/EpLUZ*).

```
$ hubble observe -n webshop -t drop

webshop/frontend-6f947cd9db-7v7t5:35310 (ID:47031) <>
  webshop/checkoutservice-5b857ffb9-ppzvv:5050 (ID:12866)
  Policy denied DROPPED (TCP Flags: ACK)
```

The output clearly reveals that traffic is being dropped, and, importantly, it includes the reason: `Policy denied`. This gives us actionable insights. Based on these dropped flows, we can start crafting more specific Cilium network policies to selectively allow the necessary traffic.

Viewing Flow Details with JSON Output

To gather more details about the source and destination of these flows, we can output the data in JSON format with the `-o json` flag and extract fields using tools such as `jq`:

```
$ hubble observe -n webshop -t drop -o json | jq
{
  "flow": {
    "verdict": "DROPPED",
    "source": {
      "namespace": "webshop", ❷
      "labels": ["k8s:app=frontend"], ❶
      "pod_name": "frontend-6f947cd9db-7v7t5"
    },
    "destination": {
      "namespace": "webshop", ❺
      "labels": ["k8s:app=recommendationservice"],
      "pod_name": "recommendationservice-5df568d8b9-fpnzs" ❸
    },
    "IP": {
      "source": "10.0.0.248",
      "destination": "10.0.2.211"
    },
    "l4": {
      "TCP": {
        "source_port": 48248,
        "destination_port": 8080 ❹
      }
    },
    "drop_reason_desc": "POLICY_DENIED"
  }
}
```

From this output, we can see that:

❶ A pod labeled `app=frontend`...

❷ In the `webshop` namespace...

❸ Attempted to connect to a pod labeled `app=recommendationservice`...

❹ On port 8080...

❺ Also in the `webshop` namespace

This is enough information to start writing a network policy that explicitly allows that communication. By repeating this process iteratively, we can build a zero-trust network model. That way, only necessary traffic is allowed, and every policy is based on observed and justified need.

Avoid the temptation to blindly allow every dropped connection you see. Doing so defeats the purpose of using network policy for security. Each policy should be deliberate. Always ask yourself: Why does this service need to talk to that one? Use Hubble to guide your decisions, but apply policy based on principle, not convenience.

The previous JSON output was shortened for clarity, as full JSON output can be lengthy. In production environments, you may want to store complete flow logs for auditing or historical analysis. That's where Hubble Exporter becomes useful.

Hubble Exporter

Hubble Exporter writes flow logs directly from the Cilium agent to a local file on each node. This makes it easy to forward logs to systems like Grafana Loki, Fluent Bit, or Splunk for long-term storage and analysis.

You can enable the static file exporter using the following Helm values:

```
hubble:
  export:
    static:
      filePath: /var/run/cilium/hubble/events.log
      fileMaxSizeMb: 10
      fileMaxBackups: 5
      fileCompress: false
```

This configuration writes structured JSON logs to disk, rotates the file at 10 MB, and keeps up to five backups.

Isovalent Networking for Kubernetes also includes a built-in datastore (Hubble Timescape) that supports long-term flow log retention. This allows for persistent search, policy audits, and historical flow correlation without the need for an external log store.

Layer 7 Visibility

So far, all observed flows included up to layer 4 packet data. To gain visibility beyond TCP and IP metadata, you must define a network policy that includes layer 7 rules. Flows that match these rules become visible to Cilium and can then be observed via Hubble. Keep in mind, though, that layer 7 policy is not just for observability; it is used to enforce traffic rules. As we saw in Chapter 13, these policies define which HTTP methods, paths, or hostnames are allowed, and traffic that does not match is actively dropped.

Enabling layer 7 visibility introduces additional processing overhead. When traffic is redirected through Envoy, it introduces a small amount of additional latency compared to traffic handled directly in the layer 3 and layer 4 datapath. This trade-off is often acceptable for the added insight and control, but it may not be suitable for high-throughput or latency-sensitive workloads.

To demonstrate this, let's prepare a new namespace and deploy a sample client:

```
$ kubectl create ns l7-visibility
namespace/l7-visibility created

$ kubectl run -n l7-visibility --rm -it tmp-shell \
    --image nicolaka/netshoot -- bash
```

Before making requests from the client pod, open a second terminal and start observing flows with Hubble using the `-f` flag (follow mode):

```
$ hubble observe -n l7-visibility -f
```

From the shell in the client pod, initiate a request to an external domain with the following `curl` command:

```
$ curl example.com
```

In the Hubble output, you will first see DNS resolution flows between the client and CoreDNS. What we want to focus on for now is the traffic that comes after the DNS exchange:

```
l7-visibility/tmp-shell:53300 (ID:6576) ->
  23.192.228.80:80 (world)
  to-stack FORWARDED (TCP Flags: SYN)

l7-visibility/tmp-shell:53300 (ID:6576) <-
  23.192.228.80:80 (world)
  to-endpoint FORWARDED (TCP Flags: SYN, ACK)
```

Here we see that `tmp-shell` is contacting the IP `23.192.228.80`. Since we just reached out to `example.com`, we can reasonably infer this IP is tied to that domain. However, many real-world applications contact dozens of domains simultaneously. Without DNS-aware visibility, it quickly becomes difficult to determine whether a given IP belongs to a known service or something unexpected.

To address this, we can apply a `CiliumNetworkPolicy` (*dns-visibility.yaml*) that uses DNS-aware functionality. We covered this already in Chapter 13, so you'll remember that the following policy routes DNS queries (UDP and TCP port 53) through a DNS proxy and allows access to all external destinations (with `toEntities: world`):

```
apiVersion: "cilium.io/v2"
kind: CiliumNetworkPolicy
metadata:
  name: "dns-visibility"
spec:
  endpointSelector: {}
  egress:
  - toPorts:
    - ports:
      - port: "53"
        protocol: UDP
      - port: "53"
        protocol: TCP
      rules:
        dns:
        - matchPattern: "*"
  - toEntities:
    - world
```

Next, execute the `curl` command again from within the client pod. The Hubble output should now include DNS-aware destination names:

```
l7-visibility/tmp-shell:46308 (ID:6576) ->
  example.com:80 (world)
  policy-verdict:L3-Only EGRESS ALLOWED (TCP Flags: SYN)
l7-visibility/tmp-shell:46308 (ID:6576) ->
  example.com:80 (world)
  to-stack FORWARDED (TCP Flags: SYN)
```

This output gives us better context: the destination is described as `example.com`, instead of being an opaque IP address. We can now ask ourselves whether or not this is legitimate access. If not, we can modify the policy to restrict it.

Layer 7 visibility is not a complete security solution—it's just one layer of observability that can help you understand a significant portion of traffic patterns. You should not rely solely on this feature for detecting or preventing malicious behavior. There will still be cases where destination IPs appear without DNS names. This often happens when an IP is accessed directly or when DNS resolution is occurring over a port that was not mentioned in the policy. Unresolved IPs may or may not be valid. Their presence should trigger further inspection. Encourage your teams to prefer DNS-based access and regularly audit flows containing bare IPs.

Next, let's extract more detailed insights about the HTTP payload itself. To do this, we will apply a layer 7 HTTP policy (also described at length in Chapter 13). This policy (*http-visibility.yaml*) sends traffic from all pods in the namespace to port 80 through an Envoy proxy, enabling Hubble to observe HTTP-specific metadata. It also grants permission to access all external destinations via `toEntities: world` so that `example.com` remains reachable:

```
apiVersion: "cilium.io/v2"
kind: CiliumNetworkPolicy
metadata:
  name: "http-visibility"
  namespace: l7-visibility
spec:
  endpointSelector: {}
  egress:
  - toPorts:
    - ports:
      - port: "80"
        protocol: TCP
      rules:
        http:
        - {}
  - toEntities:
    - world
```

Once you've applied the policy, make another request to `example.com` from the sample client. The Hubble output will now contain much richer information:

```
l7-visibility/tmp-shell:57222 (ID:6576) ->
  example.com:80 (world)
  http-request FORWARDED
  (HTTP/1.1 GET http://example.com/)
l7-visibility/tmp-shell:57222 (ID:6576) <-
  example.com:80 (world)
  http-response FORWARDED
  (HTTP/1.1 200 229ms (GET http://example.com/))
```

After the TCP handshake is established, the flows provide detailed insights into the HTTP communication. We can now see the HTTP version (`1.1`), method (`GET`), and path (`/`) of the request. Upon receiving the response, we also see the HTTP status code (`200`) and latency (`229ms`). This information can be useful for tracking service level agreements (SLAs) or monitoring for performance degradation.

Even more detail is available in the JSON output format. To explore this, we can use the following command to filter for HTTP traffic in the namespace and format the output using `jq`:

```
$ hubble observe -n l7-visibility --protocol http -o json | jq
[..]
{
  "http": {
    "method": "GET",
    "url": "http://example.com/",
    "protocol": "HTTP/1.1",
    "headers": [
      { "key": "User-Agent", "value": "curl/8.7.1" },
      { "key": "X-Envoy-Internal", "value": "true" }
    ]
  },
  "destination_names": ["example.com"],
  "verdict": "FORWARDED",
  "Summary": "HTTP/1.1 GET http://example.com/"
}
[...]
}
```

This detailed output provides additional insights that may be necessary for debugging applications or analyzing more complex behaviors.

One particularly useful aspect of the JSON view is visibility into HTTP headers. Some of these are added by the client (e.g., `User-Agent: curl/8.7.1`), while others are added by Cilium redirecting traffic through Envoy (e.g., `X-Envoy-Internal: true`).

Flow Redaction

As some information captured by Hubble may be considered security-sensitive, it should be redacted from the output. What qualifies as sensitive depends on your organization's internal policies. To demonstrate an extreme example, let's simulate a scenario where the client includes an `Authorization` header in a request.

From the client pod, issue this command:

```
$ curl -H "Authorization: Bearer MY_TOKEN" example.com
```

The JSON output from Hubble should look something like this:

```
$ hubble observe -n l7-visibility --protocol http -o json | jq
"l7": {
  "http": {
    "headers": [
      { "Authorization": "Bearer MY_TOKEN" }
    ]
  }
}
```

As seen here, the `Authorization` token (`MY_TOKEN`) is fully visible. To redact this kind of sensitive information, we need to reconfigure Hubble. You can enable redaction by adjusting the configuration. The following Helm values prevent Hubble from exposing the value of the `Authorization` header in flows:

```
hubble:
  redact:
    enabled: true
    http:
      headers:
        deny:
        - Authorization
```

You can also take the inverse approach, by using `hubble.redact.http.headers.allow` to explicitly list headers that you want to keep visible. This is useful when multiple headers might contain sensitive information. Other redaction options include `hubble.redact.http.urlQuery` and `hubble.redact.http.userInfo`. Work closely with your security team to assess your requirements and tailor this configuration accordingly.

After you apply the updated policy, Hubble will no longer show the sensitive value, replacing it with "HUBBLE_REDACTED":

```
"l7": {
  "http": {
    "headers": [
      { "Authorization": "HUBBLE_REDACTED" }
    ]
  }
}
```

With flow redaction in place, we have added an important layer of protection that helps prevent sensitive information from being exposed, while still benefiting from the powerful observability features provided by Hubble.

While the Hubble CLI is a powerful tool that works well in many environments, including CI/CD pipelines, some users may prefer a graphical interface to interpret the data more easily. Fortunately, Hubble provides a UI component that offers a visual representation of flow data.

Hubble UI

The Hubble UI runs as its own deployment and connects to Hubble Relay to retrieve flow information, which it then displays in an interactive, graphical format. To enable the Hubble UI, set the following Helm values when deploying or upgrading Cilium:[4]

```
hubble:
  ui:
    enabled: true
```

This deploys a new `hubble-ui` deployment into your cluster. To access the UI, you can use `kubectl port-forward` (alternatively, you can use the Cilium CLI command `cilium hubble ui` to open the Hubble UI in a browser window):

```
$ kubectl port-forward -n kube-system deploy/hubble-ui 8081
Forwarding from 127.0.0.1:8081 -> 8081
Forwarding from [::1]:8081 -> 8081
```

Once the port forward is active, navigate to *http://localhost:8081* in your browser. From there, you can explore traffic flows in your cluster, filter by namespace, and view dependencies between applications. Figure 15-2 is a screenshot showing the UI focused on the `l7-visibility` namespace.

4 As mentioned in Chapter 3, you can also use the Cilium CLI to enable the UI (via `cilium hubble enable --ui`). Note that if Hubble was already enabled, you must first temporarily disable it using `cilium hubble disable`.

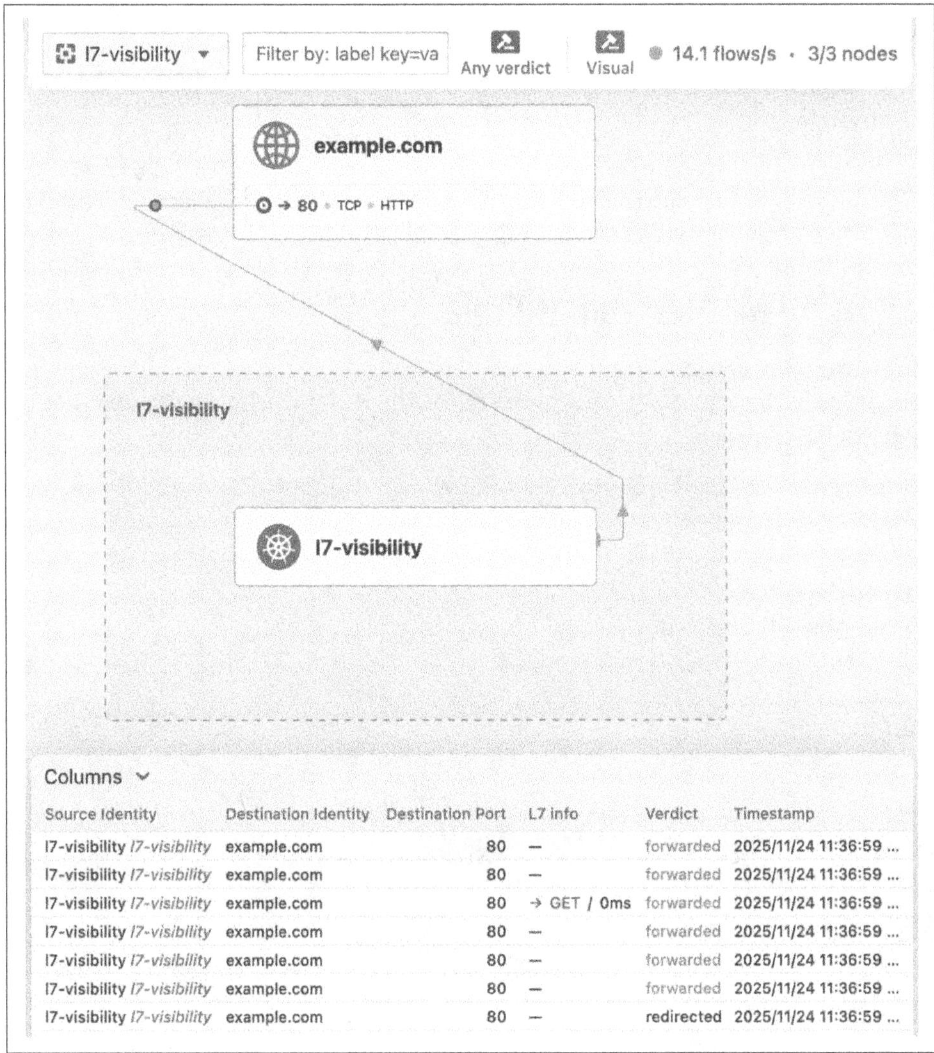

Figure 15-2. Hubble UI screenshot

The interface displays much of the same information available through the CLI, including flow direction, verdicts, and identities. However, it does not expose every detail: for instance, HTTP headers are only visible through the JSON output of the CLI.

The Hubble UI visualizes recent traffic collected by the Hubble subsystem in each Cilium agent. Each agent maintains a local ring buffer of recent flows on its node. The UI retrieves flows from these agent-side buffers via the Hubble gRPC API. Flow data is retained only within the limits of these per-node ring buffers and is not stored persistently. The aforementioned Hubble Exporter and Isovalent Networking for Kubernetes both provide long-term storage and advanced search capabilities.

Exporting Metrics from Hubble

Monitoring and alerting on Hubble's rich flow data is essential for gaining insight into network behavior and detecting anomalies. To support this, Hubble can expose a set of Prometheus metrics.

To enable their collection, update the Cilium Helm configuration with the following values:

```
hubble:
  metrics:
    enabled:
    - dns
    - drop
    - tcp
    - flow
    - icmp
    - httpV2: >
          sourceContext=workload|pod|dns|ip;
          destinationContext=workload|pod|dns|ip
```

This enables a variety of metric categories:

`dns`
: Captures DNS request and response activity

`drop`
: Tracks dropped packets and reasons

`tcp`
: Exposes TCP-level metrics like flags and connection states

`flow`
: Captures general flow metrics

`icmp`
: Provides ICMP traffic visibility

`httpV2`
: Enables HTTP metrics, such as HTTP status codes and methods

Some metrics support additional configuration using semicolon-delimited options. For instance, `httpV2:sourceContext=ip;destinationContext=ip` configures the `source` and `destination` labels used in the metric output. When multiple contexts are defined using the pipe symbol, `|`, Hubble uses the first available nonempty value in the order listed. For example, `destinationContext=workload|pod-name|dns|ip` will first try to use the destination workload (in the form *`namespace/workload`*), then will fall back to the pod name, the DNS name if that's not available, and finally the IP address.[5]

Refer to the official documentation (*https://oreil.ly/rXfqQ*) for a full list of the available metrics and context options.

Once enabled, metrics are exposed on port 9965 by the Hubble agent. Examples include:

`hubble_flows_processed_total`
: Total number of flows processed

`hubble_dns_queries_total`
: Total DNS queries observed

`hubble_drop_total`
: Total number of dropped flows

`hubble_http_requests_total`
: Total number of HTTP requests

Here is some sample `hubble_http_requests_total` metric output:

```
hubble_http_requests_total{
  destination="cilium.io",
  method="GET",
  protocol="HTTP/1.1",
  reporter="client",
  source="namespace/app",
  status="200"
} 6

hubble_http_requests_total{
  destination="example.com",
```

5 Starting with Cilium 1.17, the metrics system supports dynamic reconfiguration, meaning you can adjust the enabled metrics and their contexts without restarting the Cilium agent. This makes it easier to fine-tune observability on running clusters with minimal impact.

```
    method="GET",
    protocol="HTTP/1.1",
    reporter="client",
    source="l7-visibility/tmp-shell",
    status="200"
} 3
```

These metrics can now be scraped by Prometheus and integrated into your observability stack. You can visualize them in Grafana dashboards and configure alerts using Alertmanager to proactively respond to failures, policy violations, or unusual traffic patterns. The Cilium documentation (*https://oreil.ly/5YREc*) includes an example Prometheus and Grafana deployment you can follow.

Summary

Hubble is Cilium's observability layer, providing real-time visibility into network traffic within Kubernetes. It supports both CLI and UI access, allowing users to monitor communication, debug issues, and enforce security policies. While the CLI provides detailed information, including headers and raw flow data in JSON, the Hubble UI offers a visual representation of traffic flows and service dependencies, which can be helpful for interactive exploration.

Hubble's output clearly indicates whether traffic is allowed or dropped, along with reasons (such as `Policy denied`). This information is essential for building and refining a zero-trust model by defining only the necessary traffic flows. To protect sensitive data like `Authorization` headers, Hubble supports redaction. This can be configured via Helm values to avoid exposing credentials or personal information during flow inspection.

By default, Hubble shows layer 3 and layer 4 traffic. For layer 7 visibility, including HTTP methods, status codes, and DNS queries, specific network policies must be applied to pass traffic through the relevant proxies. This unlocks deeper insights into application behavior and external communication. Used effectively, Hubble enables teams to observe traffic, troubleshoot network issues, and enforce secure communication across Kubernetes workloads.

In the next chapter, we'll turn our attention to how to operate Cilium in production environments. Whereas observability gives you visibility into what is happening, operations are about ensuring that everything keeps running smoothly. This includes best practices around upgrades, health monitoring, and integration with operational tools.

CHAPTER 16
Operations

Over the course of this book, you have explored how Cilium provides high-performance networking, security, and observability for Kubernetes. You have learned about its key components, how packets are processed through the datapath, and how features such as service load balancing, network policies, and encryption are implemented. Along the way, you have also seen multiple methods to install Cilium and many examples of commands to verify that those features are operating as expected.

In this final chapter, we shift our focus to day-to-day operations. Running Cilium in production involves maintaining stability throughout upgrades, monitoring performance and capacity, and resolving issues when they inevitably arise. This chapter brings together operational practices, tooling, and considerations that will enable you to run Cilium and Hubble reliably in production environments.

Installation and Lifecycle Management

In the previous chapters we have shown you multiple ways to install and configure Cilium. To achieve operational success, it's important to understand that the simplest or quickest method is not always the best choice for production environments. If you don't already have a process, or are looking to improve one, this section describes a few common patterns and offers recommendations based on our experience.

If you're targeting a Red Hat OpenShift cluster, Isovalent Networking for Kubernetes (*https://oreil.ly/VVDUT*), an enterprise distribution of Cilium, provides a certified installation method with enterprise support.

Cilium CLI Versus Helm

The Cilium CLI is a powerful tool that appears frequently in the official documentation and can be used to install Cilium into a cluster, configure Cluster Mesh, auto-detect environment settings, and more. However, we generally prefer Helm, for two key reasons:

- The Cilium CLI abstracts much of the underlying configuration. This is convenient for quickstarts but not ideal for learning or understanding how Cilium actually operates. Using standard tools like Helm and Kubernetes manifests makes the system's behavior transparent.
- The Cilium CLI is difficult to operate at scale. Running imperative commands from workstations does not align with how real infrastructure is managed. Large environments rely on declarative, reproducible workflows, often using a GitOps approach. These workflows integrate smoothly with Helm charts and Kubernetes objects but not with custom CLI tools.

That said, it's fine to use the Cilium CLI for specific tasks, as long as it does not modify the cluster state (e.g., using `cilium version` to check the version or `cilium bgp peers` to list Cilium's BGP peers). The next question is how to run Helm. We present a few options in the following sections.

Running Helm from Your Laptop or Bastion Host

The least sophisticated approach is to simply run the `helm` CLI directly from your laptop or a jump host.[1] This can be appropriate for testing or experimentation, or when targeting clusters running in local virtual machines. However, for an external cluster, there are serious limitations to be aware of.

One of these is that the agent that invokes Helm needs to have very broad permissions—often the `cluster-admin` role. Many cloud providers use authentication plugins with time-limited scope to avoid storing credentials on disk, but for on-premises installations this may mean storing `cluster-admin` client certificates unencrypted in your *~/.kube/config* file.

Beyond the security concerns, there is usually no management of configuration values passed to Helm. Any upgrades or configuration changes will need to be performed manually, and if you lose or accidentally delete the applied configuration,

1 A jump host is a system that you connect to in order to access other systems on a network, serving as a secure gateway. A bastion host serves a similar purpose but is typically a more hardened, secure version designed to withstand attacks. Both are often used for managing and configuring other systems.

it won't be available anymore.[2] For these reasons, with external clusters this approach should generally be avoided for anything but demo purposes.

Running Helm from Argo CD or Flux

Argo CD and Flux are popular GitOps tools that monitor a Git repository and the cluster state and ensure they stay in sync by applying or removing differences. This approach allows us to leverage the power of Git, which brings clear benefits: in a repository, we can define exactly what we want installed and let the tools handle the rest. The repository becomes the single source of truth, making it easier to keep everything consistent. For example, as shown in Figure 16-1, we can specify a file indicating that we want to install Cilium version 1.18 with a specific values file. Git handles version control, making it easy to track all changes and understand why a change was made by reviewing commit messages. Additionally, these tools can be configured to apply the same configuration across multiple clusters, keeping them in sync.

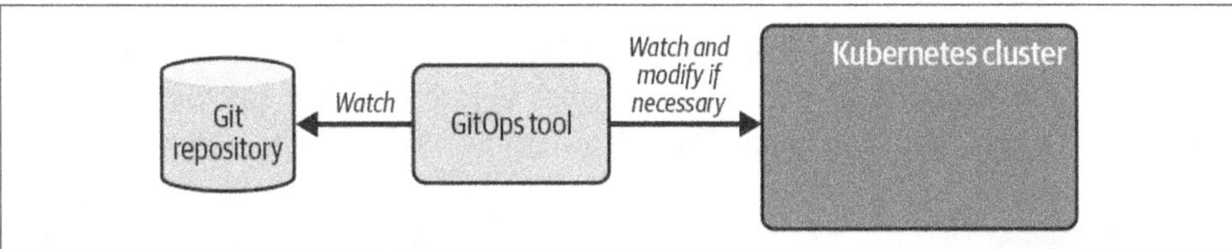

Figure 16-1. GitOps workflow from Git

However, challenges may appear when the GitOps tools are deployed on the same cluster they are supposed to manage, as seen in Figure 16-2. These tools require a functioning CNI to operate, creating a chicken-and-egg scenario: to deploy Argo CD or Flux you need Cilium, but you want to use these tools to deploy Cilium.

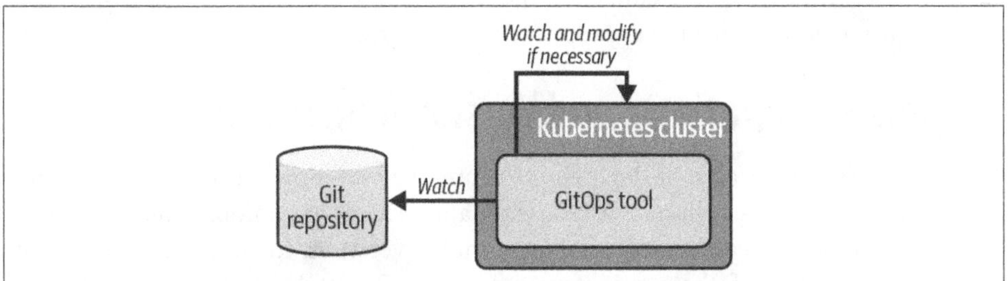

Figure 16-2. GitOps workflow with the tool dependent on the cluster it manages

2 It's possible to extract the last applied Helm values configuration from the cluster, but history beyond that is not stored.

One solution is to create a temporary cluster, for example using kind, with a fully functional CNI and deploy the GitOps tool there. The tool can then access the Git repository and be configured to deploy to the target cluster. Once the target cluster is operational, the GitOps tool can be deployed there and used to manage Cilium going forward. Another approach is to use the tool that originally created the cluster (e.g., Terraform, Ansible, etc.) to manage the initial Cilium installation. Once Cilium is installed, the GitOps tool can take over management.

Keep in mind that having a GitOps tool manage Cilium on the same cluster can create a deadlock scenario. A failing update or misconfiguration could prevent Cilium from functioning properly, which may also disrupt the GitOps tool. In such cases, fixing the malfunctioning configuration may become impossible. For these reasons, it is essential to have a disaster recovery plan that enables the restoration of Cilium functionality, for example by preparing a CI/CD job specifically designed to perform this task.

Another point to consider is that Cilium CRDs are created by the Cilium operator, so the operator needs to have run at least once before applying any Cilium-related custom resources. Planning the installation order in advance can help avoid warnings and errors.

While the specifics of Argo CD and Flux differ, the core concepts are similar. A thorough comparison of these tools and discussion of their respective options and best practices is outside the scope of this book, but Andrew Block and Christian Hernandez's *Argo CD: Up and Running* (O'Reilly) covers these topics in depth.

In short, we recommend Helm over the CLI, and we recommend using it with GitOps, provided you take the appropriate precautions.

Upgrades, Migrations, and Version Management

Now that we've taken care of deploying Cilium, we can move on to the next operational step. Upgrading Cilium is a recurring and critical operation. Cilium follows a regular six-month release cadence for new minor versions, identified by increments to the middle digit of the version format (v*X.Y.Z*). Patch versions are published periodically, incrementing the final digit (*Z*), to deliver security and bug fixes based on community demand and issue severity.

This predictable release rhythm allows platform teams to plan upgrades as part of a regular operational cycle, keeping clusters aligned with supported versions while benefiting from ongoing improvements. Because each upgrade may include kernel-level datapath changes and new CRD schema versions, it should always be planned, tested, and rolled out gradually. As with Kubernetes itself, operators should confirm compatibility, back up configurations, and validate connectivity at each stage of the process.

Upgrade or Replace?

One pattern is to not upgrade Cilium at all, and instead create a new cluster on the new version and migrate workloads across. This approach requires complexity and operational maturity elsewhere in your stack, along with an application that can be migrated without disruption—possibly using Cluster Mesh, BGP ECMP routing, or an external load-balancing layer to transfer traffic between clusters.

Such a setup is beyond the scope of this book, but in general we recommend treating Cilium as a piece of critical infrastructure and approaching upgrades the same way you would a Kubernetes upgrade.

Keep in mind that if you plan to upgrade Cilium, it is recommended to run the preflight check beforehand and to upgrade to the latest patch version before jumping to a newer minor version. The preflight check pulls the new image versions onto each node so the actual upgrade can proceed faster, which helps reduce the downtime of certain functionality (as explained in later sections of this chapter). You can enable this with:

```
$ helm install cilium-preflight cilium/cilium --version <new-version> \
    --namespace kube-system \
    --set preflight.enabled=true \
    --set agent=false \
    --set operator.enabled=false
```

Once the preflight check is done, you can remove `cilium-preflight` and proceed with the upgrade.

Traffic Stability During Upgrade

Upgrading Cilium requires restarting the Cilium agent on each node. The level of disruption to in-cluster applications depends on the features in use. Cilium's eBPF datapath continues forwarding traffic even with the agent offline, so the following will continue to function correctly:

- Routing to/from pods on the node (cluster ingress and egress)
- Routing to/from pod IPs across the cluster
- Routing to/from service IPs
- Enforcement of Layer 3 network policy (e.g., `toCIDRSet` or `toEntities`)

However, imagine a client pod is talking to a service that only has one backend pod. If the Cilium agent on the client's node restarts around the same time as the backend pod, the datapath can fall out of sync. When that happens, the client may keep sending traffic to a pod that no longer exists, because the Cilium agent isn't running to update the datapath.

Such incidents generally require a cluster operation to coincide with an agent restart, so their likelihood will depend on the expected pod churn of the cluster. They will also appear as transient errors that resolve themselves once the agent restarts. If your workloads implement traffic control features such as exponential backoff, it is likely that any disruption from this sort of failure will resolve itself without further intervention. (How tolerable that disruption is will depend on your specific situation.)

Migration from Other CNIs

You can replace an existing CNI (such as Flannel, Calico, Canal, or the AWS VPC CNI) with Cilium without rebuilding the entire cluster. However, there is no single migration path that suits all environments. The right approach depends on how tolerant your workloads are to disruption, how quickly you can recycle pods, and how your existing network is configured.

As described in Chapter 2, Kubernetes delegates pod networking to the CNI plugin configured on each node. Migrating to a new CNI therefore requires switching the active plugin for future pods and ensuring that pods created by the previous plugin are recycled or reattached to the new network.

There are four main ways to perform this transition:

Build a new cluster and migrate workloads
: The cleanest option is to create a new cluster running Cilium and redeploy your workloads, ideally through GitOps or other declarative tooling. This avoids mixed networking states and simplifies rollback, though it requires more preparation and temporary service disruption.

Reconfigure /etc/cni/net.d/ to point to Cilium
: This lightweight method switches new pods to Cilium while old pods continue using the existing CNI until they are restarted. The cluster temporarily runs with a mix of network domains until every pod has been re-created. A limitation of this approach is the need to maintain routing between the two network domains.

Node reboot or "big bang" migration
: With this approach, you replace the CNI configuration on all nodes and restart them sequentially. Each node rejoins the cluster under Cilium control, but until the rollout completes, migrated and unmigrated nodes form separate islands of connectivity.

Hybrid/controlled overlay migration

Cilium supports a hybrid mode that allows networks to coexist temporarily. In this mode, Cilium is deployed with a separate PodCIDR and overlay while the old CNI is kept active. Nodes are drained, labeled, and brought back up with Cilium as the primary CNI. During the transition, pods on both networks remain reachable as long as the CIDRs and encapsulation ports differ. This method is described in detail in the official documentation (*https://oreil.ly/F6jd5*).[3]

Monitoring, Capacity, and Observability

Chapter 15 explored how Prometheus and Hubble can be used to observe application performance and traffic behavior. In this chapter, our focus shifts from workloads to the Cilium environment itself, monitoring the health of the agents, operator, and datapath components that provide connectivity and policy enforcement.

Cilium, the Cilium operator, and Hubble all expose Prometheus-compatible metrics, but these are disabled by default. They can be enabled at installation time or during an upgrade by adding the following Helm values:

```
$ helm install cilium cilium/cilium --version 1.18.3 \
   --namespace kube-system \
   --set prometheus.enabled=true \
   --set operator.prometheus.enabled=true \
   --set hubble.enabled=true \
   --set hubble.metrics.enableOpenMetrics=true \
   --set hubble.metrics.enabled="{dns,drop,tcp,flow,port-distribution,icmp,\
httpV2:exemplars=true;labelsContext=source_ip,source_namespace,\
source_workload,destination_ip,destination_namespace,destination_workload,\
traffic_direction}"
```

These settings enable:

- Cilium agent metrics on port 9962
- Cilium operator metrics on port 9963
- Hubble flow metrics on port 9965

3 A full walk-through of hybrid migration is beyond the scope of this book, but Isovalent provides a tutorial (*https://oreil.ly/fXKH7*) and two labs that you can use to test it: Migration from Flannel to Cilium (*https://oreil.ly/ugc-j*) and Migration from Calico to Cilium (*https://oreil.ly/orJ5-*).

For quick validation or lab environments, you can deploy the example Prometheus and Grafana stack provided in the *chapter16* folder of the book's GitHub repository:

```
$ kubectl apply -f monitoring-example.yaml
```

This manifest creates a `cilium-monitoring` namespace containing:

- A Prometheus instance preconfigured to scrape Cilium and Hubble metrics
- A Grafana instance with dashboards for the Cilium agent, Cilium operator, and Hubble traffic visibility

Once deployed, access Grafana locally:

```
$ kubectl -n cilium-monitoring port-forward service/grafana \
    --address 0.0.0.0 --address :: 3000:3000
Forwarding from 0.0.0.0:3000 -> 3000
Forwarding from [::]:3000 -> 3000
```

Then open *http://localhost:3000* in your browser. (Note that in a real environment, Grafana would normally be exposed through Ingress or Gateway API, discussed in Chapter 7, rather than a port forward).

Screenshots of the dashboards—Figure 16-3 for Cilium and Figure 16-4 for Hubble—follow. (For higher-resolution images, please see the *chapter16* folder in the book's GitHub repository.) These dashboards provide a high-level view of agent health, endpoint status, policy enforcement, and Hubble flow activity. They are designed to confirm that Cilium components are operational and that Prometheus is successfully scraping metrics from all nodes.

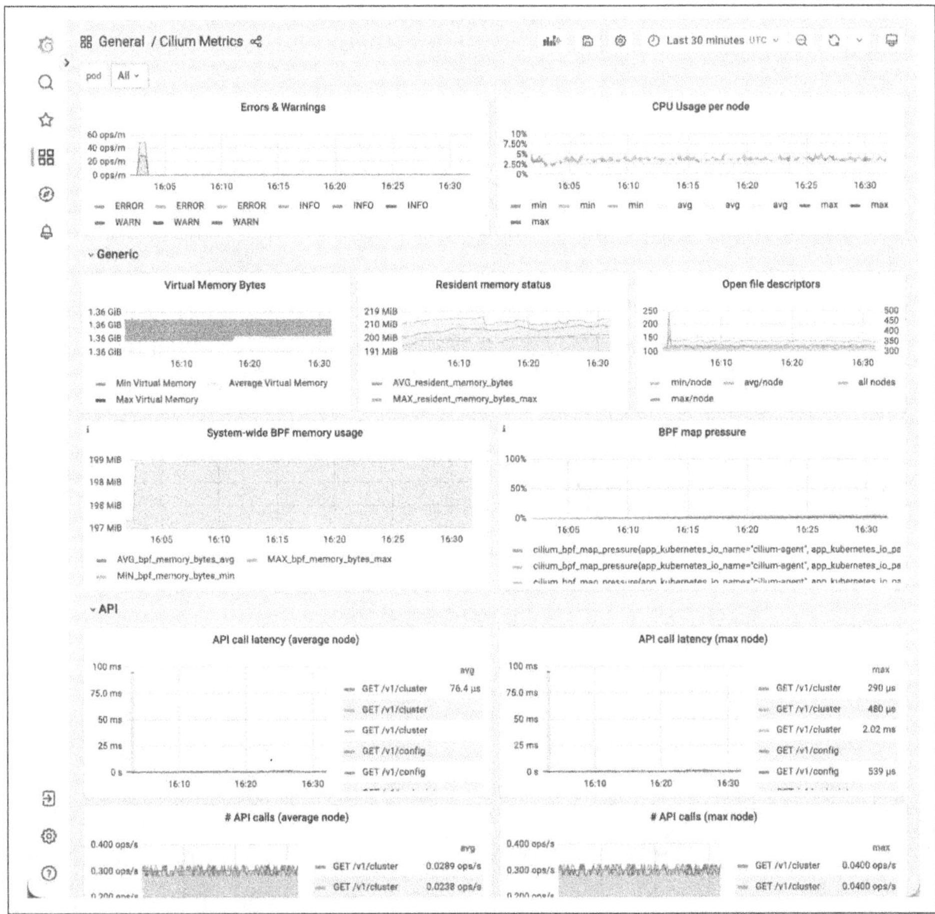

Figure 16-3. Grafana dashboard of Cilium metrics

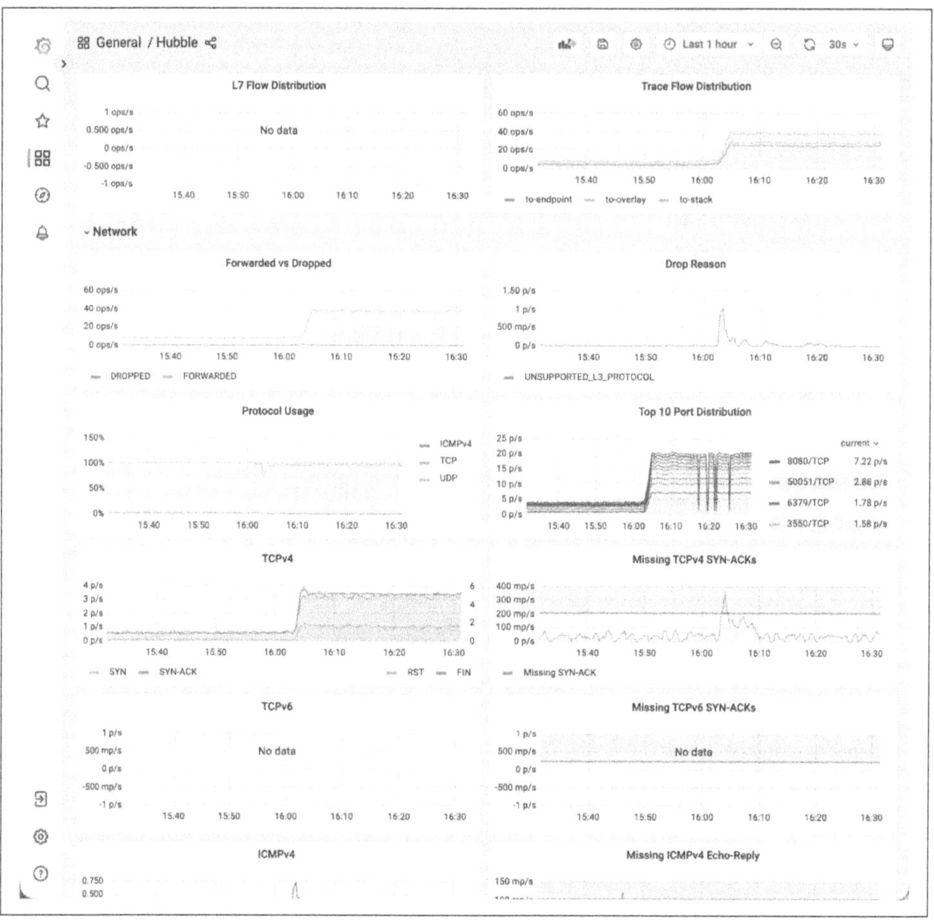

Figure 16-4. Grafana dashboard of Hubble metrics

Cilium exports a large number of Prometheus metrics, and the dashboards only surface the most common ones. For readers who need to monitor specific features, such as BGP, Cluster Mesh, or IPAM integration, refer to the "Monitoring and Metrics" section of the Cilium documentation (*https://oreil.ly/aMYV2*).

Day 2 Operations and Troubleshooting

In addition to monitoring Cilium's health through metrics and dashboards, you can use the Cilium CLI for deeper inspection and troubleshooting. In the previous chapters, you've gained experience using the CLI and the in-agent debugging tool, `cilium-dbg`. When you operate Cilium day to day, these two tools will be your most valuable companions.

Whenever something looks wrong, your first stop should be to check the status of Cilium:

```
$ cilium status
```

This command gives you a concise summary of agent and operator health and reports on the status of optional components such as Hubble and Cluster Mesh.

If the core services appear healthy, you can validate connectivity across the cluster with this command:

```
$ cilium connectivity test
```

The connectivity test automatically deploys short-lived pods to verify pod-to-pod and service connectivity, DNS resolution, and network policy enforcement across multiple nodes. It produces a clear report showing which connectivity checks succeeded and which failed. Running this test is particularly useful after upgrades or configuration changes because it confirms that the datapath, policy engine, and services are still behaving correctly.

By default, the command executes over 100 tests. If there's a specific test you want to run, you can use the flag `--test` and specify its name (for example, `cilium connectivity test --test allow-all-except-world`). You can also use regular expressions to narrow down the tests that are run—for example, the following command will skip all tests except the ones beginning with `to-fqdns`:

```
$ cilium connectivity test --test '^(to-fqdns.*)$'
[...]
🏃 [cilium-test-1] Running 123 tests ...
[=] [cilium-test-1] Skipping test [no-policies] [1/123] (skipped by user)
[...]
[=] [cilium-test-1] Skipping test [dns-only] [100/123] (skipped by user)
[=] [cilium-test-1] Test [to-fqdns] [101/123]
............
[=] [cilium-test-1] Test [to-fqdns-with-proxy] [102/123]
............
[=] [cilium-test-1] Skipping test [no-unexpected-packet-drops] [122/123]
  (skipped by user)
[=] [cilium-test-1] Skipping test [check-log-errors] [123/123] (skipped by user)

✅ [cilium-test-1] All 2 tests (24 actions) successful, 121 tests skipped,
  0 scenarios skipped.
```

If you want to verify node-to-node health continuously, use the built-in `cilium-health` service. Every Cilium agent runs this background component, which probes both host-level and endpoint-level paths. You can query it at any time for a current snapshot (use the `--verbose` flag to get more information, such as ICMP and HTTP round-trip time durations):

```
$ kubectl -n kube-system exec -ti cilium-tlnw7 -- cilium-health status
Cluster health:                    3/3 reachable   (2025-11-03T11:38:19Z)
  (Probe interval: 1m56.754608943s)
Name                               IP              Node         Endpoints
  kind-control-plane (localhost)   172.18.0.3      1/1          1/1
  kind-worker                      172.18.0.2      1/1          1/1
  kind-worker2                     172.18.0.4      1/1          1/1
```

The output of `cilium-health status` indicates whether a node can reach others with minimal latency. If any paths are marked as `unreachable`, the problem likely lies in the network fabric interconnecting the nodes.

When connectivity looks good but workloads still misbehave, turn to the logs. The Cilium agent and operator usually report clear errors when something is misconfigured. For instance, if you enable Gateway API without first installing its CRDs, the operator will log a message explaining that the resource type is missing. Similar log entries appear for policy parsing errors, IPAM allocation failures, or issues loading eBPF programs. Reviewing logs from a few representative nodes is often enough to spot the source of the problem. When you need a full diagnostic snapshot, use the `cilium sysdump` command. This collects logs, configuration, and runtime information from all Cilium components. In larger clusters, you can limit the scope to specific nodes or time ranges:

```
$ cilium sysdump \
    --node-list kind-worker2 \
    --logs-since-time 2h
🔍 Collecting sysdump with cilium-cli version: v0.18.7, args:
  [sysdump --node-list kind-worker2 --logs-since-time 2h]
🔮 Detected Cilium installation in namespace: "kube-system"
🔮 Detected Cilium operator in namespace: "kube-system"
ℹ️ Using default Cilium Helm release name: "cilium"
ℹ️ Using default Tetragon Helm release name: "tetragon"
🔍 Collecting Kubernetes nodes
🔍 Collecting profiling data from Cilium pods
🔍 Collecting tracing data from Cilium pods
[...]

🗳 Compiling sysdump
✅ The sysdump has been saved to cilium-sysdump-20251103-122032.zip
```

This command generates a zip archive that can be attached to a GitHub issue or shared in the Cilium Slack channel for community support. Before doing so, make sure to open and review the archive to understand exactly what information it contains—while it doesn't include business application secrets or configurations,[4] it does contain detailed information about Cilium as well as metadata about all pods and nodes in the cluster.

Gateway API, Ingress, and Layer 7 Policy

One important property of Cilium's eBPF datapath is that it remains loaded while the agent is restarted, for example during an upgrade. In this period of time, new information (such as new remote endpoints for services or policy updates) will not be synced from the cluster, but existing connections will be unaffected and most traffic will continue to flow unobstructed.

The same is not true for layer 7 functionality. As explained in previous chapters, layer 7 features depend on additional components to deliver the required functionality. If these components are unavailable, problems may occur.

Be aware that outages and upgrades can cause the same symptoms, because the required components run as a DaemonSet. When the DaemonSet image is changed or other upgrade tasks are performed, the existing pod is removed before a new pod is created. During that interval, no component is available to perform its task until the replacement pod becomes ready. It is therefore important to minimize the time between these operations.

There are two main sources of delay during an upgrade:

- When the new pod is created, the image must be pulled. This can take time. Pre-pulling the new image via the preflight check on all nodes before updating the DaemonSet reduces this delay.
- Configuration changes may cause the pod to start, process the new configuration, and fail due to a misconfiguration. Troubleshooting the issue and rolling back adds more time. To reduce the impact, test the changes on a noncritical cluster.

Keep in mind that these efforts only shorten the downtime window; they do not remove it. There will always be some delay between a pod starting and it becoming ready to take over its responsibilities.

If availability is critical, Isovalent Networking for Kubernetes provides high-availability functionality for these components and enterprise support.

4 This can include sensitive data from Hubble flow logs, such as authorization tokens.

This delay can have an impact on policy enforcement. Gateway API, Ingress, HTTP, SNI, and TLS interception policies all depend on Envoy, which is part of the `cilium-envoy` DaemonSet. If Envoy is shut down, existing connections and new connections will be dropped. This also applies to workloads that make use of persistent TCP connections, such as HTTP/2 streams or WebSockets.

DNS policies depend on the DNS proxy, which is part of the Cilium DaemonSet. If the agent is unavailable, for example during a Cilium upgrade, DNS requests on selected pods will be dropped. Depending on your workloads, this may not matter. Most workloads make DNS requests when they start and only reissue the request when the TTL from the response expires, caching it in the meantime. However, if you are using a service that has very short TTLs in its responses, or if caching is not possible, this may affect you.

Remember that you do not need to worry about new pods starting up and making fresh requests during an agent restart. If the agent is down, the CNI is down as well, which prevents new pods from being launched.

L2 Announcements

While Cilium's L2 Announcements feature provides load balancing across pods, it does not balance traffic across nodes. All requests are directed to a single node until that node fails. At that point, a new node becomes the leader and subsequent traffic must be sent to it.

This creates two operational challenges:

- How quickly will the new node assume leadership?
- How does a client discover the new leader?

Leader Election Timing

When you create an L2 Announcement policy, a lease object named `cilium-l2announce-<namespace>-<service>` is created in the namespace where Cilium runs. The lease includes a `leaseDurationSeconds` field. As discussed in Chapter 10, the current leader must renew the lease within this interval, or else a new leader is elected. Cilium provides a couple of settings to tune the leader election timing:

- `l2announcements.leaseDuration` defines the interval after which a missing renewal triggers a new election. Its default value is `15s` and it can be lowered to as little as `1s`. This setting must be larger than `l2announcements.leaseRenewDeadline`.

- `l2announcements.leaseRetryPeriod` controls how often the current leader attempts to renew its lease. The default is `2s`, but it can be reduced to as low as `1ns`. It must remain at least 20% smaller than `l2announcements.leaseRenewDeadline`.
- `l2announcements.leaseRenewDeadline` specifies the maximum time allowed for a renewal attempt before it is considered failed. Its default is `5s`. This value must be smaller than `l2announcements.leaseDuration` and at least 20% larger than `l2announcements.leaseRetryPeriod`.

The optimal settings depend on your specific network characteristics and desired fault tolerance. Setting these values arbitrarily low can overload the Kubernetes API server. The chosen values should reflect your network's latency—configuring them lower than the round-trip time to the API server will cause constant lease renewal failures.

Client Traffic Redirection

After a new node assumes leadership, clients must direct traffic to that node. Cilium cannot influence client behavior, as the outcome depends on how each client manages its ARP cache. Typically, clients store the MAC address of the current leader in the ARP cache. When the leader changes, the cached MAC address continues to point to the previous node until the cache expires and a new MAC address is fetched.

Lowering the ARP cache timeout on clients accelerates failover, but it also raises the volume of network traffic. This can negatively affect performance for latency-sensitive applications, because more frequent ARP requests add latency. As mentioned in Chapter 10, an alternative approach is to use gratuitous ARP (gARP). Cilium sends a gARP packet each time a node takes leadership. Clients that are configured to accept gARP will refresh their ARP cache immediately.

Many clients ignore gARP messages by default due to security concerns such as ARP poisoning. Check with your security team to determine whether enabling gARP is acceptable in your organization.

BGP

There are a few important things to watch for when using Cilium's BGP functionality. As with many features, it is difficult to claim that one specific approach is always the best choice for every scenario. Nonetheless, the following sections explore common questions and patterns with the goal of offering practical recommendations where possible by clearly outlining the reasoning behind them.

Announcing Pod IPs Versus Service IPs

Pod IPs are ephemeral and change frequently. This leaves clients with the challenge of determining which pod IP to target. Even when DNS is used to resolve pod IPs, the problem is only shifted from the client to the DNS server. On top of that, load balancing across pods must then be handled by the client or pushed onto the DNS server. Still, as mentioned in "Dynamic routing with BGP" on page 84, there are situations where advertising PodCIDRs makes sense—particularly when using native routing, to ensure routing entries are properly populated across the cluster.

Service IPs, on the other hand, tend to remain stable for long periods, which greatly reduces the frequency of DNS updates. This makes them a good fit when an external client needs to establish a connection to an application inside the cluster. Once traffic to a service IP arrives on a node, Cilium's datapath automatically load-balances across the available pods while the client continues to send traffic to a single stable destination IP.

Another important consideration is that IP ranges should be unique across clusters that use BGP, to prevent route conflicts in the network. Service IP ranges are typically smaller than pod IP ranges, which must scale to accommodate a much larger number of addresses. Especially in IPv4 environments, announcing service IPs while ensuring uniqueness can preserve valuable address space compared to exposing PodCIDR ranges.

Reliability

Cilium's BGP speaker runs inside the Cilium agent. This means that if the Cilium agent goes down, the BGP session is lost and the peer eventually removes the associated routes. While this can be useful for failure detection, it also creates a challenge during planned updates. When Cilium is upgraded, the BGP speaker restarts along with the agent, which causes the BGP peer to withdraw routes for that node. As a result, clients may experience connectivity drops even though the datapath on the node continues to work and can still serve traffic.

A practical way to reduce these interruptions is to use Graceful Restart, as described in Chapter 10. Enabling this feature instructs the peer to keep the routes for a defined period rather than withdrawing them immediately. This gives the Cilium agent time to come back up so the node can continue receiving traffic and serving both new and existing connections.

However, this setting should not always be enabled. If a node experiences an involuntary outage, such as a link failure or a power loss, the peer will keep sending traffic to that node until the Graceful Restart timer expires. This can delay failover during real failures. Choosing the right behavior depends on whether fast failover or reduced packet loss during updates is more important in your environment. For this reason, it is not possible to provide a single "one size fits all" recommendation for timer values or whether Graceful Restart should be enabled in all cases.

If fast failure detection is critical, Isovalent Networking for Kubernetes includes Bidirectional Forwarding Detection (BFD) functionality, which provides faster failure detection, with enterprise support.

Summary

Cilium provides a comprehensive set of features for a variety of use cases. However, it is important to understand what dependencies these features have and to think through different failure scenarios as well as upgrade processes and how they can affect your applications and organization. As with many things, there is rarely a single best option; there are often trade-offs to consider between performance, comfort, and reliability.

When running Cilium in production environments, you should consider the operational cost of additional features, since operational maturity with Cilium requires a solid understanding of how its components fit together. This includes the behavior of the datapath, the impact of layer 7 policies and Gateway API, and how external systems such as BGP peers react to changes.

It is equally important to choose a dependable lifecycle management approach. Using the Cilium CLI might offer a straightforward and simple experience, but it isn't the best choice when it comes to reliability and scale. Helm and GitOps workflows provide repeatability, version control, and safer rollouts.

To build safe and reliable infrastructure, it is always important to understand the tools you are using and their limitations. With that awareness, you can design architectures that tolerate failures, plan upgrades with confidence, and maintain consistent behavior across environments.

We'd like to thank you for making it this far. We've been on a journey together since the first pages of this book. Just as it has been an adventure for you as a reader, it has been a meaningful experience for us as authors. The last piece of advice that we want to share is that every successful journey starts today, not tomorrow. We truly hope you will take the insights shared in this book and build a Cilium platform that you can take pride in.

Index

K

L

M

N

O

P

Q

R

S

T

U

V

W

X

Z

About the Authors

Nico Vibert is a senior staff technical marketing engineer at Isovalent, the company behind the open source cloud native networking and security platform Cilium. Nico was the Subject Matter Lead for the Cilium Certified Associate (CCA) certification, which helped define and validate the foundational skills required to operate Cilium in production.

Prior to Isovalent, Nico held a range of technical roles spanning operations and support, design and architecture, and technical presales at companies including HashiCorp, VMware, and Cisco. He is a former Cisco Certified Internetwork Expert (CCIE #22990), one of the industry's most rigorous networking certifications.

Nico regularly speaks at industry events, from large conferences such as KubeCon and Cisco Live to smaller community forums including VMware and AWS User Groups.

Filip Nikolic is a solutions architect at Isovalent, the creators of eBPF and Cilium. With years of hands-on experience across a variety of Cloud Native Computing Foundation (CNCF) projects, Filip is not only a seasoned engineer but also a passionate advocate for open source innovation.

James Laverack is a software engineer and technical speaker with over a decade of industry experience specializing in cloud native software, distributed systems, and networking. Currently, James is a principal customer success architect for Isovalent at Cisco, and he has previously worked as a Kubernetes consultant and software engineer across a range of industries.

Colophon

The insects on the cover of *Cilium: Up and Running* are bumblebees (genus *Bombus*) on a gentian flower, a type of bee found primarily in the Northern Hemisphere, including North America, Europe, and parts of Asia. These cold-tolerant insects are commonly found in temperate climates and are especially active in cooler environments where other pollinators may be scarce.

Bumblebees are easily recognized by their large, robust bodies covered in soft hairs, giving them a fuzzy appearance. Their coloration typically features black and yellow bands, though some species also display orange, red, or white markings. Unlike honeybees, bumblebees have colonies with smaller populations, and usually nest in underground burrows or in thick grass.

The diet of bumblebees consists mainly of nectar and pollen from flowers. Nectar provides them with energy through sugars, while pollen is a source of protein that is particularly important for feeding larvae. As they collect food, bumblebees play a vital role in the pollination of both wild plants and agricultural crops, making them key contributors to biodiversity and food production.

Bumblebees are social insects, living in colonies with a queen, workers, and males. Workers forage for nectar and pollen, while the queen lays eggs. Bumblebees are known for their distinct "buzz pollination" technique, in which they vibrate flowers to release tightly held pollen.

Bumblebees are facing growing environmental challenges, and many species are in decline across their natural ranges. While some species remain relatively common, others are listed as threatened or endangered due to habitat loss, pesticide exposure, climate change, and the spread of diseases from domesticated pollinators. Many of the animals on O'Reilly covers are endangered; all of them are important to the world.

The cover illustration is by José Marzan Jr., based on an antique line engraving from Wood's *Natural History*. The series design is by Edie Freedman, Ellie Volckhausen, and Karen Montgomery. The cover fonts are Gilroy Semibold and Guardian Sans. The text font is Adobe Minion Pro; the heading font is Adobe Myriad Condensed; and the code font is Dalton Maag's Ubuntu Mono.

www.ingramcontent.com/pod-product-compliance
Lightning Source LLC
Chambersburg PA
CBHW080714220326
41598CB00033B/5416
9798341622999